India's Security Interest in her Neighbourhood

India's Security Interest in her Neighbourhood

Editor

Prof. Shekhar Adhikari

PENTAGON PRESS

India's Security Interest in her Neighbourhood

Editor: Prof. Shekhar Adhikari

ISBN 978-81-8274-848-4

First Published in 2015

Published by
PENTAGON PRESS
206, Peacock Lane, Shahpur Jat,
New Delhi-110049
Phones: 011-64706243, 26491568
Telefax: 011-26490600
email: rajan@pentagonpress.in
website: www.pentagonpress.in

Branch
Flat No.213, Athena-2,
Clover Acropolis,
Viman Nagar,
Pune-411014
Email: pentagonpresspune@gmail.com

Printed at Avantika Printers Private Limited.

Contents

	Preface	*vii*
	Acknowledgement	*xi*
	Contributors	*xiii*
1.	One Year of Modi's Foreign Policy *Diwakar Kaushik*	1
2.	Indo-Pak Geopolitical Rivalry in Afghanistan: Policy Options for India *Tej Pratap Singh*	32
3.	Environmental Degradation as a Non-traditional Security Threat to Bangladesh *Aditya Mishra*	47
4.	India-Bangladesh Land Boundary Agreement: Beginning of a New Era *Amar Singh and Shivendra Shahi*	66
5.	India's Bhutan Policy: A Critical Approach *Rajesh S Kharat*	77
6.	India-China Boundary Dispute: A Never-Ending Saga *Sana Hashmi*	91
7.	The Tibet-China Conflict: Implications for India *Simrat Kaur Virk*	106
8.	Power Struggle Between India and China *Sanjeev Bhadauria*	124

9. Evolution of Defence Policy in India: A Historical Perspective 137
P.S. Harish

10. Interference of Foreign Elements in J&K and its Implication on Internal Security 145
Jaibans Singh

11. The Importance of Maldives in South Asia 154
S. Manivasakan and Sripathi Narayanan

12. India-Maldives Relations in a Comprehensive Security Paradigm 165
T.C. Karthikheyan

13. Myanmar as a Factor in India's North East: Economic and Security Issues 181
Ashok Kumar and Kamal Kinger

14. India-Nepal Relations: Evaluating Security Implications 195
Narender Kumar

15. Maoist Insurgency in India and Nepal: An Analysis 209
Shekhar Adhikari

16. Understanding Extremism in Pakistan 231
Shalini Chawla

17. The Emerging Patterns in India-Pakistan Conflict 248
Rajpal Budania

18. Indo-Pacific Region: India's Strategic Vision 265
Hari Saran

19. Chorus or Cacophony: Varied Voices in Indo-Sri Lankan Relations 278
S. Utham Kumar Jamadhagni

20. India's External Security Conundrum: Complexities of Securing Peace in South Asia 293
Nanda Kishor M S

Index 307

Preface

Like any other country, in India peace and security have been a major concern. A lot of literature is available about external as well as internal threats to peace and security in our country. The geo-strategic location of India and its emergence as a regional power make it vulnerable to external threats. India has not only faced wars with neighbouring countries like China and Pakistan, but also has been dealing with international terrorism. We have been experiencing internal threats from insurgencies in NE and separatist movements in Punjab as well J&K in the 1960s and 1970s. India has also experienced inception of Maoist movement, which have now assumed alarming proportions. It is in this context that an approach for ensuring peace and security in India began quite early, in fact, during freedom movement itself. The approach has been reflected in the Constitution and has undergone changes over the years according to the needs and requirements.

India's neighbouring countries—Afghanistan, Bangladesh, Bhutan, China, Nepal, Maldives, Pakistan Myanmar and Sri Lanka—is a fairly complex geographical entity. They represent—individually as well as collectively—a world of historical links, shared legacies, commonalities as well as diversities which are reflected in their ethnic, linguistic, religious and political fabric.

The Indian neighbours are full of contradiction, disparities and paradoxes. In the post-colonial times, the countries of South Asia have been a theatre of bloody inter-state as well as civil wars; it witnessed liberation movements, nuclear rivalry, military dictatorship and now suffers from insurgencies, religious fundamentalism and terrorism, drugs and human trafficking. The region also has the dubious distinction of having over 540 million people who account for 44 per cent of the developing world's poor. On religious tolerance, the constituent countries range anywhere between flexibly secular minded to rigidly fundamentalist.

The SAARC has been in existence for over 27 years South Asia is considered as the least integrated of the global regions. This is despite the stipulation in its Charter that "bilateral and contentious issues shall be excluded" from its deliberations, so as the focus on areas of possible regional cooperation. PM Narendra Modi's earlier invitation to all SAARC leaders for his swearing-in-economy has ushered in a hope in regional matters. An important visit to Himalayan states have further given the strategic linkage that our nation has with this small land-locked nation (Bhutan).

On the positive side, the region has been registering a healthy growth (average 6 per cent per annum) during the past several years. Also democratic forms of governance (some flawed and feeble) are beginning to gain some ground in most parts of the region.

But the pertinent question is where does India stand in this rather volatile region? India's position is unique in more than one sense. As a matter of an interesting geographic factor, India shares borders with all her neighbours whereas no other South Asian nation (except Afghanistan and Pakistan) shares borders with any other South Asian nation. Notwithstanding some shortcomings, democracy and rule of law as instruments of political governance has been entrenched in India. In relative terms India can be arguably considered as the most stable country in the region, moving ahead on the fast tracks of development, even though the growth has of late been showing variance.

There are some unjustified and erroneous perceptions about India's neighbourly relations which are untrue. Infact, as a bigger nation, our leaders have walked the extra mile to ensure better relations in the neighbourhood. However, with China and Pakistan we continue to have long border disputes, which need to be resolved at the earliest. Pakistan is a more or less failed state in the neighbourhood and would like to see relations with India in a state of perpetual suspension. India's motives on trade are suspected even in cases of innocent proposals for economic cooperation which would lead to win-win situations.

In a scenario where we have Pakistan at one end and genuinely friendly Bhutan at the other end of the spectrum, and everyone else somewhere in between, it is perhaps difficult to write one single foreign policy prescription for the entire region. Nevertheless, there are some basic approaches which India has consistently endeavoured to adopt and apply; these include: (a) India advocates constructive, engagement despite serious provocations in the past (attack on Parliament, Mumbai terrorist attacks, etc); (b) India adheres to its benign policy of non-interference into internal affairs of others countries in the region; (c) At times, however, there are instances when it appears that the national policy is being held hostage to domestic regional politics. Bangladesh and Sri Lanka are the most glaring example; (d) India has endeavoured to deal with the neighbouring government-of-the-day, be it democracy, monarchy or military dictatorship, insisting that the choice of the form of government is best left to the people of the country concerned; (e) In a contemporary globalised world, the foreign economic policies objectives stand integrated and cannot be divorced from each other; (f) India has skillfully used its policy of non-perspective development assistance as its soft power since early 1950s. In return India has sought "good will" and "friend of India".

Despite past experiences, peace building within Sri Lanka, Bangladesh and Nepal remains a priority for India. This is not just by India's desire to safeguard own economic potential from regional poverty and economic migration but by a host of other factors. Prominent among these is a desire to build stronger allies with a view to reasserting India's position as the regional leader in the global order. Indian industry is convinced of the need to economically engage and support neighbouring businessmen as an essential prerequisite for sustained regional development.

Still then, the challenge to India's peace and security are complex and manifold and require sustained efforts. With this objective an attempt has been made to examine India's relations with her neighbours.

Shekhar Adhikari

Acknowledgement

I wish to extend my sincerest gratitude to all the contributors who have come together and laboured to examine the many facets of India and its relations with its neighbours. I must acknowledge my heartfelt gratitude to Ambassador Lalit Mansingh and Prof. N.R. Farooqi, Vice Chancellor, University of Allahabad, for their constant encouragement and support. My appreciation is also due to Dr. Shalini Chawala, Brig. L.C. Patnaik and Dr. Dhirendra Dwivedi for their kind support. A special thanks to Mr. Rajan Arya, Pentagon Press for publishing the book. Last, but not the least, I am grateful to Partibha Adhikari for showing great patience while the book got completed.

Contributors

1. Dr. Diwakar Kaushik is an Associate Professor, Department of Political Science, University of Allahabad, Allahabad, U.P.
2. Dr. Tej Pratap Singh is a Professor, Department of Political Science, Banaras Hindu University, Varanasi, U.P.
3. Dr. Aditiya Mishra is an Assistant Professor, Satyawati College, University of Delhi, New Delhi.
4. Dr. Amar Singh is a Senior Research Fellow, South Asian Studies/School of International Studies, Jawaharlal Nehru University, New Delhi.
5. Dr. Shivendra Shahi is a Project Fellow (U.G.C.), Department of Defence and Strategic Studies, University of Allahabad, Allahabad.
6. Dr. Rajesh Kharat is an Associate Professor, Centre for South Asian Studies, School of International Studies, JNU, New Delhi.
7. Ms. Sana Hashmi is an Associate Fellow, Centre for Airpower Studies, New Delhi.
8. Ms. Simrat Kaur Virk is a Research Associate, Centre for Air Power Studies, New Delhi.
9. Dr. Sanjeev Bhadauria is a Professor & Head, Department of Defence & Strategic Studies, University of Allahabad, Allahabad, UP.
10. Dr. P.S. Harish is an Assistant Professor, Department of Medieval and Modern History, University of Allahabad, Allahabad, U.P.
11. Col. Jaibans Singh is an Editor-Defence info.com, New Delhi.
12. Dr. S. Manivasakan is the Director of the Centre for South and Southeast Asian Studies, University of Madras, Chennai.

13. Dr. Sripathi Narayanan is a Research Scholar, University of Madras, Chennai.
14. Dr. T.C. Karthikheyan is an Assistant Professor, School of Politics and Public Administration, Tamil Nadu Open University, Chennai.
15. Dr. Kamal Kinger is a Professor and Head, Department of Defence and Strategic Studies, Punjabi University, Patiala, Punjab.
16. Mr. Ashok Kumar, is a Senior Research Fellow, Department of Defence and Strategic Studies, Punjabi University, Patiala.
17. Brigadier Narendra Kumar is a serving army officer.
18. Dr. Shekhar Adhikari is a Professor and Former Head, Department of Defence and Strategic Studies, University of Allahabad, Allahabad, U.P.
19. Dr. Shalini Chawla is a Senior Fellow, Centre for Air Power Studies, New Delhi.
20. Dr. Rajpal Budania is an Associate Professor, Department of Political Science, University of Allahabad, Allahabad, U.P.
21. Dr. Hari Saran is a Professor, Department of Defence & Strategic Studies, DDU, Gorakhpur University, Gorakhpur.
22. Dr. S. Utham Kumar Jamadhagni is an Associate Professor, Department of Defence and Strategic Studies, University of Madras, Chennai, Tamil Nadu.
23. Dr. Nanda Kishor MS is an Assistant Professor of Geopolitical and International Relations, Manipal University, India.

1

One Year of Modi's Foreign Policy

Diwakar Kaushik

Introduction

On 26 May 2014, Narendra Modi took oath as the fifteenth Prime Minister of India. A year has passed since then and, his government's popularity has fallen down a few notches. But the survey by "India Today Group-Cicero Mood of the Nation" published in the *India Today* April 2015 issue, serves as a reality check. The honeymoon is well and truly over but Narendra Damodardas Modi still remains very popular and is still the number one choice as the PM of India; ironically, ahead of stalwarts like Nehru and Indira Gandhi. Modi has not only continued with the old pattern of diplomacy but also gave a new direction to our foreign policy thereby giving it a more realistic, bold and a personalized touch. The critics call Modi a 'lucky' PM but the fact remains that Modi has given a new direction to the foreign policy of India.

It was clear right from the beginning that Modi's forte is external relations. It was a rare diplomatic role that all the Heads of States of SAARC countries, including Pakistan's Nawaz Sharif, came down to Delhi to attend his swearing in, at the lawns of Parliament of India. It seems that Modi is clear in his objectives, first he wants to charm the neighbourhood by his diplomatic skills and then the world. The Prime Minister is using the same mantra of 'inclusive development' on the international front as that on the domestic front.

The Lok Sabha election of 2014 saw the victory of NDA in which Narendra Modi was its Prime Ministerial candidate. It is said that foreign policy and neighbourhood policy of Prime Minister Narendra Modi emerged straight from his swearing-in ceremony. The invitation of all SAARC leaders is an important step of Modi's neighbourhood diplomacy.[1]

Paradigm Shift in India's Foreign Policy

The NDA government headed by Prime Minister Narendra Modi is slowly making a mark on the foreign policy landscape of India. There has been a paradigm shift in the functioning of India's PMO (Prime Minister's Office) and the MEA (Ministry of External Affairs). With a clear and decisive political mandate the Union Government is not bound by the limitations that the regional players pose in India's foreign policy maneuvering, which at times comes in the way of India's national interest. Most pundits have been predicting that PM Modi's foreign policy is a continuation of the policy of the previous UPA-II Government. But it is to be noted that, though in substance, India's foreign policy has been persistent, its style, shade, emphasis and pace has shaped a difference in India's foreign policy.

The forte of the new government in India will be its foreign policy was clear when the leaders of all SAARC countries were invited to the swearing-in ceremony of the new government. Since its inception the new government has given priority to diplomacy, and whether it is PM Modi, Foreign Minister Sushma Swaraj, His Excellency, The President Mr. Pranab Mukherji or the MEA all have been diplomatically very busy; in his first foreign trip as PM Modi visited Bhutan where he talked of B2B, i.e. Bharat to Bhutan of nurturing bilateral relations. He said that "The relationship between India and Bhutan is historic. The new government is committed to make this even stronger '' The Hindu, observes that, it is therefore in India's national interest to keep genuine friendly ties with Bhutan and thereby not allow any external influence on the Bhutanese territory, which will be inimical to India's strategic interests. It is perhaps an excellent move on part of the newly formed National Democratic Alliance (NDA) government (who came in power after the 16TH General Elections in April-May 2014) at the centre to choose Bhutan as the first official foreign trip by Narendra Modi, the new Prime Minister of India.[2]

While Foreign Minister Sushma Swaraj's, first visit was to Bangladesh on June 25-27, 2014, her second one was to Nepal. PM Modi also went on a two-day visit to Nepal from 3-4 August 2014, this was first by an Indian

Prime Minister in seventeen years, the last being that of Atal Behari Vajpayee in 2002. On the other hand President of India, Mr Pranab Mukherji visited Vietnam on September 15, 2014. Moreover, PM Modi visited Japan in September 2014 and had fruitful talks with his Japanese counterpart Shinzo Abe. He also met Chinese President, Xi Jinping, when he came on a visit to India on September 17, 2014, but the crowning glory of Modi's diplomatic success was to the United States in September 2014 where he swept the Americans off their feet including President Obama by his charm.

In between we had John Kerry, the U.S. Secretary of State who came to India on September 27, 2014, and the Australian PM Tony Abbot came to India in September 2014. Whether it is the BRICS or the WTO, India exercised her veto against the US sponsored food-security issue giving a clear-cut signal to the world that Modi government cannot be pressurized and will always take a decision which is in India's national interest. Therefore it becomes very clear that diplomacy is one area where the Modi government has done exceedingly well.

An editorial in the *Organiser* praises the Modi government for its foreign policy, which it says has moved for the first time towards alignment with all, away from the "old rhetoric" of non-alignment[3]: It is because while appreciating the positive change in India's foreign policy posture, a caution on domestic factors like equitable economic development and stability is necessary.

Former External Affairs Minister K. Natwar Singh heaping praise on Narendra Modi, said that the timing of PM's America visit was perfect and would be fruitful for India. He showered lavish praise on Modi saying he has not taken a single wrong step in conducting India's foreign policy. Talking on Indo-Pak relationship, he said ties between the two are "accident prone". Pakistan is weak internally and there is no clarity who India should talk to because the last call is taken by their Army. It is a complicated issue. The participation has not been resolved. People of Pakistan want good relationship with India, but the army does not want it. Singh said he was impressed by Modi. "(Former prime minister) Manmohan Singh is not a leader, though he is a good man. Modi will take up the responsibility better," said Singh. "Nobody knows better than Modi about the problems he has to face, the solutions he has to provide and the change he has to bring," he added. Singh said he had told Modi that in the foreign policy arena he should start with neighbours. "Unless our relationship with neighbours is good, how do we make it big?"

Wrapping up an account of the Narendra Modi government's foreign policy activism in its first hundred days in office, External Affairs Minister Sushma Swaraj claimed that Indian diplomacy had moved into high gear with its "fast-track diplomacy".[4] By acting "fast", the Modi government can claim it has more than neutralized, in a short period of time, the negative impact of its predecessor's months of inaction.

There are four different categories of diplomatic engagement by Modi and Swaraj: first, with South Asian neighbours, second, with East and West Asian "neighbours", third, with the five permanent members of the United Nations Security Council (P5) and finally, India's most important economic and strategic partners, led now by Japan and including Australia, Brazil, South Africa and Singapore. Within its first 100 days in office, the Modi government has engaged all.

West Asian Non-Alignment

India's West Asian 'non-alignment' meant that it would pursue good relations with all regional players, namely, Iran, Israel, Saudi Arabia, the UAE and the US. There was no better place for the region's ambassadors to meet to discuss this policy than Bahrain. The Modi government has made it clear to all regional players that it would not like to get drawn into the Muslim world's sectarian conflicts. India has, so far, been fortunate that such sectarian conflict has not entered Muslim politics here. While former defence minister A.K. Antony explained his government's decision to establish defence ties with Saudi Arabia in sectarian terms.

The BJP government has also had no difficulty in letting everyone know that maintaining good and strategic relations with Israel will not come in the way of seeking better relations with Saudi Arabia, Iran, Iraq and the Gulf states. With China reducing its dependence on Gulf oil and gas, plugging into Central Asian and Russian sources, and the US increasingly energy self-sufficient, it is India and other East Asian economies that will remain critically dependent on West Asian energy. India has also millions of productive workers living there and remitting billions home every year. Having enunciated the doctrine of high-speed diplomacy, the Modi government now needs the intellectual and administrative wherewithal to think and act fast.

Sino-Indian Cooperation

Prime Minister Narendra Modi received the visiting Chinese President Xi

Jinping in Ahmedabad on the former's birthday on September 17, 2014, symbolising the birth of new relations between India and China under the two leaders. Relations between the two countries, marred by conflict and distrust cannot, however, change abruptly unless new challenges emerge, surpassing bilateral differences, and a strategic shift becomes necessary to cope with them together.[5]

While testing whether China's move towards us are tactical, we should seriously build synergies with it in areas where both sides benefit. India and China should work together in areas of common interest, whether on climate change and WTO issues, in BRICS and the Russia-India-China format, at the G20 and Shanghai Cooperation Organisation. But then, the biggest beneficiary of a shift of power to Asia is China. Our dilemma is whether an increasingly strong China sitting atop us is better for us than the erosion of the West's long domination of global affairs necessary for a more equitable international system.

Modi's development agenda and his pragmatic approach to China create opportunities for Xi to play the economic card with India more vigorously. It is unclear, however, whether China has definitively concluded that it has earned enough Indian trust to invest heavily in India, and that tensions on the border can be isolated from burgeoning economic ties. Talk of China investing $100 billion in the next five years is unreal, as China's total investment abroad so far is about $80 billion.

India and Vietnam inked seven pacts, including one to enhance cooperation in the strategic oil sector, as they called for "freedom" of navigation in the South China Sea, over which China has been claiming territorial sovereignty. The agreements were signed during the second day of the four-day state visit of President Pranab Mukherjee who held talks with his Vietnamese counterpart Truong Tan Sang here. The leaders reiterated their desire and determination to work together to maintain peace, stability, growth and prosperity in ASEAN. They agreed that freedom of navigation in the East Sea/South China Sea should not be impeded and called the parties concerned to exercise restraint, avoid threat or use of force and resolve disputes through peaceful means in accordance with universally recognized principles of international law, including the UNCLOS-1982. China has been exerting its influence in these waters which has not been taken well by Vietnam and other bordering countries like the Philippines. Both the nations also agreed to continue closer interaction under the institutional architecture of the strategic partnership, particularly the Joint Commission meeting, the Foreign Office consultations and strategic dialogue, security dialogue and other dialogue mechanisms between the two countries, the communiqué said.[6]

The Sino-Indian cooperation is of enormous strategic value for New Delhi and such a relationship cannot be "duplicated" by its bilateral ties with any other country, an influential official Chinese daily said. State-run *Global Times*, part of the ruling Communist Party of China's People's Daily publication group, said in an editorial that the Sino-Indian cooperation is "invaluable." The geopolitical significance of the benign development of Beijing-New Delhi ties can't be duplicated, said the daily, known for its nationalistic views. The better China-India relations develop, the more advantages and initiatives India can have when dealing with the US and Japan. China has been regarded as a rival by the US and Japan, who instinctively try to rope in China's neighbours for their cause, the editorial said. A positive New Delhi-Beijing engagement would force Washington and Tokyo to cosy up to India, it said.

Xi is the first leader of a major power to visit India after the Narendra Modi-led government took charge, it said. His first stop is in Prime Minister Modi's home state of Gujarat on Modi's 64th birthday. This is viewed as a starting point for the two leaders to develop a personal friendship, the editorial said. Referring to Modi's recent visit to Japan, the daily said the floods of rhetoric such as 'joining hands to counter China' emanated from Japanese public opinion to which Modi gave a rational response at the time.[7]

Though the Indian government maintained that the Chumar and Demchok incidents are "routine in nature" due to "differing perceptions" about where the LAC lies, the fact remains that in both cases the confrontation has stretched well beyond a couple of days. This is unusual for border flare-ups that occur due to aggressive patrolling by both sides to lay claim to disputed areas. A similar face-off had also erupted in Depsang Valley's Daulat Beg Oldi sector just before Chinese premier Li Keqiang's visit in May last year. Chumar with its observation points and surveillance cameras was also the bone of contention during the Depsang face-off. It was finally defused after India dismantled what it called "a tin shed" at Chumar and the PLA troops simultaneously withdrew from Depsang.[8]

Xi's three day visit was aimed at ramping up trade and investments, besides having discussions on substantive issues including the contentious border dispute. It also coincides with Modi's 64th birthday. The three pacts were signed in the presence of Modi and Xi after the Chinese leaders and his wife Peng

Liyuan, dressed in a pale pink knee length dress, were welcomed by the Prime Minister at the entrance of the Hyatt Hotel. Modi gave floral bouquets to the couple. The choice of Gujarat as Xi's first stop in India marks a departure from protocol and many see it as a sign of warm relations between the two leaders.

The three pacts include making Guangzhou city in China and Ahmedabad as sister cities, setting up of industrial parks in this state and an agreement between Guangdong province and the Gujarat government for development of cultural and social ties between the two provinces, officials said. The agreement, aimed at developing industrial parks, was signed between China Development Bank (CDB) and Industrial Extension Bureau (INDEXTB) of Gujarat government. It envisages promoting the bilateral trade and setting up of industrial parks in the state, especially for electronics and electrical goods. While an agreement was signed between Guangdong province and Gujarat government for development of cultural and social ties between the two provinces, another MoU was inked between Guangzhou city and Ahmedabad, to make them sister cities.[9]

The visit of Chinese President Xi Jinping is an important event. Unlike other countries, which want to cooperate with us because they have business interests here, China wants to cooperate and compete with us at the same time. China and India are civilizations, and this fact lends complexity to diplomacy and trade. Xi's visit brings back memories of an earlier event. Then Chinese President Jiang Zemin visited India in 1996. Jiang was a technocrat. Yoginder K Alagh was the minister in attendance then; he writes of the incident as, "Like most high level leaders of the socialist world, he was well informed about societal developments. He asked me what I thought of Francis Fukuyama, I told him Fukuyama had got it all wrong. How could history come to an end just when it was China and India's turn to take centrestage? China and India should show the world what they can do together".[10]

Brahma Chellany said, "India's fumbling responses to the increasing Chinese incursions do not bode well for its Himalayan security".[11] The US and China are isolated in their own ways and they are two lonely powers. The process of giving up on hubris has left America neither feared nor loved. Both the left and the right in the US, somewhat disingenuously, criticize this relative modesty as an abduction of leadership. And the rest of the world says, giving up on nation-building hubris is all right, but please clean up the mess before you leave. Meanwhile, even regimes, and countries close to China take a Chinese approach to the relationship that is, being quite openly transactional.[12]

Notwithstanding the pleasant atmospherics, discussions between Prime Minister Narendra Modi and visiting Chinese President Xi Jinping in New Delhi took place in the backdrop of the standoff between Indian and Chinese forces in eastern Ladakh. The timing of the Chinese incursions in Chumar and Demchok sectors came close on the heels of President Pranab Mukherjee's tour of Vietnam that saw New Delhi extend a $100 million line of credit to Hanoi for defence purchases, including patrol boats that would be deployed in the South China Sea. Most likely it's this—along with greater cooperation between India and Vietnam in offshore energy exploration—which upset China as the latter lays exclusive territorial claim to the South China Sea.[13]

China has committed investments worth $20 billion over the next five years across various Indian sectors. This is a substantial cake if realized and compares well with the promise of $33 billion worth of investment from Japan that Modi procured on his trip there in September 2014, even if less than the wildly unrealistic figure of $100 billion that was bandied about earlier. It also set up Modi nicely for his US visit, where he sought enhanced American investment in India. A plethora of bilateral agreements have been inked in areas such as railways, industrial parks, language training and cultural exchanges—all of which will serve to build mutual confidence. New Delhi needs Chinese investments to mitigate its huge trade deficit with Beijing. Besides, the more invested China gets in India's economic growth, the less likely that it will resort to aggressive tactics. New Delhi should continue to pursue closer economic and cultural ties with Beijing, but also be prepared to play a good cop bad cop routine—just as the Chinese do—to protect its strategic interests. While it must make all out efforts to settle the border dispute, it must also be prepared to resist any Chinese blandishments that are intended to muscle it out of southeast Asia.[14]

After Modi-Xi meet, China agreed to settle border row. Prime Minister candidly said that solving the boundary issue between India and China is needed for growing economic cooperation between two countries. Modi said mutual trust and respect for each other's sensitivities and concerns, and peace and stability in our relations and along our borders are essential. Chinese President Xi Jinping said that both countries are capable of effectively managing the border situation. "Both sides are capable of effectively managing the border situation and to settle the border disputes at the earliest," Xi said after holding talks with Prime Minister Narendra Modi. Xi said that we have the sincerity to work with India on the border issue. He added that this issue should be dealt in a manner that it does not have an impact on ties. China will be opening an additional route to Kailash Mansarovar via Nathu La, Prime Minister Narendra Modi said. "I would like to thank (Chinese President) Xi Jinping on behalf of all Indians for a new route to Kailash Mansarovar. This new route, which will be opened through Nathu La, will be in addition to the existing route via Uttarakhand," Modi said during a joint press interaction with Xi at Hyderabad House.[15]

Attempting to clear the air over incursions that dodged President Xi Jinping's India visit, China said, differences over the disputed border should be handled in a way that does not impact peace and development in bilateral ties. Leaders of the two countries reached important consensus on properly handling the border issue. President Xi said that on border issues, the two sides should continue with friendly cooperation and pursue it in an equitable and fair way that is acceptable by both countries, spokesperson Hong Lei said at the regular press briefing. Hong said India had agreed to work China to properly handle and find a way to resolve the border issue. They agreed to respect and accommodate each other's concerns and deepen mutual trust, he added. On the issue of Tibet, Hong said, Prime Minister Modi said that Tibet is an integral part of China and India does not allow any separatist activities in India. On the 21st century Maritime Silk Road, Hong said Xi's proposal was aimed at pursuing common development with neighbouring countries including South Asian countries.[16]

The Congress said that its China policy found vindication in the Modi government's decision to step up a bilateral engagement. At the same time, the party expressed concern over the increasing number of incursions by China along the Line of Actual Control. Careful not to sound too critical of the Modi government vis-à-vis the visit of Chinese President Xi Jinping, former External Affairs Minister Salman Khurshid suggested that not many gains had come India's ways despite the optics. He conceived that some amount of "event management" was inevitable for a big visit like this. He wanted the government to spell out the specific gains. Also, has the Bhartiya Janata Party, which was always running us down, realized the folly of its myopic vision or is it in their nature to change their position on issues at will, he asked.

The Congress found fault with the government for not including Union Minister of State for Home Kiren Rijiju in the bilateral engagements, purportedly in deference to Chinese sensitivities vis-à-vis Arunachal Pradesh. Meanwhile, Congress President Sonia Gandhi met Mr. Xi along with former Prime Minister Manmohan Singh, Vice-president Rahul Gandhi and party members Karan Singh and Anand Sharma. The delegation sought to impress upon the Chinese leader that the party remained committed to bilateral engagement, though it was no longer in power.[17]

The visit of President Xi Jinping was remarkable for many things but mostly for the shift in the way India has done diplomacy with China. Overshadowing President Xi's visit was an incident on the Line of Actual control in the Chumar region of Ladakh, where troops and civilians were in a stand-off over construction activity on the Indian side. Prime Minister Narendra Modi's statement to the media, in the presence of the Chinese President, publicly driving home New Delhi's concerns about the "repeated incidents" at the border was addressed perhaps as much to Bharatiya Janata Party constituencies who want to see a hard line pressed on China, as it was to Beijing. The previous UPA government had preferred to send out quieter messages on the border question. This, combined with Mr. Modi's protocol and conventions to accord Mr. Xi a more than effusive welcome in Ahmedabad, succeeded in giving new signalling seems to have elicited a quick response, with the Chinese side saying that the two leaders had committed themselves to resolving the border issue "as soon as possible," and that they had reached a "consensus" on the way forward. In a joint statement, the two sides acknowledged that peace and tranquillity on the India-China border areas was an important guarantor for the development and continued growth of bilateral relations, and that pending a final resolution of the boundary question, the two sides would continue to make joint efforts to maintain peace and tranquillity in border areas.[18]

From India's standpoint, attracting Chinese investment is imperative for reviving growth. Besides, its deepening ties with Japan, Australia and Vietnam have opened up more room for manoeuvre in Asia. As China's swaggering rise rattles its neighbours, India is seen as a key player in ensuring a balanced regional order. In the run-up to the summit, Mr. Modi and Mr. Xi were projected as powerful and decisive leaders. As such, they should be ideally placed to take a serious crack at resolving the boundary dispute. Mr. Modi is supposedly free of the baggage that weighed on the Congress Party. He is certainly capable of making a persuasive public case for a settlement. Instead of going down the rabbit-hole of LAC clarification, the government should move boldly to settle the boundary dispute with China.[19]

The men are full of praise for one another, and one another's countries. Xi gushes over India as "an enchanting and beautiful land." Modi declares that their pledges to work together "will open big gates for progress and development in the world." Just a few hours into the Xi's three-day visit, newspapers were awash with accomplishments: a joint industrial park, a sister-city pact, ramped up cultural ties, business deals and investment promises from China worth well more than $20 billion. Left largely unspoken, though, are the deep worries in India over Chinese manoeuvring in the Indian Ocean, where New Delhi's years of dominance is being chipped away by billions of dollars in aid from Beijing and gargantuan Chinese construction projects. And while China's recent push for dominance in the South China and East China seas get more attention, the quite contest for influence in the Indian Ocean is being watched carefully from Tokyo to Washington. More than anything else, the worries are over energy.[20]

It is reported that Rajiv Gandhi visited China in 1988. A quarter century has passed since, then, and a future generation has now ascended to the leadership role. If ailments of the India-China relationship are neglected and allowed to deteriorate it could have significant consequences for both the regions and the world.[21] Chinese President Xi Jinping's visit to India, his first since he assumed office in March 2013 was the first state visit by a Chinese President to India in eight years. The last stop in Xi's four-nation tour in Central and South Asia, it was the most important, and the interaction between Xi and Prime Minister Narendra Modi set a positive tone for ties between the two countries. China views India's position on the BCIM (Bangladesh-China-India-Myanmar) as a barometer of its attitude towards Beijing's South Asia policy and the degree of its strategic trust. There was a positive response at least at the rhetorical level, as Modi remarked that "India believes that reconnecting Asia is important for its collective prosperity." China also reiterated its support for India's aspiration to play a more active role in the UN and the Security Council, and it will support Delhi's membership to the Shanghai Cooperation Organisation. Although the border issue will continue to hinder India-China relations and true political trust will be impossible to establish in the absence of a settlement, there is enough space to develop cooperation on common concerns. The political leaders of India and China are taking the initiative to foster a shared culture based on reciprocity and common interests. Hopefully, a deeper understanding of each other could lead to a better future.[22]

It is observed by Husain Haqqani that Modi's success with China and US, depends on ability to bring economics to the centre. Americans believe that India can achieve rapid economic growth through innovation if it opens up its economy to foreign technologies. As Modi and Obama meet, Indian policymakers must recognize that economic factors are as important to Washington as they are to Beijing. For American FDI, India must strengthen its intellectual property right regulations and protect foreign investors who are exporting new technologies to India. Greater protection for foreign technologies will not only encourage growth and innovation, but also bring in vital FDI. New Delhi cannot afford to persist with its dated modes of thought on pharmaceuticals or the defence industry either.[23]

Chinese President Xi Jinping's rhetoric about "regional war" shortly after his return from India could be a sign of his frustration over his apparent failure in persuading Prime Minister Narendra Modi to go slow on his relations with Japan, said western diplomats. Xi had asked People's Liberation Army commanders to "sharpen their ability to win a regional war in the age of information technology amid standoff with India along the defacto border in Ladakh. Japan's move towards militarization and Modi's arrival as a strongman happened at the same time. Friendship between him and Japan's (PM Shinzo) Abe is the worst thing that could happen to China, a Beijing based diplomat said. Xi is ready to put military pressure on India to keep it away from Japan, the diplomat added. The official also said that China is desperate to prove its supremacy in the region. Look at the near collision between a Chinese fighter and a US war plane in August 2014. Another diplomat echoed the reading, saying, China would woo, threaten or do whatever else it feels necessary to keep India from joining hands with Japan. He said China is determined to "be a regional bully" and India-Japan combine could destroy this.[24]

China later on clarified President Xi Jinping's recent remarks about winning "regional war" was not aimed at India. China will do nothing to disturb the tranquillity on the border, said Chinese foreign ministry spokeswoman Hua Chunying. "We will never allow border area to influence Sino-India relations," Hua was replying to questions whether Xi's remarks amounted to a threat to India amid a border standoff. "I believe that this may be a wild guess," she said. The guessing was completely "off the mark" she added. The spokeswoman dismissed suggestions that China was worried about growing India-Japan ties. The Chinese people are not fragile and petty nation. We are happy to see other countries develop friendly bilateral relations as long as such relationship is positive and conducive to regional peace, she said. Such dispute has been managed and border area is in tranquillity, she said when asked about the presence of 800 Chinese soldiers on the Indian Territory. There may be some problem between the two countries but you can be assured that the two leaders (Prime Minister Narendra Modi and Xi) have consensus to solve the disputes through friendly coordination, he said.[25]

India and the USA

Before going on his diplomatic journey to United States where he swept every one of their feet by his charm, Narendra Modi had another difficult bilateral decision to take as regards India's relations with Pakistan. In spite of repeated warnings, Pakistan went ahead and had a meeting with separatist leaders. This was not liked by the people and leaders in India, and consequently Modi called of the Secretary level talks scheduled between the two countries. Modi was lauded by the media and the leaders for his brave act while others criticised him for his unthinkable rashness in stopping all dialogue with Pakistan.

Continuing his diplomatic blitz Modi gave a speech at the United Nations General Assembly which was heard with a lot of attention. Mr. Modi questioned if institutions like the UN were operating effectively to handle contemporary challenges. He pressed for UN reforms pointing that institutions of the 20th century would no longer be effective as "no one country or group of countries can determine the course of this world"[26]. He seemed to be on a diplomatic roll chatting with UN Secretary General Ban Ki Moon and addressing the UN General Assembly for the first time. Prime Minister Modi also made some telling remarks on Pakistan, a day after his counterpart Nawaz Sharif criticized India for cancelling Foreign Secretary level talks, besides reiterating Kashmir's right to self-determination. The PM was comparatively restrained, saying he was "prepared to engage in a serious bilateral dialogue" with Pakistan, provided there was no shadow of terrorism. He admonished Mr Sharif for raising Kashmir at the UN and said Pakistan ought to take its responsibility for creating an "appropriate environment" seriously. Islamabad reacted immediately saying that it had a right to speak with Kashmiri militants conceding that such talks could be better timed.[27]

India and Other Friendly States

Prime Minister Narendra Modi visited the United States of America from September 26-30, 2014 and his visit created a surge of expectations about the likely trajectory of India-US relations. While the US and India share democratic values, political affinity between the two is still a distant dream and because of different perspectives, the two countries differently perceive their national interests in any given context. "Despite the altered geopolitical context, there are many areas where India and the US can expand their relations much beyond current levels," feels Shyam Saran, former foreign secretary, and currently chairman, National Security Advisory Board and RIS, and senior fellow, Centre for Policy Research.[28]

According to Frederic Grare, Associate Director of the South Asia Programme at the Carnegie Endowment for International Peace, "the visit can be called a success if the two countries manage to re-establish the working relationship that existed in the past but has since disappeared. The new prime minister undeniably possesses the assets to achieve that much, but the future of US-India relations will ultimately depend on India's capacity to reform itself, and therefore on the prime minister's ability to deliver on his campaign's promise to fix the structural weaknesses of his country's economy".[29]

Former foreign secretary Government of India, Kanwal Sibal opines that if the media coverage in India of Prime Minister Narendra Modi's US visit and the adulation with which the Indian-American community greeted him in New York were any yardstick, it can be called a resounding success.[30] *Hindustan Times* in its editorial on 30.9.2014 writes that the rapturous response of Indian Americans to Prime Minister Narendra Modi's visit to the United States will be long remembered. The breathless enthusiasm was on full view at the Madison Square Garden in New York. At Madison Square Garden, Modi displayed the power of persuasion, perhaps his greatest asset, and his ability to recruit participation in the story he is scripting for the new India.[31] Modi's feat is comparable to what Vivekananda did when he addressed the World Parliament of Religions in Chicago 121 years ago.

For many people, New York's Madison Square Garden still evokes images of memorable boxing matches. It has been the scene of many a memorable fights—Muhammad Ali took on Joe Frazier for the first time here, as did many others. MSG or the "Garden", as it is popularly known, has also been the choice venue for musical events like George Harrison's concert for Bangladesh, John Lennon's last public performance, Elton John and Billy Joel's record-breaking appearances as well as 'the concert for New York City' after 9/11. Located atop the Pennsylvania Station in midtown Manhattan and part of the 'Penn Complex', this multi-purpose indoor complex hosts around 300 events during the course of a year. On Sunday, September 28, 2014, it was scheduled to host the public reception and address of Prime Minister Narendra Modi to the Indian diaspora in the US.[32] The reception at the iconic venue—featuring a PM with 'rock star' status, accompanied by wall-to-wall coverage on television and social networks—created a rare unified experience for the geographically – disparate three million strong Indian American community. Mr. Modi in turn, indulged the fawning crowds and brilliantly played an audience, located far away from its 'homeland', with a speech laden with themes of nostalgia, tradition, hope, and change.

After their first meeting over dinner at the White House, Prime Minister Narendra Modi and President Barack Obama unveiled a joint roadmap for Indo-US ties by issuing a vision statement and writing a joint editorial making "chalein saath saath" or "forward together we go" the central theme of the relationship. This vision statement is comprehensive, dealing with collaborations "ranging from particles of creation to outer space," but marks a more realistic appraisal of the relationship, given the lack of forward movement in many spheres, including the nuclear deal and trade issues. This editorial, a first of its kind from an Indian and US leaders was published on the Washington Post website.[33] Barack Obama while addressing the Indian Parliament during his visit referred to Indo-US relations as "the defining partnership of the 21st Century" Narendra Modi and Barack Obama talked about a renewed US-India partnership for the 21st century. With a reinvigorated level of ambition and greater confidence, India and the US can go beyond modest and conventional goals. In this partnership, the Indian and American communities have been a vibrant, living bridge.[34]

Despite the euphoria and media-hype created by Modi's American visit, it should be remembered what Mrs Indira Gandhi once said, that on account of deep divergences on world issues both India and America cannot come closer than a certain point. All the talks of the "largest democracy" and the "oldest democracy" are just social rhetoric because both countries are governed by their national interests and nothing else. Elegantly drafted agreements and finely worded speeches aren't instruments of power. There's little sign, so far, that India has carefully considered precisely which ones it wants to acquire – and even less that it's thinking about just how to use them.

Lisa Curtis of American Heritage Foundation suggests a bit of caution. "Modi must recognise that the US government—unlike the Japanese and Chinese governments—does not announce large-scale investments in countries, but leaves it to private business to make investment decisions." She pointed out that while "this visit will create interest in the Indian market among US investors, they will ultimately base their investment decisions on the action Modi government takes over the next six months with regards to economic reforms and further opening the Indian economy to the private sector."[35]

Realistically speaking, American experts like Curtis point out that no major breakthroughs are expected. But if it can create a better understanding between the two sides and win back the confidence of the US government and business community to look at India as a major partner, it can at least create the groundwork where deeper and wider ties between the two countries remain possible. The *Hindu* writes that in a major sign of the deepening ties between India and the US, Prime Minister Modi has invited President Obama to be the chief guest at the Republic Day ceremony next year. The invitation was delivered by Prime Minister Modi during his visit to Myanmar and Australia, when he met with President Obama at the East Asia summit and the G-20 meeting of world leaders.[36]

After nine years of denying Narendra Modi a visa to visit their country, it seems the US administration was hell-bent on keeping up its efforts at courting the 15th Prime Minister of India. What appears to be a diplomatic coup, the United States President, Barack Obama, had agreed to be the chief guest at the Republic Day function on 26 January 2015 by becoming the first US president to attend the grand ceremony which showed both the military might and the cultural diversity of India. "This Republic Day, we hope to have a friend over...invited President Obama to be the 1st US President to grace the occasion as the Chief Guest," Prime Minister Narendra Modi tweeted. Official sources later confirmed that the US president has accepted the invitation.

Critics of Modi's diplomacy point out that we should not be swept off our feet at Modi's diplomatic coup of inviting President Barrack Obama as the Chief Guest at the Republic Day celebrations in 2015. There are several reasons why the US President agreed to come to India. Firstly, the Indo-US Civil Nuclear deal was in a limbo and Obama was coming here to accelerate the developments. Secondly, Obama needs India to send its army in Afghanistan when America decides to pull out. Thirdly, India has decided to allocate more money for its Defence budget and now even the private sector like Tata is going for India's defence production. In this context America also wants to have a piece of the cake. Fourthly, America needs India to keep an eye on Chinese military activities in this region and also contain it. Fifthly, America wants peace in South Asia and Obama is coming to coax Modi to begin a meaningful dialogue with Pakistan. Sixthly, Obama has an eye on the large affluent middle class of India which can be an easy market for American goods. Finally, India has the largest population of youth in the world and hence the American President wants to project a positive image of her country towards Indian youth.

"This visit marked the first time a US president had the honour of attending Republic Day, which commemorates the adoption of India's constitution. The President will meet with the Prime Minister and Indian officials to strengthen and expand the US-India strategic partnership," the statement added. Modi had met with President Obama at the White House in September for talks on two consecutive days. Modi had travelled to Washington after addressing the United Nations in New York and starring in what was dubbed as "a rock star reception" at the Madison Square Garden venue in New York. In the Washington Post, the editor commented that "Chalein Saath Saath" and after their meeting they had covered key issues including economics, climate change, and regional security besides agreeing to negotiate a 10-year extension of a military cooperation framework due to expire at the end. Modi had met with President Obama at an East Asia summit in Myanmar and a deal was struck there to allow a WTO trade deal that India had stalled over concerns that its food subsidies to the poor could face legal challenges. The President had praised Modi as 'a man of action'.[37]

Prime Minister Narendra Modi has now interacted with the leaders of different countries/regions—SAARC, countries of Indian Ocean region, Japan, China, Russia, USA, Singapore, France, Germany and Canada—on the list of foreign policy priorities mentioned in the President's address to the opening session of Parliament. It is, therefore, an appropriate time to take stock of the underlying changes in the directions of India's foreign policy. In other words, is Mr. Modi's foreign policy likely to differ from that of Sonia Gandhi and Manmohan Singh? Every country's foreign policy has elements of continuity and change following a change in government. India's policy under Mr. Modi is no different. The changes have not necessarily been explicitly articulated, but are implicit in the government's actions and view of the world. There are five areas of the emerging change: the centrality given to economic and technological development; the orientation of domestic and foreign policies toward this objective; the emphasis on national power including military power; and stress on soft power; and a reduction in self-imposed constraints on actions that other countries may construe as inimical to their interests.

"The country will no longer bend. Modi will put national interest first," Ram Madhav, Bhartiya Janata Party (BJP) General Secretary, told an audience in New York even as Prime Minister Narendra Modi was visiting the United States in September 2014. "Pakistan must know that the Modi government is different," Home Minister Rajnath Singh said while responding to ceasefire violations at the border. Mr. Modi made similar statements during the recent assembly election campaigns in Maharashtra and Haryana. The impression that is being created through all these statements is that the Modi government is pursuing a strategic policy that is different to those by previous regimes. Projecting his own uniqueness is characteristic of Mr. Modi.

So what is really new and radical is the assertiveness of the Hindu nationalistic project that Mr. Modi has globally launched in Bhutan, Nepal and New York. "A nationalistic government under a decisive leader will deal with the world with confidence. We cannot play second fiddle to anyone," said P. Muralidhar Rao, BJP General Secretary. Though Mr. Modi projects his foreign policy as being radically different, in terms of outcomes, continuity is evident. What used to be called "strategic autonomy" in saner times is now being projected as "no bending". That India cannot protect its interests by being part of any axis, and that it would pursue its bilateral relations based on its own strategic calculations is in line with the time-tested approach. What is indeed worrying is the chest-thumping rhetoric that accompanies foreign policy, regardless of the fact that we now have a 56-inch one. Balancing his nationalist convictions with the demands of a globalised world will be Mr. Modi's biggest strategic policy challenge.[38]

Modi visited Myanmar and his visit took place two years after the bilateral visit of Prime Minister Manmohan Singh in May 2012. Myanmar is now our most rapidly growing neighbour experiencing 8 per cent plus growth rates. There can be mutual benefit if both India and Myanmar can work together to truly transform the evolving connectivity corridors into development corridors, which can also be a demonstration of our 'Act East' policy. Building an interlaced economic partnership across the border can form an enduring bond between the two countries that already enjoy very good political ties.

Prime Minister Narendra Modi's visit to Australia was long overdue; it came 28 years after Prime Minister Rajiv Gandhi travelled to the continent. While the invitation to Brisbane for the G-20 summit took Mr. Modi there, the decision to travel to three other Australian cities, at a time when he had other pressing domestic commitments, was well considered. As a result, his meeting with Australian Prime Minister Tony Abbot has seen relations being upgraded and imparted with clarity. Mr. Modi's bilateral meetings came after Chinese President Xi Jinping's meetings in Canberra where China and Australia announced an FTA and enhanced strategic cooperation. The newly announced India-Australia strategic framework that structures annual meetings between the leaders, defence ministers and regular exchanges between the armed forces and non-defence forces on counter-terrorism, piracy and cyber security, is a positive step that focuses on the shared strengths of India and Australia.[39]

Prime Minister's neighbourhood—first initiative must address perceptions that Delhi only promises, doesn't deliver. Afghanistan's new government wishes to revisit its requests for Indian military assistance de novo but, the unhappy fact is that India failed to deliver the light helicopters it had promised would be in Kabul early this year, and made little progress on plans to refit Afghanistan's light transport aircraft. The UPA government, also fearful of irking Pakistan, dithered on meeting Afghanistan's requests for lethal equipment, despite having signed a strategic partnership agreement which promised just that. Kabul is thus entitled to wonder if New Delhi is a reliable partner.

Lethargy has long characterised Indian strategy in the neighbourhood: New Delhi has dilly-dallied on oil storage and port investments in Sri Lanka, proved slow in developing trade between Bangladesh and the Northeast states, and is building infrastructure that would give depth to ties with Myanmar at a glacial pace. India, it is true, has won friends with small amounts of development aid, and with low-grade military-to-military training assistance. Its record on things genuinely strategic in their scale, though, can at best be described poor. The lethargy gives reason to fear that India doesn't have what it takes to play under the spotlight reserved for genuine great powers. For Prime Minister Narendra Modi's neighbourhood-first initiative to have left, he will have to rebuild the creaking institutions to which India has entrusted the conduct of its foreign policy.[40]

Apart from Fiji, Tonga, Vanuatu and Nauru have cordial relations with

India, while Papua New Guinea, Solomon Islands, Kiribati and others have warm feelings for India. The visit of the Indian Prime Minister to Fiji comes 33 years after Indira Gandhi's visit. But the timing of Narendra Modi's visit is most appropriate because racial harmony and non-discrimination, both of which India had wished for Fiji, have just been accomplished. But the visit has to be followed up with a robust programme of co-operation in areas in which we have particular strengths.

SAARC

The much delayed South Asian Association for Regional Cooperation (SAARC) summit in Kathmandu, on November 26-27, 2014, exactly six months to the date from Prime Minister Narendra Modi's swearing-in ceremony offered him an opportunity to reconnect with India's neighbours, to revive moribund regional cooperation in South Asia. When SAARC was constituted three decades ago, India was hampered by limited resources for financing partnerships and investments in the region. This now is no longer the case. Good relations with neighbours are a priority for India. But for this, India has to commit to and accelerate its efforts towards forging closer bilateral and regional partnerships and economic integration within the subcontinent and beyond.

SAARC has remained saddled with this legacy, and India is viewed with angst by many in its neighbourhood .Sixteen years ago, the SAARC Group of Eminent Persons had charted an ambitious, three-stage road map for South Asia: a South Asia Free Trade Area, followed by a Customs Union and a broader Economic Union by the year 2020. Mr. Atal Bihari Vajpayee lent his support for the creation of a South Asian Economic Union at the previous summit in Kathmandu in 2002. The 200 Islamabad Summit called for South Asian energy cooperation and strengthened transportation, transit and communications links across the region. These good resolutions have not been realised. Intra-regional trade and investment remain well below double digit figures, making South Asia the least economically integrated area in the world. South Asian states are connected more to the outside world than to each other.

Since politics cannot be taken out of any venture between states, they also need an innovative use of diplomacy and statecraft. India must lift its game for SAARC's rescue and resuscitation. It must lead by example, building trust with its neighbours, showing solidarity, and forging with them a habit of cooperation. India has the strength to shape regional partnerships that lift neighbouring economies with its own, not as a symbol of Indian altruism but of its enlightened self-interest. It must help build a regional architecture that creates a congenial space for all its members. Such a transformation cannot come quickly. It will be conditioned by India's own growth prospects, and unpredictable circumstances can derail the momentum.

It should be remembered that the EU was made possible only due to the conclusion drawn by the people of Europe, after the experience of two terrible world wars, that a third world war would destroy Europe totally. Hence, despite a violent history of warfare, European nations sank their differences and formed the EU. But as the popular saying goes, it takes two to tango. With two of the eight SAARC nations in possession of deliverable nuclear weapons, it is imperative for the peaceful existence of SAARC nations that they effectively bind together and develop harmoniously.[41]

No previous Indian Prime Minister participated in so many high-powered multilateral and bilateral summits in his or her first months as Mr. Modi. PM Modi's focus on the grand chessboard of geopolitics to underpin national interests suggests a strategic bent of mind that only one previous Prime Minister demonstrated—Indira Gandhi. The Modi foreign policy is powered by ideas, not by any ideology and the real test ultimately will be Mr. Modi's ability to translate his ideas into transformative accomplishments. He has projected a nimble foreign policy with pragmatism as its hallmark. Nothing better illustrates this than the priority he has accorded—by shaking off U.S. visa-denial humiliation heaped on him over nine years—to restoring momentum to the relationship with America. Mr. Obama's visit as chief guest at Republic Day represents both a thank you to Mr. Modi for rising above personal umbrage and an effort to lift the India-U.S. relationship to a higher level of engagement through the major new opportunities being opened up for American businesses by Mr. Modi's commitment to pro-market economic policies and defence modernisation. The U.S. already conducts more military exercises with India than with any other country. And in recent years, it has quietly overtaken Russia as the largest arms supplier to India.

Mr. Modi has put his stamp on foreign policy faster than any predecessor, other than Jawaharlal Nehru. Yet, he appears to have no intent to enunciate a Modi doctrine in foreign policy. In contrast to the "Gujral Doctrine", which delivered little more than words, Mr. Modi wants his actions to define his policy trademarks. In fact, his actions have started speaking for themselves—from his moves to engineer stronger partnerships with Japan and Israel (countries critical to Indian interests but which also courted him even as the U.S. targeted him) to his mortars—for-bullet response to Pakistani ceasefire violations. His firm stand at the World Trade Organisation (WTO) on the food stockpiling issue, central to India's food security, stood out. After vetoing the WTO's Trade Facilitation Agreement in Geneva, Mr. Modi made the U.S. climb down on the food stockpiling issue, yet earned praise from Mr. Obama for helping to break the impasse. Even the head of the U.N.'s International Fund for Agricultural Development backed the veto, saying the real choice for India in Geneva was between "feeding" its citizens and "creating jobs" for wealthy economies.

Mr. Modi, unlike the leaders who preceded him, attaches major significance to diplomatic symbolism. For example, with the opening of the SAARC Summit coinciding with the sombre anniversary of the Mumbai terror attacks, he gave the cold shoulder to his Pakistani counterpart, Nawaz Sharif, for refusing to prosecute the masterminds of that Pakistani scripted and executed operation. Mr. Modi shook hands with Mr. Sharif only the following day at the Dhulikhel retreat. In fact, to concentrate on his broader regional and global agenda, Mr. Modi has done well to sideline Pakistan, a noxious issue that weighed down Mr. Atal Bihari Vajpayee's foreign policy. Geography demands that India evolve more dynamic and innovative approaches to diplomacy and national defence. India must actively involve itself regionally to help influence developments, which is what Mr. Modi is seeking to do. India, while building stronger bilateral linkages with other neighbours, must strengthen its "Look East" policy. Looking east allows India to join the economic dynamism that characterises the region to its east. For a politician who came to office with virtually no foreign-policy experience, Mr. Modi has demonstrated impressive diplomatic acumen, including in taking bold new directions, charting a vision to reclaim India's lost strategic clout, holding his ground in talks with world leaders, and responding to provocations by regional foes. Mr. Modi has shaken India's foreign policy establishment with his positive approach and readiness to break with conventional methods and shibboleths. All in all, the Modi foreign policy appears geared to reinvent India as a more competitive, confident and secure country claiming its rightful place in the world. A robust foreign policy, however, can sustain itself only on the foundation of a strong domestic policy, a realm where Mr. Modi must prove he can help transform India.[42]

As Dr Chintamani Mahapatra of the School of International Studies,

Jawahar Lal Nehru University, New Delhi observes, Prime Minister Narendra Modi's visit to Washington and a summit meeting with President Barack Obama has re-energised a relationship that was widely perceived to be moving towards a dead-end.[43] With Obama's visit as Chief Guest at India's Republic Day celebrations on 26 January 2015, New Delhi broke fresh ground in foreign policy. It means India and US have turned a new chapter in their relations. On his second visit to India, Obama made all proper statements and reiterated his support for a reformed UNSC with India as a permanent member but according to the state-run Pakistan Television, Nawaz Sharif told Obama that a permanent seat for India in the UN Security Council (UNSC) was unacceptable as it has not complied with the UN resolution on Kashmir. Apart from the joint photographs, back-slapping, hugs and first name terms, President Obama alongwith his wife Michelle wrapped up his visit by cautioning PM Modi over religious conversions and controversial Ghar Wapsi programmes by right-wing Hindu outfits in India. Obama also cited Article 25 of the Indian Constitution dealing with the Right to Freedom of religion and before embarking Air Force 1, told Modi unequivocally that India will succeed so long as it is not splintered on religious lines and every person has the right to practice their religion how they chose.[44]

The seismic shift in India-US engagement in the past 15 years, since the Pokhran II nuclear tests of 1998, has been domestic adversaries build on each other's work. From Bill Clinton to George W Bush to now Obama, both Democrats and Republicans have demonstrated bipartisan support for a strategic partnership with India. In New Delhi, Manmohan Singh carried forward gains of the Atal Bihari Vajpayee years. Modi has pushed ahead with much of what Singh had already started, including the nuclear deal. Modi by honouring Obama as the chief guest for Republic Day celebrations has vividly demonstrated his intent to replace some of this brittleness with steel. If he succeeds in this endeavour, historians will see Modi's bold move as a brilliant illustration of the statesmanship India, and the world, so badly needs in these troubled times. The challenge for the Modi government is to blunt the adversarial edge of the China relationship even as it looks to consolidate ties with the US. Progress on the boundary question, addressing the misconceptions on Pakistan and Tibet, tackling bureaucratic suspicions of Chinese technology will develop trust and realise economic potential. Reassuring the US and China at the same time promises to be very demanding. Appointing S. Jaishankar, former envoy to Washington and Beijing, as foreign secretary makes sense in this light.

Over the decades, a perverse political culture enveloped Indian foreign policymaking and turned Delhi into an odd-ball in the international arena. India would rather negotiate against its own long-term interests than find common ground with others. Standing up to America was considered an overriding political virtue. Whether it was on trade, climate change or nuclear policy, defending inherited positions became the dominant foreign policy tradition.[45]

External Affairs Minister Sushma Swaraj, on a three-day official trip to China said that no one country can influence our foreign policy, thereby meaning that close relations with America will not be at the cost of China.

At the 13th trilateral meeting between India, China and Russia, the two countries seemed to agree that New Delhi may soon be the right candidate to join the Asia-Pacific Economic co-operation (APEC) forum. Sushma Swaraj said, Russia and China agreed to co-operate on implementing the anti-terror proposal lying dormant in the United Nations.

Using the cricketing threats that bind South Asia, Prime Minster Narendra Modi has shown that his heart is in improving ties with the neighbourhood and he has made amends for a policy lap on Pakistan. Nearly six months after India cancelled foreign secretary level talks with Pakistan over its envoy meetings with Huriyat leaders, Prime Minister Narendra Modi called up his counterpart Nawaz Sharif and said foreign secretary S. Jaishankar will visit Pakistan as part of The SAARC Yatra. Modi spoke to Sharif as part of his "cricket diplomacy", conveying his best wishes to four SAARC leaders whose countries' cricket teams were playing in the cricket World Cup tournament. Besides Sharif, he had called Bangladesh Prime Minister Sheikh Hasina, Sri Lankan President Maithripala Sirisena and Afghanistan President Ashraf Ghani.

Modi's style of diplomacy brings a new flavour to Indian Foreign Policy. For all the talk of India as a traditional great power, a close reading of Modi's policy towards China, Japan and the US suggests that economic growth and development remain at the top of the agenda. Narendra Modi resembles Indira Gandhi because both the RSS and the BJP believe in "Vyaktipuja" or "the cult of personality". Narendra Modi has stamped his will (and whim) on the BJP. His control of his party today easily equals the domination that Indira Gandhi exercised over the Congress following her electoral victory in 1971. While Congress President Dev Kanta Baruah notoriously said, "Indira is India and India is Indira". No BJP leader has gone so far yet, but Modi has on many occasions indicated that he does see himself as the embodiment of the nation. For Indira Gandhi the sole confidant and utterly trustworthy second in command varied—between 1969 and 1974 it was P.N. Haksar, between 1974 and 1980 it was Sanjay Gandhi, and after 1981 it became Rajiv Gandhi. For Narendra Modi it is Amit Shah.[46]

Modi's US diplomacy marks a shift in India's worldview. Modi is changing the nature of India's worldview, recasting its self-image and altering the character of its diplomacy. Now India is imagining a bold trajectory of a comprehensive partnership with the US, Modi is departing from the Indian self-perception as a weak third world nation that is afraid of engaging America. Modi, in contrast, wants Delhi to see itself as an emerging power and deal with Washington with self Insurance. India has now come out of the shadow of Third Worldism and now demands boldly that the permanent membership of UN Security Council should be given to it as a right. If the UPA government panicked at the thought of America assisting India's right to great power status, Modi wants to test the seriousness of American intent, as he articulates India's strategic ambition to emerge as a responsible power. Modi's self-confidence is bringing Delhi's worldview in alignment with economic reforms in the globalised world. Like Indira Gandhi who did not let the shibboleths of non-alignment come in the way of a strategic partnership with the Soviet Union in the 1970s, similarly Modi is not going to allow ideological slogans come in the way of India's security calculus.[47]

The BJP announced a new Panchamrit or Five elixirs formula on foreign policy and pitched for peaceful engagements with Pakistan to gain the neighbours co-operation to root out terrorism in the region. BJP's national executive said that the Modi government has responded firmly and appropriately to provocations on the border, yet the party is committed to "building peaceful and friendly relations with Pakistan in order to put an end to terrorism". The pillars of Panchamrit are "Saaman—dignity and honour; Samvad—greater engagement and dialogue; Samriddhi—shared prosperity; Suraksha—regional and global security; and Sanskriti evam Sabhyata—cultural and civilisational linkages". Amit Shah unveiled a strategy to integrate the party's cadre-base with social causes taken up by the Modi government, hoping that it would help the BJP remain in power for two decades. Modi advised the party office bearers by invoking Mahatma Gandhi who had involved people in social causes to create a political support base for the Congress then.

Sino-Indian Relationship and Beyond

China and India, two fast-growing giants, are trapped in a zero-sum strategic rivalry. China, which was Asia's dominant power for centuries, wants to reassert its hegemony and regards a powerful India as an obstacle to its ambitions. India on the other hand had been a victim of Western colonialism and sees itself as South Asia's undisputed regional leader and views any attempt by China to establish its primacy in Asia as a threat to its national security and economic interests. Narendra Modi and Xi Jinping can lay the foundations for a stable Sino-Indian relationship. China must reassure India that its ambitious infrastructure program will not pose a threat to Indian national security. In particular, China should provide more transparency on its investments activities in Pakistan. In return, Modi should assuage Xi's worries that India will allow itself to be used as a pawn of the US in balancing against China. The Modi government must do an intricate dance balancing Chinese interests with Indian aspirations. The trick will be to avoid conflict, and this will require high level diplomacy by India.

Prime Minister Narendra Modi visited China, Mongolia and South Korea from May 14, 2015. Two days ahead of his visit, Chinese daily *Global Times* attacked Modi and India. It said Indians are inferior people and PM Narendra Modi is playing little tricks on the boundary dispute and should no longer visit Arunachal Pradesh for it is a disputed border region. The Chinese also published wrong maps of India in which the territory of Arunachal Pradesh was shown as Chinese and POK was shown to be in Pakistan. However, Modi has made a bold effort in recasting Sino-Indian ties; his visit to China was the fourth visit by any Indian PM in twelve years. As usual the real focus of his trip was economic cooperation as China remains India's largest trading partner. Although the border dispute with China cannot be solved overnight but a beginning has been made. India has just settled its border dispute with Bangladesh by a landmark LBA (Land Boundary Agreement) treaty by being pragmatic. A similar pragmatism on the India-China border, along the current line of actual control, would be a game changer.

A week before the marking the first anniversary of his assumption of office Prime Minster Narendra Modi ended his year of hectic diplomacy with a visit to China. For India, no other bilateral relationship is more complex and challenging than the one with its biggest neighbour. Jawaharlal Nehru's errors of judgement in dealing with China cast a long shadow on bilateral relations. Since then every Prime Minister has treaded cautiously, perhaps far too cautiously in dealing with China.[48] India and China are two major powers in the Asian region today. Deng Xiaoping once observed that a genuine Asian century could be possible only when China and India became developed countries. Both are racing ahead in that direction. Prime Minister Narendra Modi and President Xi Jinping are making sincere efforts to take India-China bilateral relation to a new hight. With Modi's visit to China, bilateral relations are expected to strengthen further. One hopes that we succeed in achieving some measured progress in the outstanding issues as Deng stated once, "There is enough space for both the countries to prosper".

The India-China relationship, today, is marked by low levels of mutual trust, pervading ambivalence in each country's approach to the other, and the lack of knowledge of the other among the people of either country. Mr. Modi's test is to introduce more rationality and coherence into the relationship than there is today, and to convince the Chinese of the same. The two countries that gave the world Panchsheel, cannot live in mutual exclusion. It is only a strong secure, economically developed India that can successfully achieve the goal of being a leader on the global stage. A partnership for development between India and China is a win-win partnership and neither side can lose in such a transaction. India, which has distances to cover in its development marathon, aims well to draw in investment and infrastructure-creating expertise from China.[49]

Modi's visit to Mongolia and South Korea reflect a robust Act East policy. While returning from China Modi visited Mongolia which was the first visit by an Indian PM and reflects new determination to actualise India's Act East policy. New Delhi needs to increase its footprint in East Asia and win over new friends. On the other hand, Modi's trip to South Korea explored new avenues of cooperation. South Korea as a miracle economy is successfully making a transition from a backward Third World nation to a First World player. There is a huge scope for cooperation between New Delhi and Seoul. On the last day of his three nations tour that took him to China, Mongolia and South Korea, Prime Minister Modi sought unity among Asian Countries and said they must work as Asians to shape the world and reform global institutions of governance including the United Nations. "If Asia must rise as one, Asia should no longer think of itself in regional fragments", PM Modi said at the sixth Asia leadership conference in the South Korean capital Seoul. Modi said: "Asia of unity will shape the world". India seeks an Asia of shared prosperity where the success of one nation becomes the strength of the other".

"We must work as Asian to reform the global institutions of governance including the United Nations and its Security Council", he said.

Act East Policy

Under Modi's "Act East policy", India has intensified engagement with key regional powers like Japan, South Korea, Vietnam and Australia. Recently, Modi had a successful "Saagar Yatra" to Seychelles, Mauritius and Sri Lanka. Modi's visit to Europe and Canada helped restore some balance to India's international engagement. Modi will be hosting a large diplomatic outreach program with Africa, the third edition of India-Africa forum summit which is scheduled to be held in New Delhi on October 26, 2015. India will invite leaders of all 54 states on the region to the five-day long summit, which is expected to be attended by nearly on thousand delegates. The meeting between the heads of the governments and states is scheduled for October 29, 2015. In June 2015, Modi visited Bangladesh and this year, Prime Minister Modi, President Pranab Mukherjee, Defence Minister Manohar Parrikar and External Affairs Minister are said to visit Russia.

India and the West

Modi was the first Indian Prime Minister to visit Canada on bilateral business in more than four decades. The decision of Modi to travel to Canada in his very first year as PM gives a signal that India not only values its friends but also shows its political appreciation. The end of the Cold War and India's economic globalisation created a lot more room for India's engagement with the Western middle powers but the UPA government was unable to seize the moment and turn new opportunities into tangible outcomes. Modi's visit to France, Germany and Canada contributed substantially to the realisation of India's new national goals. Apart from "Nav pe charcha" with the French President on the river Siene, Modi made an out of the box deal with France getting the much needed fighter planes in which 36 Raffale fighter aircrafts were bought and many more were to be given. Germany and Canada are also members ofThe NSG (Nuclear Suppliers Group) and the three nations—France, Germany and Canada also assured Modi of their support in the nuclear field and strategic support.

Prime Minister Modi made a purposeful visit to the nations in the Indian Ocean region. This was a continuation of the concept of "Saagar Mala" which was first unveiled by the Atal Bihari Vajpayee government in 2003 with the objective of rapid modernisation and expansion of India's maritime power. Modi has sought to further revitalise that idea. It can easily be extended to promote India's connectivity in the Indian Ocean, in both economic and security domains. In a survey conducted in nine countries it was found that China's image among Indians was surprisingly positive and it was also found that Prime Minister Narendra Modi is better than Chinese President Xi Jinping in handling domestic and international affairs.

Conclusion

Prime Minster Narendra Modi had no previous experience of international relations or foreign policy, but now has become a world statesman hobnobbing with the likes of US President Obama, Russian President Putin, Chinese President Xi Jinping, Australian Prime Minister Tony Abbot, Canadian Prime Minister Stephen Harper, German Chancellor Angela Merkal, and French President Francois Hollande and so on. Modi's popularity as a world statesman can be ascertained by the fact that President Barrack Obama of the United States wrote Modi's profile in the Top 100 people of the *Time* magazine by saying that he is India's reformer in chief who has risen from "poverty to Prime Minister". "Today, he is the leader of the world's largest democracy and his life story from poverty to Prime Minister reflects the dynamism and potential of India's rise as a great power."[50] Prime Minister Modi tweeted, "Dear Barrack Obama your words are touching and inspiring".

The world needs India to step up as a global power. One year in office, as Prime Minister, Prof. Pushpesh Pant, has rightly observed that Narendra Modi has given a new dimension to Indo-American realtions.[51] India has the largest reservoir of the youth in the world and has a robust economy and all the potentials of becoming a leading power in the world. With Narendra Modi directing India's Foreign policy it can be achieved.

Foreign policy is like a ghost. Everyone is talking about it but no one knows how it is. People have not seen ghosts but they will describe it in many ways, some say it is long, some short, some say it is white in colour, some say that its legs turned backwards but nobody has seen. Similarly, everyone seems to be an expert in foreign policy without knowing what it is. We only draw inferences from statements published and aired. Foreign policy is intricately connected with the security of a nation and security policy is never made public. Whatever we deduce are mere inferences. PM Modi should be careful in his diplomatic jamboree; we do not need Plato's Philosopher King but we need a Machiavellian Prince to walk on the tightrope of international relations. As the poet Bashir Badr has aptly commented:

> "*koi haath bhi naa milaega,*
> *Jo gale miloge tapak se,*
> *Ye naye mizaz ka shahar hai,*
> *Zara faaslon se mila karo*".[52]

REFERENCES

1. S. Maharana, "Neighbourhood Policy of Modi's Government", *World Focus*, Volume 417, September 2014, special issue on India & Neighbours from UPA to NDA.
2. *The Hindu*, June 14, 2014.
3. *The Hindustan Times*, September 25, 2014.
4. S. Baru, "India's fast Power", *The Indian Express*, September 16, 2014.
5. K. Sibal, "Hindi-Chini Buy Buy", *The Hindustan Times*, September 16, 2014.
6. India Vietnam Inks 7 pacts, *The Statesman*, September 17, 2014.
7. *The India Express*, September 18, 2014.
8. *The Times of India*, September 18, 2014.
9. *The Times of India*, September 18, 2014.
10. Y. K. Alagh, *The Indian Express*, September 18, 2014.
11. B. Chellany, *The Hindustan Times*, September 19, 2014.
12. P. Bhanu Mehta, *The Indian Express*, September 19, 2014.
13. *The Times of India*, September 19, 2014.
14. *The Times of India*, September 19, 2014.
15. *The Times of India*, September 19, 2014.
16. *The Hindustan Times*, September 20, 2014.
17. *The Hindu*, September 20, 2014.
18. *The Hindu*, September 20, 2014.
19. *The Hindu*, September 20, 2014.
20. *The Times of India*, September 21, 2014.
21. *The Times of India*, September 22, 2014.
22. *The Indian Express*, September, 23, 2014.
23. *The Indian Express*, September 23, 2014.
24. *The Times of India*, September 25, 2014.
25. *The Times of India*, September 25, 2014.
26. *The Hindu*, September 29, 2014.
27. Ibid.
28. S. Saran, "From Nuetral to first gear", *The Hindustan Times*, September 29, 2014.
29. F. Grare, "Lens on Modi", *The Indian Express*, September 29, 2014.
30. K. Sibal, "Not natural partners at all", *The Hindustan Times*, September 30, 2014.
31. "Arms wide open", *The Indian Express*, September 30, 2014.
32. *Outlook*, page 20, October 6, 2014.
33. *The Hindu*, October 1, 2014.
34. Ibid.

35. *Outlook*, page 24, October 6, 2014.
36. *The Hindu*, November 22, 2014.
37. *Millennium Post*, November 22, 2014.
38. Varghese K. George, "Modi meets the world", *The Hindu*, November 6, 2014.
39. *The Hindu*, November 19, 2014.
40. *The Indian Express*, November 3, 2014.
41. S. Swamy, "A case for SAARC reforms", *The Hindu*, November 25, 2014.
42. B. Chellany, "Deconstructing the Modi foreign poicy", *The Hindu*, December 4, 2014.
43. India-US ties: Reviewing the Relationship, Chintamani Mahapatra, *Strategic Analysis*, Volume 39, No. 2, March-April 2015.
44. *Times of India*, January 28, 2015.
45. C Raja Mohan, "The art of the deal", *The Indian Express*, January 29, 2015.
46. R. Guha, "How Narendra Modi resembles Indira Gandhi", *The Hindustan Times*, February 15, 2015.
47. C Raja Mohan, Modi's US diplomacy marks a shift in India's worldview", *The Indian Express*, January 25, 2015.
48. S. Baru, "India and China in a multipolar world", *The Hindu*, May 11, 2015.
49. N. Rao, "A long march to a new relationship", *The Hindu*, May 14, 2015.
50. *TIME*, Asia, Hong Kong, May 18, 2015.
51. *Rashtriya Sahara*, Hastakshep, May 23, 2015.
52. B. Badr, quoted in Culture Yaksaan (Complete works).

2

Indo-Pak Geopolitical Rivalry in Afghanistan: Policy Options for India

Tej Pratap Singh

Afghanistan is the graveyard of empires. Since time immemorial, all the empires who at the peak of their power, tried to vanquish Afghanistan met with stiff resistance from Afghan people and had to retreat without accomplishing their mission and in the process weakening and undermining the empires itself. It happened with Alexander the great, who could not conquer and move beyond the area presently called Afghanistan and had to beat hasty retreat. History repeated itself in the nineteenth century when Britain, at the height of its imperial power, invaded Afghanistan and was humbled, marking the beginning of the end of British Empire. Soviet Union, one of the two superpowers of the cold war era, intervened in Afghanistan and met the same fate. It was a disastrous intervention, a blatant case of imperial overreach. Afghan misadventure eventually led to the collapse of Soviet empire. The sole superpower, the US committed the mistakes earlier committed by other empires to invade Afghanistan and its initial decisive victory and regime change created the impression for awhile that historical trend has been reversed but soon it became evident that the US like other empires cannot change the course of history.[1] After more than a decade of fighting, the longest and costliest war in the US history[2] the US like other imperial powers came to the conclusion that Afghan war is unwinnable and so drew a plan of drawdown of troops that is going to be completed by the end of 2014.[3]

During his election campaign, President Barack Obama criticised Iraq war as a 'war of choice' and so 'unnecessary war' but termed Afghanistan as 'war of necessity', and so the US had to win Afghan War at any cost. He reiterated it later also, while addressing war veterans on August 16, 2009, "We must not forget. This (Afghanistan War) is not a war of choice. This is a war of necessity. Those who attacked America on 9/11 are plotting to do so again. If left unchecked, the Taliban insurgency will mean even a larger safe haven from which al Qaeda would plot to kill more Americans." [4]

Both Afghan and Iraq wars turned into wars of attrition sapping the US energy, willpower and raised the prospect of new Vietnam in the making. This fear first compelled the US to wrap up its military mission in Iraq and then Obama shifted his focus to Afghanistan. Despite spending trillion dollars, the US could not achieve a desired result either in Iraq or Afghanistan. The US succeeded in regime change but could not put in its place a functioning government either in Iraq or Afghanistan. Elections were held to elect a democratic government but these elections were marred by various controversies and deeply dividing the societies on ethnic and sectarian grounds. The result was anarchy in both Iraq and Afghanistan as well. The US failed miserably in its nation-state building mission in Iraq and Afghanistan. Both turned out to be costly American misadventures, reviving the memory of Vietnam fiasco and exposing 'the limits of American power and exceptionalism'.[5]

Pakistan is a critical player in Afghan end game. Without Pakistan support and acquiescence no Afghan solution is possible. The international community, regional stakeholders and Pakistan itself are aware of the centrality of Pakistan in Afghan imbroglio. Pakistan wants to exploit this favourable situation in Afghanistan to its strategic advantage even at the cost of regional and global peace, security and stability. Withdrawal of Soviet troops and end of cold war had diminished the strategic significance of Pakistan. But 9/11 and subsequent US 'war on terror' and 'operation enduring freedom' revived the fortunes of Pakistan and it emerged again the frontline state in US war against Taliban regime of Afghanistan, who had harboured Al-Qaeda Islamic extremists including its chief Osama-bin-Laden, responsible for 9/11 and other Jihadi attacks on American installations. Pakistan offered logistical support to US and its allies in their military operation against the Taliban regime of Afghanistan. The US because of its hostility to Iran was left with no option but to accept Pakistan offer, who earlier during cold war period had offered the same facility to the US and its cold war allies against the Soviet intervention in Afghanistan. India had also offered all possible assistance to the US in its 'war on terror' and 'Operation Enduring Freedom' but because of Pakistan concerns and sensitivities, the US politely declined Indian offer particularly in its Afghan mission.

Strategic Objectives of Pakistan in Afghanistan

Afghanistan is a landlocked country and has access to sea either through Pakistan or Iran. This geographical factor makes Pakistan and Iran very critical in the geopolitics of Afghanistan. Pakistan shares not only a border with Afghanistan but also shares ethnicity, religion and culture. Afghanistan, Pakistan and India in fact have shared history, geography, culture that goes back to the millennia. Afghanistan was part of many Indian empires and Buddhism flourished before the advent of Islam in Afghanistan. Bamiyan Buddha and Gandhara art are the testimony of this shared past and culture. Pakistan till recent past was part of India. Thus all three have shared a past and destined to have shared present and future. They have a common destiny. If one nation is destabilised the whole region will be affected. India and Pakistan cannot insulate against turmoil in Afghanistan. Therefore, like Pakistan, India too has high stake in the peace, security and stability of Afghanistan. However, Pakistan wants to keep India out of Afghanistan and has made it its foremost strategic objective in Afghanistan.

Pakistan is conducting its foreign policy in Afghanistan in the zero-sum-game, where any gain for India in Afghanistan is treated as a loss for Pakistan. This zero-sum-game strategy of Pakistan has vitiated the whole security scenario in Afghanistan. Pakistan does not recognise that India too has vital interest in Afghanistan. Pakistan is opposed to friendly relation between India and Afghanistan. Pakistan not only wants a friendly government in Afghanistan but also wants that Afghan government must be hostile to India. [6] Taliban government in Afghanistan from 1996 to 2001 was a type of government, which was not only friendly to Pakistan but also hostile to India. But because of 9/11 and the US 'War on Terror', Taliban were ousted from power and Hamid Karjai government, friendly to India, assumed power in Afghanistan. This is not to the liking of Pakistan and from day one Pakistan wants to see Karjai thrown out of power, because of his perceived proximity to India.

Pakistan and Afghanistan are divided by Durand line.[7] This is a disputed border that was never accepted by Afghanistan, which treats it as an imperial border imposed on it by British India disregarding ethnicity, language and culture. It divides the proud Pashtun tribe into Pakistan and Afghanistan. Even the friendly Taliban regime dependent on Pakistan moral and material support refused to recognise Durand line as a legitimate border between Afghanistan and Pakistan. Pakistan is afraid that any strong government in Kabul will try to unite all Pashtun people into one state and this will lead to further shrinkage of Pakistan territory after the heavy territorial loss suffered by the independence of Bangladesh from Pakistan. Defending Durand line and securing Afghan recognition of this line are one of the most significant objectives of Pakistan in Afghanistan. Pakistan is apprehensive of rising soft power of India in Afghanistan and believes that India wants to dismember it further and eventually to wipe out Pakistan from the global map. Pakistan is of firm opinion that India still has not reconciled to the partition and creation of Pakistan. It is because of this Pakistan paranoia, Pakistan policy towards Afghanistan is India-centric. Pakistan feels India is promoting irredentism in Afghanistan and instigating Kabul government to claim North West Frontier Province (NWFP) of Pakistan, inhabited by Pashtun tribe, who constitute almost half of the Afghan population. NWFP has been renamed recently as Khyber-Pakhtunkhwa.[8]

Afghanistan has granted permission to India to run four consulates in different parts of the country at Kandahar, Herat, Jalalabad, and Mazar-e-Sharif apart from embassy at Kabul because of close India-Afghanistan relations. Pakistan is opposed to these Indian consulates and wants Afghanistan to close it down. Pakistan is accusing India that India is using these consulates to support secessionist movement in Baluchistan to spy against Pakistan, to destabilise and if possible dismember Pakistan. India denies all these baseless allegations by Pakistan and affirms that consulates are only providing consular services to the people, promoting bilateral cultural, political and economic relations. Problem of Baluchistan is the creation of Pakistan. Instead of addressing the problem, Pakistan is unnecessarily dragging India and holding India responsible for its internal problems.

Pakistan Quest for Strategic Depth in Afghanistan

Pakistan's strategic policy is Indo-centric. India is the arch enemy, rival and existential threat. To meet existential threat posed by India, Pakistan is seeking strategic parity with India since its creation in 1947. Pakistan has not abandoned its goal of strategic parity, despite bifurcation of Pakistan and transformation of East Pakistan as a new nation-state Bangladesh and reducing of Pakistan population and territory. Pakistan strategic policy is conceived, designed, articulated and pursued by keeping India in mind. India provides the context for the Pakistan strategic policy. Unending Pakistan quest for parity with India is the most significant determinant of Pakistan's strategic policy. However, this quest for parity so far has proved to be an elusive goal. This excessive Pakistan obsession of parity with India has precluded any possibility of Pakistan's pursuit of the enlightened national interest vis-à-vis its neighbours.[9]

Pakistan is obsessed with its security, territorial unity and integrity. It feels that east-west depth of Pakistan is very narrow in comparison to north-south and so it wants to compensate this strategic weakness by having a friendly and, if possible, pliant government in Afghanistan. So that in case of need, it can shift its valuable military asset to Afghanistan for its safety and later use and also to retreat if need arises to lure the enemy inside and fight back later when it is advantageous to Pakistan. Pliant/friendly government in Afghanistan will provide a kind of cushion to safeguard strategic interests of Pakistan. For Pakistan, India is the only enemy and it feels threat to its national security from its eastern neighbour India. Therefore, eastern border with India has to be secured by Pakistan for its unity, integrity and survival. East-west depth being narrow, Pakistan wants to bring Afghanistan in its security ambit by creating a wider strategic depth encompassing Pakistan and Afghanistan to deal effectively with any security threat emanating from its eastern neighbour India.

The concept of strategic depth[10] is very controversial and Pakistan quest for it so far has been illusory. Only during the brief period of ISI created Taliban regime in Afghanistan, Pakistan enjoyed much sought after strategic depth. However, Pakistan quest for strategic depth has deeply divided Afghan polity and society on ethnic-sectarian ground. Pakistan quest for strategic depth has not only destabilised Afghanistan but the whole region of South Asia, Central Asia and West Asia as well. Even Pakistan strategic analysts have also questioned the concept of strategic depth. Sartaz Aziz, advisor to PM Nawaz Sharif on national security and foreign affairs called strategic depth an 'outdated policy'.[11] Seeking strategic depth in Afghanistan has turned out to be like digging one's own grave.[12] Noted Pakistani Journalist Kamran Shafi writing in Pakistan popular newspaper *Dawn* argued that in case of war between India and Pakistan, Pakistan army has to fight Indian army at its eastern border itself and resist its onward movement in Pakistan towards west. It is absurd to argue that Pakistan army with its weapons will retreat to west and if need arises to Afghanistan to avoid fighting Indian army. Will Pakistan Generals instead of fighting Indian army, pack up and take refuge in Afghanistan?[13] If Indian attack has to be repulsed, it has to be repulsed at eastern border itself and not allow it to overrun the whole of Pakistan and fight it on western border from Afghanistan.

Pakistan's search for strategic depth revolves around army's threat perceptions. Earlier, in the 1980s the Soviet Union was considered as a security threat along with India. But now in Pakistan perception, security threat emerges only from India. When former army Chief General Kayani argued in favour of western borders being secure he meant that strategic depth provides Pakistan the ability to concentrate on Indian borders. A friendly and subservient Afghanistan can help it to shift its military assets to Afghanistan in the event of conflict with India.[14]

However, whatever is the merit/demerit of the concept of strategic depth, it has fascinated the Pakistan security establishment and ISI has pursued it with all sincerity. This single-minded pursuit of strategic depth in Afghanistan by Pakistan has vitiated the security environment in Afghanistan, Pakistan and India.

Pakistan Strategic Ambitions in Afghanistan and its Fallout

Pakistan strategic ambitions in Afghanistan have led to excessive interference by Pakistan in the internal affairs of Afghanistan. Pakistan wants to control Afghan politics through its proxies. Taliban was created by Pakistan ISI for this very purpose. In the past, many imperial powers tried to control and rule Afghanistan but they failed miserably. The recent example is of Soviet Union, who through different proxies tried to control and rule Afghanistan but eventually was humbled. To prop up its proxy, Babrak Karmal and then Najibullah regime in Afghanistan, Soviet Union intervened militarily but had to pull back its troops because of stiff resistance of Afghan people, in the process losing money, material and men. ISAF (International Security Assistance Force in Afghanistan) led by the NATO and the US is facing the same fate, which Soviet Union faced in 1980s.

Like earlier imperial powers, Pakistan also cannot succeed in its mission of installing its proxies such as Gulubudin Hekmetyar of Hizb-e-Islami, Haqani Network or Quetta Shura. If past history is any guide, then safely it can be predicted that like earlier imperial missions in Afghanistan, Pakistan imperial mission/design in Afghanistan too is bound to fail and its efforts might boomerang, jeopardising its own national security. Like, British, Soviet and Americans, Afghanistan will be graveyard for Pakistan imperial ambition too.

Pakistan: Part of Solution or Problem

Pakistan has played a dubious role in Afghanistan. Instead of stabilising Afghanistan, Pakistan has been main factor for Afghan instability. Pakistan is a major spoiler in Afghanistan. Pakistan instead of being part of solution itself has become a problem in Afghanistan. Pakistan and Afghan problem are so intertwined that separation of the two is not possible. Even Afghan President Hamid Karjai went to the extent of saying that two are tied to one umbilical cord. During his visit to Pakistan in March 2011, Karjai observed, "India is a close friend of Afghanistan but Pakistan is a twin brother of Afghanistan. We are more than twins, we are conjoined twins. There is no separation, there cannot be a separation."[15] To address Afghan problem, Pakistan problem has also to be addressed. That is why, US has clubbed Pakistan and Afghanistan together and created a new acronym AfPak and appointed a special representative to address jointly the problems of Afghanistan and Pakistan.

Pakistan Double Game in Afghanistan

Pakistan on the one hand has joined the US in its 'war on terror' and 'operation enduring freedom' in Afghanistan and on the other hand is providing safe haven to fleeing terrorists and jihadists from Afghanistan, thereby undermining the US efforts in Afghanistan and the world at large in riding it from the scourge of terrorism and religious extremism. Killing of Osama bin Laden, the global face/symbol of terrorism and Islamic Jihadism, in Abotabad, Pakistan, near an army cantonment by the US, is the testimony of Pakistan complicity with Taliban, al Qaeda and other jihadists. Investigations in global terror strikes have always led its trail to Pakistan. Over the years, Pakistan has emerged as epicentre of global terrorism. All global terrorists head to Pakistan for training, motivation and indoctrination. Pakistan has turned blind eye towards terrorists training camps being run in different parts of its territory. In the process, Pakistan has lost control over FATA (Federally Administered Tribal Area) to the terrorists, who have even begun tormenting its master Pakistan itself. Pakistan intelligence agency ISI is actively involved in running some training camps for terrorists to be used against India and these are treated by Pakistan as 'strategic asset'[16].

Pakistan double game of running with the hare and hunting with the hound has been exposed to the international community in the wake of killing of Osama bin Laden. On the one hand, Pakistan claims to be the victim of terrorism and helping the West in its war on terrorism and on the other hand has given shelter to terrorists. All top al Qaeda and Taliban leaders including Mullah Omar are hiding in Pakistan. How long Pakistan will succeed in its double game of helping and undermining US war efforts in Afghanistan is difficult to say. Because of Pakistan centrality in Afghan imbroglio and the US hostility to Iran, the US is left with no option but to depend on Pakistan to continue its logistical support to its troops based in Afghanistan. Only other available northern route passing through Russia and Central Asian Republics is also not very reliable as Russia has only permitted non-lethal supply to Afghanistan. Deteriorating US-Russia relations over Ukraine crisis, resumption of cold-war and intensifying US-Russia rivalry has further reduced the significance of the Northern route. This northern logistical route compared to Pakistan route is very lengthy too. Therefore, even after knowing the Pakistan double game, the US has exercised restraint and silence because of its dependence on Pakistan for its military supply to Afghanistan. Pakistan seems to be lesser evil in comparison to hostile Iran and unreliable Russia.

Terrorists: Strategic Asset or Liability

Pakistan double game is backfiring as terrorists nurtured as strategic asset by its intelligence agency ISI to be used against India are turning their gun against Pakistan itself. Tahrik-e-Taliban Pakistan (TTP) popularly known as Pakistan Taliban has began targeting Pakistan security forces, civilian leaders and military-civil assets. Some of their attacks such as military headquarter in Rawalpindi, Karachi airport, naval station, Marriot Hotel; numerous mosque attacks have been audacious and daring. This also shows that these terrorist groups are no longer in the control of Pakistan ISI and the later has created a Frankenstein. Jihadi atmosphere created by these religious extremists has radicalised Muslim community in Pakistan. Radicalisation of Muslim community has not only created animosity against other minority religious groups but has also widened the sectarian fault-lines within the Muslim community. Increasing Saudi Wahabi influence has pitted majority Sunni Muslims against the minority Shia Muslims and Muslim sects like Ahmadia, Vohra, etc. These Islamic groups are being repeatedly targeted by Sunni Jihadists and these terrorist attacks have vitiated the whole atmosphere in Pakistan.

International community is now scared of the future of Pakistan. When it was created in 1947 on the basis of religion, the international community was of opinion that Pakistan is more homogeneous and the religion will bind the new state together. Whereas, international community was sceptical of Indian territorial unity and integrity, because of its vast heterogeneity based on religion, race, region, language, caste, etc. Doomsayers in case of India and soothsayers in case of Pakistan have been proved wrong. India has maintained its territorial unity, social peace and political democracy whereas in case of Pakistan, it has been balkanised, facing deep social and religious division, democracy still shaky and is on the verge of being a failed state. Prospect of Pakistan failure as a state is horrifying the whole world as Pakistan is not an ordinary state like Somalia or Yugoslavia but a nuclear weapon state. Pakistan failure will result into falling of its nuclear assets in the hands of non-state actors probably Islamic Jihadists. If this happens, nobody knows, how will Pakistan Jihadists behave? The US has made some contingency plan to secure Pakistan nuclear weapons in case of Jihadists takeover of Pakistan. But sometimes, even the best plan fails. Nuclear weapon equipped Islamic Jihadists will be a frightening proposition for the international community.

Pakistan intelligence agency ISI created and nurtured various terrorist outfits as 'strategic asset' to further its foreign policy objectives; mainly to target India in Afghanistan to oust it from there and to target India within Kashmir and other parts of the country to disturb social peace, communal harmony and weaken and undermine its sovereignty, territorial unity and integrity. However, this strategic asset has been transformed into strategic liability as these terrorist outfits apart from targeting India, US and western interests, sometimes target their master Pakistan itself. Pakistan retaliation and effort to control and manage these Jihadi groups have further alienated these Jihadists from Pakistan and these Jihadists are now increasingly targeting Pakistan strategic interests. The whole Pakistan effort to use Jihadists against India has boomeranged against Pakistan itself.

Regional Implication of Pakistan Interference in Afghanistan

Pakistan quest for 'strategic depth' in Afghanistan against India and sponsoring-nurturing terrorists as 'strategic asset' to be used against India and blackmail the international community to bail out Pakistan from the social, political, economic and financial mess created by it, has serious regional and global implications. India is the worst affected by Pakistan short-sighted policy of strategic depth in Afghanistan and Jihadists as strategic asset. Apart from India, Iran, Central Asian Republics (CARs), China, Russia are other regional powers, who are affected in various measures by Pakistan interference in Afghanistan. Globally the US is the major country affected by Pakistan dubious role in Afghanistan. AfPak has emerged as the epicentre of global terrorism and so there is hardly any region or country which is not affected by global terrorism having its root in Afghanistan and Pakistan.

Among the regional powers, after India, Iran comes next in the list of regional countries affected by Pakistan effort to manage Afghanistan through its proxies. Taliban created and nurtured by Pakistan are Pakhtun Sunni Jihadists, who are opposed to Shia and non-Pashtun ethnic groups in multi-ethnic Afghan society. Iran treats itself as saviour of Shia Muslims and interests and this self-assumed role of Iran has pitted it against Pashtun Sunni Taliban sponsored and sustained by Pakistan. In Afghan civil war, Iran is siding with 'Northern Alliance', a conglomerate of non-Pashtun ethnic groups consisting of Tajiks, Uzbeks, Hazara Shias, etc. based in the northern part of Afghanistan. Iran being the western neighbour of Afghanistan is immediately faced with the heavy influx of Afghan refugees in case of any turmoil in Afghanistan, which is a recurrent phenomenon.

Central Asian Republics on the northern border of Afghanistan are affected by any turmoil in Afghanistan as Central Asia has shared ethnicity with Afghanistan. Because of ethnic reasons, CARs are extending support to Northern Alliance against Pakistan supported Taliban. Any Afghan turmoil has spill over affects in CARs. It not only destabilises Afghanistan but its fallout is felt in CARs too. Jihadists have radicalised CARs too and all CARs governments are threatened by rising Islamic extremism. These Islamists have taken refuge in AfPak region and from there are targeting their governments in Central Asia. Drug trafficking emanating from Afghanistan under the patronage of Taliban is another threat to CARs.

Russia though not an immediate neighbour of Afghanistan has also been affected by the Talibanisation of AfPak as it has significant minority Islamic groups within its border, particularly in Chechnya. Under the influence of radicalisation of AfPak, Chechen Muslims have also been radicalised and are fighting with the Russian government for the establishment of Islamic Republic of Chechnya. Drugs originating from Afghanistan are another trouble for Russia.

Like Russia, China is also facing the fallout of Islamic radicalism in AfPak. Islamic extremists from Xinjiang, who are called Uyghur, have taken refuge in Pakistan and Afghanistan and from there have launched movement for independence of Xinjiang, which they call East Turkistan. Despite Pakistan being 'all weather friend' of China, the former has not been able to rein in Uyghur militants operating from tribal area of Pakistan and Afghanistan. Uyghur Islamic extremists have joined hand with Taliban extremists and helping each others in targeting their enemies.

Thus, there is hardly any country in the immediate or extended neighbourhood of AfPak, which is not feeling the heat of raging Islamic terrorism and extremism. Islamic extremism in AfPak has global implications too. Globally these radicalised Islamic youth are targeting Western interests in general and American interests in particular. All Islamic terror attacks in different parts of the world have their roots in AfPak region including 9/11. Without stabilising Afghanistan-Pakistan, the global menace of terrorism cannot be dealt with.

Conclusions: The Way-out

What is the way out of this Afghan crisis created mainly by Pakistan perspectives in Afghanistan, which is primarily anchored in its policy of 'strategic depth' and 'strategic asset' conceptualised against India? Since Afghan crisis has regional and global implications any solution of it must have all regional and global stakeholders on board. Any effort to exclude any important stakeholder from the resolution of Afghan crisis will not produce desired result and Afghan wound will continue to fester, exacting heavy toll from the international community. Pakistan and the US are trying to exclude India and Iran respectively from any regional or global efforts for the resolution of Afghanistan crisis. Both India and Iran are significant stakeholders in Afghanistan with vital interests in Afghanistan and any effort to exclude them will undermine and weaken global efforts for the resolution of Afghanistan.

It is ironical that American interests are closer to the countries, which are not very friendly with the US. For America, Iran is still a rogue State, part of the evil empire, which has to be contained and isolated. Russia is still not trustworthy and India though friendly cannot be befriended at the cost of Pakistan. America knows that it is mainly because of Pakistan its 'War on Terror' and 'Operation Enduring Freedom' has not succeeded in its mission of stabilising Afghanistan, despite American troops being there for than a decade. Iran might be an adversary of the US in Middle East and its nuclear weapon programme has created grave threat to the security of the US and its allies but in Afghanistan, there is complete convergence of the US-Iranian interests.[17] Any solution of Afghan crisis has to be as broad based as is possible for its successful resolution.

The following policy options can be suggested:

1. Pakistan has to surrender its policy of 'strategic depth' in Afghanistan against India. It is a flawed strategy and can never be achieved.
2. Pakistan must stop nurturing terrorist outfits like Lashkar-e-Toiba (LeT), Hizb-e-Islami, Haqqani Network, Quetta Shura, etc. and treating terrorists and extremists as 'strategic asset' to be used against India and to blackmail international community to bail it out from its economic and financial mess.
3. Pakistan and United States must be persuaded to allow India and Iran to be involved in any negotiation for the resolution of Afghan tangle. If no resolution to Afghan problem is possible without the full consent of Pakistan and United States then without active involvement of India and Iran no Afghan solution can succeed. Pakistan and the US must give up their reservations for India and Iran respectively in the larger interests of regional and global peace, security and stability.
4. Afghan security forces and police must be strengthened to take care of their internal and external security. Eventually it is going to be Afghan armed forces and police, who will provide security to Afghan people and not international assistance forces.
5. The withdrawal of NATO led forces has to be gradual. Any sudden pull out of western forces will enable Taliban to stage comeback and whole exercise of ousting Taliban from power in the wake of 9/11 will be negated in one stroke.
6. Afghan government must agree to allow a limited number of western/US troops to remain in Afghanistan in the post-2014 period to avoid any Iraq type of situation created by ISIS (Islamic State of Iraq and Syria) in Afghanistan. Even a small number of troops will

keep the US committed to future security of Afghanistan from any ISIS type of threat to its security.

7. Some kind of rapprochement between different ethnic groups of Afghanistan has to be brokered by the international community for lasting peace in Afghanistan. Multi-ethnic character of Afghan society must be respected and must be given due recognition while reaching to any solution. Any Afghan regime must give representation to all ethnic groups of Afghanistan. Exclusion of any ethnic group will be recipe for disaster.
8. Since Afghanistan problem has become a regional and global problem and so its solution has also to be regional and global. A broader regional and global approach must be adopted while addressing Afghan crisis.
9. Afghanistan should be developed as a bridge between South Asia and West Asia and South Asia and Central Asia. Afghanistan has the potential to emerge as energy hub and corridor between energy deficient South Asia and energy surplus west and central Asia.
10. Afghanistan's vast natural resources can fuel industrial growth in the region. China, India and other nations interested in Afghan natural resources must form a consortium to harness the Afghan resources for the benefit of all.
11. Afghanistan has the potential to emerge as trading hub. This will create trade linkages between the countries of the region and it will help great deal in stabilising Afghanistan.
12. Pakistan has to abandon its zero sum game approach in Afghanistan vis-à-vis India. Without allowing India due role in Afghanistan, the later cannot be stabilised. India enjoys enormous soft power in Afghanistan much more than any country of the world and this fact cannot be brushed away.

These policy options must be adopted for the stabilisation of Afghanistan in post-2014, after the withdrawal of US troops from Afghanistan. Without peace, security and stability in Afghanistan, the global peace, security and stability cannot be achieved. Afghan peace is linked to global peace. In view of this fact, Pakistan has to rise above its narrow selfish national interests and bring desired change in its perspectives in Afghanistan. This will also be in the larger interests of Pakistan as any instability in Afghanistan will destabilise Pakistan also. So the need of hour is that Pakistan must join hands with the

US and India and other regional and global stakeholders in stabilising Afghanistan.

REFERENCES

1. Seth G. Jones, *In the Graveyard of Empires: America's War in Afghanistan*, W.W. Norton & Company, 2010; Stephen Tanner, *Afghanistan: A Military History from Alexander the Great to the War against the Taliban*, Da Capo Press, 2009.
2. Afghanistan is by far the longest and costliest American war. It has overtaken Vietnam War both in terms of duration and money spent. The cost of maintaining an American soldier in Afghanistan for a year is $ 1 million. http://www.globalresearch.ca/the-most-expensive-war-in-world-history-costs-of-iraq-afghanistan-wars-could-rise-to-6 trillion/5329432 Afghanistan aid has also overtaken largest American aid programme called Marshal Plan for European reconstruction, $ 103.4 billion. http://blog.foreignpolicy.com/posts/2014/07/30/the_united_states_has_outspent_the_marshall_plan_to_rebuild_afghanistan The US wars in Afghanistan and Iraq will cost $ 4 to 6 trillion. Stephen Friedman a senior US official has to resign in 2002, when he estimated the cost of Afghan-Iraq Wars can go up to $ 200 billion. http://www.washingtonpost.com/world/national-security/study-iraq-afghan-war-costs-to-top-4-trillion/2013/03/28/b82a5dce-97ed-11e2-814b-063623d80a60_story.html.
3. The US intends to keep 9800 troops in Afghanistan even after 2014 for training and bolstering nascent Afghan National Army and Police. The US is suspending only combat operation in post-2014. The US needs its troops and bases to launch drone attacks in Pakistan against terrorists hiding there. However, the future of the US troops depends on the signing of US-Afghan Strategic Partnership by the new Afghan Govt. assuming power after 2014 election. http://www.theguardian.com/world/2014/may/27/obama-us-afghanistan-force-2014.
4. *The New York Times*, August 17, 2009, http://www.nytimes.com/2009/08/18/ cus/politics/18vets.html?_r=0.
5. A.J. Bacevich, *The Limits of Power: The End of American Exceptionalism*, Metropolitan Books, New York, 2008.
6. A. Pande, "Pakistan's Nightmare", *The Friday Times*, (Lahore), July 04, 2014, http://www.thefridaytimes.com/tft/pakistans-nightmare/
7. Durand Line was demarcated by British India and signed into a treaty in 1893 by Afghan ruler Amir Abdur Rahman Khan. The treaty was for 100 years and has expired in 1993. Since then all Afghan rulers have refused to renew Durand treaty including Taliban regime, despite Pak efforts and pressure. http://www.afghanistans.com/information/history/durandline.html
8. In 2010 North West Frontier Province (NWFP) was officially renamed as Khyber Pakhtunkhwa. It is one of the four provinces of Pakistan and only one which was not named after the dominant ethnic group of the region such as Punjabi, Sindhi and Baluch. With the renaming of NWFP this anomaly has been addressed. http://www.khyberpakhtunkhwa.gov.pk/aboutus/
9. T.P. Singh, "Unending Quest for Parity", *Defence and Security Alert*, vol. 2, issue 7, April 2011, pp.71-73.
10. The concept of strategic depth was conceptualized by former Pak Army Chief Mirza Aslam Beg in 1980s.
11. *The News*, December 19, 2013. http://www.thenews.com.pk/Todays-News-13-27399-Strategic-depth-an-outdated-policy,-Sartaj-tells-Senate

12. I. Gul, *The Friday Times*, July 11, 2014, http://www.thefridaytimes.com/tft/is-this-the-end-of-the-strategic-depth-doctrine/
13. K. Shafi, "Defining 'Strategic Depth'," *Dawn*, 19 January, 2010. http://www.dawn.com/wps/wcm/connect/dawn-content-library/dawn/the-newspaper/columnists/14-defining-strategic-depth-910
14. P. M. Kamath, "Pakistan's Strategy after Osama," *Defence and Security Alert*, vol. 2, issue 11, August, 2011, p.32.
15. *The Times of India*, March 11, 2010. http://timesofindia.indiatimes.com/world/south-asia/India-close-friend-but-Pak-conjoined-twin-says-Afghanistan/articleshow/5672129.cms
16. "Terrorists as Strategic Assets," *Pakistan Today*, May 12, 2014. http://www.pakistantoday.com.pk/2014/05/12/comment/terrorists-as-strategic-assets/
17. T. P. Singh, "Stabilisation of Afghanistan", Defence and Security Alert, vol.2, issue 11, August 2011, p. 75.

3

Environmental Degradation as a Non-traditional Security Threat to Bangladesh

Aditya Mishra

Introduction

Since the end of the cold war the definitions of security and national risk have been undergoing tremendous transformations. The nature of the security environment is changing from the traditional meaning of state defense security to non-traditional threats, or so-called "gray area phenomena", revealing states' vulnerability to the potential for turmoil and disorder. One of the most significant aspects of this change is the inclusion of the growing impacts of the degradation of environment—nationally, regionally as well as globally. More attention is thus focused on reality of global economic and ecological interdependence. Along with its traditional aspects—economic, social, political and military—now international security invariably encompasses environmental issues. The arguments for the broadening of national security to include non-traditional threats were to constitute the nucleus of 'post-realist' thrust linking the global environment with security.

Many countries, whether developing or developed, are facing different types of environmental problems, like extensive flooding, droughts, land degradation, water-sharing problems, resource conflict and the adverse effects of climate change and global warming. Although less recognized, the impact of the potent challenges being posed by environmental degradation is noteworthy in many states, particularly those that have fragile socio-political and economic structures. South-Asian region is home to some of the most fragile states in the modern world. South Asia is the most densely populated region in the world, with few natural resources. Land, forest, and other natural resources are thus being degraded and gradually becoming scarce. On the other hand, natural disasters and man-made interventions have also complicated environmental security and the ecological balance in South Asia.[1]

Among these countries Bangladesh, is severely affected with all the previously mentioned problems, along with political confrontation, poor governance and state incapacity to manage the huge population and natural resources. The geographical location and downstream position of Bangladesh has been a vital factor in the proper sharing of trans-boundary water coming from outside of the border. Ongoing global warming and climate change have significantly impacted the environmental security and ecological balance of Bangladesh. Natural disasters, cyclones and sea level rise are potential threats arising due to climate change. These three climate-induced factors have already affected the human-environmental chemistry of Bangladesh and will continue to do so in the future; putting the very existence of Bangladesh at stake. The main objective of the paper is to show that how environmental degradation constitutes a non-traditional security threat to Bangladesh. So first of all an attempt is made to conceptualize non-traditional security threat. Secondly, by discussing briefly the status of environmental degradation in Bangladesh, an attempt is made to identify the nexuses of environmental degradation and the security of Bangladesh. Finally, an attempt would be made to draw some conclusions from the discussions on the issues and project an outlook for the future.

Conceptualizing Non-traditional Threat

With the end of the Cold War, the study of international security added a new aspect of security considered that the traditional notion of security was inadequate to explain emerging threats.[2] The era of cold war was based on military supremacy and the post-Cold War, as analysed by economic performance rather than military capability, emerged as a measure of state power although economic interest of countries is still manifest through their military actions. Recent Iraq war is testimony to this fact. Simultaneously, the slogan of sustainable development encompassing social, economic and environmental concerns has brought to the fore issues of overall human welfare in the present time as well as in the future.[3]

The post-Cold War security agenda has been characterised in some views, by two developments specifically. The first is the emphasis on individual security and not only the security of the state, and the second is the increasing recognition of non-military threats to security. Traditionally, 'security" was the security of state; it was threatened by the military power of other state.[4] Even today, some commentators still argue that military threats are bigger than ever in the post-Cold War era, exempt from the military balance of power, which, for decades, had ensured state and individual security.[5] However, even if these threats were bigger now days, they certainly are not the only menace to the lives of people all around the world. Environmental degradation, poverty, famines and diseases are huge threats to the lives of millions of people all around the world. Thus, a new concept of security had to be developed.

Bzan was one of the most prominent exponents of the broadened concept of security in the immediate post-Cold War period. Stating that the "range of potential national security issue is wide..., he classified types of threats according to five sectors, namely the military, political, economic, societal and ecological.[6]

Today, most consider security from a global perspective rather than only from the perspective of individual nations and the idea of common security. More recently, analysts, following the United Nations Development Programme's (UNDP) 1994 Human Development Report and their notion of security as "freedom from fear and want,"[7] have settled on the phrase "human security" to emphasise the people-centred aspect of these efforts.

Advocates of human security began to claim a paradigm shift in security studies—a disciplinary and policy shift from traditional to non-traditional security threats (NTST). The Human Development Report of 1994 shifted the emphasis from national security in terms of external threats to a country's territorial integrity, towards human security that encompasses security "against poverty, hunger, diseases, unemployment and environmental degradation". This implies that security of each individual needs to be guaranteed through human development. The Commission on global governance in its report on Our Global Neighbourhood calls upon the world community "to make the protection of people and their security an aim of global security policy".[8]

Proponents of the paradigm shift and NTST advocates claim that in many parts of the world, non-military challenges are perceived as being more threatening than the military power of some prospective enemy states. Increasing globalisation and interdependence make countries more vulnerable to certain non-traditional threats. The term "common problems" is used to indicate issues that transcend international boundaries, especially environment and resource issues. Some of these issues cannot be addressed by a single state or group of states.[9] Thus, the NTST discourse calls for a deepening and broadening of the field of security studies by including the economic, environmental, health and social problems.

In the 2004 Report of the United Nation (UN) Panel on Threats, Challenges and Change, it is stated that leads to large-scale death or lessening of life chances and undermines States as the basic unit of the international system is a threat to international security. In this regard, six "clusters of threats" were identified, which seem to represent a mixture of traditional and 'new' or non-traditional security threats. These are as follows:[10]

- Economic and social threats, including poverty, infectious disease and environmental degradation.
- Inter-state conflict.
- Internal conflict, including civil war, genocide and other large scale atrocities.
- Nuclear, radiological, chemical and biological weapons.
- Terrorism.
- Transnational organized crime.

In order to have a clear definition of non-traditional security threat, we can distinguish it from the traditional security by examining the result of insecurity rather than source of insecurity. That is to say non-traditional security refers to the threat to national security without military clashes between formal military forces and traditional security means threat usually resulted in military clashes.[11]

Many security issues, which currently preoccupy policymakers and analysts, such as nationalism and ethnic conflict, the proliferation of weapons of mass destruction and regional political and military instability, are relatively consistent with the conventional national security concerns and practices. Non-traditional challenges, however, are now commanding increased attention. Among the various policy issues framed by the NTST perspective as the most important are unchecked environmental degradation; the spread of infectious diseases, particularly HIV/AIDS and SARS; cross-border migration; transnational organized crime, such as arms and drugs smuggling and human trafficking, and natural disasters.

Environmental Degradation as a Non-traditional Security Threat

The threat caused by environmental degradation seems less clear-cut and direct than most other dangers to human life. Thus, the potential threat of global warming and ozone depletion appears far-off, when compared to more imminent threats, such as natural disasters and military or terrorist attacks.[12] However, the negative modifications in environmental conditions heighten peoples' vulnerability to other threats, such as disease, and are thus largely an indirect threat to human security. Hence, some studies have revealed that close to a third of deaths related to diseases worldwide have some environmental causes, such as air or water pollution.[13] Human induced environmental degradation, and the resulting scarcity of resources, can be the case of political instability and conflict. Furthermore, environment as a resource has strategic significance for nation-states who build power through natural resources like water, oil, gas, and various other minerals. Increasing state control over environment and natural resources has spillover effects such as environmental degradation, resulting in undue catastrophes. These include uncontrolled migration, high population growth, and human casualties. Such catastrophes have become real security concerns for the affected states.[14]

Thus environment-threat-vulnerability nexus plays a vital role in proving that environment is a real security threat. Firstly, ecosystem integrity is crucial for the population's sustainable livelihood. Therefore, certain environmental conditions—often resulting from environmental change, such as pollution depletion, or natural disasters—can pose an acute threat to security. Environmental degradations and climate change increase an individual's vulnerability. Moreover, environment is linked with international security as it becomes evident that national solutions to environmental problems would not be sustainable in the long-run without international cooperation. Secondly, another aspect is the direct relationship between environment and transnational conflict.[15]

Environment Degradation—Security Nexus in Bangladesh

At the beginning of the 21st century, Bangladesh seems to be continuing its trend of remaining as a potential site of insecurities, instabilities and conflicts. An overwhelming dependency on water resources and a high population density (exceeding 1100 per sq km) with chronic poverty, make Bangladesh one of the most environmentally vulnerable areas in the world (Compendium of Environment Statistics of Bangladesh 2009). Competition for limited resources, environmental degradation and environmental change threaten most people's lives and livelihoods yearly. Frequent devastating floods, droughts and water scarcity in the dry season, salinity intrusion, deforestation, arsenic contamination, river erosion, degradation of wetlands, pollution of water and land and so on are very common phenomena in Bangladesh.[16] Water resources in the country have not been managed effectively through the ages. As water is central to the livelihood of Bangladesh, the crisis related to water and its consequences have push Bangladesh into a very threatening situation.[17]

The geographical setting of Bangladesh makes the country vulnerable to natural disasters. The mountains and hills bordering almost three-fourths of the country, along with the funnel-shaped Bay of Bengal in the south, have not only made the country a meeting place of life-giving monsoon rains, but also make it subjected to the catastrophic ravages of natural disasters. Its physiography and river morphology also contribute to recurring disasters. Abnormal rainfall and earthquakes in the adjacent Himalayan range add to the disaster situation. Effects of *El-Nino*-Southern Oscillation (ENSO) and the apprehended climatic changes have a great impact on the overall future disaster scenarios. Bangladesh faces a growing number of multifarious environmental problems. The following are several environmental issues that significantly affect Bangladesh's security.

Population and Poverty

Arguably, one of the most critical sources of the degradation of environment in Bangladesh are rooted in factors like high concentration of population in the country, scarcity of resources, underdevelopment and the chronic poverty. About 164.4 million people live in Bangladesh with a surface area of 144 thousand square kilometers (Foreign and Commonwealth Office 2011). The situation is urgent as the country is poised to lose a good part of its territory to the rise in sea levels because of global warming; while its very population increases at an unsustainable rate. The current estimate of population growth in the country varies from 1.5-2 percent per year depending on the source of data. If one takes a middle ground and considers a growth rate of say 1.75 percent/year, the population will double in the next 40-47 years. High population growth rates lead to more intense use of resources, exacerbating existing scarcities and over-exploitation.[18] This enormous size of population has posed a serious challenge for future development of the economy in following ways: putting huge pressure on environment and available resources; limiting agricultural growth and food grain production through reducing arable land for housing and non-agricultural purposes; raising requirement for food grain; and raising the number of poor population thus slowing down the rate of poverty reduction.[19]

In addition to the elevated population, the gravest factor that is interlinked with environmental stress in a complex way is 'poverty'. About 80 percent of Bangladesh's population live on less than $2 a day and 25 percent (40 million) are classified as 'extreme poor'. The extreme poor are food-insecure, unable to afford 80 percent of their minimum food needs (Australia's Aid Programme 2011). More than two-thirds of the rural population is landless or functionally landless (owning less than 0.2 ha of land). Even productive land is subject to regular flooding (Participatory Small-Scale Water Resources Sector Project 2009). Total farm land in the country is decreasing at about 1 percent rate annually due to loss of land to urbanization, infrastructure, housing settlement, etc., as a consequence more and more people become landless.[20] The critical point is that most Bangladeshi who are poor and live in rural areas, are highly dependent on natural resources for their lives and livelihoods. Agriculture contributes 21.77 percent of GDP of Bangladesh while Industry and Service contributes 29.73 and 49.67 percent. Since agriculture is largest employment sector of the country, logically national growth depends on it (Agriculture Long March 2011). In the total number of workforce (70.86 million), agriculture, forestry, and fisheries account for 63%.[21]

Thus, ecological resource dependent people are most susceptible and disadvantaged, though their number is larger in the country. Their vulnerable situation gets more intensified and threatened as they have to depend on degraded resources. Environmental scarcity thus is directly or indirectly associated with underemployment and overall livelihood insecurities. Whether environmental scarcity adds to poverty or poverty increases environmental degradation, in both ways it is threatening to human security. Overpopulation and environmental resource scarcity both have destabilizing potentialities. These two factors together are thus strong roots of insecurities and conflicts.

Water Crisis

Water is the most essential constituent among the environmental resources, and is important for the survival of all living organisms. The environment, economic growth and development of Bangladesh are all highly determined by water and its regional and seasonal availability, and the quality of surface and groundwater. The sources of water in Bangladesh are rivers and groundwater. Bangladesh is a lower riparian, river-reign country.[22] There are 808 rivers in Bangladesh where most rivers rise from Himalayan range and fall into the Bay of Bengal. There are 57 trans-boundary rivers that Bangladesh shares with her neighboring countries; 54 with India and 3 with Myanmar. Bangladesh is situated in the deltaic part of the region. The country lies at the confluence of three of the world's major rivers—the Ganges, the Brahmaputra and the Meghna, which originate from the Himalayan system and flow through China, Nepal and India before passing through Bangladesh as they drain out into the Bay of Bengal. As a result, 93 percent of the waters passing through Bangladesh come from outside its boundaries. The GBM (Ganges, the Brahmaputra and the Meghna) river systems drain a total catchment area of about 1.72 million sq km through Bangladesh into the Bay of Bengal. Out of this large catchment area, only 7% lies in Bangladesh. The other co-riparian countries are India, Nepal, Bhutan and China.[23]

With physically rich water resources, Bangladesh is still suffering from very critical water crisis both from water shortage and water abundance. While Bangladesh has plenty of water resources but at the same time distribution of water resources is extremely irregular; excess of water in the monsoon and inadequate in the dry season. Thus flood and shortage of water hangs like a double-edge sword over Bangladesh. This uneven accessibility of water creates various types of environmental stress. On one hand, Bangladesh faces flood and sedimentation problem and on the other hand it faces drought, salinity intrusion, deforestation, and so on due to scarcity of water.

Flood

Floods are annual phenomenon in Bangladesh and their severity is seen in the months of July and August. Regular river floods affect 20% of the country, in extreme situations; about 68% of the country is affected. Catastrophic floods, on the scale of those that took place in 1974, 1987, 1988, 1998 and 2004 occur in every 10-20 years resulting in large-scale destruction and loss of lives. Approximately 37%, 43%, 52% and 68% of the country is inundated with floods of return periods of 10, 20, 50 and 100 years respectively. Floods have become much more unpredictable than earlier times, in terms of both onset and scale.[24] The full scale of damages caused by floods is unknown in the country. According to government officials total death toll was 1000 in 1998, 747 in 2004 and more than 500 in 2007. The economic damages at the current price were estimated to be US$2.8 billion in the 1998 flood, US$ 2.2 billion in 2004. A preliminary estimate by the Department of Agricultural Extension estimates the floods to have damaged crops worth about US$286 million in the 39 flood-hit districts out of the country's 64 districts in 2007.[25] Loss of agricultural production, damage and destruction of immobile infrastructure, disruption to essential services, national economic loss, evacuation, and loss of human live and biodiversity, displacement and sufferings of human population and biodiversity are the obvious impingements of flood in Bangladesh and which are clearly threat to the human security.

Drought and Salinity

On the contrary the water scarcity and its outcome are also a great problem in Bangladesh. Drought is a recurrent phenomenon in some parts of the Bangladesh in post-monsoon and dry season. The North part of the country suffers most from the drought problem due to water scarcity of surface water. During the last 50 years, Bangladesh suffered about 20 drought conditions. Despite the recurrent and devastating nature of droughts in Bangladesh, it has attracted far less scientific attention than floods or cyclones. However, losses from drought are likely to be more severe than from floods in Bangladesh. The percentage of drought affected areas were 31.63% in 1951, 46.54% in 1957, 37.47% in 1958, 22.39% in 1961, 18.42% in 1966, 42.48% in 1972 and 42.04% in 1979. During 1981 and 1982 droughts affected the production of the monsoon crops only. The drought condition in northwestern Bangladesh in recent decades had led to a shortfall of rice production of 3.5 million tons in the 1990s. The drought in 1995-96 caused immense damage to crops, especially in the case of rice and jute that are the main crops of North West Bangladesh. These are followed by bamboo-clumps, a major cash earning crop of many farmers in the region. In the recent times, this was most persistent drought in Bangladesh.[26] One major crisis or consequence of water problem is salinity intrusion. Over 30 percent of the net available cultivable land of Bangladesh is located in the coastal areas. But it has been observed that all the coastal cultivable lands are not being utilized for crop production, mostly due to soil salinity. Increased soil salinity limits growth of standing crops and affects overall crop production, and also makes the soil unsuitable for many potential crops. It is believed that the impact of climate on physical systems, in combination with the effect of sea level rise, would cause a net increase in salinity in the already affected soils of the coastal regions.[27]

The apprehended sea level rise would bring more of the coastal area under inundation. Coastal waters are likely to become more saline, and soil salinity will increase. In addition, even groundwater aquifers will face salinity intrusion. Winter crops in the coastal area that depend on groundwater for irrigation would be negatively affected. Agriculture, forestry, and fisheries might face severe adverse effects due to increased water and soil salinity. The extent of increase in soil salinity in a particular area within the coastal zone would determine the extent of crop loss. Reduced water flow from upland during winters will accelerate the inland saline water intrusion.[28]

Arsenic Contamination

Another most dangerous threat emanating from environmental degradation is the arsenic contamination of its ground water, almost the sole source of drinking water in the country. The risk is of wide range. Arsenic contamination, first noticed in 1993, has already assumed a gigantic scale. The permissible level of arsenic in water is 50 ppb (Parts per billion) according to experts. But according to the Bangladesh Atomic Energy Commission, the level of arsenic is between 150 and 200 ppb in tube-well water in the districts boarding West Bengal. According to the data provided by UNICEF in 2008, there are approximately 8.6 million tube wells in Bangladesh. Of these, 4.75 million tube wells (55%) have been tested for arsenic among which 3.3 million (39%) were marked green indicating that the ground water is safe; while 1.4 million (16%) were marked red indicating that they are unsafe to use as sources of drinking water due to the high arsenic level. Recent findings show that about 20 million people in Bangladesh are using tube wells contaminated with arsenic over the permissible level (>50 ppb).[29]

The overall situation indicates that Bangladesh is in the highest risk of an epidemic of arsenic poisoning and arsenic related diseases. Arsenic affects a wide variety of human organs: skin, lungs, liver, cardiovascular system, nervous system, hematopoietic system and reproductive system. The effect could be anywhere from disorder and deformity to cancer. It is estimated that nearly 80 million people of the country are affected by arsenic and one in ten has the probability of developing cancer from the poisoning. Arsenic affected people suffer from enormous social stigma here as people consider it as a contagious disease or a curse. As indicated, arsenic contamination of its ground water remains one of the most serious environmental challenges facing Bangladesh.[30]

Wetlands

Wetlands, one of the most important water-related resources in Bangladesh, have been exploited and used exhaustedly, without having proper conservation policies or having any long-vision plan. Degradation of wetlands has caused several problems including extinction and reduction of wildlife, extinction of many indigenous wild and domesticated rice varieties, loss of many indigenous aquatic plants, herbs, shrubs and weeds, loss of natural soil nutrients, loss of natural water reservoirs and of their resultant benefits, increase in the occurrence of flooding and degeneration of wetland based ecosystems, occupations, socio-economic institutions and cultures. Over emphasis on irrigation and flood control has a negative impact on wetlands. Many wetlands are destroyed and their capacity and productivity negatively affected. Fish resources become scarce in these wetlands and valuable flora and fauna are also threatened. People in the wetlands also suffer due to a lack of access to the water resources. Thus, even though the wetlands are very rich in natural and water resources, the people in the wetlands have long suffering and struggles.

Trans-boundary Water Sharing Issue

Water crisis and conflict in Bangladesh is not only limited to the domestic sphere as Bangladesh is the lowest riparian country. The geographical location of Bangladesh has been a vital factor in the proper sharing of trans-boundary water coming from outside the border. There are 54 common rivers that crisscross the geographical contours of the two countries. The problem of resource allocation and sharing, primarily for irrigation purpose, is sensitive and politically charged in Bangladesh.[31] With about 80 percent of the total Bangladeshi population in the rural sector, 61 percent of the total land area arable and 4/5th of the arable area under paddy cultivation, water for agriculture is vital.[32] The Ganges Water Treaty in 1996 greatly reduced political friction but issues relating to the sharing of the Teesta waters and the Tipaimukh Hydro project that India plans on the Barak have opened up a new set of riparian concerns.[33]

As per Bangladesh, its economy, agricultural practices and production, and the general environment have been threatened due to water shortage during the dry season and water abundance during the rainy season. Bangladesh claims that this dichotomous situation is the result of the Farakka Barrage and its controlling of the water flow into downstream Bangladesh.[34] The migration of Bangladeshis due to the environmental impacts of upstream projects in India received little attention in the bargaining process between India and Bangladesh.[35]

On the other hand India claims that due to silt deposition and flooding patterns, the Ganga is actually naturally sifting eastward and has begun to leave the Gorai-Madhumati high and dry in the lean season.[36] Farakka diversions are not the cause of this phenomenon but could have hastened the process. Furthermore, the variation in the river flow has perhaps stemmed more from the absence of basin-wide integrated planning and management than from the barrage itself.[37]

The sharing of Teesta waters has also assumed priority in the discussion between the two states. In the dry season, the exclusive control of the river water at Gazoldoba renders the Dalia Barrage almost useless for diversion of water due to low flows. Moreover, sudden release of excessive water through the Gazoldoba Barrage during the rainy season causes floods, bank erosion and damages huge amounts of crops downstream.[38]

India has recently proposed the construction of the Tipaimuki Barrage in its territory and Bangladesh has concerns about this project because they claim that it will adversely affect the greater economy, environment and river morphology of the Sylhet district of Bangladesh.[39] India has also initiated the Inter-River Linking Project. This project would also keep Bangladesh on an acute straiten towards her socio-economic and environmental ecology.[40]

In reality, the water-related tensions between the two states seem to represent the twin dangers of big-country insensitivity and small-country paranoia because, in fact, both Bangladesh and India face critical challenges of how to manage shared water resources during their excesses and acute scarcity. It is particularly difficult for Bangladesh as it has only 7 percent of the catchments areas of the major shared rivers, the Ganges, the Brahmaputra and the Meghna, but at the same time it is almost completely dependent on them for its water security.

Pollution

Bangladesh is still at the formative stage of modern industrial development and urbanisation. Therefore, the environmental consequences of modernisation have not become quite remarkable yet. Nonetheless, some of such consequences are already assuming alarming proportions. These are pollution of air in the big cities and industrial areas, pollution and depletion of surface and ground water and so on. In this regard, the most alarming case is the pollution of the air in Dhaka. According to a recent study, Dhaka appeared to be one of the most polluted cities of the world. Thousands of people in capital are dying prematurely because of air pollution. An estimated 15,000 premature deaths, as well as several million cases of pulmonary, respiratory and neurological illness are attributed to poor air quality in Dhaka, according to the Air Quality Management Project (AQMP), funded by the government and the World Bank. The World Health Organization (WHO) says vehicular air pollution is a major cause of respiratory distress in urban Bangladesh. According to the DoE (Department of Environment), old, poorly serviced vehicles, brick kilns (there are currently about 1,000 in and around Dhaka), dust from roads and construction sites, and toxic fumes from industrial sites are major sources of air pollution.[41] According to the National Institute of Diseases of Chest and Hospital (NIDCH), nearly seven million people in Bangladesh suffer from asthma; more than half of them children. The report also said that cases of children suffering from bronchitis and chronic coughs have also shot up in recent years.[42]

Furthermore, a World Bank study said four major rivers near Dhaka—the Buriganga, Shitalakhya, Turag and Balu—receive 1.5 million cubic meters of waste water every day from 7,000 industrial units in surrounding areas and another 0.5 million cubic meters from other sources. Unabated encroachment that prevents the free flow of water, dumping of medicinal waste and waste of river passengers have compounded the problem, making the water unusable for humans and livestock. Not only the air and ground water, surrounding of the city and its surface water are also being polluted by industrial waste. In this regard, the worst pollutants are the tanneries. Ninety percent of the 270 tanneries of the country are located in the populous Hazaribag area of Dhaka. According to one estimate, these tanneries release 8.47 million liters of liquid waste and 98 tons of solid waste per day.[43] Clearly, pollution has been a constant threat to the quality of life of people and ultimately security of the country.

Cyclones and Storm Surges

With a very narrow resource base and endemic poverty, Bangladesh, since its birth, was suffering from recurring natural calamities. Tropical cyclones from the Bay of Bengal accompanied by storm surges are one of the major disasters in a country with large-scale loss of property and lives. The height of storm surge in excess of 9m is not uncommon in this region. For example, the 1876 cyclone had a surge height of 13.6 m and in 1970 the height was 9.11 m. In fact, the 1970-Cyclone was the deadliest cyclone that hit Bangladesh coastline. With a wind-speed of about 224 km per hour and storm surge of 6.1 to 9.11 metre, the death toll was about 300,000 people.[44] The most recent cyclone, Cyclone Sidr, hit Bangladesh on November 15, 2007, with an enormous intensity. Winds of 220-240 km/hr and the cyclone's width of 600 kilometers caused over 3,000 deaths and projected costs of $2.3 billion dollars due to widespread devastation to houses, infrastructure, and livelihoods.[45] Needless, to say, all these have been a constant threat to the food security of the country and the human security threat to the people.

Climate Change

As indicated, unrestrained and unplanned exploitation of nature by man without adequate concern for its far-reaching consequences is the root-cause of the environmental degradation. Climate change is another very significant factor as Bangladesh is an agro-based country and is largely dependent on nature. The World Water Development Report, published in March 2003 reveal, that by the middle of this century (2050), 7 billion people in 60 countries including Bangladesh are likely to face acute shortage of water. Only 50 cm rise in the sea level would engulf two-thirds of the country. A rise of only 1.5 m would have the impact on Bangladesh a 17 million (15%) affected population and 222,000 km-square (16%) affected land.[46] The probable impacts of global climate change (GCC), particularly sea-level rise and the associated impact on ecosystems and economic loss, adds to the already daunting array of environmental issues. Climate change will change the physiography and demography of Bangladesh. By 2050, 70 million people could be affected annually by floods; 8 million by drought; up to 8% of the low-lying lands may become permanently inundated. In addition to direct inundation of a large population, the sea level rise will certainly result in increased frequency and severity of flooding along the major estuarine rivers. Saltwater intrusion problems will also be exacerbated in coastal aquifers. Some impacts manifesting in erratic weather patterns and unexpected extreme climatic events have already been evident.[47]

According to the United Nations Development Program (UNDP) Bangladesh is vulnerable to the impacts of climate change for three reasons: 1) Bangladesh is located in a delta of a major river basin, making it susceptible to floods and cyclones. 2) The country has a small area and is heavily populated, one of the most densely populated countries in the world. 3) The country is also very poor and a majority of the population lives below subsistence level, making them already vulnerable.[48]

Conclusion

As apparent from the above explanations, by now, Bangladesh is exposed to a host of severe threats to its security, which is usually referred to as non-traditional security or non-conventional security, emanating from a combination of domestic, regional and global sources. Recurrent cyclones and storm surges, floods followed by droughts, loss of top soil and soil nutrients as well as agricultural and forest land, pollution of water and air, depletion and degradation of resource base are some of its worst manifestations. The impacts of these threatening factors are devastating as the socio-economic context of Bangladesh is also vulnerable. These social and environmental stresses have various negative social effects such as loss of economic productivity, decline in agro-production, increase in livelihood insecurity, increase in competition on limited resources, and so on. Directly or indirectly these negative social effects and environmental stress cause enormous threats to the well-being of Bangladesh, especially these environmental stresses threaten the majority people's livelihood. As livelihood is the core of human security and the 'security' of the majority people is basically related to environmental factors, such as the quantity, quality and availability of environmental resources. In present reality, people need much attention to be secure from environmental threats and livelihood insecurity.

The notion of threat in Bangladesh therefore, is very much related to environmental factors than any other territorial threats. In the case of Bangladesh, these vulnerable situations not only concern threats, but they also contribute to huge loss of lives and breeding conflict. Water crisis in Bangladesh involves both domestic and interstate level conflict. The victims of the rise of sea level naturally become environmental refugees in India and this may lead to political tensions. Nowadays, 'push back' is a common experience in Bangladeshi newspapers. This phrase means pushing alleged illegal Bangladeshi people from India to Bangladesh by Indian Border Security Force (BSF). Environmental refugees created by climate change will cause even worse situation that are likely to trigger conflict between the two countries.[49] Bangladeshi migrants will generate political tension as they traverse the region's many of the contested borders and territories, such as those between China, India, and Pakistan. The India-Bangladesh border is already a site of significant political friction, demonstrated by the 2,100-mile, two-and-a-half-meter high, iron border fence that India has started to build. Due to be completed in 2007, this fence is being constructed at a time when there are numerous signs of the rise of Islamic extremism in Bangladesh. The combination of deteriorating socio-economic conditions, rise of radical Islamic political groups, and dire environmental insecurity brought on by climate change can lead to a volatile mix with severe regional and potentially global consequences.[50]

The environmental challenges posed to Bangladesh emanate considerably from the regional and global sources. Therefore, while the mobilisation of national efforts with a view to facing the challenges is indispensable, their success would significantly depend on the actions taken at the regional and global levels. In this regard, the role played by the international community and the country's ability to involve the neighbours in co-operative endeavours would be of crucial importance.

The treaty between Bangladesh and India envisaging the sharing of Ganges water is an encouraging sign. However, in order to respond to the environmental challenges faced by Bangladesh and its neighbours, much more needs to be done. First of all, it is necessary to mobilise the collective will and efforts of the countries of the Ganges and the Brahmaputra river basins. For a long time, this seemed to be an impossible task. Geography dictates that no co-operative effort could be initiated without the participation of India.

For Bangladesh, pursuing 'environmental diplomacy' would be of crucial importance not only for facing the challenges emanating from regional and global sources, but also from domestic sources. Naturally occurring inorganic arsenic contamination of Bangladesh's ground water, almost the lone source of drinking water, has already been characterised as a challenge potentially more devastating. For Bangladesh, a challenge of such gigantic proportion would be impossible to face on its own. Therefore, mobilisation of substantial assistance on the part of international community for initiating effective measures of arsenic mitigation would be indispensable.

This need for international assistance applies also to challenges thrown by recurring devastating floods. In this regard, along with attracting international assistance, co-operation with the neighbours, India in particularly, aimed at the proper management and utilisation of common water resources is of crucial importance.

To sum up, Bangladesh's ability to face the challenges to its security thrown by the process of environmental degradation would significantly depend on the ability of the country's diplomacy to galvanise international support and develop effective co-operation for management of common resources and environment with the neighbours, particularly India.

REFERENCES

1. T. Dissanaike, South Asia Disaster Report Special Copenhagen Issue, 2009 http://practicalaction.org/media/download/7087. [01.01.2012]
2. N.R. Biswas, "Is the Environment a Security Threat? Environmental Security beyond Securitization," *International Affairs Review* 2011, 20 (1).
3. S. Bhardwaj, "Cooperative Security in South Asia: The Future Outlook," in Farooq Sohban (eds) *Strengthening Cooperation and Security in South Asia*, Dhaka: The University Press Limited, 2004.
4. M. Hough, and G.P.H. Kruys, Non-military Treats To Security: Selected United Nations and other Multilateral Documents, Institute of Strategic Studies November 2009, University of Pretoria: South Africa.
5. P. Hough, *Understanding Global Security*, London: Routledge, 2004.
6. M. Hough and G.P.H. Kruys, Non-military Treats To Security: Selected United Nations and other Multilateral Documents, Institute of Strategic Studies November 2009, University of Pretoria: South Africa.
7. P. Hough, *Understanding Global Security*, London: Routledge, 2004.
8. S. Bhardwaj, "Cooperative Security in South Asia: The Future Outlook," in Farooq Sohban (eds) *Strengthening Cooperation and Security in South Asia*, Dhaka: The University Press Limited, 2004.
9. P. Hough, *Understanding Global Security*, London: Routledge, 2004.
10. ibid.
11. X. Yan, "Nontraditional Security in East Asia", Accessed 21st January 2009, URL: http://rwxy.tsingua.edu.cn/xi-suo/institute/english/production/yxt/6.htm.
12. P. Hough, *Understanding Global Security*, London: Routledge, 2004.
13. ibid.
14. N.R. Biswas, "Is the Environment a Security Threat? Environmental Security beyond Securitization," *International Affairs Review* 2011, 20(1).
15. ibid.
16. M. Walsham, Assessing the Evidence: Environment, Climate Change and Migration in Bangladesh. International Organization for Migration (IOM), Switzerland, 2010 http://

publications.iom.int/bookstore/free/environment_climate_change_bangladesh.pdf. [10.1.2012]

17. WWDR3 2009: Facing Water Challenges in Bangladesh at the confluence of the Ganges: Brahmaputra and Meghna Rivers : A WWDR3 Case Study http://waterwiki.net/index.php/Category:.Asia_%26_Pacific [10.1.2012]
18. U.K. Sinha, Strategic Analysis, Vol. 30, No. 3, Jul-Sep 2006© Institute for Defence Studies and Analyse, http://www.idsa.in/system/files/strategicanalysis_uttam_0906.pdf [10.1.2012]
19. D. Talukder, and C. Love, Estimation of Population and Food Grain Production in Bangladesh by 2020: A Simple Moving Average Approach to a Time Series Analysis. Bangladesh e-Journal of Sociology 7/2011, 8 (2) http:// www.bangladeshsocilogy.org/BEJS %208.2%20Estimation %20of%20Population%20and%20Food%20Grain%20Production %20in%20Bangladesh%20by%202020.pdf. [10.1.2012]
20. World Food Programmer Agricultural Production & National Food Balance. Food Security Atlas for Bangladesh 2011, http://foodsecurityatlas.org/bgd/country/availability/agricultural-production. [10.1.2012]
21. Bureau of South and Central Asian Affairs 2010: Background Note: Bangladesh, http://www.state.gov/r/pa/ei/bgn/3452.htm. [10.12.2011]
22. Water Pollution and Scarcity Bangladesh: State of the Environment, http://www.moef.gov.bd/html/state_of_env/pdf/bangladesh_water.pdf. [10.1.2012]
23. Bangladesh Institute of Peace and Security Studies Water security: The threat facing Bangladesh. Bangladesh Institute of Peace and Security Studies 22/2009, http://www.bipss.org.bd/download/water_security.p [15.05.2011]
24. Gain, A.K. and M.A. Bari Effect of Environmental Degradation on National Security of Bangladesh. Asia Pacific Journal on Environment & Development 2007, 14 (2): 35-54.
25. Bangladesh's Haunting Floods 2011, http://www.climateavenue.com/cl.imp.sealevel.Bangladesh.htm [10.12.2011]
26. Banglapedia, National Encyclopedia of Bangladesh (2008), http://www.banglapedia.org/httpdocs/HT/D_0284.HTM [10.12.2011]
27. Water Pollution and Scarcity Bangladesh: State of the Environment, 2001, http://www.moef.gov.bd/html/state_of_env/pdf/bangladesh_water.pdf. [10.1.2012]
28. ibid.
29. Huda, Riaz Uddin, Naz Hasan, Department of Pharmacy, Stamford University Bangladesh, http://www.omjournal.org/fultext_PDF.aspx?DetailsID=107&type=fultext [10.12.2011]
30. ibid.
31. Compendium of Environment Statistics of Bangladesh (2009), available at http://www.bbs.gov.bd/WebTestApplication/userfiles/Image/Other%20Reports/Environment.pdf. [10.12.2011]
32. M. Nasiruddin, and M.S. Hassan 2009: Agricultural Research Priority: Vision-2030 and beyond available at, http://www.barc.gov.bd/documents/Final-%20Dr.%20Nasir.pdf. [10.1.2012]
33. IDSA Task Force Report 2010: *Water Security for India: The External Dynamics*. Institute for Defence Studies and Analyses 2010, New Delhi.
34. N. Verma, G.K. Sarangi and A. Mishra, The Impact of Climate Change on a Hydro-Geographic "Region of Conflict" Case study of the Ganga Basin. *World Affairs Summer* 2009, 13 (2).
35. A. Swain, 1996: The Environmental Trap: The Ganges River Diversion, Bangladeshi Migration and Conflicts in India. Uppsala: Department of Peace and Conflict Research 1996, 135.

36. Verghese, 2009: Water conflicts in South Asia. Studies in Conflict & Terrorism 2/2009, 20
37. ibid.
38. S. Suryanarayanan, India and Bangladesh: Teesta River Agreement. May 2010, Available at http://www.strategicforesight.com/teesta_river.htm [01.05.2010]
39. IDSA Task Force Report *Water Security for India: The External Dynamics.* Institute for Defence Studies and Analyses 2010, New Delhi.
40. BIPSS 2009: Water security-The threat facing Bangladesh. Available at https://docs.google.com/viewer?url=http%3A%2F%2Fwww.bipss.org.bd%2Fdownload%2Fwater_security.pdf [10.12.2011]
41. Bio Earth 2009: Bangladesh Pollution Threatens Millions, http://www.bioearthinc.com/bangladeshpollution.htm [10.12.2011]
42. ibid.
43. ibid.
44. A.K. Gain and M.A. Bari Effect of Environmental Degradation on National Security of Bangladesh. *Asia Pacific Journal on Environment & Development* 2007, 14 (2): 35-54.
45. USAID: Bangladesh: Environment 2011: Bangladesh Has Rich But Dwindling Biodiversity. Current Conditions: Environment. http://www.usaid.gov/bd/programs/environ.html [10.1.2012]
46. BIPSS 2009: Water security-The threat facing Bangladesh. Available at https://docs.google.com/viewer?url=http%3A%2F%2Fwww.bipss.org.bd%2Fdownload%2Fwater_security.pdf [10.12.2011]
47. USAID: Bangladesh: Environment 2011: Bangladesh Has Rich But Dwindling Biodiversity. Current Conditions: Environment. http://www.usaid.gov/bd/programs/environ.html [10.1.2012]
48. Matthijs van der Hoorn 2010: Climate Change and Conflict in Bangladesh, http://geography2.ruhosting.nl/masterthesis/scripties/HoornMatthijsvander.pdf. [10.1.2012]
49. A.K. Gain and M.A. Bari 2007: Effect of Environmental Degradation on National Security of Bangladesh. Asia Pacific Journal on Environment & Development 2007, 14 (2): 35–54.
50. ibid.

4

India-Bangladesh Land Boundary Agreement: Beginning of a New Era

Amar Singh and Shivendra Shahi

The re-emergence of the Bay of Bengal in regional strategic calculus has immense geopolitical consequence. As this opens up enormous economic opportunities, there is a need for the littorals to chart out a shared vision of building a community based on peace, prosperity and stability.[1] In this context improving political relationships with the Bangladesh and the settlement of long-standing territorial disputes provide an opportune time to explore bilateral cooperation in resources sharing, inter-linking connectivity and joint efforts to enhance security. India–Bangladesh relations have had a chequered past, essentially due to frequent changes in the political dispensation in Bangladesh and compounded by, what some commentators insist, "benign neglect" by India. India's preoccupation with its western and northern neighbours, polarization in political and popular opinions within Bangladesh on relations with India, presumption and perception within Bangladesh about India's "intentions", unhappiness—on both sides—on the issue of water sharing, illegal migration, etc., further vitiated the atmosphere.[2]

Boundary dispute is one such issue that is there between India and Bangladesh before the latter was born as a state. Disputes about the position of a boundary often take different forms as they arise out of different causes and certainly retain the potential to too often be unduly bitter, costly and time-consuming before their peaceful resolution. As they concern two or more countries, boundary disputes are primarily concerned with the legal and technical issues of determining the line of the boundary between or amongst them or may be a result of the prevailing state of the relationship amongst the neighbours involved.[3]

The deep historical bonds between Bangladesh and India evolved from centuries of shared history, religion, and culture, materializing long before the latter's assistance during the Bangladeshi War of Liberation against Pakistan in 1971.[4] The India-Bangladesh boundary is no ordinary one. It was the longest international boundary which was hastily constructed in the dying days of British colonialism. The border was intended to separate a contiguous majority area of Muslims from that of non-Muslims—but for only about a quarter of its length separates a Musim-majority in Bangladesh from a Hindu-majority in India. As many as 162 tiny enclaves (111 Indian and 52 Bangladeshi) dot a section of the frontier: in the extreme an Indian enclave sits with in a Bangladeshi enclave, itself situated within a larger Indian enclave, all surrounded by Bangladeshi territory. Shifting rivers, mapping errors and 'adversely possessed lands'—that is, lands unwittingly encroached upon and (illegally) occupied by both countries—added to the maze of identity, loyalty and insecurity along the Bengal border land.[5]

Both India and Bangladesh conducted a joint census between 14-17 July 2011 to determine the total population in these enclaves ('chhintmahals') and found their number to be around 51,549. Of them, 37,334 persons were in Indian enclaves within Bangladesh, while 14,215 people were residing in Bangladesh enclaves within India.[6] These people have been rendered stateless due to a cartographic anomaly. Devoid of basic services such as electricity, hospitals or schools, the residents are stuck without any relief.[7] These enclaves are virtually ungovernable as they are inaccessible from the mainland. Being landlocked, the enclaves have become a haven for criminals. A delay in the ratification of the agreement would not only further dent India's credibility but also create safety and security concerns as well.[8]

Background

The origin of India-Bangladesh border disputes goes back to the time of partition. The former East Pakistan was cut out of the territory of Assam and Bengal. Being a part of Pakistan, Bangladesh has a common land boundary of approximately 4096.7 km, which was determined as per the Radcliffe Award of 1947, then with East Pakistan.[9] It passes through flat and hilly terrain, rivers and jungles and traverses five states of India, viz., West Bengal (2217 kms), Assam (262 kms), Meghalaya (443 kms), Tripura (856 kms) and Mizoram (318 kms), including nearly 781 kms of riverine border.[10] About 85 per cent of this border is porous, having no natural feature to identify the border.[11]

Folklore has it that the islands of enclaves in India and Bangladesh were the result of a series of chess games between the Maharaja of Cooch Behar and the Faujdar of Rangpur. These noblemen used these villages as a wager. Thus, some villages in Cooch Behar became the properties of Rangpur while villages within Rangpur came to be owned by the Cooch Behar Maharajas. This informal arrangement between the two rulers allowed collection of revenues and administering of the respective 'enclaves'. But after the Partition, Rangpur became part of East Pakistan (now Bangladesh) while Cooch Behar became part of India when its Maharaja Jitendra Narayan acceded his princely state to India in August 1949.[12]

Although the demarcation of the border between India and the then Pakistan had started soon after the partition, progress was slower than expected, due in part to the difficulties in determining precisely where the border ran. Even though some of these boundary disputes were sought to be settled by the Nehru-Noon agreement of 1958, subsequent hostilities between the two countries left the task unaccomplished. Even after the creation of Bangladesh, the boundary dispute between the two countries inherited the legacy of history and fractured politics. On May 16, 1974, shortly after the liberation of Bangladesh, Prime Minister Indira Gandhi and Bangladeshi premier Sheikh Mujibur Rahman signed the India-Bangladesh Land Boundary Agreement (LBA), under which the two countries agreed to transfer these enclaves to each other's sovereignty. Though, the Bangladesh legislature ratified the agreement soon after, India's legislature, preoccupied with the Emergency of 1975, did not. Though the agreement got implemented in its entirety without ratification by India, yet the three issues pertaining to:

(i) Undemarcated land boundary of approximately 6.1 km in three sectors viz. Daikhata-56 (West Bengal), Muhuri River-Belonia (Tripura) and Lathitila-Dumabari (Assam);
(ii) Exchange of enclaves; and
(iii) Adverse possessions.[13]

These remained in a state of limbo bringing both the countries and its leaders to a point of never-ending conflict, mistrust and unlimited tension, which has vitiated the good neighbourly relations and converting the region into a theater of power play by other vested interests.[14] However, in respect of Dahagram and Angarporta enclaves of Bangladesh, article 1(14) of the 1974 LBA provides for access to these enclaves by leasing in perpetuity an area of 178 metres × 85 metres near "Tin Bigha". This was implemented through letters of Exchange on October 7, 1982, between the then foreign minister of India and foreign minister of Bangladesh[15] and later in 1992, for enhancement of mutual trust and promotion of good neighbourly relations, India courageously announced its decision to permanently lease out the Teen Bigha Corridor to Bangladesh in 1992, despite local opposition.[16]

Despite the limited nature of dispute on the border, the non-settlement of adverse possessions has led to tension between the border guarding forces of the two countries. Muktapur, Pyrdiwah and Naljuri along the Meghalaya-Bangladesh border had witnessed firing incidents in the recent past. In Dumabari area (Assam) firing took place between the two security agencies as early as in 1962 and again in 1965. In Muhuri river area (Tripura), 10 incidents of firing were reported between Border Security Force (BSF) and Bangladesh Border Guard (BGB), the last reported in 1999. In Boroibari (Assam), in a firing incident in 2001, 16 BSF personnel were killed. Thus, the adverse possession areas have been flashpoints between India and Bangladesh exacerbating the tensions along the border and between the two neighbouring states. The issue got further complicated with the increasing population pressure in Bangladesh, use of Bangladesh soil for anti-India terrorist activities, and refuge for terrorists, militants and criminals. All of this necessitated the need for an early settlement of the outstanding land boundary issues between India and Bangladesh.[17]

Proposed Deal: In September 2011, during Prime Minister Manmohan Singh's visit to Dhaka, the two Prime Ministers signed a Protocol to the Land Boundary Agreement that would enable its implementation. The 2011 Protocol will settle:

- Unresolved issues pertaining to the un-demarcated land boundary of approximately 6.1 km; exchange of enclaves; and adverse possessions.[18]
- Exchange of enclaves (India agreed to receive 51 out of the 71 Bangladeshi enclaves (from 51 to 54 of the 74 chitts) inside India comprising about 7,110.02 acres, while Bangladesh to get from 95 to 101 of the 103 Indian enclaves (111 out of 119 chitts) which are inside Bangladesh proper (17,160.63 acres). [19]

Transfer of Territories in Adverse Possession

S. No.	*States*	*Territory to be transferred to India (in acres)*	*Territory to be transferred to Bangladesh (in acres)*
1	West Bengal	2398.05	1957.59
2	Meghalaya	240.578	41.702
3	Tripura	138.41	-4
4	Assam	—	268.39
	Total	2777.038	2267.682

Source: Radha Kumar, (2013), "Failing Bangladesh: Legislators against the National Interest", Delhi Policy Group, New Delhi, pp.5. http://www.delhipolicygroup.com/uploads/publication_file/1048_Bangaldesh_LBA_-_Policy_Brief.pdf

- Bangladesh would retain the 4617 acres of its Dahagram Angarpota exclave, involving about 14,215 people who were residing in Bangladeshi enclaves in India whereas 37,269 people residing in Indian enclaves in Bangladesh.
- The exclaves' populations, over 50,000 people, were to have a say in the matter, and each person, would be empowered to ultimately choose their nationality remained on paper.[20]

At last after 41 year, the Indian Parliament ratifies the long awaited Land Boundary Agreement between India and Bangladesh (May 2015). It is an issue, which has remained a sour point between the two countries. The delay was mainly because India's foreign policy has been held hostage to domestic politics. While on paper, the exchange of enclaves between India and Bangladesh may seem like a loss of Indian land to Bangladesh, the actual scenario is quite different as the enclaves are located deep inside the territory of both countries and there has been no physical access to them from either country. In reality, the exchange of enclaves denotes only a notional exchange of land as the protocol converts a de facto reality into a de jure situation. The inhabitants in the enclaves could not enjoy full legal rights as citizens of either India or Bangladesh and infrastructure facilities such as electricity, schools and health services were deficient. Further, due to lack of access to these areas by the law and order enforcing agencies and weak property rights, certain enclaves became hot beds of criminal activities.[21]

Why it was Needed

Economic Interactions: India's economic interactions with Bangladesh have grown gradually in recent years. Bangladesh has replaced Sri Lanka as India's largest trading partner in South Asia, with bilateral trade touching US$ 5.7 billion in 2012-13. The duty free access given by India to Bangladesh for all items except 25 has been an important factor for this dramatic growth. Since the signing of the Bilateral Investment Promotion and Protection agreement, Indian investment in Bangladesh has been growing. For historical reasons and because of the porous nature of regional borders, informal trade among these countries is much higher than formal trade. In the recent past, India has established the 'Border Haats' concept, a local market across borders, with Bangladesh, hoping to encourage cross-border trade and minimise illegal transactions. The challenge, however, is to make legal trade across borders more attractive than smuggling. China's growing economic footprint in the region also presents another dimension of the challenge for India. China is today the largest trading partner of Bangladesh.[22]

Cross-Border Security Cooperation: The under-developed borderlands of Bangladesh and India have long been characterised by ethnic conflicts, gun-running, smuggling, narcotics and human trafficking. They are far away from the political and economic centres of two countries and the absence of effective administrative controls have led to these areas becoming breeding grounds for all sorts of illegal activities. Cross-border security cooperation has been a major concern of India's bilateral cooperation with Bangladesh. In fact, the progress made in dealing with Indian insurgent groups taking shelter in Bangladesh has deepened mutual trust and enabled India to develop closer political and security interactions with its eastern neighbours. One of the challenges in cross-border cooperation has been the issue of unsettled land and maritime territorial boundaries.[23]

The election of the Indian Prime Minister Narendra Modi and his repeated emphasis on promotion of closer regional cooperation, interconnectivity, and trade has enlivened the hopes of people for an early resolution of this outstanding dispute. It has also been said that the new PM is favourable of such a step within his government's good neighbourhood policy as it will provide content to his much stated policy of reaching mutually beneficial solutions to the neighbours' problems though BJP while in opposition during UPA-2; it had stalled Congress' attempts to resolve this border dispute. Further under his leadership, the ready acceptance by India of the United Nations Tribunal verdict on the long-disputed sea border between India and Bangladesh, which awarded around 80 percent of the

25,000 km^2 of disputed waters to Bangladesh has also struck a positive note with the Bangladesh leadership, its people and the outer world, earning for India, the much required goodwill and further enhanced mutual understanding with the neighbours.[24]

Advantages

The major features of the 2011 protocol regarding the India-Bangladesh boundary are also its advantages. These are as follows:

- As the protocol is the outcome of bilateral negotiations, it is mutually acceptable and durable and paves the way for settlement of the long pending land boundary issues.
- It takes into consideration the situation on the ground and the wishes of the people.
- It takes into account the views of the concerned State governments and has their written consent.
- The exchange of enclaves will mitigate major humanitarian problems as the residents in the enclaves and others on their behalf had often complained of the absence of basic amenities and facilities.
- The settlement of adverse possessions will lead to tranquillity and peace along the border.
- The protocol provides for a comprehensive package solution involving "give and take" on both sides.
- It represents a permanent solution to a decades old issue, land will be exchanged; the protocol does not envisage the displacement of populations.
- The newly demarcated boundaries are a fixed boundary, thereby adding to certainty regarding the future and also paving the way for closer engagement and mutually beneficial relations between India and Bangladesh and the region.
- A settled boundary reduces friction, helps neighbours consolidate mutually beneficial exchanges and promotes confidence in building better relations. This also helps on issues of strategic concern, including security cooperation and denial of sanctuary to elements inimical to India. [25]

The border settlement will open up and create huge economic opportunities for both Bangladesh and the Border States including Assam,

West Bengal, Meghalaya and Tripura. They can garner huge economic benefits by getting connected with Bangladesh. Dhaka could be a gateway for India to open to the East Asian countries. India could seek from Bangladesh as a goodwill gesture transit rights to its northeast, bringing development to the region. Bangladesh will also benefit immensely by the deal.

The newly elected Prime Minister of India has been talking of 'neighborhood first' concept and the ratification would show that he means what he says despite opposition from his own party's Assam unit. The land swap deal would go a long way to improving India's image in the neighborhood as well as in the international arena. The neighbours often view India with suspicion because of its size, economy and military might and see New Delhi as a bully.

Conclusion

However since there are such border disputes amongst the countries in the region, which stand a chance of being escalated and complicating the already fragile ties that the countries share, it is important that proper mechanisms are worked out for proper resolution of such disputes and in the light of the aforesaid concerns.

Two fundamental principles and processes that underlie New Delhi's calculus of territorial dispute settlement are particularly noteworthy. First, an imperative of good neighborliness has been a fundamental prerequisite for settlement—New Delhi was willing to meet the Bangladeshi Prime Minister mid-way, even beyond, but only after the latter had met India's security concerns and walked the extra mile to extend the hand of friendship. The significant credit for the settlement belongs at the Bangladeshi end. Second, and more important, is a practice of Indian boundary diplomacy which has seen New Delhi admit to the exigencies of "Zamini Haqeeqat" (ground realities) in disputed border areas—formally seeking to resolve territorial disputes according to the status quo, with least disturbance to local inhabitants. "Ground realities" is formally acknowledged in the India-Bangladesh Joint Statement. Paired with the acceptance of a political parameters based approach to dispute resolution, it has also unlocked potential for resolving the long dormant Sino-Indian boundary dispute.[26] In the context of this boundary deal Indian people and political establishment need to introspect, Why has there been a difference of views between both the main political parties on this issue and if their actions of support and opposition at different times are purely politically motivated or by their concern for protection of India's national interests?

With the Modi regime there is an indication of India's resolve to continue its focus on its immediate neighbours. There is a strong recognition that India's destiny is inextricably linked to its neighbourhood. The challenge before India is to act upon this vision. "as the land deal is sealed India and Bangladesh have entered a new phase in bilateral relations with a pragmatic and practical approach based on sovereignty, equality, friendship, trust and understanding for the mutual benefit of their peoples and collective prosperity of the region".[27] Dhaka and Delhi need to go far beyond just an assertion of their traditional political and historical links. Gen next expects much more than just platitudes and hopes to see tangible results leading to visible benefits, right at its doorsteps. Mutually beneficial projects and agreements will always find favour irrespective of the governments of the day in New Delhi or Dhaka.[28]

REFERENCES

1. K. Yhome (2014), "The Bay of Bengal at the Crossroads: Potential for Cooperation Among Bangladesh, India and Myanmar", FES India paper, New Delhi, [Online: Web] Accessed 14 June 2012, http://www.fes.de/cgi-bin/gbv.cgi?id=11043&ty=pdf
2. "India and Bangladesh—A new phase in Bilateral Relations", *Indian Foreign Affairs Journal*, Vol. 6:4: 365-406, October–December, 2011.
3. B. Mohapatra (2014), "India Bangladesh Relations and the Land Boundary Agreement: Tackling the Seeds of Discord", [Online: Web] Accessed 14 April 2015, http://www.academia.edu/12301946/India_Bangladesh_Relations_and_the_Land_Boundary_Agreement_-_Tackling_the_Seeds_of_Discord.
4. M.C. Poplin, "India Bangladesh Relations: A Review of Bilateral Opportunities and Constraints," India Development Cooperation Research (IDCR) Project, Background Paper no. 1, [Online: Web] Accessed 14 June 2014, http://idcr.cprindia.org/blog/india and bangladeshreview bilateral opportunities
5. S. Gupta (2011), "India and Bangladesh: calculus of territorial dispute settlement", 10 October, East Asia Forum, [Online: Web] Accessed 4 July 2012,http://www.eastasiaforum.org/2011/10/10/india-and-bangladesh-calculus-of-territorial-dispute-settlement/
6. S. Mohan (2014), "India-Bangladesh Land Boundary Agreement and enclave populations", 31 December 2014, [Online: Web] Accessed 1 May 2015,http://www.theindependentbd.com/index.php?view=article&catid=169%3Aop-ed&id=242635%3Aindia-bangladesh-land-boundary-agreement-and-enclave-popu
7. K. Shankar (2015), "Empowering the Traditional Institution", *The Shillong Times*, 9 May, [Online: Web] Accessed 24 May 2015, http://www.theshillongtimes.com/2015/05/09/empowering-the-traditional-institutions-2/
8. J. Bhattacharjee, (2014), *"India-Bangladesh Relations: A Ten-point Agenda"*, Observers issue brief:71, [Online: Web] Accessed 3 January 2015,http://orfonline.org/cms/export/orfonline/

modules/issuebrief/attachments/issue_brief_71_1409294274331.pdf
9. M. Bhaskar (2014), "Indo-Bangladesh Land Swap Deal: A Move Towards Settlement of Border Disputes", Munich, GRIN Verlag, [Online: Web] Accessed 7 March 2015, http://www.grin.com/en/e-book/286531/indo-bangl
10. Zahoor Ahmad, "India-Bangladesh Cattle Smuggling—Challenges and Opportunities", *International Journal of Scientific Research*, Volume, 2014, 3:3, March.
11. M.H.A Rashid, "Let us Prove that Past Is Past" in "India and Bangladesh—A new Phase in Bilateral Relations", *Indian Foreign Affairs Journal*, 2011, Vol. 6:4: 365-406, October–December.
12. K. Shankar, (2015), "Empowering the Traditional Institution", *The Shillong Times*, 9 May, [Online: Web] Accessed 24 May 2015, http://www.theshillongtimes.com/2015/05/09/empowering-the-traditional-institutions-2/
13. Government of India (2014), "India and Bangladesh: Land Boundary Agreement", Public Diplomacy Division, Ministry of External Affairs, New Delhi.
14. B. Mohapatra, (2014), "India Bangladesh Relations and the Land Boundary Agreement: Tackling the Seeds of Discord", [Online: Web] Accessed 24 May 2015, http://www.academia.edu/12301946/India_Bangladesh_Relations_and_the_Land_Boundary_Agreement_-_Tackling_the_Seeds_of_Discord
15. Government of India (2014), "India and Bangladesh: Land Boundary Agreement", Public Diplomacy Division, Ministry of External Affairs, New Delhi.
16. B. Mohapatra (2014), "India Bangladesh Relations and the Land Boundary Agreement: Tackling the Seeds of Discord", [Online: Web] Accessed 24 May 2015, http://www.academia.edu/12301946/India_Bangladesh_Relations_and_the_Land_Boundary_Agreement_-_Tackling_the_Seeds_of_Discord
17. Government of India (2014), "India and Bangladesh: Land Boundary Agreement", Public Diplomacy Division, Ministry of External Affairs, New Delhi.
18. Ibid.
19. R. Kumar (2013), "Failing Bangladesh: Legislators against the National Interest", Delhi Policy Group, New Delhi, [Online: Web] Accessed 4 May 2015, http://www.delhipolicygroup.com/uploads/publication_file/1048_Bangaldesh_LBA_-_Policy_Brief.pdf.
20. B. Mohapatra (2014), "India Bangladesh Relations and the Land Boundary Agreement: Tackling the Seeds of Discord", [Online: Web] Accessed 24 May 2015, http://www.academia.edu/12301946/India_Bangladesh_Relations_and_the_Land_Boundary_Agreement_-_Tackling_the_Seeds_of_Discord
21. Government of India (2014), "India and Bangladesh: Land Boundary Agreement", Public Diplomacy Division, Ministry of External Affairs, New Delhi.
22. K. Yhome (2014), "The Bay of Bengal at the Crossroads: Potential for Cooperation Among Bangladesh, India and Myanmar", FES India paper, New Delhi, [Online: Web] Accessed 14 June 2012, http://www.fes.de/cgi-bin/gbv.cgi?id=11043&ty=pdf
23. Ibid
24. B. Mohapatra (2014), "India Bangladesh Relations and the Land Boundary Agreement: Tackling the Seeds of Discord", [Online: Web] Accessed 24 May 2015, http://www.academia.edu/12301946/India_Bangladesh_Relations_and_the_Land_Boundary_Agreement_-_Tackling_the_Seeds_of_Discord
25. Government of India (2014), "India and Bangladesh: Land Boundary Agreement", Public Diplomacy Division, Ministry of External Affairs, New Delhi.

26. S. Gupta (2011), "India and Bangladesh: calculus of territorial dispute settlement", 10 October, East Asia Forum, [Online: Web] Accessed 4 July 2012,http://www.eastasiaforum. org/2011/ 10/10/india-and-bangladesh-calculus-of-territorial-dispute-settlement/
27. K. Yhome (2014), "The Bay of Bengal at the Crossroads: Potential for Cooperation Among Bangladesh, India and Myanmar", FES India paper, New Delhi, [Online: Web] Accessed 14 June 2012, http://www.fes.de/cgi-bin/gbv.cgi?id=11043&ty=pdf
28. S. Data (2011), "Show Tangible Results Leading to Visible Benefits" in "India and Bangladesh—A new phase in Bilateral Relations", *Indian Foreign Affairs Journal*, Vol. 6:4: 365-406, October–December.

5

India's Bhutan Policy: A Critical Approach

Rajesh S Kharat

Indian Prime Minister Narendra Modi's maiden visit to Bhutan had surprised many academicians, policymakers and statesmen not only in India but also in the world. Even Bhutanese did not expect this honour to their country following resentment against India few months back. However, being one of the small and weak states of South Asia, Bhutan always felt that its relations with India have been characterised as relations between unequal neighbours. In fact, geo-strategic location and considerations decide Bhutan's destiny as it is sandwiched between two powerful neighbours, India and China, who tend to be hostile towards each other. In Bhutan, India always has an edge over China, due to its geographical proximity and more importantly colonial legacy and cultural affinity.

Designated Prime Minister Modi's decision to invite all the HOG (Heads of Government) from SAARC countries, including Lobsang Sangay the Prime Minister of Tibetan Government-in-exile, for the oath ceremony signaled a new perspective in India's foreign policy. Since, Indian government have prioritised to develop proximity with its immediate neighbours than other countries, the speculations were made that the Bhartiya Janata Party (BJP) led government might think of Nepal for Modi's first maiden visit to any foreign country. Historically, geographically, ethnically and culturally India is much closer to Nepal than Bhutan. But this did not happen and India chose Bhutan over Nepal. This sudden change in India's neighbourhood policy, particularly vis-à-vis Bhutan, compels the researchers to re-assess India's Bhutan policy in the contemporary period and analyse the factors responsible for this change.

Bhutan has a very small area of 18000 sq. miles and a population of about 742,000 with the population density of 19.3 per sq. km. Thus, the small population and territory of Bhutan leave it with inadequate human and natural resources.

It is a buffer state between two giant Asian neighbours—India and China—and landlocked in nature which isolates it from the rest of the world. Geo-strategically, Bhutan is not only isolated from the rest of the world but also from within. On the north it is bounded by the Tibetan plateau, whereas on the southern side it is surrounded by plains of the Jalpaiguri district of West Bengal and Golpara, Kamrup and Darrang districts of Assam. Bhutan is sandwiched between the Chumbi valley of Tibet; Sikkim and Darjeeling in the west; and the Kameng district of Arunachal Pradesh in India on the east. However, it maintains its relations and contacts with the rest of the world only through the Indian territory.

Mahayana Buddhism is Bhutan's state religion and it has impact on Bhutan's national life as Buddhism enjoys state patronage in Bhutan. In the domestic sphere, it maintains a separate identity, values and traditions—whereas at the international level, Bhutan follows *Panchsheel*, five core principles of Buddhism as one of the basic principles of its foreign policy. *Madhyam Marg* (Middle Path) has been observed and followed to resolve the crucial and critical issues. Moreover, being a Buddhist nation it is able to establish a cordial link with other Buddhist countries in order to procure development assistance as well as their support in world politics. Thus, Bhutan's religious identity has become an important asset in its external policy management.

With low industrial growth, its economy is dependent upon other countries and international financial agencies like IMF, World Bank, etc. According to the World Bank Report (2014) its Gross Domestic Product per capita was last recorded at US $2037.16 in 2013.

As Bhutan is economically and militarily weak (its army has only 10,000 men), it cannot defend its boundaries in a situation where conflict is involved. Under such circumstances, it has to look to other friendly neighbours like

India and regional/international organisations like SAARC, NAM and the United Nations.

An Overview of Indo-Bhutan Relations: 1949-2007

As far as foreign policy of Bhutan is concerned, it is conscious about its inability to play a major role in the region because of its own limitations of topography, untapped resources, inadequate infrastructure, and dependent economy and to some extent due to colonial legacy of the Indo-Bhutan Treaty of 1949, which was revised later in February 2007. Bhutan always had reservations about the implementation of Article Two of 1949 Treaty, which says, 'the Government of India undertakes to exercise no interference in the internal administration of Bhutan. On its part, the Government of Bhutan agrees to be guided by the advice of the Government of India in its external relations. Thus, the Indian government assured Bhutan that it will strictly adhere to the principle of non-interference in its internal affairs, which shows India's respect to the principle of *Panchsheel.*

From the Bhutanese point of view, the incorporation of Article 2 in this treaty has a different meaning altogether. As far as the first part is concerned, 'non-interference in the internal administration of Bhutan', it did not create any misinterpretation concerning the sovereign and independent status of Bhutan. But it was not happy with the second part of Article 2. It implied that the treaty restricted Bhutan from extending her relations beyond India. Therefore, Bhutan always felt India has adopted the colonial model of relationship with it and continued the legacy of previous treaties like Treaty of Sinchu La of 1865 and Treaty of Punakha of 1910, signed basically between British India and succeeding Kings of Bhutan. The basic aim of these treaties was to extend influence and engage Bhutan economically.

Whereas, for India Article 2 of this treaty has its own significance. In the first place, the treaty was a logical continuation of the British Indian arrangement. Bhutan is strategically located on India's northern border. 'It is crossed by three rivers: Raidak, Sankosh and Manas. A line of mountains runs through it, rising from about 5,000 feet at the Indian border to the great peak of Jula Kangri which is over 24,000 feet.'[1] S. Gopal observes, 'Nehru did not expect armed attack on India by China from Tibet, but he did not rule out infiltration by groups or even occupation of disputed areas.' (Nehru's note, 18 November 1950) Therefore, Nehru had emphasized that India should take care not to get involved in the internal squabbles of Bhutan (which he thought, in turn, might encourage China or other foreign influences within its territory).[2] Also in a private meeting with B.M. Kaul, Nehru said that

> ...how important it was from India's point of view to strengthen Bhutan's friendship in view of her key position on our border and how we must do everything possible to help her. He also said we must treat smaller countries like Bhutan as our equals and never give them an impression that they were being 'civilised' by us.[3]

Thus, from the point of view of defence, India benefits from this security arrangement. As an ally of India, Bhutan provides a natural barrier to protect the Himalayan frontier of India. In other words, it prevents the Chinese from entering into India. Bhutan's loyalty to India is dictated by the fact that her landlocked position of Bhutan makes her dependent on India for trade, transit and contact with the outside world.

Moreover, if any foreign power tries to violate this security arrangement, either party can invoke the relevant provisions of the 1949 Treaty which is reinforced by mutual security arrangements like presence of IMTRAT (Indian Military Training Team) in Bhutan. In spite of changed international political environment, the 1949 Treaty seems to serve a useful purpose for both. But, Bhutan considered the treaty as unequal and loaded in favour of India. Therefore, in due course of time whenever Bhutan had an opportunity it expressed its resentment and demanded revision of the treaty, India succeeded in postponing the revision till the February 2007. Nevertheless, the revised treaty addressed Bhutan's concerns by readjusting and revising Article 2 which was the bone of contention between India and Bhutan. For instance, in the revised version, changes have been done in the word—now it is 'mutual cooperation' rather than 'advice'.

While analyzing India's compulsions to revise this treaty one should not also overlook that Bhutan was quite assertive in its foreign policy in various sub-regional and regional forums like BIMSTEC and SAARC and the international forums like NAM and the United Nations. The decision of opening of traditional Sino-Indian border at Nathu La Pass in Sikkim in June 2006 and its geographical proximity with Bhutan has obviously attracted the Bhutanese people. In particular the Bhutanese traders demanded to rejuvenate their age-old traditional, cultural and trade relations with Tibet. Obviously, India had no other option but to accept Bhutan's demand to revise the treaty without further delay, which was quite justifiable.

Moreover, Bhutan's preparation for introducing of parliamentary democracy as political system in Bhutan since 2006 onwards could be one of the reasons that New Delhi cannot sustain anymore with its own paradoxical policies towards the Himalayan Kingdoms, Bhutan and Nepal. For instance, while supporting the democratic movement in Nepal because of its varied interest in the region, it did not react or come out with any policy in regard to the movement for democracy in Bhutan led by the political group, which is a combination of Bhutanese of Nepali origin as well as the Drukpas. Thus, India's predicament in formulating foreign policy towards the democratic issue of Bhutan might have forced the Indian government to take this wise decision to revise the Treaty of 1949. In addition to this, the GOI was also not sure of the next generation of Bhutan, who will be entrusting the democratic values and principles of civil and political rights, whether they may or may not accept Indo-Bhutan Treaty in totality. If not, it may opt for abrogation of the treaty itself and remove the obstacle that prevents Bhutan on paper to extend its external relations with the countries other than India. Hence, India played a safe game and decided to revise the treaty and it was the first time in the South Asian context, that India adopted a pro-active foreign policy vis-à-vis Bhutan. As a result, India can be assured of smooth peddling of its politico-strategic and economic relations with Bhutan in the coming years and it would be accepted by the young generation of Bhutan.

Once Bhutan became democratic after the enactment of Constitution of Bhutan in 2008, many democratic institutions evolved in Bhutan. One of these institutions was a general election which was assisted by the Indian bureaucrats and experts. At the same time, the new government made its intention that being an active member of SAARC and BIMSTEC (Bay of Bengal Initiative for Multi-Sectoral Technical and Economic Cooperation) Bhutan wanted to diversify its economic relations with the countries other than India, especially, with Bangladesh and Nepal and the South East Asian nations. As a result, on 17 December 2009, coinciding with the 102nd National Day of Bhutan, the Royal Bhutanese Consulate was inaugurated in Kolkata by the Governor of West Bengal in the presence of the Bhutanese Foreign Minister. Thus, by this time relations between India and Bhutan reached the height of success, despite the constant pressures from Chinese side to accept their economic package and deal in order to settle the Sino-Bhutan boundary dispute and minimise Indian influence in Bhutan.

China as a Factor

Chinese occupation of Tibet in 1950 caused grave apprehensions in Bhutan which were confirmed when in July 1958, Communist China laid claim not only to vast portions of Indian territory, but also to some 200 sq. miles of Bhutanese territory as being part of Tibet.[4] Further, in July 1959, in pursuance of its policy of integrating Tibet with the heartland, China seized control of the Bhutanese-administered enclaves in western Tibet in the vicinity of Mount Kailash and the Gartok region.[5] The area of southwest Bhutan is rich in timber and is strategically important due to its topographical features. It 'provides an excellent observation point over the Chumbi valley and the roads leading to it.'[6] Moreover, this area is much closer to the strategic Jaldhaka barrage in the Indian state of West Bengal. China does not want to relax its claim on this disputed area. Hence, the Chinese have constructed a road linking the Chumbi valley with Bhutan.[7]

Thus, the demarcation of boundary with China created serious problems for Bhutan. It has become a more crucial part of its foreign policy objectives, as China did not want any Indian interference in this matter. 'In fact, Chinese armed intervention and territorial encroachment into Bhutan aimed at pressurising Bhutan to accept the idea of direct talks.'[8] So Bhutan initiated direct talks with China in 1984, to sort out its boundary problems and the first round of boundary talks was held at Bejing in 1984. Since then Twenty Two rounds of boundary talks have taken place between Bhutan and China, but no consensus has been reached.

During the first round of talks, China made it clear that it would not accept Bhutanese claims on strategic points which are more advantageous to Bhutan and India[9] and added that it would be more generous on less important territorial claims. While during the fourth round, which was held in Beijing from 10 to 14 May 1988, both countries concurred on a four-point pattern of guiding principles which would govern their mutual relations and issued a joint statement to this effect. These guiding principles are:

(1) Observing the five principles of peaceful co-existence: mutual respect for sovereignty and territorial integrity; mutual non-aggression; non-interference in each other's internal affairs; equality; and mutual benefit and peaceful co-existence.
(2) Treating each other on an equal footing and entering into friendly consultations on the basis of mutual understanding and mutual

accommodation with a view to reaching a just and reasonable settlement.

(3) Taking account of the relevant historical background based on traditions, custom, usage and administrative jurisdiction while accommodating the national sentiments of the people and the national interest of the two countries.

(4) Pending final settlement of the boundary question, maintaining tranquility on the border and status quo of the boundary as before March 1959 and refraining from unilateral action or the use of force, to change the status quo of the boundary.[10]

Both sides exchanged views and reiterated their desire to maintain a peaceful and friendly border, and expressed their keenness to make every effort for an early demarcation of the boundary. However, the substantive talks were initiated only during the Fifth round of Boundary talks. Both countries had claimed the 495 sq. km areas of Pasamlung and Jakarlung valleys as part of their territories respectively. In particular, the Bhutanese delegation claimed that these valleys were Bhutan's territory on the ground that these valleys lay below the source of *Bazaraguru chhu* (river) of *Kurote Dzongkhang* of Bhutan.[11] In response to the Bhutanese claims, the Chinese delegation offered a package proposal to Bhutan at the sixth round of talks at Thimpu in August 1990. According to this proposal, Chinese had 'offered to give Bhutan the Pasamlung and Jakarlung valley, with an area of 495 sq. km in the central sector of the boundary if Bhutan agreed to concede the 269 sq. km disputed area in the western sector.'[12] This offer was made to Bhutan, as the 269 sq. km area in the western sector had great strategic significance to China for its security. However, Bhutanese delegation did not agree to the Chinese proposal as they must have thought that it will affect their relations with India, upon whom they are dependent for the development assistance and accessibility.

However, Twelfth round of Sino-Bhutan border talks held in Beijing on 8-12 December 1998 concentrated on three important points:

1. The establishment of diplomatic relations with Bhutan;
2. The establishment of trade relations with China; and
3. The question of the exchange of land.[13]

During this time, both countries signed an *Agreement to Maintain Peace and Tranquillity* on the Bhutan-China border in 1998, which is the first Sino-Bhutanese agreement or treaty till date. Nevertheless, there was no final decision on the exchange of territories as the proposed areas to be exchanged have borders with the Indian state of Sikkim. It shows Bhutan's concern not to jeopardise India's interest in the Himalayan region while maintaining its formal relations with China.

The fourteenth round of boundary talks was held in Beijing in November 2000. Both countries 'expressed their satisfaction with the progress being made on the boundary discussions and agreed to continue the dialogue in accordance with the Five Principles of Peaceful Co-existence.'[14] More importantly, during the sixteenth round of talks at Beijing on 12 October 2002 Chinese Premier stated that China and Bhutan are resolving their boundary issues through mutual understanding and reconciliation.[15] He further said that China appreciated the Bhutanese government's support on the issues like Taiwan and human rights, and hoped to develop cooperative relations based on the principle of equality, mutual benefit and non-interference in each other's internal affairs.[16] In response, Bhutan's Foreign Minister Jigmi Thinley said, 'Bhutan and China should further promote mutual understanding between the two peoples and reiterated Bhutan's consistent stand on the issues of Taiwan and human rights and emphasized that Bhutan would continue to firmly support China on the issues.'[17] Indirectly, Bhutan proposes that it is not interested in China's contentious issues and rather it is more interested in maintaining politically correct relations.

Till April 2004 seventeen rounds of talks had been completed but there was no permanent resolution to this issue. Delay in any concrete decision by both parties has created apprehensions between Indo-Bhutan relations, since India's strategic interest is much involved in the Himalayan Kingdom. When Foreign Minister was asked for the reasons for further delay in final decisions on boundary talks, he gave a typical diplomatic answer: 'Big Objectives take time to fullfil'.[18] To quote the Foreign Minister of Bhutan, "I am optimistic about the final outcome of the boundary talks.' He added, 'it would be better to conduct the talks without haste and with great care and patience as it involves the national interest of the country".[19] The Foreign Minister said that a small country like Bhutan must be tactful in its approach to its boundary negotiations with its large neighbour because it cannot afford to lose even a single square kilometre of land.

In spite of cautious foreign policy exercised by Bhutan, Prime Minister Thinley's meeting with his Chinese counter part Wen Jiabao at the sidelines of the Rio+20 summit on 21 June 2012 has created furor. It was assumed that Bhutan was negotiating with China for formal diplomatic relations and once again, one of the most sensitive and contentious issues of Bhutanese foreign policy back into the public domain. The reason behind this uproar was that it was the first time the two Heads of the Government had met and discussed bilateral issues of mutual interest and multilateral cooperation including Bhutan's bid for a non-permanent seat on UN Security Council for the term 2013–14, elections which are to be held in fall this year.[20] Although Bhutan refuted these allegations, it was reported that Thinley purchased a fleet of 20 buses from the Chinese motor vehicle company and the contract for his son.[1] Moreover, Bhutan's bid to establish diplomatic ties with China was confirmed by the official Press Release of PRC (People's Republic of China) on 22 June 2012.[21] The press release was appreciative and went as follows:

> Bhutan's staunch support to One China Policy and her position on issues concerning Taiwan and Tibet and willing to settle border issues in an cooperative manner, enhance bilateral economic and trade cooperation and people-to-people and cultural exchanges, and carry out close communication and coordination in international and regional affairs.[22]

In the backdrop of the meeting at Rio in June 2012, the Twentieth round of border talks was held in Thimpu, between Chinese Vice-Foreign Minister Fu Ying and acting Bhutanese Foreign Minister Khandu Wangchuk. During this meeting Chinese Minister said:

> China hopes to make joint efforts with Bhutan on the basis of previous talks, continue to seek fair, reasonable and mutually acceptable solutions through friendly consultations and make the border line a bridge of friendship and cooperation between the two countries.[23]

In other words, she suggests while engaging boundary talks with Bhutan, China intends to open up other channels like diplomatic relations at the moment and keep critical issues pending. In response the Bhutanese Minister re-reiterated:

> Bhutan firmly pursues the one-China policy, thinks highly of China's long-term foreign policy of treating all countries as equals, no matter large or small and good-neighbourly friendship and is willing to strengthen coordination with China on the international arena.

Thus, the Twentieth round of talk almost prepared the ground to establish the diplomatic relations between the two. However, the Twenty First round of talks were held in August 2013. No major decisions were taken in this meeting. Bhutan did not continue further dialogue with China about diplomatic ties. Probably, Bhutan must have realised India's uneasiness and considered India's strategic stakes in Bhutan vis-à-vis China. In fact, earlier, New Delhi expressed its concern over the developments on Bhutan-China borders. In Haa, as it was reported in *Times of India* on 26 June 2013, the Chinese army entered into Bhutan's northeastern region and set up three military camps. 'According to intelligence reports, the PLA entered through the Sektang region in the east and Pang La in the north, and carried out a series of patrols along their shared border.' Bhutan was in a great difficulty either to resist China's military advancement or to accept China's aggressive postures in order to minimize India's presence in Bhutan, because in both the situations, it is Bhutan who would suffer most.

Despite this dilemma in its foreign policy Bhutan during Thinely's period chose to continue hobnobbing. All these developments raised serious concerns in the security and foreign policy establishment of India. India expressed its unhappiness over this and discontinued the subsidy on LPG and kerosene it supplied to Bhutan when Bhutan was at the peak of its Second General Election campaign in July 2013. Later on Indian government cleared the air and announced that Bhutan did not renew the agreement which was expired in June 2013 and Bhutan did not ask to renew it so India had no other option but to discontinue the subsidies given to it. However, the matter was resolved immediately when the new government was formed by PDP (People's Democratic Party). Bhutan's new Prime Minister Tsering Tobgyal took official position that his government's priority is to maintain friendly relations with India and maintained status quo. In a nutshell, Bhutan must have realized that it cannot do away with India whether they like or not. Later on it had direct impact on Bhutan-China relations when the Twenty Second round of border talk was held in July 2014. It did not yield any result in favour of China. In the meantime India honoured Bhutan when Indian Prime Minister Narendra Modi chose to visit it as the first foreign destination.

After so many rounds of talks between Bhutan and China, one can surmise that the Chinese have been reluctant to reduce their claims on the western sector, which is strategically important for them or to interfere in the question of Tibetan yak herders' intrusion into Bhutanese territory unless and until the Bhutanese accept the proposal of exchange of an area of 495 sq km with the pasture lands covering an area of 269 sq km. On the other hand, Bhutan cannot accept this kind of Chinese proposal, as a large number of Bhutanese people depend on livestock for their livelihood, these pasture lands being vital for their survival. The Bhutanese also claim that both the areas had always belonged to them. Bhutan wants to ensure that its traditional grazing land is not affected and that the boundary is demarcated according to traditional lines. Based on these facts, it is construed that on the issue of demarcation of boundary lines between Bhutan and China there will be debates and dialogues which may continue even in near future.

Besides, Sino-Bhutan boundary disputes China is also trying to intensify its expansionist policy in Bhutan by offering economic packages to Bhutan and creating situations to accept these assistance in order to make its presence in Bhutan.

Withdrawal of Subsidies: A Curse or Bless?

As mentioned earlier, India's decision to withdraw subsidies on oil and kerosene supply to Bhutan when the country was facing its second general election was unwarranted and unfortunate. In other words, Bhutan was trying to imbibe the principles and virtues of a democratic political system which is totally unknown to its people. During this critical juncture the policy makers in India have dented the traditional relationship with it. Educated youth in Bhutan resisted India's policy of taking their country for granted. Additionally many Nepali newspapers also expressed solidarity with Bhutan and reminded them that Nepal too had to face this Indian attribute in 1989 and now it was Bhutan's turn, the most trusted neighbour of India. It was quiet an embarrassing situation for Indian policy-makers.

Perhaps, besides, China factor there were other issues which compelled India to take these drastic steps. For instance, DPT then ruling party had their manifesto in which they paid attention to Bhutan's role in the United Nations, SAARC, NAM, BIMSTEC and other international forums. The Manifesto also focused on 'economic diplomacy and self-reliance by 2020'. Whereas, the then opposition leader of PDP, Tsering Tobgyal, in his party's manifesto described that 'massive diplomatic expansion with 52 countries was 'unnecessary' and was Indo-centric with a special focus on close relations with bordering Indian states of Assam, West Bengal, Arunachal Pradesh Sikkim and Bihar.'

However, after the PDP's sweeping win in Bhutan, the newly elected Prime Minister Tsering Tobgyal visited India in September 2013. During his visit he has sought Indian investment in manufacturing, mineral-based industries, education, health, tourism, information technology, financial services, infrastructure development, industrial estates, special economic zones (SEZs), dry ports and townships. He also urged:

> The private Indian investors to invest in Indian currency as 100% foreign direct investment (FDI) is allowed in Bhutan. Investment in hydro-power projects should be the "driver for diversification into other sectors like manufacturing, mineral-based industries, education, health, tourism, information technology, financial services, infrastructure development, industrial estates, special economic zones (SEZs), dry ports and townships.

Indian government took a very positive note of this and proposed to increase the financial aid to Bhutan significantly in its interim Union Budget presented to the parliament. In the Parliament, former Finance Minister P. Chidambaram, proposed to provide aid and grants worth Rs 50.5 billion to Bhutan during the fiscal year 2014–15, so that it will cover for India's resumed fuel subsidy and contribute to Bhutan's 11th Five Year Plan. In continuation of this development assistance, the GOI has extended its support in the field of education including the prestigious Nehru-Wangchuk Scholarship which has enabled talented and deserving Bhutanese students to study in India.

Further, National Democratic Alliance led Modi's government took an opportunity to pacify Bhutan while respecting the century-old relationship between the two. Modi's visit to Bhutan should be seen in view of the proposed bilateral talk between Bhutan and China in July 2014 which alarmed the bells in the minds of policymakers to neutralize Chinese intensified efforts to woo Bhutan for full-fledged diplomatic relations with it. As a result, Modi government took the initiative to build confidence among the people and statesmen of Bhutan and inculcate the feelings of brotherhood and fraternity between the two. To do so, Modi government announced many programmes and signed new trade agreements with Bhutan.

During his visit to Bhutan in June 2014, he gave populist slogan "*B4B—'Bharat for Bhutan' and 'Bhutan for Bharat'*" and through this policy he promised to nurture the bilateral relations between two countries. In this visit he laid the foundation stone of the 600 MW Kholongchu hydro-electric project in Bhutan as an Indo-Bhutan Joint Venture. There are three hydro-electric projects (HEPs) totaling 1416 MW (Chukha, Tala and Kurichu) in operation. Three more HEPs [Punatsangchu I (1200 MW), Punatsangchu II (1020 MW) and Mangdechu (720 MW)] are under construction. They are scheduled to be commissioned in 2017–18. It is a classic example of win-win cooperation as the hydropower projects generate export revenues for Bhutan while cementing economic partnership and provide clean and low-cost electricity to power crisis neighbouring states of India.

During this visit Bhutan also promised not to allow its territory to be used against India, an assurance that comes against the backdrop of militants from north-eastern India taking shelter there. The two countries agreed to continue with their close coordination and cooperation on issues relating to their national interests and not allow each other's territory to be used for interests inimical to the other. Modi announced doubling of scholarships being provided to Bhutanese students in India which will now be worth Rs 2 crore. Prime Minister Modi also promised to assist Bhutan in setting up a digital library which will provide access to Bhutanese youths to two million books and periodicals. India has committed Rs.4,500 crore (750 mn USD) towards Bhutan's 11th five-year plan and is involved in infrastructure projects, agriculture, information communication technology projects among others in the landlocked kingdom.

While Bhutan has India's full fledged support in each and every sector at the same time China is also engaging Bhutan. There are reports that many scholars are being invited in China with fellowships and academic exchanges. Besides, once Bhutan is prepared to establish diplomatic relations with China, China might complete its policy of encirclement and campaign against India in the region. Moreover, Chinese assistance may neutralize Bhutan instead of pro-India on international occasions. It is to mention that there is increase in the number of aspirant FDI investors in Bhutan after the revision of FDI policy in 2010. Out of total 17 approved FDI, Indian FDI are only 8, this figures are challenging India's economic interest in Bhutan. It is not only China who is competing with India there are countries like Singapore, Japan and Thailand which are equally interested in investing in Bhutan and look for an opportunity to pierce in the serene Eastern Himalayas.

Therefore, India should respond as a true neighbour and a friend in need and friend indeed.

Since, India has damaged the century old trust and faith and left a permanent mark in minds of young Bhutanese the development assistance given to Bhutan is a policy of appeasing Bhutan.

REFERENCES

1. Lt. Gen. B.M. Kaul, *The Untold Story* (Bombay: 1967), p.247.
2. As mentioned in, S. Gopal, *Jawaharlal Nehru: A Biography*, Vol. Two, 1947-56 (Delhi: 1984), p. 176.
3. Lt. Gen., B.M. Kaul, n.19, p. 248.
4. L.S. Rathore, *Politics of Bhutan*, 1978, pp. 20-21.
5. S.D. Muni, "Sino-Bhutanese Boundary Talks", *The Indian Express* (New Delhi), 12 June 1984.
6. *The Hindustan Times* (New Delhi) 7 December 1996.
7. Ibid.
8. S.D. Muni., op.cit.
9. S.D. Muni., op.cit.
10. *The Times of India* (New Delhi) 15 May 1988.
11. Ibid.
12. Ibid.
13. Bhutan-China Border talks", *The People's Review*, 24-31 December 1998. Online Edition, see website, www.yomari.com/p-review/1998/12/241298/bhut.html
14. *The Kuensel*, 2 December 2000, p. 1.
15. Ibid.
16. *The Times of India*, 26 June 2013.
17. *The Times of India*, 11 July 2013.
18. *Awaz*, 2 September 2013.
19. Ibid.
20. Bhutan News Network, 20 February 2014.
21. *The Economic Times*, 16 June 2015.
22. *The Hindu*, 16 June 2014.
23. Ibid.

6

India-China Boundary Dispute: A Never-Ending Saga

Sana Hashmi

India and China are two ancient civilisations whose relations date back to centuries and both countries share historical, cultural and social linkages. However, with the advent of British to the Indian subcontinent, both countries lost direct contact with each other. It was only in 1950s that these countries began to look towards each other. Resistance against colonial and imperial powers and solidarity of Asian and African countries were few of the issues which brought them together. Both countries were established as modern nation-states almost simultaneously; India gained independence from the British rule on August 15, 1947 and after approximately two years, on October 1, 1949, communists came to power in China and the People's Republic of China (PRC) was established.

Though both India and China adopted different political, social and economic systems after independence, both found a long-lost friend in each other. India established diplomatic relations with China on April 1, 1950 and became one of the first few non-communist countries to recognise the PRC. Their relations were laid down on the Five Principles of Peaceful Existence. In fact, the early years of the decade of 1950 witnessed the burgeoning bonhomie between India and China so much so that the former Indian Prime Minister, Jawaharlal Nehru, in the initial years of their friendship, had pronounced both countries as brothers by the promulgation of the notable slogan *Hindi Chini Bhai Bhai (*Indians and Chinese are brothers). The cordial relations led to the signing of Panchsheel Agreement consisting Five Principle of Peaceful Coexistence in 1954 followed by the landmark visit of Jawaharlal Nehru to China in October in the same year. It is beyond the shadow of doubt that the first ever milestone in their relations was achieved this year.

On April 29, 1954, the Governments of the Republic of India and the People's Republic of China signed the Agreement on Trade and Intercourse between Tibet Region of China and India. As per the agreement, the Government of India agreed to withdraw its armed forces from Tibet and hand over all post, telegraph and telephone offices with all equipment to the Chinese government.[1] Nevertheless, cordial relations lasted only a brief stint and became increasingly fragile with mounting tensions over undemarcated India-China boundary. Interestingly, China has always been of the opinion that the common boundary between India and China had never been formally delimited, therefore, required to be negotiated between the two Governments, and, if necessary, settled through joint surveys. On the other hand, the Indian Government claims the McMahon Line as the valid boundary between India and China.[2] In general, the Chinese Government claimed that the momentary alignment of the boundary was the result of British imperialist aggression against China especially regime in Tibet and further argued that the India-China frontier had never been formally delimited.[3] The Government asserted that the entire length of the boundary had been defined, either by treaty or by custom, or both.[4]

Notably, India-China relations are multi-faceted and complex and their boundary question is the most prolonged and exasperating issue of all. An important point here is that while China was quick enough to resolve its boundary disputes with other neighbours, it has not resolved the long-standing border problem with India till yet. Intriguingly, India along with Bhutan remains the only country with which China still has differences over their shared boundary. When India became independent, it acquired a latent boundary dispute with China in the east, the McMahon Line, and a more complex dimension was added in the west on the accession of the state of Jammu and Kashmir to India on October 26, 1947.[5]

The more serious India-China border conflict started in 1951 when the Indian Government brought to the notice of the Chinese Government some Chinese maps which showed traditional Indian territory as part of China;

however, Zhou Enlai, the first Premier of China, assured Nehru at that time that these were old maps produced by the "pre-liberation regime" in China and that China had no time to revise them.[6] Despite this assurance from the Chinese side, Nehru clarified that "India's boundaries with China were clear and not a matter of further argument".[7] Nevertheless, incursions at the Indian borders by People's Liberation Army (PLA) began to occur on territories like Bara Hoti, Damzan, Nilang and Shipki Pass, Lapthal and Sangcha Malla and others by 1954. The boundary dispute erupted into open on August 28, 1959, when Nehru disclosed in Parliament that on August 25, 1959, a strong Chinese detachment had crossed into the Indian territory of Longju in the Subansiri Frontier Division at a place south of Migyitun and open fired.[8] As a consequence of the clashes in late 1950s, Jawaharlal Nehru and Zhou Enlai met in New Delhi from April 19-25, 1960, to discuss the differences that had arisen between the two Governments.[9] A joint committee was set up to look into the matter and was designated to examine the factual data from both the sides. However, no substantial gain was yielded through the findings of the report submitted by the committee and the relations began to worsen in the following years.

Divergence over the India-China boundary led to a brief but appalling war in October 1962. There was a strong realisation that the argument extended by India in the discussion leading to the 1961 report were strong, valid and supported by legal documents, whereas the Chinese territorial claims were unconvincing. Unable to succeed in its aims to achieve a large chunk of the Indian territory by peaceful means, China attacked the northern border of India.[10]Consequently, the 1962 war heavily damaged China's 'good neighbourliness policy'.[11] In addition, the war also resulted in the loss of credibility of the famous slogan *Hindi Chini Bhai Bhai*. Another major upshot of the war was the loss of Aksai Chin, an uninhibited part of Ladakh in Jammu and Kashmir which share its border with Pakistan, to China. After occupying a large tract (approximately 38,000 square km) of Aksai Chin, which is considered by India as an illegal occupation, China built a highway (National Highway 219) through it to connect with its eastern province of Xinjiang, one of the restive regions in China.[12] China has felt a great need for a road across the Aksai Chin and a territory in Ladakh to ensure the defence of the road. The Chinese authorities also felt that the Tibetan rebels and Khampas might use the territory, if it was not under their control, for guerrilla activities against the Chinese regime.[13] As expected, war had an adverse effect on India-China relations that only worsened in the times that followed. Both countries normalised their diplomatic relations at ambassadorial level only in 1976andK. R. Narayanan was appointed as India's first ambassador to China since 1962. Nonetheless, 10 years later, in 1986, Chinese and Indian patrols began confronting each other in the Sumdorong Chu valley of the Tawang district of Arunachal Pradesh just east of Bhutan which touched off a border crisis that continued for months, with both sides refusing to back down, stepping up their patrols in the disputed area and moving substantial military forces in the region.[14] Before going any further, it is important to throw more light on the causes and repercussions of the 1962 war. While exploring the aspect of provocations in India-China war is an exceedingly contested issue, several reasons can be cited for the war. The main reasons are listed below:

1. **Forward Policy:** By 1960s, Indian government began to claim that the Chinese were trying to occupy all the vacant areas along the India-China border. It was reported that the Chinese had built seven roads inside the Indian territories of Ladakh, several roads close to India's border in Punjab, Himachal Pradesh and Uttar Pradesh, six in Sikkim and Bhutan borders, and eight in the North-East Frontier Agency (NEFA) border. It was also reported that the Chinese had established as many as seven new posts in Ladakh, fourteen in the central sector of Punjab, Himachal Pradesh and Uttar Pradesh, twelve across Sikkim and Chumbi valley, and three across NEFA.[15] Through these developments, Indian leadership and top-level officials concluded that Chinese efforts had been directed at seizing more Indian territory wherever possible and creating evidence in support of their 1960 claim by pushing forward the line of actual control.[16] In retaliation, India also started deploying its troops against the Chinese soldiers which came to be known as 'the forward policy'. The policy was basically the idea of and promulgated by Gen. B.M. Kaul. Nehru, though reluctantly, gave a green signal to the enforcement of the policy. Under the purview of this policy, the Indian side deployed troops and established border outposts in massive number along the India-China boundary. It was basically to keep a check on Chinese incursions on the Indian territory. In the opinion of Gen. Kaul, the so-called policy would act as a deterrent and, in turn, rule out the possibilities of India-China war. He stated that, "The Chinese would not react to our establishing new posts and that they were not likely to use force against any of our posts even if they were in a position to do so".[17] However, the policy proved to be the main provocative element and fuelled China's desire to teach India a lesson.

2. **Tibet Factor:** Though India had given up all its extra-territorial rights

on Tibet after signing the "1954 Agreement on Trade and Intercourse between Tibet Region of China and India", it has long been an established and irrefutable fact that Tibet is a determining factor in India-China relations since 1959. Owing to China's crackdown in Tibet in 1950s, Dalai Lama along with 80,000 Tibetans fled to India in 1959. He took refuge in India which was whole-heartedly granted by Nehru. This further angered the Chinese. The proposition that the Tibetan exiles and the Dalai Lama in particular are responsible for many of the problems of India-China relations is one that is made often.[18] Many sinologists are of the opinion that India-China boundary issue is just a symptom and a result of deterioration in the relations between the two countries, and that the deterioration set in because of the official and unofficial Indian support and sympathy of the Tibetan revolt of 1959.[19] Scholarly view suggests that India's Tibet policy which was discomforting for China was undeniably one of the main triggers.

3. **Burgeoning US-India Friendship:** Although India-US cordial ties are not widely considered as a major reason for the war; however, its indirect implications on China's motives of waging war on India cannot be entirely ruled out. It was only in 1970s that the US and China restored ties, before which Mao Zedong had an anti-US posture. On being questioned on the reasons for the 1962 war by the President of Mongolia, Zedenbal, Mao replied that, "The war was not about territory but it was to teach a lesson to India which was moving too close to the US".[20] Being in the Soviet camp in 1950s, China was never comfortable with India's close proximity with the US. Hence, perceived it as a threat to its national interest.

4. **India's Influence:** It was in 1950s that the Chinese leadership began to get wary of Nehru's attitude and assessed that he was, on one hand, a leading member of the Indian bourgeoisie' that had led the fight for independence and on the other, could not let go of his 'lust for expansion'.[21] It is an established fact that Nehru-Mao ideological rivalry played a great role in deteriorating India-China relations. When Mao Zedong decided to launch his war against India, he had categorically asserted that he must crush Nehru whom he was envious of due to various reasons. One reason, according to him, was that he felt that India was getting undue attention from the international community, attention that he, along with PRC, deserved for their revolutionary war.[22] Apart from ideological rivalry between Mao and Nehru, a very important cause for the Chinese invasion of India was the ideological difference between the two countries, one swearing by sectarian

communism and the other by democratic socialism, one by alignment and the other by non-alignment, one by dictatorship and the other by democracy.[23] It was felt that China had a grand design for the Afro-Asian world and the elimination of India as a serious obstacle to Chinese ascendancy.[24]

Above-mentioned factors indisputably contributed to ever-escalating differences and trust deficit between India and China. Out of the three, Tibet still continues to haunt the stable cordial India-China ties and has, time and again, proved to be a bone of contention in the relations. After analysing the reasons for the war, it might be suffice to say that the factors leading to India-China war were not sovereignty driven, rather were an outcome of India's domestic and foreign policy dispositions.

The 1962 war and the following incursions at the India-China boundary are not the end of the story of tension between India-China. The unresolved boundary dispute still remains a bone of contention in their relations. The fundamental problem is two-faceted. While the India-China boundary is divided into three sectors, namely western, middle and eastern, India and China have disagreements only in western and eastern sectors. Out of India-China 4,000 km long boundary, approximately 2,000 km long boundary of India and China lies in the western sector which separates Indian state of Jammu and Kashmir from China's northwestern Province, Xinjiang Uyghur Autonomous Region (XUAR).In the undefined northern part of the frontier, India claims an area the size of Switzerland, occupied by China, for its region of Ladakh and in the eastern part, China claims an Indian-controlled area in the eastern sector three times bigger, including most of Arunachal.[25] Additionally, India claims a Chinese-controlled territory which was ceded to China by Pakistan in the northern sector. The particular territory including Shaksgam valley was, as claimed by the Indian side, compromised during the signing of China-Pakistan boundary agreement of 1963.

China's Claim over Arunachal Pradesh[26]

China never ratified the McMahon Line which became a cause of concern when China began to lay its claim of sovereignty over Indian-controlled territory of Arunachal Pradesh. Disagreement over boundary in the eastern sector is mainly due to China's non-recognition of McMahon Line, drawn between British India and Tibet. It is intriguing, since China's occupation of Tibet, Arunachal Pradesh has been a frontier as well as a buffer between China's controlled Tibet and India's north eastern region. Historically, Arunachal

Pradesh was not a state; it was incorporated in India as a territory and till 1980s it was known as North-East Frontier Agency (NEFA) created in 1955. The McMahon Line was drawn in 1914 when Simla Accord was signed which was initiated by the plenipotentiaries of the British India, Tibet and China. However, at later stages, on the grounds of difference of opinion regarding the boundaries of Tibet, since China always recognised Tibet as its part, under Nationalist forces China withdrew its consent to ratify the agreement. China has opposed and challenged the very legitimacy of the line on the ground reiterating that it was signed by erstwhile Tibetan officials who did not have an authority to do so since Tibet is an inalienable part of China. They also claim that it was a British ploy to weaken and humiliate China and regards it as a constituent of British imperialism.[27]Later, China also claimed that the Tawang Region, which was shown as a part of India after the demarcation of the McMahon line, has been part of Tibet for centuries and thus belongs to China. The Chinese uphold that the disputed territory in the eastern sector is historically Tibetan land encroached upon by British imperialism and then turned over to the Indian heirs of the British Empire.[28]

To substantiate its claim, China turns to history claiming that Tawang which is a part of Arunachal Pradesh has been its part since centuries. It cites that 6th Dalai Lama was born in Tawang in the 17th century and Tawang Region being part of Tibet belongs to China. Tawang is a centre of Tibet's Buddhist culture with one of the biggest Tibetan monasteries outside Lhasa and traditionally, its ethnic Monpa inhabitants offered fealty to Tibetan rulers.[29] China cites the Tawang Monastery, one of the last vestiges of Mahayana Buddhism, as evidence that the mountainous district of Tawang in Arunachal Pradesh once belonged to Tibet and that India should hand it back to help settle the row.[30] This is also in consonance with China's 'One China theory'. The Chinese have based their specific claim on the territory on the premise that Tawang was administered from Lhasa, and the contiguous areas owed allegiance to the Dalai Lama, the spiritual and temporal ruler of Tibet.[31] While China has cited a number of reasons to prove its legitimacy over Arunachal Pradesh, India has always refuted Chinese claims. However, despite India's consistent refusal to such claims, China which only claimed Tawang previously has now expanded its claims from Tawang to the entire state of Arunachal Pradesh.

In 2006, just a week before the Chinese Premier Wen Jiabao's first ever visit to New Delhi, Chinese Ambassador to India, Sun Yuxi stated that, "The whole of the state of Arunachal Pradesh is Chinese territory and Tawang is only one of the places in it. We are claiming all of that. That is our position."[32] This assertion led China to claim over 90,000 square km long Indian territory in the North-eastern front.

This problem further aggravated when China started issuing stapled visas to the citizens of Arunachal Pradesh stating that they do not have to apply for visas to come to their own country which further annoyed the Indian Government. Every now and then, there have been various reports of issuing stapled visas and denial of visas to the residents of Arunachal Pradesh. Furthermore, China has always been protesting against any visits by 14th Dalai Lama as well as by any Indian leaders to Arunachal Pradesh. In 2009, visit by the former Indian Prime Minister, Manmohan Singh, to Arunachal Pradesh triggered tensions between India and China. The foreign ministry spokesperson of China at that time, Liu Jianchao, was quoted as saying on October 13, 2009 that China was 'seriously dissatisfied' by the visit of the Indian Prime Minister, who was accused of 'ignoring China's concerns by visiting southern Tibet' and further called the visit as 'provocative and dangerous'.[33] Visit of the 14th Dalai Lama's to Tawang in November 2009 invited similar protests from the Chinese side. Beijing criticised the visit as undermining Chinese territorial integrity and slammed the Dalai Lama's "scheme to wreck China's relations" with India.[34] In November 2013, India's President, Pranab Mukherjee, visited the state of Arunachal Pradesh to which, surprisingly, China reacted mildly.

Strategic Importance of Tawang for India and China[35]

Tawang holds enormous importance in both India and China's strategic manoeuvres. The tactical location of the region coupled with its rich natural resources and fresh water, makes it one of the most important regions for both India and China. China repeatedly terms Tawang as Indian-Occupied Territory and refers to it as Southern Tibet.[36] The question to be asked is why has China been hell-bent on claiming Tawang? With Tawang under its control, China can get closer in proximity to the Indian states of North-eastern region and also pacify its fear of India becoming a major world power. Additionally, this gives China unhindered access to Bhutan, a neighbouring country with which China has trifling differences over its border. It will also bring China closer to other Southeast Asian countries, thus satisfying China's expansionist need as the fastest growing economy in the world. By occupying the passes in Ladakh, China has ensured that India cannot launch an offensive to cut-off the Western highway.[37] If China occupies Tawang, the Indian approach from the eastern sector will also be severed. On February 14, 1979, when the India's External Affairs, Atal Bihari Vajpayee, visited Beijing, he was told by China's Former Paramount Leader, Deng Xiaoping, that the eastern sector is of economic value and the area of biggest dispute.[38]

Likewise, from the Indian perspective, Arunachal Pradesh is highly imperative. The state acts as a buffer between India and Tibet Autonomous Region (TAR), thus providing the much needed strategic depth against China. Additionally, India cannot afford another setback like 1962, when China attacked India on Western and the Eastern sectors, including Tawang, Thag-La ridge and Tseng-jong and Indian army was humiliated due to lack of preparedness and astrange assumption that China would not become aggressive.[39] The Tawang region borders China-controlled Tibet and it acts as a barrier between the two nuclear powers. It is like a floodgate, which holds the advent of the Chinese military might. Furthermore, Arunachal Pradesh is one of the four states of Northeastern India which shares its border with Myanmar; hence it is India's gateway to Southeast Asia and crucial for India's Look East Policy now rechristened as Act East Policy by the Narendra Modi Government.

Infrastructural Development at North-eastern Border of India

In retrospect, India has never felt the need for having a strong defence system at its borders with China for the simple fact that the Himalayan range was perceived to be a natural boundary for India. For more than 3,000 years, the Himalayas have been regarded as the natural frontier of India.[40] It was only after the 1962 War with China that India understood the need for having a robust infrastructure along the India-China border. The war took India by surprise and it was realised by the Indian leadership that the country suffered huge losses mainly because of lack of a proper network of transportation and infrastructural development.[41]

Since independence, China's infrastructure has been much better than that on the Indian side. Over the years, China has constructed a recommendable network of air, road and rail links along the border. These include 40,000 km of roads and a 1,118 km rail link from Lhasa in the TAR to Gormo in Qinghai province of mainland China. This massive infrastructural build-up makes it possible for Beijing to amass a huge number of troops at the border in a very short time. In contrast, Indian troops have to deal with sloppy infrastructure, with many roads ending 60-70 km short of the LAC and the nearest railhead being at least 100 km away, impeding swift troop mobility.[42] China, at the cost of US$ 2.16 billion, completed the extension of the Qinghai-Tibet railway line to Shigatse, a town near the Nepal border, in September 2014. The Lhasa-Shigatse line extended over 253 km, carrying trains at 120 km per hour through valleys and over three bridges that run across the Brahmaputra river, or Yarlung Tsangpo as it is known in China.[43] In the 13th Five-Year Plan (2016-2020), China states that it plans to extend this railway line further and bring it closer to the Indian side of the border in Arunachal Pradesh which would connect Shigatse to Kyirong in Nepal and the Chumbi Valley between Sikkim and Bhutan.[44] Another railway line from Lhasa to Nyingchi Prefecture, which shares the border with Arunachal Pradesh is on the cards.[45]

The rapid pace of this development of air, rail and road infrastructure in Tibet have raised concerns in India as it provides massive advantage to China to move its troops and equipment overcoming the adverse geographical problems in this remote region of the world. In a boost to infrastructure in the strategic Himalayan region, China has announced plans to build the seventh airport near Tibet, where the world's highest altitude aerodrome is located.[46]

Apart from developing its rail-road-air network, China has deployed a substantial number of Intermediate Range Ballistic Missiles (IRBMs). With these developments, India is also waking up to the need of developing infrastructure in the entire Northeast region particularly to avoid any 1962 war-like situations again in future. Initiatives by India might not bring it at par with China but could certainly provide a strategically vital response to China's expansionist policies.[47]

China's Win, India's Loss[48]

The 1962 war and subsequent claims by China on Indian territories had indeed made Nehru cautious of China. Nehru signed the Panchsheel Agreement so as to have lasting and cordial relations with China. However, since the very beginning, China took the agreement lightly and barely followed its provisions. Surprisingly, the treaty was never renewed.[49] What makes the matter worse is India's recognition of Tibet as part of China because China is laying its claim of sovereignty over Arunachal Pradesh solely on the basis of Tibet being under its control. Recognition of Tibet as an autonomous part of China by Jawaharlal Nehru in 1953 and then Atal Bihari Vajpayee in 2003, in a hope that China would give up its claim on Indian territories, added credibility to its control over Tibet. Sadly, in practical terms, India has no big card to play in the border negotiation that had sold out Tibet chiefly to China. It is now paying the price of potentially losing territories in this mutual adjustment deal which was an outcome of Nehru's failed foreign policy of appeasing China that still prevails in the Indian diplomatic book of wisdom.[50] As A.G. Noorani, in his book, *Credulity and Negligence* rightly pointed out that Nehru was credulous about China's intentions thus neglecting India's defence with a policy of appeasement that has proved so disastrous in the past.[51] Only with respect to China was Nehru faulted, he tragically misjudged Chinese intentions and policies towards India.[52] Notably, despite the war in 1962, India wanted to deescalate the tension. However, China has always been systematic with regard to its policies. It took great advantage of India's blind faith on China and went step by step, first invaded Tibet and established its foothold there and later expanded its claims to Tawang.

The vitality of this region can never be overemphasised, but India, for the last few decades has somehow understated its importance. There has been a lack of strong diplomatic and even security policy to counter the Chinese claims in this region. India has lacked the assertive approach in putting forward its stand, which is evident from India's lukewarm responses to dozens of Chinese incursions along the border every year. This lack of assertiveness and strong response can be gauged by the hapless condition and absence of proper infrastructure in the border regions of the Northeastern India, particularly Tawang. The transport and military infrastructure, on the Indian side, lags far behind to that on the Chinese side. Infrastructure is an essential element in the defence of the country and can prove to be a turning point should there be a war between the two nations. Quite evidently, it demonstrates that India's policies and strategies towards settling the dispute are full of defects, ignorant assumptions and erroneous decisions which have proved to be favourable for China but ruinous for India.

Conclusion

The point to be noted is that till now seventeen rounds of border negotiations have been held but with no substantive outcome. In fact, in 2013, so as to stop incursions and improve coordination among Indian and Chinese soldiers, an agreement namely Border Defence Cooperation Agreement (BDCA) was inked between the two countries as a confidence building measure. The agreement was in the aftermath of a border stand-off at Depsang valley in April-May 2013. Just a month before Chinese Premier, Li Keqiang's maiden visit to India, Chinese soldiers entered 19 km into the Indian side of the line of control and established tents there for three weeks. That was not the first time that such incident happened. Longju incident is still an unforgettable event which proved to be a disastrous turning point in India-China relations. In 1986, Sumdorong Chu Valley incursion in NEFA is also a case in point. However, in contemporary times, it may be noted that the Chinese incursions on the Indian territory, by land, sea and air, have increased after 2005, with as many as 233 violations in 2008 and more than 500 transgressions from 2010 to 2012.[53] In March 2014, just five months after the signing of the BDCA, Chinese soldiers tried to penetrate into the Chumar area in Leh. Such repetitive incursions have made it clear that no agreement is useful in pacifying the situation. Similar agreements were signed and joint committees have been set up earlier. The 1993 Agreement for Maintaining Peace and Tranquillity along the Line of Actual Control in the India-China Border Areas and Joint Working Group (JWG) for border negotiations set up by Rajiv Gandhi in 1988 are two of the many examples of unsuccessful endeavours between India and China.

It has been more than 50 years that the conflict has been intact and both sides have been unable to find a mutually agreeable solution to their prolonged issues. Evidently, both do not want to give any concessions to the other. However, if overall India-China relation is taken into consideration, it displays a different trend. In a globalised world, competition and cooperation are inevitable for both countries. To deal with such a precarious situation, both India and China have adopted two-pronged strategy. On one hand, both are in favour of a status quo while reinforcing their claims time to time, while on the other hand, their cooperation, sometimes, overshadows their boundary dispute. India and China being the second and third largest economies in the world respectively are bound to cooperate at several regional and global fora. The pressure of portraying themselves as responsible stakeholders in the world makes them more accommodating towards each other. While this approach evades any future conflict, the boundary question still remains unanswered. What is in the best interest of India, if not of China, is the resolution of the dispute with utmost urgency. However, as of now, this seems to be a far-fetched reality as both countries are mainly focussed on maintaining a status quo with an aim to enhance their military capabilities.

In a situation where there is no hope for the resolution of India and China's long-drawn boundary dispute, India needs to proactively focus on its strengthening relations with its neighbours and other countries in Asia to be able to balance out with China. More importantly, it is high time for India to improve its border infrastructure particularly in the northeastern region. Improving connectivity with and within the northeastern region has become a prerequisite for the Indian leadership. Finally, internationalisation of the legality of the McMahon Line would greatly work in India's favour too.

Undoubtedly, India-China relations are one of the most complicated relationships in contemporary time. While there are issues of differences, cooperation still weighs more than conflict. However, till date, boundary issue is one of the most important defining features in India-China relations. It is evident that boundary dispute and the frequent border clashes still have the potential to derail the existing relationship because a basic lack of trust underscores it. It is not that the dispute cannot be resolved; it is just that China does not want to compromise with its bargaining position with respect to India. It does seem that India will keep persuading China to address the boundary issues whereas China will keep avoiding a solution for the dispute. Therefore, status quo with repeated border incursions is what is likely to be the scenario in the future.

REFERENCES

1. "Agreement between the Republic of India and the People's Republic of China on Trade and intercourse between Tibet Region of China and India", (Beijing: Ministry of External Affairs of India, April 29, 1954).
2. Ministry of External Affairs Government of India, Report of the Officials of the Governments of India and the People's Republic of China on the Boundary Question (New Delhi, 1961), pp. 233, 110-115.
3. Notes, Memoranda and Letters exchanged and Agreement Signed between the Government of India and China, White Paper II, 1959 (New Delhi: Ministry of External Affairs, Government of India, 1959), p. 52-57.
4. Ibid, p. 85.
5. A.G. Noorani, *India-China Boundary Problem 1846-1947: History and Diplomacy* (New Delhi: Oxford University Press, 2011), p. 1.
6. B.L. Sukhwal, *India: A Political Geography* (New Delhi: Allied Publishers, 1971, p. 197-198.
7. Same as n. 3, p. 49.
8. Noorani, n. 5, p. 1.
9. Same as n. 2, p. 1.
10. Sukhwal, n. 6, p. 202.
11. The Good Neighbourly policy was first initiated in 1954 with a clandestine aim of parting ways with China's once prominent foreign policy principle of Leaning to One Side towards the Soviet Union.

12. Why China Claims Arunachal Pradesh, available at http://www.rediff.com/news/2006/nov/16sld1.htm (accessed on September 26, 2014).
13. Sukhwal, n. 6, p. 196.
14. V.G. Kulkarni, "Eyeball to eyeball on the Himalayan border," *Far Eastern Economic Review*, April 9, 1987, pp. 38-40.
15. B.N. Mullik, *My Years with Nehru: The Chinese Betrayal* (New Delhi: Allied Publishers, 1971), p. 313.
16. Ibid.
17. Quoted in Neville Maxwell and A. G. Noorani, "India's Forward Policy", *The China Quarterly*, vol. 45. 1971, pp. 157-163.
18. T. S. Murty, *India-China Boundary: India's Options* (New Delhi: ABC Publishing House, 1987), p. 66.
19. Ibid.
20. Jasjit Singh, "Two Front Saga: China's Local-Border War and Pakistan's 5th War Against India", *Focus*, October 2011, pp. 22.
21. Ranjit Singh Kalha, *India-China Boundary Issues: Quest for Settlement* (New Delhi: Pentagon Press, 2014), p. 100.
22. Ibid.
23. Sukhwal, n.6, p. 196.
24. Ibid, p. 197.
25. India and China's territorial disputes: Taking the high ground, available at http://www.economist.com/blogs/banyan/2010/08/india_and_chinas_territorial_disputes (accessed on January 26, 2014).
26. This section on China's Claim on Arunachal Pradesh draws heavily on material from the author's previous article on China's Tawang Temptation published in October 2012 in Defence and Diplomacy, Journal of the Centre for Air Power Studies.
27. Surya P. Sharma, "The India-China Border Dispute: An Indian Perspective", *The American Journal of International Law*, Vol. 59 No. 1, January 1965, pp. 16-47.
28. John W. Garver, "Sino-Indian Rapprochement and the Sino-Pakistan Entente", *Political Science Quarterly*, Vol. 111 No. 2, Summer 1996, pp. 323-347.
29. "Why China Claims Arunachal Pradesh", Rediff, November 16, 2006 at http://specials.rediff.com/news/2006/nov/16sld1.htm (accessed on September 26, 2014).
30. "Arunachal is Chinese land: Envoy", November 20, 2006 at http://ibnlive.in.com/news/arunachal-is-chinese-land-envoy/26108-3.html (accessed on January 26, 2014).
31. Mohan Guruswamy and ZorawarDaulet Singh, *India-China Relations: The Border Issue and Beyond* (New Delhi: Viva Books, 2009).
32. "Arunachal Pradesh is out Territory: Chinese Envoy", Rediff, November 14, 2006 at http://www.rediff.com/news/report/china/20061114.htm (accessed on October 23, 2013).
33. "How To Counter China on Arunachal Pradesh" Rediff, October 14, 2009 at http://www.rediff.com/news/column/how-to-counter-china-on-arunachal-pradesh/20091014.htm (accessed on November 17, 2012).
34. Dalai Lama Visits Arunachal Pradesh, available at http://in.reuters.com/article/2009/11/08/idINIndia-43780920091108 (accessed on November 2, 2014).
35. This section on strategic importance of Tawang for India and China draws heavily from the author's previous article on China's Tawang Temptation published in October 2012 in Defence and Diplomacy Journal of the Centre for Air Power Studies.
36. Sujit Dutta, "Managing and Engaging Rising China: India's Evolving Posture", *The Washington Quarterly Post*, Spring 2011, pp. 131.

37. Sheru Thapliya, "Sino-Indian Border Impasse: Strategy for Resolution", *CLAWS Journal*, Summer 2010, pp. 206.
38. Same as n. 2, p. 230.
39. Neville Maxwell, *India's China War*, (Dehradun: Natraj Publishers, 1997), pp. 356.
40. Sukhwal, n.6, p. 196.
41. Sana Hashmi, "Military Infrastructure along the Northeastern Border of India", *Defence and Diplomacy*, vol. 1, no. 2, January-March 2012, pp. 103-112.
42. Rajat Pandit, "Chinks in the Armour", *The Times of India*, October 3, 2009 at http://timesofindia.indiatimes.com/world/china/Chinks-in-the-armour/articleshow/5083423.cms?referral=PM (accessed on March 31, 2014).
43. Ananth Krishnan, "China to Extend Tibet Rail to Town near Nepal Border", *The Hindu*, March 6, 2014 at http://www.thehindu.com/news/international/world/china-to-extend-tibet-rail-to-town-near-nepal-border/article5757520.ece (Accessed on March 6, 2014).
44. Sana Hashmi, "Tibetan Railway Signals Trade Imbalance", *Asia Times Online*, September 17, 2014, http://www.atimes.com/atimes/South_Asia/SOU-01-170914.html (accessed on September 17, 2014).
45. Ibid.
46. "China to build 7th airport in Tibetan region", The Economic Times, September 9, 2013 at http://articles.economictimes.indiatimes.com/2013-09-09/news/41903530_1_highest-altitude-civilian-airport-garzi-tibetan-autonomous-prefecture-bangda-airport (accessed on September 9, 2013).
47. Hashmi, n. 41.
48. This section on China's Win, India's Loss draws heavily from the author's previous article on China's Tawang Temptation published in October 2012 in *Defence and Diplomacy Journal* of the Centre for Air Power Studies.
49. Same as n. 3, pp. 98.
50. "Tibet is India's Legitimate Ticket to Claim Arunachal", Rediff, November 9, 2011, at http://www.rediff.com/news/column/tibet-indias-legitimate-ticket-to-claim-over-arunachal/20091109.htm (accessed on September 26, 2011).
51. A.G. Noorani, *Our Credulity and Negligence* (Bombay: Ramdas G. Batkal, 1963), pp. 142.
52. Michael Brecher, "Nehru's Foreign Policy and the China-India Conflict Revisited", *Pacific Affairs*, Vol. 50 No. 1, Spring 1977, pp. 99-106.
53. Suman Sharma, "Army Accessed China War-Game Plan, did not Enhance Security", *The Sunday Guardian*, April 27, 2013 at http://www.sunday-guardian.com/news/army-accessed-china-war-game-plan-did-not-enhance-security (accessed on May 15, 2013).

7

The Tibet-China Conflict: Implications for India

Simrat Kaur Virk

China's endless interests in the Tibetan Autonomous Region (TAR) are well-known. While on one hand, Tibet fits into China's sense of *nationalism*; on the other, even geopolitically speaking, it has served as a strong wall of defence from Europe and the rest of Asia. Even Mao Zedong is believed to have said that, Tibet is fundamental to national security. This is amply clear when we look at Tibet with its terrain, thus being a hurdle for numerous invading armies and significant from a military point of view. Moreover, traditionally Tibet also acted as a buffer between China and the rest of Eurasia; the realisation of which came with the British invasion in 1903.

More recently, however, there has been an acknowledgment of the environmental significance of the Tibetan Plateau. The inauguration of a massive hydropower project on the Brahmaputra (in the Tibetan Autonomous Region) in November 2014 is indeed reflective of this fact. Besides this, China has undertaken several infrastructure and mining projects within the resource-rich region. This is primarily because after having seen unprecedented growth, China realises that in order to sustain its economic rise, it ought to tap into Tibetan resources. As a result, it is undoubtedly keen on using Tibet's abundant natural resources for its economic interests, which partly explains why it is aggressively pushing for integration of the TAR with the Mainland.

China's renewed interest in Tibet can also be explained in terms of its abundant water resources. With an average altitude of 4500 meters, the Tibetan Plateau is often referred to as the Third Pole (being the largest repository of freshwater after the two poles). Moreover, many of the world's greatest rivers flow out of the Tibetan Plateau, example, the Yellow, Yangtze, Mekong and more importantly for India, the Brahmaputra, all originate in the Tibetan Plateau. Tibet therefore, provides China with water security, as well as water superiority; both of which are important for it to sustain its economic growth keeping in mind its population growth.

Tibet, however, continues to be one of China's restive regions. With the Dalai Lama living in exile in India, and a growing resentment among the locals, the Chinese government faces a tough task in trying to integrate the region. The leadership has consistently been of the view that while one way to integrate is an enhanced security. Presence, the other is to accelerate infrastructure development. There is no doubt that China has invested several million dollars in the region, but many believe that not much has changed on ground for the local population. This shows, as many believe, that most development inside the TAR is just a step to consolidate China's control over the restive region.

Tibet has been an eternal source of conflict between India and China, with China repeatedly accusing India of trying to undermine its role inside the region, particularly on giving asylum to the Dalai Lama and a number of Tibetan refugees.

With this in mind, the following chapter deals with the historical background of relations between China and Tibet, and how this had played out in the context of India-Tibet relations. The chapter concludes that this conflict will have implications and delves on what these will be for the India-China relations.

Tibet and China

It is important to remember at the very outset that both China and Tibet often cite historical evidence, dating back to several hundred years, when they make their respective claims and counter-claims. Therefore, for a better understanding of the conflict, a historical study of Sino-Tibetan ties is primary.

Relations between China and Tibet can be divided into 3 phases

- Pre 1911

- Post 1911—with the Nationalist Government
- Post 1949—with Communist China

Pre 1911

Much of China's claim that Tibet is its part and has been so from the time when the *Yuan Dynasty* (1271-1368) was flourishing in China, at the time of the Mongol conquests. Interestingly, prior to this Tibet is known to be an independent state, being essentially a feudal society made up of ethnic groups. Further, it is believed to have been unified somewhere around 600-630 AD.

It was during this period that Buddhism was adopted as a State religion. The introduction of Buddhism led to the start of the significant Choe-Yon[1]relationship. It was somewhat similar to that of Priest and Patron. What it meant was that, in return for spiritual guidance the *famas* would be given military protection. However, this has been exploited and to a large extent, conveniently misconstrued by China, who interpreted the relationship between the priest and patron to be like one between a sovereign and subject. China, therefore, claims that Tibet has been a protectorate of China since the time of the Mongols. However pro-Tibet thinkers are of the view that China fails to make a distinction between the Mongols and itself, despite the fact that the Mongols have categorically stated that they ruled Tibet and China as separate states.

There is a dearth of factual evidence of deep Sino-Tibetan ties during the Ming Dynasty (1368-1644). China too, is seemingly uncomfortable discussing ties between Tibet and itself during this period. What are the possible reasons behind this? One explanation for this caution is perhaps that most evidence suggests that during this period the Phagmodun kings ruled Tibet. Further, strengthening the Tibetan stand is the fact that for the first time, Tibet required absolutely no foreign aid, managing its affairs relatively independently. Also, during this period, known as the 'Golden period'[2] of Tibetan history, the King challenged the powers of the Sakya Lamas, and emerged as the new King of Tibet, therefore, suggesting that the Lamas' hold had weakened tremendously.

As previously mentioned, the fact that Tibet sought protection (primarily military) from successive Chinese emperors is often cited by China when it makes its claims over Tibet. For example, the *Qing Dynasty*, which succeeded the Ming, aided the Eighth Dalai Lama (1758-1804) when Tibet was attacked by the Gurkhas in 1788. Only a small Manchu contingent was sent at that time but by the time of the Second Gurkha war in 1792, the Chinese and the Tibetan soldiers fought under one unified Sino-Tibetan command. The joint forces were successful in pushing back the Gurkhas. This is when China seized the opportunity and in an attempt to have a more governance-based role in Tibet, issued a 29-Point document called, 'Regulations for Governance'. On the basis of this document, Ambans[3] were given the same status as that of the Dalai Lama. Although this was never accepted by the Tibetans who regarded the Ambansas mere ambassadors, it was China's way to have more direct control over Tibet. The Tibetan side however, accepted only those parts of the 29 point document that suited them and choose to ignore the rest.

It will be noteworthy to reiterate that while Tibet only sought protection from the Qing rulers by invoking the *Choe-Yon* relationship, it did not realise the Chinese intentions of using this at a later stage to strengthen its claim.

Protection sought from the Qing emperors by Tibet based on the Priest-Patron relationship deteriorated with the decline of the Qing Dynasty. This was primarily a result of the weakening of the *Choe-Yon* relationship when Qing troops invaded Tibet in 1909 which was seen as a breach of trust. For a large part of the eighteenth and the early nineteenth centuries, Tibet managed its own affairs. In fact, records suggest that Lhasa solely fought the Dogra invaders (1841-1842), the Gurkhas (1855-1856) as well as the Young Husband expedition (1903-1904). Finally in 1912, when the Nationalist forces defeated the Qing army, Tibet too expelled the Qing Amban and declared independence.

Post 1911

The period between the fall of the Qing Dynasty in 1912 and the invasion in 1950, is believed to be the time when Tibet enjoyed freedom and fairly less interference from its neighbouring countries. But as we will see clearly in the following section, the Chinese leadership never let go of the understanding of the strategic importance of Tibet. New China's leader, Mao Zedong, took up the cause of Tibet with renewed vigour. The issue of the integration of Tibet in China now seemed like a personal goal that he had set for himself.

As previously mentioned, the Choe-*Yon* relationship had weakened considerably by this time. Several advances were made by Chinese troops into eastern parts of Tibet, particularly Kham. The result being the Dalai Lama leaving Lhasa only to return after the Revolution. This absence of the Dalai Lama in the years preceding the 1911 Revolution was exploited by China who looked to strengthen its political position in Tibet. In yet another attempt to achieve its goal, China restored the status of the Dalai Lama as "loyal and submissive vice-regent bound by the laws of the sovereign state".[4] However, the Dalai Lama refused to accept any such titles given by China stating that he did not need any Chinese seal to establish his spiritual and temporal role. The Thirteenth Dalai Lama used this rejection and thought it was enough to declare Tibetan independence, something unequivocally rejected by China.

By 1914, the Tibetan Army that had been strengthened at the behest of the Thirteenth Dalai Lama interestingly defeated the Chinese army from eastern Tibet, further setting up its military line along the region between the Salween and the Mekong Rivers.

Soon after, another occasion brought China and an independent Tibet face to face. This was when the British convened a Tripartite Convention famously called the Simla Convention, with the aim of adopting a more aggressive policy towards Nationalist China that had issued a doctrine stating that Tibet was its integral part. The Simla Convention which divided Tibet into Inner Tibet and Outer Tibet (Inner Tibet, which included Kham and Amdo were to be under Chinese control) was rejected by China and, as a result, not signed by the its representatives.[5] This rejection is widely believed to be because China had specific problems with Tibet's independent representation. What stands out here is the oft mentioned concept of the "loss of face". The idea of an independent Tibet did not go down well with China. The claims and counter claims with regard to Sino-Tibetan boundaries defied a resolution. McMahon had therefore devised the concept of Inner and Outer Tibet and related it with the concept of suzerainty. Outer Tibet was—western Kham, central and western Tibet while Inner Tibet was—eastern Kham and Amdo. (The British interest lay mainly in outer Tibet). Owing to China's refusal to ratify the Simla Convention, it stood to lose certain rights. One of the primary privileges that China lost was the British recognition of its suzerainty over Tibet, and a right to station a Chinese Amban along with a certain number of troops at Lhasa. One can thus say that for all practical purposes, Tibet was an independent nation.

Another momentous year in Tibet's history was 1933. This was the year that the Thirteenth Dalai Lama, who played an epic role in rebuilding Tibet, passed away. China, by sending a Condolence Mission headed by General Huang (Chiang Kaishek's Vice Chief of Staff), got another opportunity to establish itself in Tibet. General Huang, who set up office in Lhasa was given an agenda, which included, among several suggestions, the fact that 'Tibet must form a part of China' and 'obey the Chinese Government'[6]. Furthermore, it went on to state that the 'Central Government shall grant Tibet autonomy within the framework of Chinese sovereignty.'[7] Tibet did accept this subordination to China but they agreed to this only within the framework of the Simla Agreement. So the proposals that were made included, that Tibet would be a part of China but it would not be turned into a Chinese province; that absolutely no interference from China in its religious and cultural affairs would be allowed by Tibet. It is also important to note here that Tibet did not have a strong enough army to fight off the Nationalist army but at the same time it did not want its entire eastern border to fall with the Chinese. As a result, it adopted a rather reconciliatory approach. This resulted in the Kham area being incorporated into China. This was also due to the fact that the Kham and Amdo areas were not under the direct control of Lhasa.

Soon after these events, China was too involved with the Japanese War (1937-1945) and so Tibet became low priority. This, however, did not last too long and soon after Liberation in 1949, China's new leadership under Mao Zedong took up Tibet with renewed fervour, which ultimately led to the invasion of Tibet by Chinese troops.

Post 1949 (The Invasion)

It is important to note the events leading up to the invasion of Tibet in 1950. For this purpose, it is of prime importance to apprise ourselves of the situation in Tibet at that time. The Fourteenth Dalai Lama was still a teenager and hadn't attained ruler status yet. The government was divided into various factions; the Panchen Lama was in exile and the members of the Kashag[8] who were meant to be representatives of the Dalai Lama were divided. Further, the Tibetan army was no match for the troops of China's Peoples' Liberation Army (PLA).

As stated earlier, Mao lost absolutely no time in his task of the "liberation" of Tibet[9]. A year after declaring liberation in China, Mao sent PLA troops into Tibet. He clearly used historical records to justify China's invasion of Tibet. But was he legitimate in the invasion? The Chinese would perhaps agree with Mao's actions but when seen from a Tibetan point of view, Tibet had now been free for several years; added to that was the view that its relationship with successive Chinese dynasties was more spiritual than political in nature. For Communist China, however, it was hard to make this distinction. Further, China was also confronted with the problem of its minorities who primarily inhabited its periphery like, Tibet, Inner and Outer Mongolia and Xinjiang. Mao, following Stalin's model chose to refer to these states as autonomous regions, corresponding somewhat to provinces.

In October 1950, three divisions of China's Eighteenth Army launched an attack at Tibet's Western Kham frontier. Kham area, as we know was mainly populated with Khampa nomads who were not under the direct control of the government in Lhasa. The Khampa soldiers did indeed put up a defence that were eventually decimated. The military invasion did not last a very long time. The PLA troops that had crossed the Jingsha River in eastern Tibet on the 6th and 7th October defeated the Tibetan troops by the 19th of the same month. Western Kham was set up as Chamdo territory, which eventually became a part of Tibet Autonomous Region (TAR), while eastern Kham (previously Xikang) was merged into Sichuan province. A conflicting question that appears from the above is, as what is often asked—what was the need for China to invade Tibet if it considered it part of the Chinese territory?

Once the PLA troops had been deployed, China surprisingly did not continue with its military campaign and offered to Tibet what it called a "peaceful" proposal.[10] This famously came to be known as the *Seventeen Point Agreement for the Peaceful Liberation of Tibet*. It was soon decided that a group of officials would travel to Beijing to negotiate a deal. What is important to note here is the fact that China has used the Seventeen Point Agreement to legitimise its sovereignty over Tibet but Tibet claims that the circumstances under which the deal was signed, were entirely illegal. The Tibetan side claimed that they were forced to sign the agreement despite the fact that they had not been authorised to sign. Further, they were not allowed any communication with their government in Lhasa and had no permission to make any recommendations or alterations to the document. In other words, therefore, China allowed absolutely no negotiation and simply asked the Tibetan officials to sign the document. Clearly the Seventeen Point Agreement doesn't in any way legitimise Chinese sovereignty over Tibet since Tibet was made to sign it under duress. Although China claims that it received an authorisation letter from the Dalai Lama, there is no proof of that; further, the Dalai Lama himself has rejected the Agreement on several occasions.

However, on the basis of this Agreement, Tibet became a part of China and thus allowed to station its troops inside Tibet. Further, all matters relating to defence were now under Chinese control. Tibet's foreign affairs too were to be looked after by Communist China. As a result of this, no country recognises the Central Tibetan Administration (CTA).[11] In a surprising concession that Mao made (although it is widely believed that this was because he had no local Communist government to look after Tibet when he had invaded), he allowed the authority of the Dalai Lama and the traditional government to remain in power. Thus allowing Tibet's religion to be respected. The Dalai Lama, did attempt to work on the Agreement through the early 50's but with tension brewing in eastern Tibet, which spread to mainland Tibet, he left Tibet for India where he remains till date.

Several reasons for China's stand on Tibet now come to the forefront; however, identifying one can be a difficult task. Firstly, Tibet was relevant as a 'buffer' between China and other countries. As we are well aware, that in the 'great game' Tibet was used as a 'pawn' in the hands of bigger players. There is no denying that the British in the early twentieth century, maintained relations with Tibet in an attempt to counter the growing influence of the Soviets. Another rather conflicting reason that is often given by China is that the intention behind the invasion of Tibet was also to rid it of serfdom that was highly prevalent in society. China claims that prior to the invasion of Tibet in 1950, it was 'hell on earth'. In fact supporters of the invasion suggest that 95 percent of Tibetans lived in feudal serfdom before 1950, and go on to cite cases of severe cruelty and abuse in the traditional Tibetan system. According to the PRC, 'there was a historically imperative need for progress of Tibetan society and welfare of Tibetan people to expel the imperialists and shake off the yoke of feudal serfdom. The founding of the Peoples' Republic of China in 1949 brought hope for the deeply distressed Tibetan people.'[12] To this, the Tibetan Government in exile responds, 'the Chinese justifications make no sense. First of all, international law does not accept justifications of this type. No country is allowed to invade, occupy, annex and colonize another country just because its social structure doesn't please it. Secondly, the PRC is responsible for bringing more suffering in the name of liberation.'[13] For the Chinese therefore, one can say, it was a 'sacred duty' to liberate Tibet and 'to make the east wind prevail'.[14]

The Role of the Dalai Lama

The 'institution' of the Dalai Lama is now more than ever at the centre of the Sino-Tibetan conflict. Most of the somewhat 'weak' evidence given by China in its claims over Tibet revolves around the ties between the Mongol

Khans (clearly, as mentioned previously, failing to make a distinction between them and China) and Tibet, and the bestowing of titles on the Dalai Lama by successive Chinese dynasties. Therefore, suffice to say that there are primarily two main reasons that China cites to legitimise its claim over Tibet. Firstly, that owing to the conquest of Tibet by the Mongol Khans in the thirteenth century, Tibet became a part of the Mongol empire and as a result part of the Chinese Empire. Secondly, and more significantly, China claims that it played an important role in the selection of the Dalai Lama and the bestowing of various titles on him. In fact, even the origin of the title of Dalai Lama, as the Chinese News agency, *Xinhua News Agency* states, "was granted by the central agencies of China's dynasties"[15] and not created by Tibetan Buddhism or granted by the old ruling class of Tibetans.However, these attempts by China have been unsuccessful so far as even at present the 'cult' of the Dalai Lama only seems to be growing and getting stronger. With a sharp increase in the number of self-immolations (since 2009 there have been a total of 125 confirmed self-immolations, 12 in 2009, 86 in 2012, and 27 in 2013)[16] by Tibetans fighting for independence, and the Dalai Lama's return to Tibet, it is hard to overlook the hold that he has over the people of Tibet.

Several remarks by China's top political leadership highlight the tactics that China is trying to employ in order to, what they call, 'expose' the Lama's façade, accusing him of encouraging self-immolations. For example, the newly elected President Xi Jinping is believed to have stressed the need to "fight against the separatist activities by the Dalai Lama group and completely destroy any attempt to undermine stability in Tibet and national unity."[17] Another report in the Tibet Daily states senior Tibetan official, Padma Choling, Chairman of the Standing Committee of the Tibet Autonomous Regional People's Congress, that the exiled Tibetan government based in India is two-faced, because it claims to ban self-immolations, but actually "fans extremism in China".[18]

Why the role of the Dalai Lama is central to the conflict is because China sees him as one of the biggest hurdles on its way to integrate the region into the Mainland. This is mainly due to the support that the Dalai Lama finds with the people of Tibet who have revered the institution for centuries. Not just this, the Dalai Lama is seen as the face of Tibet's international campaign. With this in mind it may be correct to say, as it is widely believed, that the Tibetans themselves might lose the commitment to the Tibetan cause with the death of the 14th Dalai Lama.

This section therefore seeks to explore how the Dalai Lama has come to be the face of the Tibetan struggle for independence. While doing this it attempts to trace the historical background of the evolution of the institution, and how the Dalai Lama by virtue of the position he holds in the hearts of the Tibetan people, is playing a vital role in Sino-Tibetan relations. An attempt will also be made to highlight the role that the Dalai Lama played in Sino-India relations.

The institution of the Dalai Lama came into prominence with the advent of the *Gelugpa* or the Yellow Hats Sect. It was founded at the end of the fourteenth century and flourished thereon. It was in the fifteenth century, primarily, that the sect rose to eminence and its influence spread to central Tibet. Altan Khan, a descendant of Kublai Khan was the first to give the title of the Dalai (originally *Talei*), Lama, meaning the 'Ocean of Wisdom' to Sonam Gyatso, who was his Guru. The title of the First and the Second Dalai Lama was given retrospectively to Tsong Khapa and Gedun Gyatso respectively after the death of Sonam Gyatso. With the ascent of the Gelugpa sect, the clerical office of the Dalai Lama also rose and he also began to serve as the head of the Tibetan traditional council. During the Ming Dynasty (1368-1644), there was a surge in the number of titles that were bestowed on senior Lamas from Tibet. The Chinese perhaps thought that through these titles given to the 'priests' they could manipulate the 'patrons'. Two important questions that arise here are—What was the status of Tibet during the Ming Dynasty? Is it true, that for all practical purposes, Tibet was independent at the time of the Ming Dynasty?

It was during the reign of the Fifth Dalai Lama, also known as the Great Fifth that the political structure in Tibet became relatively more organised and definite. Under the patronage of Gushri Khan, the Dalai Lama set up a new form of government known as the Kashag and appointed himself as its head. The Dalai Lama remained the head of the Kashag until 1959 and came to be the spiritual and the temporal head of Tibet. The Kashag is still being maintained by the Central Tibetan Authority (CTA) in Dharamsala with Lobsang Sangay as its Kalon Tripaor, the Prime Minister. This was shortly after the Dalai Lama gave up his temporal role and resigned as the leader of the CTA in 2011.

The Thirteenth Dalai Lama who, seizing the opportunity of a weakened Qing Dynasty in 1912 declared an independent Tibet, also expelling the last of the Chinese officials stationed at Lhasa. The Chinese, for whom the idea of the 'loss of face' is prime, were deeply angered by this, and part of the anti-Dalai Lama propaganda can be viewed as an attempt to avenge this 'humiliation'.

It is true that the Chinese realised, although a little late, that the only way to exert influence over Tibet was through their leader, therefore the Dalai Lama. The people of Tibet revered the Dalai Lama and looked to him not only for guidance on spiritual aspects but also on all other aspects (despite him having given up his temporal role). China knew that once it succeeded in controlling the Dalai Lama, there would be a sense of legitimacy of Chinese rule in the minds of the Tibetan people. So, their historical claim on Tibet centred on the history and the origin of the Dalai Lama.

Dalai Lama and Sino-Indian Relations

It is also worth underlining how the Dalai Lama influenced bilateral ties between India and China and thereby impacted the peace and stability of the entire Asian region. The Dalai Lama became the tipping point of the breakdown in Sino-Indian relations. We know that it was the flight of the Dalai Lama and him being granted asylum by the Government of India that led to the ultimate breakdown in Sino-Indian relations. As Natwar Singh states in his book, My China Diary, "The day the Dalai Lama walked into India in the end of March 1959, the character and content of Sino-Indian relations altered drastically. By the time Zhou Enlai came to India in 1960, the point of no return had almost been reached."[19] The fact that India has provided a safe haven for the Dalai Lama and thousands of other Tibetans hasn't gone down well with the Chinese, and continues to be a bone of contention between the two neighbours. Tibet, under the guidance of the Dalai Lama established the Central Tibet Administration which is said to be the representative of the people of Tibet. This fact irks the Chinese the most, who feel that there is too much interference by India in its internal matters (Tibet being an internal Chinese issue). In fact, one of the primary reasons for the Sino-Indian war in 1962, as experts say, is that China (under the leadership of Mao) wanted to "teach India a lesson." Despite repeated assurances given by successive Indian Prime Ministers that anti-China protests by Tibetan activities will be controlled on Indian soil, yet there exists a trust deficit between the two countries.

Even China's reaction to the Dalai Lama's Nobel Prize was centred on claiming that there had been too much interference by other countries in its 'internal' issues. All matters related to Tibet and the Dalai Lama are claimed as strictly China's concern where no other country should interfere.

The Middle Way Approach

The Fourteenth Dalai Lama has proposed, what is called the '*Middle Way of Autonomy*', to resolve the issue of the independence of Tibet; a solution that should be acceptable to Tibet as well as China. The Dalai Lama pioneered efforts all through the early fifties to rework the Seventeen Point Agreement, which he claimed was signed under duress. Not achieving much success and also owing to the Khampa revolt he was forced to seek asylum in India. The Middle Way approach was adopted by the Dalai Lama after talks with Deng Xiaoping who told him rather categorically that, "Except independence, all other issues can be resolved through negotiations".

The Middle Way Approach, as proposed by the Dalai Lama does not seek independence for Tibet. However, treading on a cautious path, it suggests autonomy for the three traditional provinces of Tibet within the framework of the People's Republic of China (PRC). This autonomy would be governed by an independently and democratically elected legislature and executive. In a clear softening of stand, the Dalai Lama agreed that once the above criteria are fulfilled he will not seek separation of Tibet from China and would work within the framework of the PRC. It proposed that while the central government of PRC would be responsible for the political aspects of Tibet's international relations and defence, the people of Tibet would concern themselves with all matters relating to Tibet such as religion and culture, education, economy, environmental protection, to name a few. The approach goes on to propose that China should stop all human rights' violations and the transfer of Chinese nationals to Tibetan areas. The Dalai Lama, it says, will be responsible for all negotiations pertaining to this approach with China. To give a sense of the hold that the Dalai Lama has over the Tibetans, nearly 64 percent of the Tibetans were in support of the Middle Way Approach and did not feel the need for a referendum. However, the Dalai Lama's Middle Way of Autonomy has been rejected by groups such as the Tibetan Youth Congress and the Young Tigers, who are willing to consider violence as an approach to independence.

India and Tibet

Relations between India and China can be divided into two phases: Pre

1947(relations with British India), and post 1947 (relations with independent India).Relations between British India and Tibet were mostly in terms of expeditions sent into Tibet. Britain recognised the immense importance of Tibet in opening up trading routes along the Himalayan region and also saw it as away to curb the growing Russian influence. As a result, one of the first expeditions was led by Bogle who successfully recognised the influence that China wielded in Tibet primarily through trade. Furthermore, China also showed its presence in the region with the stationing of its Amban. It is important to note here that prior to such expeditions, in 1890, Britain signed a treaty with China, called, 'The Convention between Great Britain and China relating to Sikkim and Tibet'. Through the signing of this treaty, China recognised that Sikkim became a protectorate of the British.

Following this, the other prominent expedition that was led by Colonel Young Husband in 1904 was part of Britain's final efforts to finalise the Sikkim Convention in 1890. Not just this, the expedition was driven by the fact that Britain,based on certain intelligence reports, was aware of the seemingly growing proximity between Tibet and Russia, which it wanted to curb. It was also effectively a temporary invasion by Britain to resolve the dispute over the border of Tibet and Sikkim. Interestingly, in 1906, Britain again signed an adhesion agreement with China, which is when it officially recognised China's rights over Tibet. Between 1906 and 1912 the situation in Tibet deteriorated. This was also the time of the Revolution. At the same time, there was a growing concern regarding the influence of the Nationalist Party, and moreover, Britain was also keen on maintaining Tibet as a buffer. As a result the British called for a convention, which came to be known as the Simla Convention of 1914.

As mentioned previously, through a clear demarcation of "Inner" and "Outer" Tibet, Britain achieved its aim of keeping Tibet as a buffer. *Outer Tibet* comprising U-Tsang and Western Kham would be with the Tibetan Administration with no interference from China. *Inner Tibet* would include Amdo and Eastern Kham and would be under the Chinese government.

Interestingly, although China initialled the accord, it did not sign the agreement. As a result, the Chinese Government to date does not recognise the McMahon line as the official boundary. It is precisely this confusion that has resulted in the long standing boundary dispute.

Was there much of a difference between the British attitude and Nehru's attitude towards Tibet? The answer to this question is in the negative. Many historians are of the view that Nehru's understanding of the Tibet issue is often referred to as being 'vague'. In fact, the Panchsheel Agreement even restricted and regulated Tibetan trade with India. Many also believe that by signing this agreement, India recognised China's complete control over Tibet. The Indian Government, one can therefore conclude, stuck to its policy of not angering the Chinese as it saw a potential ally in it or and wanted to appease them. In the later years, providing military aid to the Khampa revolt in the mid-50s' and a safe passage to asylum seekers, is what is widely believed to be one of the tipping points in the souring of India China relations.

Implications for India

So what has been the major impact of the conflict for India? As stated earlier, there is no denying to the fact that one of the primary fallouts has been that India now shares its boundary with its formidable neighbour, something that in retrospect could have been avoided. One of the primary impacts has been on the security of the region and this can be related to China's large-scale military buildup inside the TAR. This mainly has consequences for India owing to the geographical proximity of the two countries.

Border Dispute

It should be remembered at the very outset that China's refusal to ratify the Simla Agreement is the primary cause of the present border dispute.The entire boundary between India and China is divided into the Western, Central and the Eastern Sectors. The *Western Sector* is the boundary of the Jammu and Kashmir with Xinjiang and Tibet. The disputed territory is somewhere between 13,000 to 15,000 kilometers. The *Central Sector* is the boundary between Himachal Pradesh and Uttar Pradesh with Tibet; The *Eastern Sector* is the boundary of Arunachal Pradesh with Tibet.

When Sino-Tibetan tensions arose, India's relations with China also hit a low. (The common border has been a source of dispute between the two).

Both sides have built transportation infrastructure, airstrips and outposts, and have deployed large number of troops along the border.

The two major regions that remain in focus are the Aksai Chin region (Western sector), which is claimed by India as being part of Ladakh but administered as a part of the Chinese Xinjiang Autonomous Region, and Arunachal Pradesh claimed by China as being part of south Tibet and administered as an Indian state. Arunachal Pradesh is especially significant since it has the holy place, the Tawang Monastery belonging to the Gelugpa sect and founded at the behest of the Fifth Dalai Lama. The Chinese claim that the issue of boundary rests on the fact that if Tibet is indeed a part of China, a place with religious significance for the Tibetans should then, essentially be a part of China too! The fact that Arunachal Pradesh borders Tibet undoubtedly is one of the most uncomfortable political issues for China given the continuous questioning of the legitimacy of its presence there. China fears that the exiled Tibetan government could use Arunachal Pradesh as a base to provide external support to the Tibetans inside the TAR to resist Chinese occupation. A strong Tibetan Buddhist culture along the border districts of Arunachal Pradesh like Tawang and Upper Siang could provide the vital link to Tibetans residing in Tibet looking for outside support. Tawang became a part of India when Tibet signed a treaty with India in 1914 (Simla) but this was not recognised by China.The presence of the Dalai Lama in India and his visits to the Tawang Monastery for religious purposes further create anxieties for China and Tawang continues to be a flashpoint in Sino-India relations.

Until recently border skirmishes continue and Sino-India relations are marked with a deep sense of suspicion from both sides despite the presence of a Border Dispute Cooperation Agreement (BDCA). Moreover, Chinese officials have publically claimed the entire territory of Arunachal Pradesh as being part of southern Tibet and have periodically engaged in small scale skirmishes in the region.Regarding the infrastructure development inside the TAR, although China claims that it is aimed primarily for regional integration (also quelling economic unrest in the bargain), the possibility of using it against India still exists.

Military Implications

As discussed earlier, the other major result of China's presence inside the TAR has been is the fact that India now has a shared boundary with China. As a consequence of this rapid militarisation of Tibet can hold serious implications for India.

Infrastructure development inside TAR, although primarily linked to the Western Development Plan, is also aimed at improving the military preparedness of the PLA. Construction of rail and road links began soon after the invasion in 1950. Presently, 90 highways are complete and almost

97% of Tibet is connected to the mainland. There is a strong impetus towards improving logistics capability of the PLA.

There are a total of fourteen airbases—of which the established ones include Hoping, Bangda, Shiquanhe and Bayixincun and Kongka. More recently, what should be of special interest to India, is the airfield that is constructed at Nyingchi in south-east Tibet, which is only 20 kilometers from Arunachal Pradesh.

Presently there are close to 3,000,000 PLA troops stationed in Tibet and six rapid reaction forces in Chengdu with the ability to reach at the India-China border within 48 hours.

Water Sharing

China is furiously pursuing inter-basin and inter-river transfer projects with the aim to divert water to eastern part of the country which has relatively fewer resources. Most of water-transfer projects are being carried out on the Tibetan plateau, which is the world's largest freshwater repository.

Approximately, 354 billion cubic metres (BCM) of water flows from Tibet to India out of which 131 BCM is accounted in the Brahmaputra River on which China is allegedly planning to build twenty-eight dams. In November 2014, China inaugurated one of the five-phased hydroelectric projects in the Zangmu region and plans to build similar electricity generating projects in Dagu, Jiexu and Jiacha regions.

The proposed damming of the river can have serious consequences for not just the Indian region but can affect other lower-riparian countries like Bangladesh. Many analysts in India also fear that China could easily deprive India of much-needed water during a lean season as India and China are yet to sign a river-water sharing treaty. At 160.5 million hectares, India has more arable land than China's 137.1 million hectares. Environmental experts estimate that there will be approximately a 60 percent drop in the water flow in the north east region if China successfully diverts waters from the river.

Security

Historically, refugees from Tibet were central to Sino-Indian relations. Now, economy and trade may appear to be overtaking it as the primary concern, India giving shelter to Tibetan refugees is inherent to our strategic culture based on soft power and undoubtedly affects India-China relations.

Viewed from a security point, there is no doubt that anti-China protests have indeed always been a security challenge for China and a diplomatic test for India. Indian leaders have given repeated assurances for not allowing anti-China activities on Indian soil to their Chinese counterparts but at the same time faces criticism for providing asylum to thousands of refugees. Of primary concern is that amongst the thousands of refugees who live in India, there exist groups that advocate a more aggressive approach to protesting and controlling these becomes a tough task for security forces in India. There is also a fear that if the situation inside the TAR was to deteriorate, there could be a spillover effect in regions with a high refugee population. For India, therefore, the best possible solution could be to engage with the exiled government to look for ways to control such violent and aggressive protests.

Conclusion

To conclude, India remains in a precarious situation; it has given asylum to Tibetan refugees for over fifty years now; the largest population of Tibetans outside Tibet is in fact in India. This can be reasoned on the fact that firstly India and Tibet share deep cultural ties, and secondly and more importantly, Tibetans generally are of the view that to continue their struggle for independence, India is a perfect ally primarily because of its geographical proximity to Tibet. But India must also seriously look at the internal security threat that it faces by having a large number of refugees on its soil.

Therefore, one can say that the major challenges that India faces include not only the unresolved border dispute with China but also a whole bevy of issues ranging from environmental and internal security and also the security at its borders. It is important to note however that both India and China indeed have a lot to lose in case of an armed conflict; one of the major concerns being that a conflict could possibly undercut bilateral trade. Not only this, from China's perspective it could further include India's growing closer to US while for India it could mean a strengthening of ties between China and Pakistan—a situation both countries would ideally like to avoid.

What then of Tibet and the Tibetan cause? With an ageing Dalai Lama and a China that seems to be biding its time until it can prop up its choice of the highest Lama, an end to the struggle isn't in sight. In the past, Tibetans have often been referred to as being 'orphans' (although it has been used in the context of the Cold War). With little support from the rest of the world this description probably seems more accurate today, than ever.

REFERENCES

1. Literally, Priest-Patron, roughly corresponding to Guru-Disciple.
2. History of Tibet, Tibetan Alliance of Chicago, at http://tibetan-alliance.org/nomads/?page_id=21 (accessed September 2013).
3. A Manchu word meaning High Official.
4. M.C. Goldstein, A History of Modern Tibet, 1913-1951: The Demise of the Lamaist State (University of California Press, 1989), p. 49.
5. N.C. Sinha, The Simla Convention 1914: A Chinese Puzzle at https://www.repository.cam.ac.uk/bitstream/handle/1810/243068/bot_1987_02_01.pdf?sequence=1 (accessed July, 2013).
6. Goldstein, p. 238.
7. Ibid.
8. See Kashag, The highest executive office of the Central Tibetan Administration.
9. Claude Arpi, *Tibet: The Lost Frontier*, New Delhi: Lancer Publishers, 2008, p. 165, pp. 165–8.
10. Ibid.
11. Previously the Tibetan Government in Exile, TGIE.
12. M Goldstein, p. 37.
13. http://en.wikipedia.org/wiki/Serfdom_in_Tibet_controversy.
14. Claude Arpi, Tibet The Lost Frontier, (New Delhi: Lancer Publishers, 2008).
15. Liu Wei, The Origin of the Title of "Dalai Lama" and its Related Backgrounder, Xinhua News Agency, March, 2009, at http://news.xinhuanet.com/english/2009-03/01/content_10921943.htm (accessed July 2013).
16. Map: Self Immolations in Tibet from 2009-2013, International Campaign for Tibet, December 19, 2013, at https://www.savetibet.org/resources/fact-sheets/self-immolations-by-tibetans/map-tibetan-self-immolations-from- 2009-2013/ (accessed December, 2013)
17. Ranade (Knowledge World Publishers: New Delhi, 2011), p. 269.
18. Tibetan Exiled Government called Two-faced, *China Daily*, March 6, 2013, at http://www.chinadaily.com.cn/china/2013npc/2013-03/06/content_16280933.htm (accessed July 2013).
19. K. Natwar Singh, *My China Diary*, New Delhi: Rupa & Co., 2009, p. 86.

8

Power Struggle Between India and China

Sanjeev Bhadauria

At the outset, it may be useful to mention one thing about India's security practice. Ever since Nehru's brief stint with his romantic notion of building an alternative paradigm of "dynamic neutralism" (which later became the Non-Aligned Movement), India has been a hesitant practitioner of the 'power balance', and the Realist thinking has lately crept into its security and foreign policy-making. While attention has been focused on the rise of China and its impact on relationships in Asia, the emergence of India is now attracting increased attention and there is growing concern about the possibility of strategic competition between China and India and its possible impact on the region.

Sino-Indian Dynamics

In recent years, the 'rise of China' has become a frequently evoked term of reference, as has the 'rise of India'. There may still be debate over exactly how far both have risen, and about their precise Great Power status, but one can say that theirs is a significant relationship and are significant powers as well. Both have widening geopolitical horizons, yet as adjacent major states they both strive to stamp their authority on the same region. Geopolitics starts off here in its straightforward 'classical' sense, the way in which geography affects politics, or rather international politics.

It is important for understanding Sino-Indian dynamics; overlapping territory and location are at stake; strategic space matters for them and hence something of a 'Power Struggle' seems to be at play between these two rising powers where the concept of 'Power Struggle' is referred to as competition in influence, hegemony and profits. Such competition is at stake in the current Sino-Indian relations—and it is in this sense that their relationship can be described as another great contest. From India's viewpoint, the current challenge posed by China's tight grip on Tibet and her growing influence in Asia and close land links with Pakistan are of utmost importance,

The Oceanic elements are also a geopolitical factor in the Sino-Indian relationship, evoking Mahan and his emphasis on sea-power enabling power projection and control of the Sea Lines of Communication (SLOCs).India's geostrategy is being contested by Mackinder and Mahanian images and some of India's strategic ambivalence can be traced to the lack of a well-defined geopolitical image to ground a debate on grand strategy. A Mahanian solution to the China challenge is that India can overcome some of its continental disadvantages vis-à-vis China by posing a nuisance to China's sea lines of communication (SLOCs) or even involving itself in East Asian disputes.[1] But, only time will tell how far this can be actualized.

Struggle for Power

As states on the rise, China and India face each other in the international system, spatially and power-wise. The Sino-Indian relationship presents attitudes of optimistic cooperative engagement and of pessimistic antagonistic containment, which are discernible in both countries. The government rhetoric currently stresses cooperative dynamics, yet we notice an image of competition and rivalry. The media has been rife with speculations almost everyday in the recent past covering areas like military-security, economics and diplomacy. It would be pertinent to analyse whether globalization has replaced regionalism and where does geo-economics stand vis-à-vis geo-politics while dissecting the issue at hand. The stakes are high as both have similar need for securing access to energy resources for their economics-led rise to 'Great Power' status along with 'pursuit of primacy' in geo-political sense. On the political front, India like any other rising state desires to be recognized as a great power in the international order.

Chinese Challenge

India's unresolved territorial and boundary dispute with China and an undemarcated Line of Actual Control (LAC) on the India-Tibet border do not augur well for long-term peace and stability between these two Asian giants. Though the border is relatively stable, a future border war with China, though improbable, cannot be ruled out. China has had serious border disputes with many of its neighbours, and it chose to resolve those disputes only when it felt that the concerned neighbour was weak or when the latter acknowledged China's superior status. The frequent intrusions by Chinese troops into Indian territory are signals meant to assert China's growing political and military stature as well as means to test India's resolve. Moreover, India also has to bear the brunt of Chinese aggressiveness for being aligned with the United States.

China's carefully orchestrated plan aimed at the strategic encirclement of India is evident from its unjustifiable opposition to India's nuclear weapons programme; its strong military support to the ruling regime in Myanmar; its diabolical assistance to the LTTE in Sri Lanka; its increasing proclivity to build and acquire ports in the Bay of Bengal and the Arabian Sea—the so-called "string of pearls" strategy; its attempts to isolate India in the ASEAN Regional Forum (ARF) and to prevent India's entry to the Shanghai Cooperation Organisation (SCO); and, its relentless efforts to increase its influence in Nepal, Bhutan and Bangladesh. China is also blocking India's membership in regional and international institutions. It created hurdles in India's membership to the ARF (ASEAN Regional Forum), APEC (Asia Pacific Economic Cooperation), ASEM (Asia-Europe Summit Meeting), the UN Security Council, etc. Beijing also resents India-led regional initiatives such as the Mekong-Ganges Cooperation (MGC) and BIMSTEC (Bangladesh, India, Myanmar, Sri Lanka, Thailand Economic Cooperation). Clearly, China's growing power and influence in Asia poses a long-term strategic challenge to India as a competing regional power.

Positive Developments

On the political front, having fully normalized relations in 2003, Beijing entered into what it calls a "Strategic and Cooperative Partnership for Peace and Prosperity" with New Delhi in 2005. This development signals an important upgrade in relations between the two countries, and a sign that Chinese officials recognize India will become a significant Asian power. The two nations share a desire to see the international sphere transition to a multi-polar structure in which each country has an increased voice in global affairs. Military relations between the two neighbours have also steadily improved, with an agreement in 2006 to begin undertaking joint military exercises, as well as high-level exchanges between their respective armed forces.

On one hand, economic cooperation and enhanced political ties benefit both nations: bilateral trade between the two Asian giants stands at nearly $60 billion which the two are expected to do with each other this year (230 times the total in 1990). China has recently displaced the United States (US) as India's largest trading partner while India is China's ninth-largest market. China may have replaced the US as India's number one trading partner, but India is a secondary source of commerce for China when compared with the United States, Taiwan or Japan. Moreover, the trade relationship is profoundly unbalanced and increasingly a source of anxiety in the Indian business community. This is due to India's soaring trade deficit with China, India's economic weakness vis-à-vis China may actually spark conflict rather than dampen it.China has effectively turned asymmetrical trade into another instrument to prevent India's rise as a peer competitor.[2]

Despite improving relations with India, China has not been less warm towards Pakistan; if anything their ties have grown stronger. China actively assisted Pakistan with its nuclear program from the late 1980s onwards, and has provided it with ready-to-launch M-9, M-11 and Dong Feng 21 ballistic missiles, thus helping it bridge its military capability gap with its Indian rival.

All three of Pakistan's first nuclear plants in Kahuta, Chasma and Khushab were built by the Chinese. China has not only supplied Islamabad with nuclear and missile components, it has given it the technology to allow it to indigenize these weapon systems. The Indian strategic community tends to view Sino-Pak relations in a zero-sum game perspective. But, India needs to view Sino-Pak ties in new perspective and with new thinking. It is high time to de-hyphenate India-China-Pakistan relations. India and China are no longer in an 'either-or' or 'zero-sum game' kind of situation. Sino-Indian relationship is not dependent on the state of Sino-Pak relationship or vice-versa.[3] With the maturing of ties, China's close relationship with Pakistan should have no bearing on the momentum of New Delhi advancing the impetus of Sino-Pak ties.

Potential for Discord

Balancing these positive developments, however, is the long-standing friction: their 1962 war inflicted a humiliating defeat on India and created an unresolved border dispute. Such security tensions are not helped by China's on-going military buildup. Furthermore, China has been a principal supplier of weapons technology, both conventional and nuclear, to Pakistan, India's South Asian *bete noire*. In July 2007, Beijing deepened this "all-weather friendship" when it signed a free trade agreement with Islamabad.But of far greater concern to India are China's gestures of support for Pakistan in its periodic confrontation or conflict with India.

China's ambitions in the Indian Ocean are another source of worry to India which has been seen as 'China's next frontier'. According to an American Pentagon study, General Zhao Nanqi, Director of the General Logistics Department of the People's Liberation Army (PLA), issued a top-secret memorandum that disclosed the PLA's strategy to consolidate Chinese control over the South China Sea and the Indian Ocean. He noted: 'We can no longer accept the Indian Ocean as only an Ocean of the Indians.'

The potential for discord between the two countries can also be clearly seen in the energy sector. Beijing is desperate to secure hydrocarbon resources for its expanding economy, while India is increasingly reliant on similar energy sources. In recent years, China has beaten India in head-to-head competition for oil assets in Kazakhstan, Ecuador, and Nigeria. Despite the pledges of future cooperation in pursuit of energy supplies, it can be argued that India is in a fundamentally competitive if not conflictual relationship with China in their joint quest for energy resources. China's efforts to secure its access to overseas energy resources have brought it into India's backyard. Oil from East Africa and the Persian Gulf must cross the Indian Ocean to make its way to the market in China. In an effort to secure its interests, China has helped establish a network of ports and partnerships with countries in the littoral region-including several nations that have traditionally been hostile to India.

China and India

As China and India rise in tandem, their relationship will shape world politics. It is a shame they do not get on better. These two Asian giants, which until 1800 used to make up half the world economy, are not mere nation states but in terms of size and population, each is a continent. India and China—the two oldest civilisations, for the first time in more than half a millennium are simultaneously marching upward on their relative power trajectories. Both see Asia's rise on the world stage as bringing about the end of Western dominance. Both have a long history of bitter rivalry and a contested border. Both have their weak points—regional conflicts, poverty and religious divisions for India; the contradiction within the 'Market-Leninist' system for China. Both are plagued by domestic linguistic, ethno-religious and politico-economic fault lines that could be their undoing if not managed properly.[4]

As for changing the 'power balance', the People's Liberation Army's steady upgrading of its technological capacity, its building of a blue-water navy and its fast-developing skills in outer space and cyberspace do not yet unnerve India. Its humiliation at Chinese hands in a brief war nearly 50 years ago still rankles and a tradition of strategic mistrust of China is deeply ingrained. India sees China as working to undermine it at every level: by pre-empting it in securing supplies of the energy both must import; through manoeuvres to block a permanent seat for India on the United Nations Security Council; and, above all, through friendships with its smaller South Asian neighbours, notably Pakistan. India also notes that China, after decades of setting their border quarrels to one side in the interests of the broader relationship, has in recent years hardened its position on the disputes in Tibet and Kashmir that in 1962 led to war. This unease has pushed India strategically closer to America—most notably in a deal on nuclear co-operation.

The two countries are seen as serious long-term rivals—especially if India continues to tilt towards America. As recently as the early 1990s, India was as rich, in terms of national income per head. China then hurtled so far ahead that it seemed India could never catch up. But India's long-term prospects now look stronger. While China is about to see its working-age population shrink, India is enjoying the sort of bulge in manpower which brought sustained booms elsewhere in Asia. It is no longer inconceivable that its growth could outpace China's for a considerable time. China has marched far ahead of India on a whole gamut of development indices. The two countries were, by and large, on a par when they set out on their different development paths more than sixty years ago. India recognising the reality, is not aiming to catch up with China. The more likely scenario is that China will stay well ahead of India. But India can still capitalize on its advantages-a growing economy, an attractive political democracy, a vibrant model of secularism and tolerance, and a special relationship with America.[5] It has the advantage of democracy, at least as a pressure valve for discontent. India's army is, in numbers, second only to China and America. India does not threaten the West; it has powerful friends both on its own merits and as a counterweight to China.

Although, the Indo-US strategic partnership is still very much in its infancy and one needs to give it more time to mature and evolve before delivering any definite prognostics, US strategic thinkers are suggesting containment policy towards China. In this business of containing or counter balancing China, the significant Asian powers like India and Japan assume importance for the US. John Mearsheimer argues, 'in the not-too-distant future, the United States may need other Asian countries to help it contain China. It would be difficult to fashion an effective coalition of Asian countries without India as a central pillar'.[6] Further, a strategically enhanced 'Look East Policy' in an attempt to counter Chinese pre-eminence in Asia. Parallel to its strategic alignment with the US, India has been engaging ASEAN states as well as Australia and Japan. Adhering to the age-old precept of "the enemy of my enemy is my friend," India has been stepping up its military ties with countries traditionally wary of China's power in the region, such as Vietnam, and, looking even further a field, to Mongolia. New Delhi has also managed to create, after a decade of painstaking groundwork, a sub-regional organization, BIMSTEC, or the Bangladesh-Sri Lanka-Thailand Economic Cooperation, which effectively links South Asia to Southeast Asia.

"String of Pearls" versus "Necklace of Friendship"

Beijing aspires to have command over vital sea lanes between the Indian and Pacific Oceans through a string of bases, naval facilities and military ties. This has been described by the strategic community as 'String of pearls' strategy. The term 'string of pearls' was first used by an American scholar, Booz Allen Hamilton, in a report titled 'Energy Futures in Asia', prepared for the Pentagon. Since then it has become popular in strategic parlance in South Asia. The report says, 'China is building strategic relationship along the sea lanes from the Middle East to the South China Sea in ways that suggest defensive and offensive positioning (not only) to protect China's energy interests, but also to serve broad security objectives.'[7] It would be worthwhile to analyse how far has China succeeded in encircling India with its "String of Pearls" and how has India responded with its "Necklace of Friendship" with other countries.

Over the past two decades, New Delhi has undertaken a concerted effort to direct its foreign, economic, and military policies eastward. What began as economic cooperation with the nations of Southeast Asia has expanded into full-spectrum engagement with the major powers of East Asia, such as Japan and the United States. India's expanding role in the Asia-Pacific has been facilitated by countries such as Singapore, Vietnam and Indonesia that look to the South Asian giant to help hedge against Beijing's growing regional influence. A steadily expanding economy, paired with a growing partnership with key regional actors and an increasingly capable Navy, positions India to have an impact on the emerging security architecture of the Asia-Pacific. India's emerging influence in East and Southeast Asia is driven by a host of factors including geography, economics, and historical ties. Nevertheless, in understanding India's push toward the Pacific Ocean, it is difficult to ignore the role played by its northern neighbour. India's relations with China have become complicated.

Strategic experts suggest that the goal of this so-called "string of pearls" strategy is to secure access to locations that could be used to project Chinese power into the Indian Ocean. Regardless of whether or not the "String of Pearls" is an accurate characterization of Beijing's Indian Ocean strategy, China has certainly been active in the regionand Hambantota is the latest jewel in this so-called string of pearls that will pave the way for China's rapidly expanding navy to operate routinely in the Indian Ocean from secure bases in the region. The aim would be to challenge U.S. and Indian naval dominance in the area and ensure that China itself could protect vital trade and energy supply lines instead of having to rely on potentially hostile powers.However, it seems highly unlikely that the commercial port facilities China has helped to build at Hambantota and Gwadar will be converted into bases for the Chinese Navy.

There are only two alternatives before the Asian countries: either accept Chinese hegemony or take steps to balance Chinese power. New Delhi hopes and believes that the latter will be more acceptable to China's neighbours.[8] As a counterbalancing action India is trying to match China's "string of pearls" strategy with a "necklace of friendship" with countries which are not on good terms with China.

Future Prospects

The rise of India has been greatly overshadowed by what has happened in China over the past twenty years. If the development in China had not occurred, then it would be India that would be considered the new darling of global growth. To some extent, that has enabled India to commence its own growth curves without the media attention that has been focused on China. In other ways, however, there is little doubt that the phenomenal growth of China has served to spur India into action.

In terms of resources, India also appears to hold some aces. Its available workforce is now double that of China's, and is crucially growing younger. Its birthrate is nearly three times that of China, suggesting that future cheap global labor requirements and labor intensive industries will start to migrate. What used to be China's main economic driver—the provision of cheap labour to service global demand—is being whittled away.

That goes hand in hand with natural resources. India possesses 800,000 square kilometers more usable arable land than China, and 10 times the natural fresh water resources. This has huge implications for the agricultural and textile industries. If India is smart, and manages these resources properly, it will begin to emerge as a highly competitive player in these global markets. This will affect India's domestic demand as well—increased demand for Indian agriculture will lift hundreds of millions of Indian farmers out of poverty and into meaningful consumption and wealth creation models.

Much has been made of India's lack of infrastructure, and again, when held up against the current Chinese systems it looks ramshackle. A currently miserable 70,000 kilometers of highway (express routes) pales against China's 1.4 million kilometers. India has plans however to develop and invest significant amounts into building a national highway system, and these are currently well underway. This is expected to double India's available highways in length in the next five years.

By 2030, hopefully based on current trends, India would have overtaken China in terms of population, and almost certainly in GDP growth rates. With double the amount of available workforce, a younger population and a consumer economy of its own of about half a billion people in its new middle class, India's tortoise against China's hare would have caught up significantly. When that happens, the bet for who reaches the finishing line on top by 2099 will look very different than it does today. China is on the eve of a demographic shift that will have profound consequences on its economic and social landscape. Within a few years the working age population will reacha historical peak and then begin a precipitous decline.[9] So, it is advantage India in such a futuristic scenario.

The Genesis

Sino-Indian relations present a mixed picture. In the aftermath of the end of the Cold War, much of the debate on security in the Asia-Pacific was dominated by how geo-economics would emerge as a dominant theme as opposed to geo-politics. In fact the opposition is too forced; geopolitics at times involves geo-economics when it comes to questions of how easily or difficult a state might find it to access resources, especially in the energy field. Sea Lines of Communication are not only a question of geopolitics, but also of geo-economics. Trade and investment patterns are not necessarily global; they remain at times much regionalised. Geopolitics remains an important vehicle for analysing both powers. Such dynamics of interstate tensions in Asia continue to be defined most accurately in geopolitical terms. Mackinder-Mahanian paradigms on land-maritime power projection remain relevant for understanding India and China's drive and responses to each other.

The simultaneous emergence of India and China as Asian and global powers, in fact, makes it imperative for them to be sensitive to each other's interests and aspirations and they should work together to mutually support their rightful place. The only trouble is that the immediate spaces in Asia where they are going into, i.e., Southeast and Central Asia, and their respective backyards of East and South Asia, are ones where their interests are involved, often in diverging rather than converging ways. China's "String of Pearls" geopolitical projection cuts across India's SLOC, whilst India's "Necklace of Friendship" with countries like Singapore, Vietnam and Japan can seem more like a choker for China. India's quest for strategic autonomy and Japan's fear of strategic abandonment by Washington will bring India and Japan closer to each other to forge common strategies vis-à-vis China.[10] Probably, in the coming years, a major realignment of forces is likely to take place that may pitch India against China, as the two leading Asian heavyweights.

China has probably established a more comprehensive encirclement of India than has India of China. China's ability to directly threaten the heartland of India from its adjacent base of Tibet is unmatched by any comparable Indian land position. China's links with Pakistan, and also Myanmar, are not matched by India's land presence in Afghanistan, Tajikistan and Mongolia, either in terms of depth or size.

However, there are some countervailing trends, where India's links with Japan and most of all with the United States make India a worrisome factor for Chinese strategists. India as the premier rim land power will have to quickly consolidate its comprehensive military strength and choose its options wisely in order to play the key role of system balancer and stabilizer, whose support can tip the balance for or against mainly maritime US in its tussle with the prospective Eurasian heartland giant, China. The three Tsviz Taiwan, Tibet,

Trade &Currency are major irritants between China, USA, and India could emerge as the swing state in the global balance of power. It will have an opportunity to shape outcomes on the most critical issues of the twenty-first century and to play a key role in the great struggles of the coming decades.

Conclusion

Faced with each other, both China and India have similar policies. India's 'Great Game', its Grand Strategy in effect, vis-a-vis China is a hedging strategy, one of 'congagement', with elements of containment along with USA and Japan while trying to retain and further consolidate its pre-eminence in the Indian Ocean. China's Great Game with India is a similar hedging one, i.e., containment (through encirclement and 'strategic proxies') as well as engagement, whilst driving for in Pacific Asia. Both are hoping to gain enough resources and time to complete their respective peaceful rises by the mid-twenty-first century. As two rim land powers, they may, over time emphasise a Mahan path to the oceans and sea power, or they may seek a Mackinder path to establish land power and pre-eminence inside Asia. Conflict or cooperation remains possible in either direction. Geopolitics and 'the logic of geography' remain relevant for these two emerging Great Powers from, in and around Asia.

Collectively, India's expanding economic ties, its growing partnerships with key regional actors, and its increasingly capable navy will have an important impact on the evolving regional order in the Asia-Pacific. After nearly half a century of "confinement" to the sub-continent, India is increasingly making its presence felt across Asia's various sub-regions, reprising a role that it played in centuries past. While this conclusion generally concurs with the thrust of recent assessments of India's foreign policy goals in Asia and its potential role in shaping the region's future security architecture, it is somewhat more circumspect about India's present level of influence in the Asia-Pacific. In the near term, India's presence and influence will be felt most strongly in Southeast Asia. However, it has clearly signalled an ambition to play a leading role in the international politics of the broader Asia-Pacific region. Although it will be some time, if ever, before India's power projection and political influence match the full extent of its regional ambition, it is clear that India is much more than a state that merely "interacts with the Asia-Pacific in various ways."

It has been suggested that India would like to prevent the emergence of another dominant power between Singapore and Aden. While it may be difficult for India to prevent the rise of China in the region, given its current capabilities, it certainly would like to make it difficult for China to have complete sway over the region. It makes sense for India to stress cooperation while working to narrow the power disparity with China and build greater stability in Asia through strategic ties with other democracies, including the US and Japan. The US and Japanese interests also converge with India on this count and it is this dynamic that will go a long way in shaping the regional security architecture in the coming years.

Both the rising powers China and India are insecure enough about each other. Taking advantage of hindsight, the two regional powers have never been on good terms. They have always engaged in stiff competition to march ahead of the other and to achieve this objective they have also tried to contain and counter-balance each other. The weaker of the two has always roped in the extra regional powers to counter-balance the rival. Precisely, because of this reason, India is trying to rope in US against China in its hedging strategy. Since China is a potential challenger to the superpower status of the US, the US also needs India to contain China.

Both India and China have huge list of internal problems. They would do themselves immense good if they can focus their energies in fighting poverty, over-population, diseases, poor infrastructure, imbalanced development, corruption and human rights violations. Both countries have neighbours who share antagonistic relations with them. Conflictual relations will benefit the minions who won't mind largesse from both sides and play up for short sighted benefits. Asian values should drive the governance in both countries and together they should ensure that the twenty-first century truly belongs to Asia.

Time will tell exactly how the relationship will mix competition and cooperation. These two nations both aspire for the "first-world" status—and economic gains could be the incentive for a more tightly allied Asia. The two countries are not mutually dependent.

REFERENCES

1. *The Tribune*, Thursday, April 26, 2013, Chandigarh, India.
2. Brahma Chellaney, The risk of lopsided trade with China, Live mint, 29th May, 2013.
3. M.K. Bhadrakumar, "De-hyphenating" Sino-Indian ties", *The Hindu* (Chennai), July 17, 2010.
4. Mohan Malik, "India and China: As China Rises, India Stirs", in Harsh V. Pant (ed.), *Indian Foreign Policy in a Unipolar World* (New Delhi: Routledge, 2009), p. 163.

5. Fareed Zakaria, *The Post-American World: And the Rise of the Rest* (New Delhi: Penguin Books, 2008), p. 165.
6. Brahma Chellaney, *Asian Juggernaut: The Rise of China, India and Japan*, (New Delhi: HarperCollins Publisher India, 2006), p. 142.
7. John J Mearsheimer, "India Needs the Bomb", *The New York Times*, March 24, 2000.
8. Mohan Malik, "China-India Relations in the Post-Soviet Era: The Continuing Rivalry", *The China Quarterly*, no.142, June 1995, p. 322.
9. Mitali Das and Papa N'Diaye, Chronicle of a Decline Foretold: Has China. Reached the Lewis Turning Point?; IMF Working Paper, WP/13/26, January 2013.
10. Mohan Malik, "India and China: As China Rises, India Stirs", in Harsh V. Pant (ed.), *Indian Foreign Policy in a Unipolar World*, (New Delhi: Routledge, 2009), pp. 185-186.

9

Evolution of Defence Policy in India: A Historical Perspective

P.S. Harish

The aspect of military had played a significant role in the progress of civilization from time to time. Many mighty empires had sustained for a longer period owing to the application of sophisticated defence mechanism for security and protection. In the present scenario, numerous conflicts are being waged around the world for various reasons and the constant fear of being attacked is on the rise day by day. Due to this development, nations had to focus more, not only on developing weaponry, but also on a higher allocation of defence budget and drafting an effective policy in order to meet any eventuality. Modern weapons with maximum destructive capacity were also manufactured and in this regard the production of nuclear weapons has become the point of major focus. The foreign domination for thousands of years in some way or the other had a greater impact on the building up of external relations and it can be considered as a pre-cursor for the growth of the defence policy in India in course of time. Keeping this in the background, the present paper deals on the growth of defence policy in India from a historical perspective.

Defence Policy is said to be a program or a set of principles prepared by a country to defend itself from its enemies.[1] It is more focused with the protection of the state and its citizens from direct or indirect military threats. As human beings began to settle in one place from the Neolithic period, the aspects of security and defence became very significant. The Early period witnessed the invasions of Aryans and later Greeks, Scythians and others had come over to India. One of the earliest treatises that spoke about the defence of an empire and its policy making was Kautilya's *Arthasastra*. In this regard, his *Mandala* theory of foreign policy is very relevant and it had elaborated on various aspects that a king had to follow in order to protect his empire from enemies. It had also stressed that nations act in their political, economic and military self-interest and a state should not always depend on its neighbours for its survival.[2] But in course of time, the growth of heterodox religions like Buddhism and Jainism fostered the concept of *ahimsa* and the Mauryan ruler Ashoka came under the influence of this principle to such an extent that he abandoned his policy of expansion and warfare and completely devoted his time in the propagation of peace and it could have certainly impacted his foreign policy. The later empires like the Guptas would have maintained an elaborate defence mechanism as it would have been impossible to maintain a huge empire without effective foreign policy. With the beginning of the 8th century, when Arabs and subsequently Turks invaded India, there was political interaction and numerous transformations in the military and defence aspects. As their empire expanded in India, defence became the foremost priority as there was constant threat from Central Asian region and also from Mongols. Iltutmish, one of the earliest rulers of Delhi Sultanate, was said to have averted Mongol invasion over India through his diplomatic skill and strategy. This clearly shows that in order to protect his empire, Iltutmish successfully overcame a major attack through his effective defence policy. However, during Muslim rule there was a clear divergence of security perspectives between the Muslim rulers and the Indian subjects. The former perceived threats to their empire from the North-west and the Indian kings. The latter only perceived threats to their way of life. It was only with the coming of the Europeans, especially British, that both began to understand the threat from the sea.

Till the coming of the Europeans, there was no standard and concrete defence policy for the country as India had been witnessing numerous external invasions as well as internal instability from time to time. With the establishment of British as the paramount power of the country, the aspect of defence of its empire became very significant. The reason was that India was considered as a prime colony of the British Colonial Empire and that India had been a bone of contention between the various European powers right from the seventeenth century when their presence increased over South-

East Asian countries. The post-Buxar period witnessed the entire country practically under the British administrative machinery and in this regard, military policies and defence system too came into the forefront. The borders were effectively equipped with necessary military apparatus and internally too the British began to get a stronghold in the course of the next one century till its colonial base was shaken due to the revolt in 1857.

The post-revolt period witnessed India coming under the direct British control and hence changes were necessitated in all the spheres of administration including military. Most of the 19th century witnessed British military strategy strongly focused on defending and indeed expanding the Indian empire. With regard to the military, the interdependence between Indians and British was the basic characteristic of the policy and it was a liability that the British would protect India in case of emergency and, similarly, India would reciprocate to the imperial needs when desired. During the same time, Russian threat and the problems at the Northwest India were one of the major military challenges. Hence Indian defence was thoroughly reconstructed with substantial finances and thus provided her with internal as well as external protection due to various constraints in Indian finances.

The foreign policy of the British over India was aimed at securing the alliance and integrity of the border areas of the Indian empire. This resulted in the formation of 'Ring Fence' which consisted of two or less circles.[3] It could be maintained for nearly a century successfully in midst of internal rivalries due to the effective British diplomacy and its naval domination over Indian Ocean. By the beginning of the 20th century, British colonial base expanded its stronghold in most parts of Asia. The First World War experienced the loyalty of the Indian forces by fighting on the British side, but the post-war period saw the growth of frictions between British and Indian military. The reason being that British colonial empire had expanded to the newer territories in the Middle East and it aimed at stationing Indian forces in those regions, but there were voices against it owing to the financial constraints and the increasing influence of Indian nationalists.[4] However, in course of time, there was gradual deployment of Indian forces as the British with great difficulty had accepted to provide financial assistance to India. Even after this, there were sufficient forces available for subduing the country's tribesmen (Pathans) rebellion in the Northwest Frontier region. From this period till the beginning of the Second World War in 1939, both Britain and India found the Northwest as a troubleshooting and provocative area and consequently invested more time to ensure peace in the region. This further became significant as conditions became inevitable for the Second World War and stability was necessary on the Indian Northwest.[5]

Thus, the defence policy during the British rule basically aimed to fulfill its military needs as army from its colonies, especially from India played an important role in various wars and colonial expansion of British. With the beginning of twentieth century, when nationalist wave began to emerge and subsequently voiced its concerns, reforms in Indian military was one of the key aspects, where there was protest that Indian military forces were under the foreign control and that they were being referred as 'mercenaries'. Along with this, the Indianization of the army which had also been an important issue right from the 1920s remained unaddressed under the British policy.[6] Though this issue was brought in several times, it was rejected by the British on the point of potential threat to the military efficiency. Inspite of all this, Indian influence in defence matters did not show any signs of improvement and remained minimal till the end of British rule.[7]

India's Defence Policy during Post-Independence Period

With India becoming an independent nation, free from colonial yoke, all the aspects of the country, including military and defence came under its control. But the immediate challenge for the country was certainly with regard to its security, as it was surrounded with various neighbors who were still under some form of colonial control. The newly formed boundaries required immediate attention and its protection became an important task in front of the country. The northwest province and equally the northern borders were in a vulnerable situation and it was essential that India muster its forces for the defence of the newly formed nation. However, Nehru was confident that 'no danger threatened India from any direction and even if there was any danger, India can cope up with it.'[8] With regard to his impressions about the importance of having a defence policy, Nehru had a lot of confidence on Indian potential which he had expressed in the following manner:

> There is no doubt that India can built up an efficient defence apparatus...We live in an abnormal world, full of wars and aggression, when international law ceased to be and treaties and undertakings have no value and an unabashed gangsterism prevails among nations...The only thing to be done to protect oneself is to rely on ones strength as well as to have a policy of peace.[9]

The early phase of freedom was the beginning for all the policies to take shape along with the international understanding and diplomacy as the key constituents. Nehru had been instrumental in building up the foreign policy based on peace and mutual co-existence among the nations. Inspite of Nehruvian policy, India was sensitive with regard to its border areas and left no stone unturned to thwart any attempt of external aggression as Indian foreign policy was also equally concerned on its security considerations. The 1950s witnessed India taking a lead in mobilizing Asian and African countries to fight for their independence on one hand and envisaging its idea of Non-Alignment on the other, though it hadn't taken its full shape. This was viewed by America as an obstacle in the containment of Soviet due to the Cold War situation. Along with this, India taking up the lead in south-east Asian region and its vibrant support in the decolonization process was also not acceptable to the Western world.

The next decade witnessed the policy of Non-Alignment or the *Panchsheel* implemented and India hoped that it would be able to settle the border issues relating to the Mac-Mohan Line and the Chinese incursions to Tibet through mutual discussions. The reason was that India did not possess sophisticated military apparatus to counter Chinese coercive diplomacy. The defeat of India in the 1962 war against China made India to ponder seriously on its defence and foreign policies. It also became clear that Indian statesmanship and diplomacy could not prevent a war with its neighbor and hence a change became inevitable in India's foreign policy.[10] Similarly, the war with Pakistan also made India to rethink about its future course of action in order to develop a strong regional base. This resulted in India keeping its Non-Alignment policy backdoor for the time being and had to depend from outside for equipping itself with sophisticated defence machinery due to the non-availability of strong economic base and technical expertise.

The period of 1970s saw the deepening of the Cold War effect over the world and particularly on Asian countries. But India began to show that it was capable of becoming one of the greatest powers of Asia. With an intention for the balance of power, India entered into a Treaty of Friendship with USSR opposite to the US-China alliance.[11] The 1971 war, which led to the creation of East Pakistan and with great tension around, was neutralized with the influence of USSR and in this manner India was able to minimize the American effect.[12] Hence India created a new strategic environment and began to emerge as one of the leading powers in the region. This was further strengthened with India carrying out its first nuclear test in 1974 and it was also an indicator of India's up gradation of its defences and also its policy. The later period witnessed the need for India to connect more with the outside world and hence there were various bilateral agreements. But regarding its strategic concerns, India had to become extra vigilant as US began to step up its presence over Indian Ocean region through the expansion of its facilities at Diego Gracia. Similarly the developments in Sri Lanka too became a major security concern due to the involvement of outside powers like China, Israel and Pakistan. But the late 1980s witnessed a gradual improvement in the Indo-US ties with numerous cultural exchanges, scientific co-operation and other bilateral relations.

The collapse of the Soviet during the beginning of the nineties had a lasting effect all over the world. The weakening of the socialist system required the countries not only to redefine their status, but also to mould the defence policy based on the changed circumstances. During this period, India began to launch a comprehensive 'Look East' strategy which aimed at fostering closer politico-military ties with in Southeast Asian region.[13] In this regard, India began to conduct joint naval exercises with Indonesia, Malaysia and Singapore in the area around the Andaman Islands in 1991.[14] Singapore, in order to test some of its guns and missiles had utilized India's testing facilities at Chandipur on the east coast.[15] Similarly India signed a MOU (Memorandum of Understanding) with Malaysia in 1993 in order to promote defence cooperation between the two countries and this was the first defence MOU that India signed with an ASEAN (Association of Southeast Asian Nations) country.[16] The visits by the then Prime Minister PV Narasimha Rao to Thailand and Vietnam signaled India's new relationship with these countries. This visit was fruitful for India as it could sign a protocol on defence cooperation with Vietnam. Even by the beginning of the 21st century, India made an offer to Vietnam for joint naval training to combat piracy and in turn Vietnam offered to train Indian army in jungle warfare and counter-insurgency.[17]

With regard to Singapore, India had signed a Defence Co-operation Agreement in 2003 and in 2007; India leased one of its airbases in West Bengal to Singapore in order to train its air force personnel.[18] Hence, India strived hard to develop a cordial defence policy and foster a relationship that would usher a positive environment in the region.

Hence, it can be concluded that Indian defence policy was a gradual evolution in the course time. Though, initially there was no steady and concrete policy owing to the numerous external invasions and internal instability, the base for the emergence of defence policy could be attributed to the British rule, although Indian participation in the decision making was very minimal during the colonial rule. It was only with the independence that the entire authority and the right to formulate a policy with regard to security of the boundaries came in the hands of India. However, the immediate challenge for the country was to protect its borders as it was vulnerable for attacks from its neighbouring areas and India was successful in this regard. The early phase of freedom was the beginning for all the policies to take a shape along with the international understanding and diplomacy as the key constituents. It was also a delicate phase as it witnessed the growth of 'Cold War' phenomena and India had to be tactful in remaining as a neutral country. Jawaharlal Nehru, the first Prime Minister of independent India was instrumental in chalking out a policy based on mutual co-existence and co-operation among nations. Throughout this phase, India had effectively communicated that it would follow a balanced policy based on peace, but at the same time would not keep quiet, if its borders were threatened. But from 1970s India began to play an important role in the outside world by improving its ties with Soviet and with US in the next decade when the intensity of the 'Cold War' was gradually on the declining trend. With the end of cold war in the beginning of 1990s India began to emerge as the key power in Southeast Asia.

While the process of liberalization ushered a new phase in the economic relations, the collapse of the Soviet made the surrounding countries alter their policies to the changed circumstances. In this regard, India showed marked interest to foster defence ties with the Southeast Asian countries through its 'Look East' policy. These mutual agreements harboured feel good factor, trust and one to one co-operation thus preparing a base for developing effective defence mechanism in the region.

REFERENCES

1. www.freedictionary.com
2. www.defencejournal.com/2003/mar/kautilya.html
3. J.L. Kavic, *India's Quest for Security: Defence Polices: 1947-65*, University of California Press, California, 1967, p. 9.
4. Leake, Marico, Elizebeth, "British India versus British Empire: The Indian Army and an impasse in Indian Defence," 1919-1939, *Modern Asian Studies*, July 2013, p. 1.
5. Ibid., p 2.

6. A. Deshpande, *British Military Policy in India, 1900-1945: Colonial Constraints and Declining Power*, Manohar, 2005, pp 104-05.
7. S.P. Cohen, *The Indian Army: Its Contribution to the Development of a Nation*, Oxford University Press, New Delhi, 1990, pp. 93-94.
8. Kavin, J, Lorne, op cit, p. 23.
9. Roy, Kaushik, *Hinduism and the Ethics of Warfare in South Asia: From Antiquity to the Present*, Cambridge University Press, New Delhi, 2012, p. 242.
10. A. Kumar, "An Historical Perspective in Indian Foreign Policy," *World Affairs*, Vol 14 (no. 1), p. 106.
11. Ibid., p. 107.
12. Ibid.
13. S.M. Pardesi, "Southeast Asia in Indian Foreign Policy: Positioning India as a Major Power in Asia," in *India's Foreign Policy: Retrospect and Prospect*, Edited by Sumit Ganguly, Oxford University Press, New Delhi, 2010, p. 119.
14. G.V.C. Naidu, Whither the Look East Policy: India and Southeast Asia, *Strategic Analysis*, Vol 28 (2), p. 338.
15. Ibid, p. 339.
16. S.M. Pardesi, op cit, p. 119.
17. Ibid., p. 120.
18. Ibid., p. 119.

10

Interference of Foreign Elements in J&K and its Implication on Internal Security

Jaibans Singh

If there is one region that figures most in the media through statements made by a plethora of so-called experts, critics, policy makers, strategists and thinkers it is Kashmir. Almost everybody who is anybody or has pretensions to being somebody in world affairs, Muslim affairs or South Asian affairs would like to express an opinion on this small, beautiful and otherwise insignificant land mass. In fact, one could compile volumes of the printed page simply on "Kashmir-speak".

The sources from where opinions and prescriptions on Kashmir emanate vary. They range from those directly involved, those who are obliquely involved, those who wish to be involved and those who pretend to be involved.

Those directly involved with this issue are state and non-state actors of Pakistan who wish to take the whole of Jammu and Kashmir on a destructive path as in the case of Pakistan occupied Kashmir (PoK). Those obliquely involved are countries like China who wish to exert pressure by proxy. Those who wish to be involved are entities like the Organisation of Islamic Conference (OIC), which has no visible stake and yet does not refrain from issuing statements on Kashmir; those who pretend to be involved are the neutral but decisive players in world geopolitics like the United States and the European Union or other international organisations.

Despite all that has been written and talked about, the violence that envelopes the state defies a definition—is it an indigenous insurgency or foreign sponsored terrorism? Is it propelled by the aspirations of the people or by some strong and determined foreign elements who want to exploit the region both economically and strategically? Is it a political movement, a social movement or simply a law and order issue?

While addressing the issues involved one thing is undeniable—the centre of gravity lies with the people. The term "people," however, does not constitute only inhabitants of the area; it also refers to pressure groups of foreign origin who have vested interests in the region.

The history of foreign interference and influence in the Kashmir valley in post-independent India goes back to the first Indo-Pakistan war of 1947–48. The war was fought because Razakars (Mercenaries), sponsored by the newly formed dominion of Pakistan, invaded the Kashmir valley and areas in Poonch and Rajouri. Since Maharaja Hari Singh of Jammu and Kashmir had chosen to join the dominion of India and had signed the Instrument of Accession, the Indian Army was called in to evict the Razakars. What followed was a long and debilitating war over two campaigning seasons. Certain political considerations did not give the Indian Army the time and space required to culminate the war with absolute control of the complete state. The unfinished military agenda laid the seed of the conflict that has not seen a closure in the last six decades; the situation also opened the gates for foreign interference.

During the Indo-Pakistan war of 1965 Pakistan made yet another attempt to engineer an uprising in the Kashmir valley through the intervention of foreign mercenaries. The operation code named Operation Gibraltar was unsuccessful. Pakistan finally realised that it would not be able to wrest Kashmir from India with military might. It was then that the country evolved the infamous "policy of a thousand cuts". It played upon public dissension and political frustration in Kashmir to export a cult of terrorism. Pakistan terrorists were sent across in great numbers; they were joined by indoctrinated local youth to give rise to an uprising against the Indian state.

Foreign terrorists, however, had a larger religious agenda in mind! They committed untold atrocities on the minority communities (mostly Kashmiri Pundits and Sikhs) and forced their exodus from the valley. By so doing they successfully dismantled the liberal and secular culture (well known as the concept of *Kashmiriyat*) that had been practiced in Kashmir for ages.

The next more malevolent religious agenda was breaking down the culture of Sufi Islam and replacing it with what prominent writer Asit Jolly has described as the "The Wahhabi Invasion". Wahhabism is an austere, puritanical interpretation of Islam promoted by Saudi Arabia. A well-planned effort to replace the Sufi form with this religious interpretation continues to make deep inroads into the Kashmiri Muslim society due to the foreign sponsored efforts of the Jamait Ahle Hadith, which calls itself a welfare organisation but runs its activities through hundreds of mosques spread across the Kashmir Valley.

Ahle Hadith, which began as a 19th century Sunni reformist movement, is now viewed by Western analysts as far more conservative and aligned to the Salafi Islamic movement of West Asia.

"Young Kashmiris are restive and disillusioned. To them Ahl-e-Hadith is a new, more committed and determined option," is an informative explanation of the malaise given by Mohammad Yousuf Tarigami, CPI (M), legislator of the Jammu and Kashmir Legislative Assembly.

Foreign interference in Kashmir has been taken a step further with the establishment of an al-Qaeda branch called—al-Qaeda in Indian Sub-continent (AQIS). Kashmir will remain a special focus of this group with the intent to exploit polarised political sentiment. Al-Qaeda's considerable experience in the proliferation of terror will get ample support from the already well-established Pakistan Inter Services Intelligence (ISI) sponsored and Wahhabi-motivated terror groups like the Lashkar-e-Toiba (LeT) already operating in the Kashmir valley.

There are reports that al-Qaeda has already released videos calling upon Kashmir Muslims to follow their "brothers" in Syria and Iraq. Experts opine that this movement will gain momentum as the US leaves Afghanistan.

"We should take this seriously. They are trying to attract a constituency. They have local assets and networks in Kashmir and we will have to see what they do now. There is the prospect of a spectacular action," says analyst Praveen Swami.

There is also the security threat from the Taliban which is fighting America and NATO troops in Afghanistan. It is being speculated that Taliban fighters will turn their guns against India and engage its forces in volatile Jammu and Kashmir following the withdrawal of US and NATO troops from Afghanistan. Militant organisations active in Kashmir like LeT and JeM have their roots in Afghanistan as well. These and similar groups can become potent generators of splinter cells and radicalisation of individuals.

The role of Pakistan's ISI in sponsoring terrorism in Kashmir needs no elaboration; however, there is a need to understand its modus operandi. The ISI has a sub-section called the Joint Intelligence Bureau (JIB) that has been specifically created to conceive, execute and oversee Kashmir operations. Millions of dollars earned from the illicit trade of narcotics and funds from multifarious sources support the ISI. ISI, in turn, supports six major terror organisations including the LeT besides several fringe groups.

Operations of these groups are closely coordinated by the JIB. Religious teaching and indoctrination for potential recruits is carried out at madrassas followed by rigorous military training before moving them to secret camps in Pakistan occupied Kashmir for infiltration.

The overseas operation of the ISI, that involves even larger sums of money, came to the forefront post the arrest of Ghulam Nabi Fai in the US in 2011. Fai was the head of the Washington-based Kashmiri American Council (KAC). The US Federal Bureau of Investigation (FBI) maintained that Islamabad is a 'state sponsor of terrorism' and mentioned in its report one Brigadier Javed Aziz Khan, an ISI officer who handled Fai.

Pakistan, along with sponsoring terrorism is also supporting drug smuggling to the Kashmir valley in a big way mainly through ISI. There have been major drug recoveries in the recent past in which Pakistan's hand was clearly evident. On January, 17, 2014, 114 kilogram brown sugar was recovered at Trade Facilitation Centre, Salamabad. Earlier on August, 13, 2013, 10 kilogram cocaine was recovered by Army at Sheri followed by another recovery of 1kilogram brown sugar on September, 18, 2013, at Tangdhar.

Drugs like opium and cannabis are freely available. Then there are the medical opiates like cough syrup, neuro-toxic tablets, etc., that are available from chemist shops and spurious dealers; finally those who are desperate indulge in intake of fevicol, thinner, glue sticks, etc.

This problem has been around for almost a decade now. According to a United Nations Drug Control Program (UNDCP) sponsored survey, Kashmir division alone had 70,000 drug addicts, including 4000 women, in the year 2008. A recent survey titled, "Community drug abuse study survey in Kashmir" by a renowned psychiatrist, Dr Mushtaq Margoob, and his team asserted that there are 24.32 lakh substance abusers in Kashmir, which includes

2.11 lakh opium, 1.37 lakh cannabis, and around 38,000 alcohol abusers. According to this study, around 35% boys of very prestigious schools from 8th standard to 12th standard use these substances daily. Statistics issued by the lone drug de-addiction centre at Police Control Room (PCR) Srinagar reveal that in 2013, the centre has received 1441 drug addiction cases which are more than double the cases registered in 2012.

Increasing drug use among women and girls in the Kashmir valley has also been reported from time to time. According to a survey conducted by a local NGO under United Nations Drug Control Programme (UNDCP), Kashmir has around 4,000 female addicts. The survey points towards an alarming situation wherein girls receiving higher education and professionals are falling prey to drug addiction.

When we talk of the people of Jammu and Kashmir we must also consider the people of POK and Gilgit-Baltistan who are under the illegal occupation of Pakistan. In this region the foreign interference is not only by Pakistan but also by China.

China has been Pakistan's most abiding ally; till the 1980s, China supported Pakistan's view that the people of Kashmir were entitled to the right of self-determination. Later, the need for trade accretions prevailed and in the 1990s China took the position that Kashmir is a bilateral matter that needs to be solved through peaceful negotiations between India and Pakistan.

China's policy towards PoK and Gilgit-Baltistan is, however, guided by its strategic interests in the region. It needs the region for its outreach to the Arabian Sea and for establishing connectivity with the resource rich Central Asian Republics (CAR's). China is, therefore, actively conniving with Pakistan towards subjugation and colonisation of these territories; it has a viable military presence in Gilgit-Baltistan while being in control of the Karakoram Highway (KKH).

Pakistan's recent overtures to virtually cede large chunks of Gilgit-Baltistan to China have come as a shocker. This wholly illegal move has affected Asian geopolitics in particular and the world in general. By increasing its 'footprint' closer to India, China can have a upper hand during any conflict in the future.

People's Liberation Army (PLA) soldiers have been seen in Gilgit-Baltistan, working on dams, expressways and railroads, extending the Karakoram Highway. Unconfirmed reports hint at the construction of tunnels at secret locations, ostensibly for a proposed gas pipeline from Iran to China. These can also be secret missile storage sites. KKH is today a bone of contention being the nodal point for a drug trade directed at India. The highway can also act as a carriageway for transport of military and nuclear arsenals and other illegal activities.

Another lobby, the Organisation of Islamic Conference (OIC), which is a creation of the Saudi Royal family, loses no opportunity in making pretence of being involved in the affairs of Kashmir; the volte face is also almost immediate since none of the member nations wish to annoy the much stronger India.

Statements on Kashmir, howsoever superfluous and misleading, are elicited from forums like the OIC and other Muslim bodies and then quoted as fact. Such manipulation is normally done by the All Party Hurriyat Conference (APHC) to create a standing for itself and remain flush with funds. It has always been the endeavour of Pakistan and its stooges to generate misinformation on the Kashmir issue at regional and international forums.

No presence of the Islamic State of Iraq and Syria (ISIS) has been registered in Jammu and Kashmir. However, in a recent development masked men waving ISIS and al-Qaeda flags and banners appeared on the streets of Kashmir to protest against Israel. This put security forces on alert.

The importance being given to the perceived presence of the ISIS in the Kashmir valley is yet another step aligned to the objective of radicalising the Kashmir valley. It would be inappropriate to brush aside this development. It would also be inappropriate to read too much into it. A balanced view will not only put the matter in perspective, it will also lead to a logical assessment of the threat being posed and the most viable counter-measures to be put in place.

The ideology of the ISIS is not different from that espoused by other fundamentalist terrorist organisations like the Lashkar-e-Toiba (LeT) and the Jaish-e-Mohammad (JeM) that operate against Jammu and Kashmir. The brutality of the terrorist movement in Kashmir was of no less intensity than that being practiced by the ISIS. One cannot easily forget the rape, murder and torture that terrorists inflicted upon the Kashmiri Pundits to engineer their exodus from their homeland. Later, the atrocities unleashed on the Muslim population of Jammu and Kashmir to keep the terrorist writ intact were no less brutal. The manner in which terrorists have beheaded and decapitated Indian soldiers only a year or so back is yet another example of their inhumane viciousness. Their acts are no different from the horrifying images of western civilians being beheaded by the ISIS which have caused worldwide revulsion. The ISIS is not giving any new lessons to the terror mongers in Kashmir; in fact, it is simply following precedents set by the organisations like the LeT, JeM, etc.

What is notable is that there are some in Kashmir who actually support such a monstrous activity. It is not the physical threat posed by the ISIS that one needs to fear, it is the element of inhumanity creeping into the people of Kashmir that is of concern.

There are some who say that hoisting of flags of this ISIS is a manifestation of the deep anger and alienation the youth of the Valley harbour towards India. Who is being harmed more by this sadistic demonstration—the Indian state or the Kashmiri society? Is this not a classic case of cutting your nose to spite your face?

It is difficult to digest the fact that the Chief Minister of the State, who is also a Kashmiri Muslim, is unperturbed by the development. This thought process would lead one to believe that even the highest level in the valley has become immune to the cult of violence.

Consistent religious indoctrination and the inability of the state government to meet rampant unemployment are leading to a revival of "home grown insurgency". Shakil Ahmed Wani of Budgam, who carried out a daring strike at the Pakharpura Shrine on June 16 this year has three postgraduate degrees from various universities. The alleged mastermind of the Delhi High Court blast (September 2011) that killed 15 persons and wounded 80, is Wasim Akram Malik. He is a medical student in his early 20s from Jammu's Kishtwar region. Recently, the state police has claimed to have busted a Lashkar module in Sopore with the arrest of seven militants, all in their early 20s. Police sources put the number of Kashmiri men to have taken up the gun from 2010 onwards at over 40, including those who lost their near ones in the 2008 and 2010 violence.

Social media is playing a big role in igniting this malaise. According to Jammu and Kashmir Police the use of social media has increased drastically in the terror hotbeds of Sopore, Pulwama, Tral, etc. Foreign-sponsored terror groups have found in Facebook, Twitter, YouTube, WhatsApp, etc., a cheap means of communicating rabid fundamentalism via continuous communication. Facebook pages like "Frontline Kashmir" and "Aalaw" are being managed from POK.

Observers in Srinagar feel that Ayam al Zawahiri's call for Jihad in India will find few takers in today's Kashmir, howsoever restive it may be. Political scientist Noor Ahmad Baba says, "despite the simmering discontent and disillusionment with India, Kashmiris have no appetite for more violence and al-Qaeda's extremist ideology."

Religious fundamentalism can be countered by promoting the Hanafi sect of Islam, whose standard bearer is the influential Islamic school Darul Uloom at Deoband in Uttar Pradesh. This can give a response to the Ahle Hadith sect. Moderate Hanafia Maulvis need to be encouraged to voice their views in all districts of the Kashmir Valley. Hanafi represents one of the four schools of Sunni Islamic thought and is popular in the subcontinent.

It would be in India's interest to bring Gilgit-Baltistan into the limelight and give moral support to the people who are, in any case, deprived citizens of the Indian nation. Ways and means have to be found to end the terrible suffering of the people. The demands of the people, as articulated by their freedom fighters operating from overseas, can be taken up through diplomatic channels. These are condemnation of ongoing human rights violations, restoration of state subject rule in Gilgit–Baltistan, opening up of trade routes with Kargil, an end to inhumane attacks on Shias, exclusive rights to the ethnic population, grant of political rights and genuine autonomy. India should not shy away from extending wholehearted support to the people of Gilgit-Baltistan

As the threat of terror is reducing in Kashmir the need to move the younger generations away from the shadow of the gun and onto a path of progress and development is most significant. If people start moving on the path of moderation the death knell for the forces of terror in the valley will automatically be sounded. Obviously, terror masters sitting in Pakistan will do everything in their power to stop any such development from taking place.

A conscious effort has to be made to change the negative perceptions that some parts of the Kashmir society harbour due to relentless propaganda by forces of evil. It is very important to further the initiative being taken by the Prime Minister. Basic methodology in this regard can be akin to that being followed by the army in its WHAM campaign. It is time for the state government, the civil society and above all parents and elders in the Kashmir valley to challenge the ogre of religious fundamentalism

The buck finally stops at the door of good and effective governance as well as at proactive diplomatic/information posturing. India's constant effort to assist the beleaguered and terrorist afflicted people of Jammu and Kashmir and fulfill their aspirations has been construed as her weakness by inimical foreign forces. While Pakistan frequently makes arrogant and brash statements grounded in total falsehood, the Indians are for some reason even shy of stating the truth. An assertive government following the path of righteousness can contain this debilitating foreign influence that is eating up Kashmiri society.

11

The Importance of Maldives in South Asia

S. Manivasakan and Sripathi Narayanan

Introduction

The Maldives, an archipelago nation of the Indian Ocean stretches in a north-south direction, off India's Lakshadweep islands, between the Minicoy Island and Chagos Archipelago. It stands in the Laccadive Sea, about 700 km south-west of Sri Lanka and 400 km south-west of India. The archipelago chain of the Maldives consists of approximately 1,190 coral islands grouped in a double chain of 26 atolls, spread over roughly 90,000 sq.km. The archipelago is 823 km long and 130 km at its greatest width. This makes the Maldives one of the most dispersed countries in the world. Of all the islands, only 202 are inhabited. The average height of the islands is about 1.5 m above sea level and the highest point is 2.5 m above sea level. This makes the island-nation a country with the lowest high point in the world.

The total population of the Maldives is estimated to be around 394,000.[1] This includes the immigrant labour force that constitutes a quarter of the population. For a country that converted to Islam completely as far back as the twelfth century, religion in Maldives continues to remain moderate though citizenship is granted only to Sunni Muslims. From a tradition of autocracy of both Republican and earlier forms, the country took to multi-party democracy as recently as 2008.

This Indian Ocean archipelago was a Protectorate of the British Empire till 1965 without being a colony, like much of South Asia, including the immediate neighbours of India and Sri Lanka. Under the Protectorate arrangement, the internal administration of the archipelago continued under the traditional system of the Sultanate, while the British, based in Ceylon were responsible for the security and foreign policy of the Maldives. After the withdrawal of Britain from the east of the Suez, the Maldives witnessed a period of internal political turmoil, which saw the rise and fall of the 'First Republic' and the reinstatement of the Sultanate. Subsequently, the Sultanate as a form of governance was abolished in November 1968, with Ibrahim Nasir, until then Prime Minister, being named the first President of the 'Second Republic'. In the face of stiff political opposition Nasir resigned in 1978 and Maumoon Gayoom replaced him as President. Gayoom remained in power till November 2008.

During this period of 30 years, Gayoom won six consecutive elections to the office of the President. The elections were held under a system of a single candidate cleared by a near-nominated Parliament. It was not till 1998, when multiple candidates' elections were introduced, but even then the nation lacked democratic characteristics and credibility as is commonly understood as theelection system lacked a credible opposition to the candidature of Gayoom as President.

When faced with political protests in 2004-05, President Gayoom undertook a series of political reforms. This culminated in the drafting of a Third Republican Constitution in 2007 that included, amongst other changes, a multi-party democracy and fresh elections for the presidency a year later, which anyway was due. The 2008 elections paved the way for Mohamed Nasheed, popularly known as 'Anni', representing the newly-formed Maldivian Democratic Party (MDP), to be elected as President; in what was the country's first truly multi-party/multi-candidate election to the office of the President; and thus ending the long and uninterrupted reign of President Gayoom. The Constitution of 2007 had adopted the Presidential system of governance with a directly-elected Executive President and a legislator, People's *Majlis*, or Parliament, a system that was anyway prevalent in this archipelago.

Since Democracy

The Maldives' first experience with democracy was in the year 2008. Till then, this island nation functioned under a totalitarian model of administration.

The Constitution of 2007 not only introduced a multiparty democracy but also a system of governance that is based on the executive-presidency. Thus, the election to the office of the President is a two-round polling system with the winner having to acquire 50 per cent plus one share in the popular vote polled.

Thus, in the 2008 election Nasheed of the MDP won the race to the presidency in the second round by winning over the then incumbent Gayoom. However, Nasheed's victory was not won easily since he had to face Gayoom in the runoff (second) round. In the first round of polling Nasheed won just 25 per cent of the popular vote, as against President Gayoom's 40 per cent. But in the second round with the support of the other candidates, MDP secured the race of the office of the Presidency.

However, the advent of democracy in the archipelago confronted its first shock and its first test with President Nasheed resigning from office within three years of his five-year term. His Vice President Waheed Hassan Manik succeeded Nasheed as the first citizen of the nation in February 2012. However, the resignation of President itself became a matter of contention since Nasheed and the MDP claimed that the resignation was result of a *coup*. This prompted the new government to constitute an inquiry commission which included representatives from each one from the international community (nominated by the Commonwealth for the UN as well) and by Nasheed for his MDP. This commission dubbed as the Commission of National Inquiry (CoNI) released its report on August 30, 2012, where it dismissed the claims of President Nasheed and the MDP.

Since the release of the CoNI report, the political climate in the nation has been geared towards the presidential elections in 2013, which anyway under the normal scheme of things were due and were slated to be held on September 7. The political climate in the Maldives charged up on multiple counts and post February 2012, the political issues in the Maldives was largely centred on President Nasheed.

The Second Poll

The run-up to the elections was marked by significant developments. One such development that pertains to India took place in February 2013, when Nasheed sought refuge in the Indian High Commission in Malé fearing arrest by the Maldivian authorities.[2] This placed Delhi in a delicate situation on the one hand, while on the other, it also created a situation that highlighted the importance of India in the Maldivian context.

For India, it was an unprecedented experience to host a high profile leader in its embassy premises under such circumstances. At the same time, India was walking the diplomatic tightrope since the situation at hand was complicated. For a start, the circumstance that led to President Nasheed seeking shelter in the Indian mission was a domestic issue that briefly took a bilateral character.

Though brief, the internationalisation of the domestic politics of the Maldives is of particular significance in that, India, was sucked into what was a purely a domestic legal issue, because Nasheed sought protection in the Indian mission to avoid arrest. The warrant of arrest that was drawn in the name of the former president was a legal procedure and was within the ambit of the Maldivian Judiciary.

The second issue was the airport contract. GMR, an Indian construction major, was awarded a contract to modernise the Ibrahim Nasir International Airport, Male. The US $511 million contract was annulled in November 2012, after it became a political issue for some time. This project of GMR was by far the single largest Foreign Direct Investment (FDI) into the Maldives and a significant commercial engagement by India.

The third issue was the perceived role of India. The Adhaalath Party, a minor political entity, had accused India of "meddling in the internal affairs of the country" and "for assisting a criminal fleeing from trial".[3]

Besides, at the same time, India was the first country to recognise the change in guard in February 2012, even when the MDP claimed that Nasheed resignation was a result of a coup.

This delicate political deadlock was resolved and paved the way for elections which also was not free from controversy. The run up to the elections witnessed heavy campaigning by all political players, each hedging his opportunity in becoming the first citizen. Nevertheless, this time around the elections unlike the one held in 2008 was of a different variant.

The 2008 elections carried with it a degree of idealism of the new-found democracy, while the 2013 was politics at its finest. Abdulla Yameen, won the presidency even while the elections were mired in controversy.

For a start, the first round was annulled by the Supreme Court, stating some anomalies. This largely pertained to a number of invalid votes being cast. The first round was held on September 7, nullified and the re-election for the same was held on November 9. The runoff was held on the November 16.

One common trait of both the 2008 and 2013 elections was that the leading candidate in the first round failed to win the elections. Maumoon Gayoom secured a comfortable 40 per cent in the first round in 2008 but lost the second round to Nasheed, who only secured a quarter of the votes in the primary poll. Nasheed too, in 2013 faced a similar situation. Even though he secured 45 per cent of votes as against Yameen's 25 per cent, Nasheed managed a final total of only 48 per cent, while Yameen crossed the half way mark by just a 1.4 per cent.

The heated campaign and controversial elections did come to rest with the final announcement of the results on November 16, when Yameen was declared as a duly elected President. The new president made his first official oversees visit to India on the very first day of the New Year, 2014, thus cementing the bond between these two nations. This visit is also significant given the manner in which New Delhi was dragged into the stalled first round of the elections. Incidentally, one of the candidates, who did not make it to the runoff, claimed that the Indian supplied electronic voting machines that were defective and were tuned to register votes wrongly.

Geo-strategic Location of the Maldives

The geostrategic location of the Maldives has never been lost to the world. This is quite evident through the history of the Indian Ocean; when the era of colonialism witnessed much warfare between the European nations for colonies, the Maldives was spared this plight.

The foremost reason for this privilege was that, this archipelago of the Indian Ocean offered little in terms of resources for the resource hungry Europe. But once the powers to be established themselves in the Indian Ocean region, they realised the importance of securing them. It was in this context that the Maldives gained prominence and it was also for this very reason that the Maldives became a protectorate of the British and not its colony.

For London, its incentives in the Indian Ocean were largely driven by the need to securing India, the *Jewel in the Crown* from its European rivals; and thus was the strategic importance of the Maldives. As a result of this, the British interests were driven by an exclusionist policy of ensuring that the external relations of this archipelago was limited and confined to the British Empire. A similar approach can be witnessed in the Himalayan foot hills, wherein the two Himalayan Kingdom's, Nepal and Bhutan were recognised as independent nation-states with the foreign policy being dictated by the Delhi, the capital of British India.

In the case of the Maldives, Ceylon became the nodal centre that guided the external affairs of the Maldives, while it recognised the authority of the local Sultanate. However, the British interests in the Maldives ran parallel to London's withdrawing from the "East of the Suez". The Maldives gained complete independence from the British in July of 1965 while the British withdrew completely from Asia in 1971.

Since 1965, the Maldives has been in the eye of a number of nations. The United States, the Soviet Union and Libya under Gaddafi, had expressed their desire to mark their presence in the Indian Ocean by establishing a base/ military facility in the Maldives. For the United States, the Maldives was a nation of interest in the '70's, especially after it established its naval base in the central Indian Ocean archipelago of Diego Garcia. The Maldives provided an attractive rest and recuperation centre for its troops based in Diego Garcia.

Incidentally the British air strip of the Second World War vintage in the Sothern Atoll of Gan too attracted the interests of the powers-to-be during the Cold War. This air strip was primarily built and used by the Allied forces after the fall of Singapore to the Japanese and when Ceylon become the headquarters for the Allied Force in Asian theatre of the war.

Throughout the Maldives was impervious to the overtures of the superpowers, but the events of the late 1980s changed this position. The coup attempted by the militants of Sri Lanka's People's Liberation Organisation of Tamil Eelam (PLOTE), and the subsequent rescue efforts by the Indian military, code named Operation Cactus, exposed the vulnerability of the archipelago to external threats.

Op Cactus resulted in suppressing the threat imposed by PLOTE and restored the sovereignty of the Maldives. Since then both India and Maldives have deepened their security related ties extending to wide spectrum involvements.

Today, the military ties include the regular bi-annual naval exercises between the two Coast guards, since 1991. This in 2012 expanded to include Sri Lanka while at the same time the three nations concluded a Trilateral

Maritime Security Agreement in July 2013. This agreement is also expected to be expanded to include Mauritius and Seychelles.

Incidentally, in light of the threat emanating from Somalia based piracy, the Indian Navy and Coast Guard have undertaken the responsibility of securing the exclusive economic zone of Maldives, Mauritius and Seychelles.

In this regard, a fleet of helicopters of the Indian Navy is based in the Gan Atoll, which complements all other Indian assistance, including naval vessels, training for Maldivian security authorities. Apart from this, the Maldives is a part of Indian maritime radar surveillance network.

The strategic location of Maldives in the present day context is also well recognised by other nations as well, especially by China and United States. The United States in the era of Jihadi terrorism, sought the assistance of Malé in offloading the pressures on the Guantanamo Bay detention centre in Cuba. Malé was not enthusiastic of the proposal that was put forth Washington.

On the other hand, China has extended an invitation for Malé to become an integral part its Maritime Silk Route (MSR). The MSR also includes the other South Asian nations like India and Sri Lanka. The MSR till recently was received with pessimism by India as it was a view based on the prism of the String of Pearls (SoP) theory.

The SoP, an American construct, was proposed to be a series of Chinese funded and executed ports and maritime facilities around the Indian periphery and thereby encircling India. This theory gained significant traction in India which feared a Chinese initiative to box it within its near waters. The theory in recent times has died a natural death and has paved the way for a greater acceptance for MSR, both in India and in the Maldives, which in turn contexts the MSR as a means for greater economic cooperation between these nations.

Where from Here

India does not face any grave threat from the Maldives nor does its pose a challenge or give rise to any cause for concern for India. New Delhi's ties with this nation have been more than cordial. Nonetheless, there are a few key issues that one needs to keep in mind when it come to dealing with India's neighbours, especially smaller neighbours including the Maldives. What holds good to other nations in the Indian Subcontinent also holds good in the case of Maldives.

The issues that are of concern and need to be kept in mind would begin with the asymmetric nature of the ties. This is not just limited to the mere question of size of the nations and their population but also the perception of each other.

For Maldives, India apart from Sri Lanka is its closest country among all nations in the world, both in terms of proximity and in bilateral ties. However, its domestic politics and its external ties, in some parts, is a derivative of its internal affairs, and does hinge strongly upon its notion and idea of India. A small section of the Maldivian polity has expressed their opinion of India that is anything but charitable. The Adhaalath Party, has already accused New Delhi of its involvement in alleged electoral malpractices in the 2013 presidential elections. Such issues along with the case of the Malé Airport project that was undertaken by GMR only feed to the frenzy of such fringe elements.

The GMR matter could have been handled more deftly, more delicately with greater empathy and lesser panache. The timing of and the course of the contentious issue immediately took a nosedive in the bilateral ties. From Delhi's perspective, the airport was a commercial contract between an Indian firm and the State of Maldives, but for Maldives it was primarily a question of sovereignty.

On the other hand, for a small nation like the Maldives, not to mention its neighbour, Sri Lanka, they seek commercial and economic partners when it comes to development. For them India is not the sole partner nor do they expect India to be the only partner in this regard. Thus, their relationship with China and others need not be seen in the context of India-China ties alone but more on commercial lines, when at a time Delhi's economic and trade ties with Beijing is only reaching from great highs to greater heights.

It is in this context, that the Chinese President Xi Jinping's three-nation visit that included the Maldives, Sri Lanka and India in September 2014, has been welcomed by the region. At the same time China has invited all three nations to become a part of its MSR, which too has been welcomed by the region.

It is important to note that many in India till a couple of years ago were apprehensive of Maldives' ties with China, especially in terms of the strategic dimensions to the bilateral ties. At the same time the then prevailing environment in India, was apprehensive of the Chinese Navy that was participating in combating piracy that emanated from the coast of Somalia.

The Chinese diplomatic mission in the Maldives was inaugurated by the then President Nasheed a week before the Indian Prime Minister's scheduled visit to the Maldives for the 17th SAARC Summit, in 2011. For many in India, the timing of this event was seen in a negative light and the GMR issue that followed subsequently, added fuel to speculations.

However, any apprehensions of either a Chinese design for the Maldives in the context of India or Maldives hedging China against India has to be taken in an altogether different calculus.

Strategic Ties versus Economic Engagement

The touchy subject of upgrading the Ibrahim Nasir International Airport has now entered the history books. This is so as the original contract with GMR has been terminated and the Chinese President during his visit to the nation, has expressed China's interest in undertaking the same project, along with others.

On the other hand, in July of 2013, India and the Maldives along with Sri Lanka entered into a trilateral maritime security agreement. This agreement was signed at a time when the bilateral ties between both India and the Maldives and India and Sri Lanka, were perceived to have hit the rock bottom. On the Maldivian front, the GMR question loomed large, whereas with Sri Lanka it was its domestic challenges on the ethnic front that threw the spoke in the bilateral wheels.

The trilateral maritime security agreement which largely focuses on issues of Maritime Domain Awareness, has also factored in the inclusion of both Seychelles and Mauritius. At the same time since 2008, the Indian Navy and Coast Guard have been entrusted the responsibility of securing the exclusive economic zone of the latter two nations and that of the Maldives also.

In the light of the 26/11 terrorist attack in Mumbai, and the up gradation of coastal security in India, New Delhi is in the process of installing a number of radars to monitor its near seas. The Maldives is also a part of this project, wherein Indian installed surveillance systems in the archipelago will be integrated with those of New Delhi's. While the Indian helicopters at the Gan airfield are meant for securing the Maldivian waters.

Thus, the strategic and security related ties of the Maldives are largely in partnership with India, while its economic and trade ties are not necessary so. In fact, for a nation that is largely dependent upon international tourism, the Chinese contribution in this sector is more than significant. Nearly a quarter of all inbound tourists are from China. In fact, President Xi in his visit to the nation had requested his fellow countrymen to refrain from having instant noodles and savour the local cuisine. Xi's observations are not an opprobrium on the dietary practices of countrymen but also impact of the same in to the economy of the host nation, the Maldives.

Conclusion

The Maldives has moved far away from the days of Operation Cactus. In these many years, the Maldives has undergone significant changes. For a start, the nation has embraced democracy with full vigour and has accepted the challenges that it brings with it. Since 2008 domestic issues have become a matter of concern and importance.

In the past, the international perception of the Maldives was largely confined to its geostrategic location. However, in recent times, the domestic factor is also gaining prominence. Two reasons contribute to this. One is the structural change in the nature of Maldivian polity and two is the advent of multilateralism in world affairs.

As regards South Asia, principally India, the importance of the Maldivian archipelago is twofold. On the strategic front, the location of the archipelago influences the commercial shipping lanes that crisscross it. The shipping lane of the Indian Ocean, of which the Maldives is an integral part, is the lifeline for a number of nations. Thus the security concerns of the Maldives, which are both of internal origins and external threats, will have an impact on the sea lanes of communications. The incidence to the Operation Cactus is a pointer, though at that time the global scenario was not similar to what it is today. In the present day context, of international terrorism and piracy, multi-polar global security architecture, the Maldives is in the centre stage, at least in the context of the Indian Ocean.

Conversely, the domestic affairs of the Maldives, with respect to the region are of greater importance. Given the inherent contradiction is the style and systems of governance, the Maldives' tryst with democracy is seen with great interests. For India, New Delhi's relationship with most, if not all, neighbours has been partially held hostage by the internal political contradictions of the nations in question. Thus far, the Maldives has not fallen under this bracket but the possibility of the same cannot be ruled out.

At the same time the limited experience of Maldives ballot box can be attested as a negative vote in the past two elections to the office of the President. Both Gayoom in 2008 and Nasheed in 2013 lost the runoff round to their challenger; even when their individual share in the votes polled in the first round of polling was much higher than their nearest competitor.

Even though the electoral experience of this archipelago is limited, there lies a pattern that reflects a vibrant polity. This facet is welcomed and duly appreciated by the world's largest democracy. India clearly understands the complexities of a multiparty democratic system. Thus, for New Delhi the challenge lies not in engaging only with the state but also with individual constituents at all levels.

In short the importance of the Maldives is not only those attributes in the past that those that will make its presence felt in the near and distant future. And all this and more in the environment of climate change and global warming!

REFERENCES

1. Maldivian Population 2014, http://worldpopulationreview.com/countries/maldives-population/
2. Dr. N. Manoharan, Political Crisis in Maldives and India's Dilemma, http://www.vifindia.org/article/2013/february/22/political-crisis-in-maldives-and-indian-dilemma#sthash.Lgn5nIJk.dpuf
3. Ibid.

12

India-Maldives Relations in a Comprehensive Security Paradigm

T.C. Karthikheyan

Introduction

The Maldives is more than just pristine beaches and cocktail venues, and there are enough signs it will be proved right sooner than later. The island nation had consistently denied requests from the world and regional powers for any kind of military base, even refusing refueling facilities for the ships in one of their islands. There are two main reasons behind this. Firstly, given its inherent vulnerabilities in the form of its geographic structure, lack of natural resources and economic disadvantages, they had always maintained good relations with its neighbours. Secondly, it is their resolve to maintain the policy of non-alignment during the cold war, to derive possible benefits from the international community, antagonising none. Even after the end of the cold war, Maldives didn't contemplate letting any regional or world power to utilise their islands for military activities. Maldives had also been a prominent active member of the Alliance of Small Island States (AOSIS) that spearheads efforts in highlighting the problems of small island states on the issues of environmental degradation and economic problems for decades.

Maldives and the Indian Ocean Region

India has a larger stake in the India Ocean that inherently connects with its security and prosperity. Given its strategic importance and the emerging competition between the extra regional powers, the vast Indian Ocean and its contiguous waters present a wide range of security issues. It is thus imperative for India to address and to evolve a cooperative regime in the maritime security of the Indian Ocean where Maldives plays an important part.

On the backdrop of recent developments like piracy and seaborne terrorism, India has now taken the role of a leader in its sphere of influence using its naval capabilities. The Indian Navy is helping the Maldives to tackle piracy and its security concerns, and it has become increasingly important to secure the island territories, especially the ones that are uninhabited which could be used by the terrorists. India has initiated the process of putting viable cooperative mechanisms to harness the collective strength of states to secure the maritime domain in its vicinity. Consequently, it has beefed up its defence cooperation with Maldives commendably in recent years.

Maritime Security Cooperation

After the 2008 Mumbai 26/11 attack, the defence community took cognizance of the need to seal the permeability of India's costal security apparatus. Though there had been proposals to modernize and strengthen the coast guards even before the Mumbai attack, the need for urgent implementation was realized only after 26/11. This scenario prompted the defence establishment in India to ponder over the possibilities of putting in place an effective foolproof network on its waterfront areas and high seas to safeguard its national interests.

At the external level, India decided to increase its naval surveillance capabilities in the high seas on the Indian Ocean, where the possibility of terrorist attacks could emanate from and also putting in place of a well-coordinated mechanism to safeguard its territorial waters from intruders. Accordingly, the importance of cooperation with the Maldivians comes into prominence, wherein mutual assistance generates mutual benefits. The geographical structure of the Maldives itself poses numerable hurdles for its comprehensive security and India's role gains prominence in such a scenario. Lately, there had also been some extra regional powers' interest in Maldives and therefore, it is only sensible on part of India to create a cooperative structure for securing relevant national interests.

Advantages of Cooperation with Maldives

This cooperative mechanism has two advantages which is mutual in its outcomes. First, it serves the purpose of consolidating India's position in the Indian Ocean region and also ensures to be a reliable partner for the security of the Maldivian state. Secondly, it serves the economic interests of Maldives enormously by safeguarding its marine resources from poaching. This is of great significance given the fact that fishing is the mainstay of Maldivian economy.

Nevertheless, two major reasons could be attributed for India's assistance to Maldives. They are:

1. Extension of Indian military and economic influence in the South Asian region.
2. Curtailing possible Chinese influence on Maldives, thereby pre-empting the further strengthening of the Chinese strategy of "string of pearls".

India and Maldives has joined hands to keep the seas in their sphere of influence free from unwanted visitors. The Maldivians have understood the importance of cooperation with Indian security apparatus and they are more than willing to do so. This was emphatically put on by Maldivian Foreign Minister Mr. Ahmed Naseem at the end of his first visit to India in April 2011. The emerging cooperation follows the realisation that sanitation of the waters around the Maldives is vital to securing the Indian coast. If we cannot defend the Maldives, we cannot defend the Indian soft belly and cannot defend peninsular India.[1] Indian assistance was instrumental in the Maldives beefing up its surveillance and patrolling capability in the recent years.

Robust Engagements

India has always been more receptive to the demands of the Maldivian government of its security needs. The best example is "Operation Cactus",[2] to thwart the attempted coup on the Maldivian government in 1988 by the Sri Lankan mercenaries. The threat of non-state actors has plagued the Maldivian security system ever since. It is evident that the small island territories are particularly vulnerable to aggression by mercenaries, terrorists and even pirates.[3] To strengthen its security, Maldivian authorities requested for a patrol craft from the Indian government, to perform multiple tasks such as patrolling the exclusive economic zone. Consequently, India decommissioned one of its ships from the Indian Navy and transferred it to Maldives in April 2006 renaming it as '*Tillanchang*'.[4] It was a major part of the cooperation between the two nations in the fight against terrorism, piracy and smuggling under the broad framework of United Nations conventions. India has always been sensitive to the security needs of Maldives, a real source of strength indeed; and the later too has utmost regard to India's security sensitivities. Much of the context for evolving a mutually beneficial relationship is provided by the tension-free socio-historical settings under which both India and Maldives interact,[5] unlike India's relations with its other SAARC neighbours which are mired in ethno-religious socio-cultural tensions, border disputes, etc.

India–Maldives relation has been witnessing an increased cooperation on various fronts and the military strategic relationship stands out distinctively. While the two countries already have a security cooperation agreement against sea-borne terrorism and piracy, the framework of a detailed agreement to include Maldives into the Indian coastal security grid was drawn in 2009. It was conceived to be an exclusive security arrangement with India and the island nation will not approach other regional countries for similar agreements. The driving force behind these developments was triggered largely by fears of a hostage crisis in Maldives whose economy is driven largely by tourism. The threats of terrorists taking over populated islands and holding the nation for ransom has been a lingering problem.[6] But concerns about the possible ramifications on pursuing an independent policy and sovereignty, raised by local opposition parties in Maldives had cast a shadow on the realisation of these strategic plans. Despite this imbroglio, there has been improved cooperation on other strategic security needs.

Increased Strategic Cooperation

As noted earlier, besides transferring the fast attack craft *'Tillanchang'* to Maldives, a large number of officers of the armed forces of the island nation are given training regularly in various officers training academies in India. The Indian Army also conducts a joint exercise '*Ekueuvrin*' (meaning friends) with the Maldivian National Defence Forces (MDNF) from 2007 on counter-terrorism.[7] The MNDF officials acquired some of the Indian Army's invaluable operational experience through this training. This helps foster military-to-military cooperation and enhanced inter-operability, as against the 1988 operation undertaken to thwart the coup attempt, where the military used only a tourist book map of the island nation for their operations in the absence of a detailed one. It is to be noted here that the challenge was not to just remain alert or reactive to given situations but to be pro-active in dealing with disruptive forces like pirates, poachers and terrorists.

The effective implementation of the combined Indian Navy–MNDF exercises, hydrographic surveys, integrated surveillance and coordinated patrolling would address the security concerns of both the countries phenomenally. The Indian Coast Guard conducts an exercise on maritime rescue operations and patrolling of seas around Maldives called *'Dosti'* (meaning friendship). These joint operations are highly valuable for the MNDF in facing the modern challenges of terrorism, poaching, piracy, etc. Besides, Military teams from Maldives are also visiting the tri-services Andaman Nicobar Command (ANC) to observe how India manages security and surveillance of the critical island chain. Maldivian security personnel are also undergoing training at the Karnataka Police Academy in the Indian State of Karnataka on regular basis. In April 2010, India provided the '*Dhruv*' helicopter manufactured by Hindustan Aeronautics Ltd (HAL) re-painted with Maldivian flag and a sign saying MNDF. This was a result of India's commitment to deliver security equipments to Maldives according to its requirements.

India also undertook a refit work of the Maldivian Coast Guard Ship 'Huravee' of the MNDF and delivered it in February 2010.[8] 'Huravee' has now greatly enhanced the defence capabilities of Maldives at high seas. India has plugged an important missing cog in its defence structure in the Indian Ocean by channelising Indian Navy's capabilities to foster lasting strategic security cooperation with the Maldives. This is only the beginning of the valuable partnership, which will prove critical in validating India's strategic depth in the Indian Ocean. This has been validated in a US report that says "as its military capabilities grow, India will contribute to Asia as a net provider of security in the Indian Ocean and beyond".[9]

Furthering the maritime cooperation, a trilateral agreement on maritime cooperation was reached by India, Maldives and Sri Lanka on 9 July 2013 in the context of the need for a more robust maritime security environment in the Indian Ocean region. They signed an Outcome Document outlining further collaborative measures in the areas of Maritime Domain Awareness (MDA); strengthening coordination of maritime Search and Rescue (SAR); promoting marine oil pollution response cooperation; expanding 'DOSTI' (friendship) exercises; and sharing of information on illegal maritime activities and piracy.

The roadmap for future cooperation in all these areas was confirmed and some important aspects among others are as follows:

(a) to provide Maldives and Sri Lanka access to the Indian Long Range Identification and Tracking (LRIT) data to monitor and track their own flagged merchant vessels;
(b) to utilise the Merchant Ship Information System (MSIS) for exchange of unclassified information on white shipping (a fair and safe shipping procedures); and
(c) to share Automatic Identification System (AIS) data in a trilateral format over the MSIS platform.

India's maritime role in safeguarding the security, sovereignty and integrity of the Maldives is credible with consistency. The maritime trilateral agreement enables India to continue its traditional role in the region to patrol and safeguard the EEZs of its southern neighbours. Some of the aspects of the agreement specifically keep the Indian Navy and its security apparatus of being informed about what is happening in its southern neighborhood, thereby avoiding any exigency of being surprised by adverse developments in its vicinity. The current agreement provides the best opportunity and effective official mechanism to address some of the maritime security concerns shared by India and Maldives, and it is up to India to use these in a prudent manner to fulfill its national interest and strategic goals without giving any leeway to a third party.

The Political Relations

Maldives is a country which has never cited any concerns about India being a dominant player in the region and it has always maintained a smooth and friendly relationship with India. This stems from the historical linkages and interdependence exemplified by the way in which India has helped Maldives in ensuring is security in the realms of social and political. As seen earlier, the 1988 military intervention by India not only thwarted the takeover of the country by non-state actors, it also established political stability and continuity without any repercussions in the Maldivian society. India has regularly conducted training programmes for the Maldivian administrators and executives, and also played a major part in bringing democracy in Maldives through institutional cooperation. It was this kind of assistance in times of both peace and crisis situation that built mutual confidence and has kept India–Maldives relations intact.

Meanwhile, events took a critical turn in Maldives in February 2013, when in an unprecedented move, the former President Mr. Mohamed 'Anni' Nasheed took refuge in the Indian Mission in Malé to evade an arrest warrant issued by a magistrate's court in a case concerning the detention of the Chief Judge of the Criminal Court during his Presidency in January 2012. This particular episode created an intense diplomatic activity between the two countries. The background of this crisis shall be tracked back to the events that happened on 7 February 2012 when the transfer of power took place in Maldives under controversial circumstances. It is controversial because Nasheed says that he resigned his presidency "under duress" and the government of the day said that he resigned by himself. Some deeper analysis on this episode gives an impression that it was a well-orchestrated coup combining political opportunists, religious fundamentalist and some self-serving individuals. Nevertheless, the Indian leadership extended its "warm felicitation" to the new president and his government, immediately after the new president took office. At that time, India took a pragmatic decision of not interfering in its small neighbour's internal matters, which had repercussions within the Maldivian territory.

New Delhi witnessed these developments closely, though nothing concrete emerged on the normalization of the democratic ethos and governance in Malé as assured by the new government then. The former president Dr. Waheed, even failed to honour his assurance in protecting the $500 million investments of the Indian firm GMR infrastructure in developing the nation's main international airport and also to hold free and fair inclusive elections as soon as possible. The bone of contention was because; Malé viewed that there were terms in the GMR agreement concluded by Nasheed's regime that could not be implemented under the current Constitution and the legal system in Maldives. According to Maldivian law, no taxes could be levied without parliamentary approval, but the opposition parties claimed that the Nasheed's regime had authorised GMR to levy taxes in the agreement.

India's Approach towards the Political Crisis

Throughout that political crisis in Maldives, India had sought to maintain a balanced approach by giving equal importance to both the serving and the former Presidents of Maldives. Whenever they requested a meeting with the higher officials of the Indian government they were treated equally, though the former president Mr. Nasheed had enhanced existing cooperation by bringing in various initiatives that took India-Maldives relations to a new plane in his stint as President. By establishing a coordinated security apparatus by means of installing radars in the different atoll islands of Maldives in monitoring the crucial Indian Ocean region in its vicinity and linking it with the Indian coastal security grid, sharing intelligence on religious radicals and opening the large investment opportunities for the Indian firms and along with his democratic credentials, Nasheed gained the confidence of Indian leaders and administrators, before he was forced to "resign" on 7 Feb 2012.

India's unavoidable situation of diplomatic intervention when the former Maldivian president Nasheed took refuge in its Malé mission was necessitated by the fact that Maldives is now integral to India's maritime security policy in the Indian Ocean Region. As both the concerned parties in Maldives valued Delhi's support, India's intervention made the task of restoring democracy easier and earlier. Nonetheless, it has to be remembered that sustaining the democratic ethos entirely remains with the people of a country, which had been evident from the events unfolded after the Arab Spring. Realising this, on 18 February 2013, the former Indian External Affairs Minister Salman Khurshid observed, "The people of the Maldives have India's support. Whoever the people of the Maldives elect will have India's support. The Maldives can't change its history. The Maldives cannot deny the history of somebody who was President of Maldives. And we cannot deny the Maldives' present by saying that whatever there is at present is not to our liking. It's the people of Maldives who decide and whoever they decide as their elected leadership, we will respect".[10] This clearly stated India's perspective without any ambiguity and any preference for one person or the other. Intensive Indian diplomacy in those few days successfully defused the crisis when the former president left the Indian High Commission in Malé after his 11-day stay as a "guest".

From India's point of view, Nasheed taking refuge in its Malé office had provided an unintended and unprecedented occasion to restore contacts with the then Maldivian government and political leadership after the cancellation of the GMR contract on airport development. It positively gave both sides an opportunity to understand and appreciate that there is much more to bilateral relations than might have been understood by both sides. It is in this earnest effort, India is trying to further improve its relations with Maldives.

Rising Challenges to Democracy

The Maldives is facing a disturbing phenomenon with the growing religious extremism and this sometimes with political patronage too. There have been some instances of abduction of several men in recent times by a vigilante group in a push to identify and remove some activists advocating secularism or professing atheism. Currently Islam is being misused for undue advantage and political gain in Maldives. There are apprehensions from the opposition parties that the Maldivian authorities are using few extremist individuals for their short-term political gains, thereby giving these extremists a voice and influence in politics that they don't deserve. The fear is that the lack of actions by the authorities against these few individuals could endanger the hopes for a functional democracy and a peaceful society. In this context, former President Nasheed has accused leaders of the religious conservative Adhaalath Party of radicalising and indoctrinating youth to carry out these vigilante actions in the name of Islam.[11] He also opined that radical Islam is getting very stronger in the Maldives with their significant strength in important government institutions as well. The involvement of radicalized groups in abductions and killings has been brought out by the findings of the private investigation—conducted by Glasgow-based Athena Intelligence and Security—commissioned by human rights NGO Maldivian Democracy Network.

There are concerns that kidnappings, human rights violations and lack of transparency has caused waning of democratic ethos in Maldives. These developments greatly compromise the hopes for democracy and in turn the effective functioning of the pragmatic civil society will be at stake. Henceforth, it becomes imperative for India to strengthen the democratic process along with the economic and social security of Maldivian youth that could eventually weaken the radicalization of the Maldivian society. This in turn, in the long run shall minimize the negative ramifications on India's security.

With the formation of the "Al Qaeda in the Indian Subcontinent", India needs to be vigilant with what is happening in its southern neighbourhood. After the twin explosions aboard a train at the Chennai central railway station on May 1, security officials believed Pakistan's Inter-Services Intelligence directorate may have made inroads into Tamil Nadu. The arrest of a Sri Lankan, Zaheed Hussain, a couple of days before the blasts only substantiates the links. This has also been reinforced by the developments in September 2014 when the National Investigation Agency (NIA) arrested a Sri Lankan national, Arun Selvarajan in Chennai on the charges of spying on behalf of

Pakistan. On this backdrop, Pakistan's activities in Maldives should be followed closely so that the radical elements in Maldives were not used against India.

India's Economic Assistance to Maldives

India has been a committed partner in ensuring different aspects of security of the Maldives, in a variety of fields such as education, health, infrastructure, technology and equipment, environment, etc. The Indian government provided Rf. 5 billion worth of aid to the Maldives during the three-year period, 2009–11. In addition, line-of-credit facilities, bond purchase, standby credit facility and items, equipment and financial assistance worth $268 million was provided to hold the SAARC summit in Addu, according to the statistics of the Indian High Commission in Malé.[12] One of the largest contributions from India was towards the construction of Faculty of Tourism and Hospitality building. $2.5 million was granted as free assistance of the Indian government to assist in the development of human resources. India also agreed to assist with the military hospital established by the Maldives National Defence Force (MNDF). Private Indian companies are also vying for increased investments in different sectors.

India's Aid to Maldives in Recent Times (in US$ million)

Funds provided for	*Amount*
Development of Indira Gandhi Memorial Hospital	4.5
Towards building of Police Academy	25
Towards purchase of police vehicles	9
To Coastal Management Centre	1.15
For purchase of sports equipments and drugs	1
For the Institute for Information Technology	5.3
To build 500 housing units	40

Source: Raajje 2012.

During his visit to Maldives for the 17th SAARC summit in November 2011 the Indian prime minister announced a standby credit facility of $100 million for Maldives and promised help in setting up the Maldives Police Academy. The State Bank of India also subscribed fully to the $100 million in bonds issued by the Maldives Monetary Authority. Ambitious plans to enhance connectivity between the two countries to enhance trade and people-to-people contact were also signed.

Apart from heavy spending on military, another main shortcoming for the economic security of Maldives is the lack of quality higher education and skilled personnel on various fields. To address this, capacity building programmes and scholarship are provided by the international community to Maldivian students on a regular basis. Maldives Institute of Technical Education (MITE) was set up as a grant-in-aid project of Government of India in 1996. Having the capacity to train at least 200 students a year in various technical/vocational disciplines, in order to better reflect the academic programmes conducted by it, MITE was renamed as Faculty of Engineering Technology (FET).[13] This was the first higher learning institute in the country for technical education and without the active participation of India this would not have been possible. At present, this has been brought under the new Maldives National University established in 2011.

Pole and line method of fishing is the pride of Maldives, but this is becoming a bane due to the increased use of FADs (Fish Aggregation Devices) by international fishing companies, belonging mainly to Spain, France and Japan, and also Iran. The Maldivian fishing fleet is simply unable to compete due to its reliance on pole and line fishing methods. The under-resourced Maldivian coastguard is also unable to monitor the vastness of the Maldivian EEZ, and local fishermen rarely go beyond the 100 nautical miles (the EEZ is 200 miles). The maritime security cooperation agreement between India and Maldives addressed this concern by keeping a tag on the problem of poaching and over fishing by international companies in the EEZ of Maldives and thus helping to stabilize its economy.

Competitive Economic Scenario

While India may have the edge in terms of political clout and military cooperation, that is not the case when it comes to trade and economy. Apart from providing some regular financial assistance and aid facilities, India's presence in Maldivian trade and economy is not that much vibrant. In fact Sri Lanka and Thailand have more shares in these sectors and it is a matter of time before China becomes the largest trading partner with Maldives, unless India takes a pro-active policy measures in this regard.

China plays an important role in the Maldives' $1.5 billion economy. China provides maximum visitors to the tourism industry (30 percent of 1 million plus tourists in 2013), which earns 28 percent of gross domestic product and 90 percent of foreign exchange, with stays costing up to $1,000 a night at luxurious resorts. To negate these kind of strong Chinese influences on the other aspects of Sino–Maldivian relations, it has become important for India to continue to engage them, to stress opportunities for working together, on the economic, socio-political and military levels.

It the case of Maldives, China's interest and engagement has been steadily increasing over the years. China set up its embassy in Maldives in 2011 and has since been lobbying hard to get involved in the development of infrastructure in some of the strategically located islands of the archipelagic nation. Furthermore, during the turbulent political condition in 2012, there were open statements from some prominent Maldivian politicians and administrators to engage with China while shunning India in economic and strategic cooperation. On the strategic front, the former President Nasheed himself claimed that just a week before his ouster in February 2012, there was pressure on him from within Maldives to sign a defense cooperation agreement with China, which he ultimately refused to do. It has to be noted that China has long been actively wooing Maldives with the offers of economic assistance, infrastructure development and financial loans/grants, which the Maldives would find it difficult to refuse given the vulnerable condition of Maldives' economy.

In September 2014, Maldives passed a bill to facilitate and creating of Special Economic Zones with an aim to attract investment in manufacturing, free-trade, and offshore finance.[14] According to the Economic Minister Mohamed Saeed, it will push much industrial developments throughout all the major regions of the country that includes construction of harbors and establishment of bunkering facilities. India should seize the momentum to get hold of its share in these new developmental activities, or else it runs the risk of losing another important neighbor in terms of economic and strategic opportunities.

Environmental Cooperation

Sea-level rise is of particular concern to an atoll island state like Maldives. It is more vulnerable to the projected sea-level rise and the whole nation could go under the sea in the next 50 to 100 years as predicted by the United Nations Framework Convention on Climate Change report prepared by the Intergovernmental Panel on Climate Change. Rising sea level will also affect the marine environment with possible damage to coral reefs and fisheries. There is also the danger of inundation of outlying islands and damage to vegetation and freshwater resources through saline intrusion, as predicted by the IPCC. In Maldives, a far greater proportion of the population suffers from the potential effects of mere one metre sea-level rise and the survival of the people would be a challenge due to loss of land. On this background, in 2008 the former President Nasheed said that he would be setting up a "sovereign fund" to buy home land for his people, in case the effects of global warming and sea-level rise causes the country to disappear. One of the possible places, he said, would be India due to socio-cultural ties. It is a testimony of Maldives' faith and confidence on its neighbour and the cordial relationship it has developed without the problem of "Indophobia". But this project never took off as there is no international law to deal with these kinds of issues. In spite of this, India will be the prime destinations if a refugee situation occurs due to climate change and sea level rise, as India has a larger landmass and has a secular polity to accommodate the people of Maldives, unlike Sri Lanka where there had been instances of violent attacks on minorities of different religion in recent times and that will deter many Maldivians going to Sri Lanka. India's role during the 2004 tsunami has been commendable is helping Maldives by providing rescue missions, medicines and other equipments needed at that time.

India could also benefit from Maldives in safeguarding its island territories in Lakshadweep Islands and Andaman and Nicobar Islands by following some efficient environmental management practices that has been followed in Maldives for many years. India can benefit from the knowledge and training provided by Maldives in this aspect. It will also be helpful in protecting the coastal structures, villages and towns in the mainland India which are threatened by sea level rise. India will only benefit from its cooperation with Maldives in the environmental sphere.

Conclusion

Comprehensive cooperation between India and Maldives is indispensable in the Indian Ocean region, based on each state's dependence on the other, particularly in the military security and optimum utilisation of their knowledge, resources and capacities. They need to pool their assets, efforts and intelligence to deter security threats through mutual cooperation, complementing global arrangements placed within a comprehensive security structure.

Maldivian authorities had consistently expressed concerns over the crucial tasks of safeguarding their uninhabited islands and protecting their vast Exclusive Economic Zone (923,322 square kilometers), and India has been assisting this small nation, time and again to develop and enhance its maritime surveillance with aerial mobility capabilities and operational acumen. This is mainly due to the realisation on part of India that the national security concerns of Maldives cannot be de-linked from the security of the region. Efficient joint mechanisms with high technological inputs should be developed and installed on a continuous basis, to hinder the capacity and capability of the pirates and terrorists to disrupt and destroy maritime enterprise, and thus ensuring peaceful use of the Indian Ocean.[15]

Though India helps Maldives in upgrading its security, ties between the two were not uni-dimensional but also encompass economic, cultural and educational fields which have lot of scope for further development. The Indo-Maldives maritime cooperation agreement provides the much needed focus for India in improving its capacity to defend its vital interests in the Indian Ocean, as well as to reinforce its regional strategic pre-eminence. Meanwhile appropriate policy measures have to be devised to keep the Chinese and Sri Lankan influence on Maldives at a distance. India's relations with the Maldives have always been good and the maritime dimension offers greater prospects for trust-building through cooperation and mutual benefits, which will only grow from strength to strength ensuring a non-zero-sum matrix. For India, the strategic and investment priorities undertaken with Maldives will better enable success in today's operations, while preparing for tomorrow's threats.

While the pressure from international community did force the autocratic regime of Gayoom to respect the popular sentiments and initiated the democratic transition in 2004 is recognised, the truth is that sustaining a democracy and the institutional independence is a task that is best accomplished by domestic actors. If events in the past few years were to be a yardstick, then it has not been satisfactory and there are still some unrest lingering in the socio-politico space of Maldives. The Maldives' social-politico security has been hindered by a lack of consensus on religious extremism in the national political and societal framework. The situation is more complicated, as Maldives has entered into the world of being a functioning democracy just a few years ago. Since Maldives has been a closed society for a long time before its transition to a functioning democracy 2008, it has to witness a turbulent transition period, as proposed by Ian Bremmer in his 'J-curve' phenomenon,[16] before the fruits of changes are accepted and enjoyed by everyone.

India should make its presence felt by vigorously involving in trade and economic activities of the island nation other than providing financial assistance and aids. India should take the opportunity provided by the economic and liberalisation policies that are underway in Maldives, particularly on infrastructure and financial services. Maldives could become a serious competitor in financial services for many of the small countries which are tax havens at present. Rising sea level drastically affects the existence of Maldives and as a big neighbour it's a concern for India too with long term implications on its own security. Maldives also faces the mammoth challenge of successfully integrating its environmental concerns into their national policies and programmes, without affecting their economic and infrastructural development.

India's relationship with Maldives tends to have a Chinese dimension to it and that can't be avoided given the increasing nature of interdependence between them. It should also be kept in mind that Maldives is not a "shadow state" anymore vying for security of different nature from India alone. It has learned a lot from Sri Lankan policies and behavior, and will not hesitate to go and get anything it wants from china. The enthusiasm showed by Maldives and Sri Lanka on the Chinese proposal of a new maritime silk route is a case in point. These things should be taken seriously by the Indian policy makers and should not let another neighbour in the south go out of its influence.

REFERENCES

1. S. Dikshit, 'A Team of Three to Sanitise the Seas', The Hindu, 2011 [Online: web] Accessed 18 Sep. 2014. URL: http://www.hindu.com/2011/04/27/stories/2011042765541500.htm
2. Bewoor, A.G. undated, 'Operation Cactus: Reminesenses' [Online: web] Accessed 18 Sep. 2014 URL: http://www.bharat-rakshak.com/IAF/History/1988Cactus/Cactus01.html
3. Ibrahim H. Zaki and P. R. Mulay, *Small State Security Dilemma: A Maldivian Perception*, Lancer's Books, New Delhi, 2008, p. 104.
4. S. Dikshit, 'India transfers naval ship to Maldives', 2006, The Hindu, Online: web] Accessed 25 Sep. 2014. URL: http://www.hindu.com/2006/04/17/stories/2006041706371200.htm
5. P. Sahadevan, "Maldives", inMaj. Gen. Dipankar Banerjee (ed), *Security in South Asia*, Manas Publications, New Delhi, 1999, p. 254.
6. Jim Neff, andJustin Mayo, 2001, 'U.S. Ports Represent Weakness in Nation's Defenses: Analysis Shows', Tribune, [Online: web] Accessed 18 Aug. 2014 URL: http://www.military.com/Content/MoreContent/1,12044,FL_ports_103001,00.html
7. Ministry of Defence, 'India and Maldives to Tackle Sea-borne Terrorism', Press Information Bureau, India, 2009, [Online: web] Accessed 12 Aug. 2014 URL: http://pib.nic.in/newsite/erelease.aspx?relid=47230
8. *The Hindu*, '"Huravee" Handed over to Maldives After Refit', 2010, [Online: web] Accessed 8 Sep. 2014 URL: http://www.thehindu.com/2010/02/12/stories/2010021253660200.htm

9. United States of America, Quadrennial Defense Review Report, Department of Defense, 2010, [Online: web] Accessed 26 Aug. 2014 URL: http://www.defense.gov/qdr/qdr%20as%20of%2029jan10%201600.PDF p. 60.
10. Minivan News, 23 Sep. 2014, Nasheed accuses Adhaalath leaders of radicalizing the youth, [Online: web] Accessed 24 Sep. 2014 URL: http://minivannews.com/politics/nasheed-accuses-adhaalath-leaders-of-radicalising-youth-90225
11. Ibid.
12. J. J. Robinson and N. Ahmed, 'China's top legislator visits parliament, President', Minivan News, 2011, [Online: web] Accessed 22 Jun. 2014 URL: http://minivannews.com/politics/chinas-top-legislator-visits-parliament-president-20772
13. Ministry of External Affairs, 'India–Maldives Relations', 2012, [Online: web] Accessed 28 Sep. 2014 URL: http://mea.gov.in/Portal/ForeignRelation/Maldives-January-2012.pdf
14. Ministry of Trade and Economic Development, Government of Maldives. Special Economic Zones Act, 2014, [Online: web] Accessed 28 Sep. 2014 URL: http://www.trade.gov.mv/downloads/54080acf86332_SEZ%20Act%20Translation.pdf.
15. B. Chellaney, 'India—Regional Security Challenges', 2010, [Online: web] Accessed 16 September 2014 URL: http://www.kas.de/upload/dokumente/2010/06/PolDi-Asien_Panorama_02-2010/Panorama_2-2010_SecurityPolitics_Chellaney.pdf
16. I. Bremmer and J. Curve, *A New Way to Understand Why Nations Rise and Fall*, Simon & Schuster Paperbacks, New York, 2006.

13

Myanmar as a Factor in India's North East: Economic and Security Issues

Ashok Kumar and Kamal Kinger

Introduction

The North-Eastern tip of India consisting of contiguous states—Arunachal Pradesh, Assam, Manipur, Meghalaya, Mizoram, Nagaland, Tripura and Sikkim—constitutes a unique narrow passage way connecting the Indian sub-continent to Southeast Asia and East Asia and acts as a crucial corridor for human migration and development between these areas. The North Eastern Region (NER) occupies its favourable and strategic location as it shares international border with China, Myanmar and Bangladesh. Therefore, it is the only gateway for India to reach Southeast Asia and East Asia via Myanmar. India's NER is unique in terms of growth and opportunities which it offers by interlocking the region with the country's neighbours in the South Asia and South East Asia.[1] In terms of geographical size, Northeast India constitute about 8% of the total India's size, Northeast India's population (all 8 states combined) is approximately 40 million (2011 census). The Siliguri Corridor in West Bengal connects the NER with the main part of India. Northeast India is one of the most panoramic and strategic landscape of India.

Strategic Significance

The significance of this region has only grown over the years with its land linkages to Southeast Asia, and the 1080 km disputed border that it shares with China. There are some significant developments in this region, which have both regional and strategic implications. Apart from this, Northeast India has an extraordinarily important international strategic dimension and is a vital part of the nation's defence architecture. It is not only India's land bridge to Myanmar but also a gateway to Southeast Asia and beyond. The NER is endowed with human and a variety of natural resources such as uranium, coal, hydro-power, forests, oil and gas. Gifted with highly fertile land, the Northeast region is the world's largest producer of tea as well. It sits right in the hub of a geographical space which is home to nearly a billion people comprising the population of Bangladesh, Myanmar, Nepal, Bhutan, South Western China and the Association of South East Asian Nations (ASEAN). The ecstatic beauty of India's Northeast serves as an attractive tourist spot and its infrastructure is a hub of immense business potential.

Myanmar Factor

Myanmar occupies an important geographic location in Southeast Asia. The union of Myanmar lies in the northwest region of Southeast Asia, between the Tibetan plateau and the Malay Peninsula. Myanmar represents the 2nd largest landmass in Association of South East Asian Nations. Myanmar covers an area of 676,578 square kilometer and has population of 55 million (2013). Myanmar geo-strategically located at the tri junction of South Asia, East Asia and Southeast Asia, which serves a golden land bridge between India and prospering economies in the East Asia and Southeast Asia. Myanmar shares its international border with India (1643 km) and Bangladesh (193 km) in the west, with China (2185 km) in north, with Thailand (1800 km) and Laos (235 km) in the east. It also occupies a critical geostrategic position which often perceived to be a buffer state between the two Asian giants—India and China, who share a complicated relationship, with elements of cooperation and competition in their engagements, especially in the Asian region.

India and Myanmar's relationship officially got underway after the Treaty of Friendship was signed in 1951, after which the foundation for a more meaningful relationship was established. Myanmar is becoming increasingly important for India in both a strategic and economic context.[2] India has to tackle insurgency in the Northeast whose activities have had an adverse effect on development in the country. Porous border with Myanmar is attributed as contributing towards the insurgency problems in India's Northeast. As the long International boundary between India and Myanmar formally demarcated on 10 March 1967. The agreement between the two countries remains an artificial line dividing tribes such as the Singphos, Nagas, Kukis, Mizos, etc. These tribes however, continue to maintain strong linkages with their kin across the international divide. To maintain their age old ties, a unique arrangement called the Free Movement Regime (FMR) is in place, which permits the tribes residing along the border to travel 16 km across the boundary without visa restrictions, which has become a serious problem for both the countries as Kachin Independent Army (KIA), Chin National Front (CNF), National Socialist Council of Nagaland-Khaplang (NSCN-K), National Socialist Council of Nagaland-Isak-Muviah (NSCN-IM) and United Liberation Front of Assam (ULFA) like groups have been known to have cross-border linkages in providing shelters.[3] Four of India's politically sensitive North-eastern states, Arunachal Pradesh (520 km), Nagaland (215 km), Manipur (398 km) and Mizoram (510 km), share international border. On the other side, Kachin, Chin states and Sagaing region of Myanmar share land border with India.[4] These parts have been facing insurgency-related problems. Due to their ethnic connections, insurgent groups from the northeast of India not only receive shelter in Myanmar but also have operational bases.[5]

India's Look (Act) East Policy and Importance of Myanmar

India's Look East Policy has morphed into a proactive Act East Policy (AEP), which envisages accelerated across the board engagement between the two growth poles of a vibrant Asia. It has become an important focal point which is a solid domain in orchestrating India's AEP. There are ample possibilities for Northeast India to reap benefits from India's thriving relations with South East Asia as the process of globalisation provides the countries with the opportunities to grapple with cross-market accessibility and enabling them alleviate their poverty and economic backwardness. Commerce, culture and connectivity are the three pillars of India's robust engagement with ASEAN. In the economic arena, the India-ASEAN relations are poised to scale new frontiers.

India's Northeast is still striving for an enduring and uninterrupted connectivity with its eastern neighbours. In other words, India's AEP cannot be realised unless the land to land links are fortified and consequently borders made immaterial on matters of trade and economic collaboration between these regions. India's Northeast states and Myanmar are inescapable on this roadmap to greater connectivity and collaboration between India and Southeast Asia. In fact these regions that have been long neglected and undermined have found pre-eminence as a crucial focus and a means to India's AEP. Moreover, Myanmar is also unique for being strategically significant to India's security. Myanmar has also taken on along with India the onus of common regional problems like drug trafficking, arms smuggling and insurgent movements.

As Myanmar is an immediate neighbour of vital importance for defence and internal security needs, stability and development in the NER and expansion of India influence in the Bay of Bengal area and Southeast Asia.[6] Myanmar has been considered a gateway to South East Asia and the only country in Association of Southeast Asian Nations (ASEAN) with which India shares a 1643 km long land border most part of it is unfenced and a substantial coastline of 1930 km wide open on the Andaman Sea and the Bay of Bengal posing strategic challenge to India's eastern frontier.

Myanmar is being a part of the Golden Triangle including Thailand and Laos, though, the border region has been the theatre of criminal activities such as smuggling and illegal trade in narcotics, fake currency and sources of arms supplies which have caused serious problems to India's security. India also shares the strategic waters of Bay of Bengal including the strategically important area of Andaman and Nicobar Island where the two closest Andaman and Myanmar's Coco islands are barely 30 kilometres apart. This geographical proximity between the two countries translated into long-standing trade relations across land borders and the sea route. Myanmar is perceived to be a Chinese proxy for balancing India in the region. While for China, Myanmar acts as a gateway to India's sphere of influence the Bay of Bengal and the Andaman and Nicobar Islands.[7] These factors contribute to India's rising security concerns as China's strategic interests in Myanmar pose serious threats to India's maritime and economic interests in the Indian Ocean.[8] Based on these geographical proximities, India's strategic interests in Myanmar through Northeast are also pragmatically calculated as:

(i) India sees Myanmar as an active player in suppressing the insurgents in northeast India;
(ii) The bridge for India's implementation of its 'AEP';
(iii) An important energy resource base; and
(iv) A significant barrier to the Chinese presence in Indian Ocean.

China–Myanmar Strained Relations

China's relation with Myanmar has undergone change in recent times. The military junta of Myanmar had been dependent on Beijing for support for decades but after Myanmar started taking baby-steps towards democracy, the over-dependence on China began decreasing. Anti-Beijing sentiments also became visible in Myanmar where the Chinese made massive investments over the years. As Chinese were exploiting Myanmar's own resources and President Thein Sein even suspended the Myitsone Dam project which was meant to supply electricity to China.

These rapid changes in Myanmar's domestic politics brought serious challenges to both China's existing interests in the country and its strategic planning for the future. Early in the year, after the March inauguration of the new Myanmar government, China possessed a well-developed strategic blueprint for its relations with its south western neighbour. Key elements of this blueprint—border stability, energy transportation, and economic cooperation remained China's basic considerations in Myanmar.[9] Beijing, however, began to envision and foster an additional layer of strategic cooperation based on the traditional fraternal friendship and economic ties between the two nations. This has certainly made China nervous. On the other side, India can utilise this opportunity to revive and enhance its relation with Myanmar and so on.

But, this point cannot be neglected that Myanmar is of great strategic significance to both India and China. China's continuous presence and its role in Myanmar is a matter of worry for India. In the early years of the military regime, India pushed hard that a democratic system should be established in Myanmar. Meanwhile, China has become an increasingly attractive source of low-interest loans, grants, development projects, technical assistance to Myanmar. India has already realised that the main beneficiary of strained India-Myanmar relations was China, whether for access to all important hydrocarbon energy sources and transport corridors. China is investing heavily in infrastructure, mining projects, hydropower dams and oil-gas pipelines to help southern China's growing energy needs and gaining greater access to the Indian Ocean through Myanmar. The China-funded Kyaukphyu port project with road link and gas and oil pipelines to Yunnan in China is likely to be completed in the next few months. This would provide China a direct strategic access to the Indian Ocean by passing the choke point at Malacca Strait.[10] Its natural presence in the Coco Island of Myanmar is in the name to ensure the security of piracy affected Strait of Malacca through which its oil carrying tankers pass is also a cause of worry for India.[11]

India's Northeast and Southeast Asia

The AEP is being embarked upon with the presupposition that the improving trade ties between India and ASEAN will certainly elevate the Northeast out of the menace of insurgency, poverty and economic backwardness. The AEP is expected to usher in a new era of development for the Northeast through network of pipelines, connectivity, communication and trade.[12]

The ASEAN-India vision document 2020 and India-ASEAN car rally was a notable initiative undertaken by the Indian government to emphasise on the geographic proximity between Northeast India and Southeast Asia. Moreover, India has undertaken some bilateral and multilateral projects for boosting connectivity between the Northeast and Southeast Asia. The important ongoing and potential infrastructure projects in this regard are Moreh-Tamu-Kalewa Road, India-Myanmar-Thailand Trilateral Highway, Trans Asian Highway, India-Myanmar rail linkages, Kaladan Multimodal project, the Stilwell road, Myanmar-India-Bangladesh gas or oil pipeline, Tamanthi Hydroelectricity project and optical fibre network between Northeast India and Southeast Asia.[13] But certain obstacles like lack of infrastructural development, absence of enthusiastic response from local people, frequent insurgencies, poor governance in the states, the easy availability of arms and weapons from across the international border to be utilised in armed movements and criminal activities impede increased relations between Northeast India and South East Asia. Moreover, the geographic location of the North-Eastern region makes it more vulnerable to be the core of hostility with massive negative outcomes. There are enough avenues through which Northeast India can be related to Southeast Asia. Racial, linguistic and cultural similarity prevails among the people of Northeast India and those of Southeast Asia. If the concerned governments really strive to translate their policies into reality their collaborative endeavours would invariably revive age old cultural and historical bonds.

There has been exchange of peoples, goods and services between our Northeast and countries of Southeast Asia through centuries. The Ahoms of Assam migrated several centuries ago from the Shan state of Burma where the language spoken is almost identical to that spoken in Laos and Thailand. The Chins from Myanmar migrated over the past centuries to Manipur and

Meiteis of Manipur have ties for over 2000 years with the Burmans of Myanmar. Similar migration has also occurred to Northeast from Yunan province of China. Boosting people to people contact transcending political barriers is an imperative for facilitating cultural interaction among various regions.[14]

With the economic rise of China and India, Asia has become the cardinal point of global geopolitical change. In the process of redistribution of spheres of influence between China and the United States, Southeast Asia has a key role. There Myanmar's location between India and Southeast Asia, as well as common land borders with China, gives the country a unique bridging function. Myanmar long coastline on the Gulf on Bengal provides control of the eastern Indian Ocean. Here major transport routes are located for oil from Africa and the Middle East to China, Japan and South Korea.[15]

In contemporary era, physical connectivity is of utmost importance as it channelizes the means to accelerate the movement of goods, people and services and thereby acts as a gateway to reviving economic enterprise. Advanced communication and interaction would foster trade, commerce and tourism prospects in the entire NER. But because of the existing hurdles the people of NER are quite apprehensive about the developmental strategies and consider it as mere rhetoric. The people of the Northeast should not feel ostracised from the mainstream one and simultaneously need to be convinced of the genuine concern of the government about the overall betterment and security of the region. The development of the region is a stepping stone towards the success of the policy. For utmost achievement India and ASEAN should be steadily oriented towards their innovative measures with the adequate knowledge of their common interests and gains. India should devote its potential to utilise the available resources in the Northeast in their best possible way. The existing opportunities and the challenges are to be assessed and grappled skilfully. Northeast India and Southeast Asia must grasp the skill of understanding each other proficiencies, should pay tribute to each other potential and must reveal greater endurance towards each other drawbacks. Cooperative endeavours based on mutual trust and confidence will lead to enduring development and proper accomplishment of the Policy.

Myanmar as an Economic Opportunity

Myanmar is located in a region which has experienced tremendous economic growth over the past two decades. Myanmar is one of the most resource-rich countries in Southeast Asia. Myanmar has abundant natural resources including land, water, forest, coal, mineral and marine resources, natural gas and petroleum.[16] Its wealth is not limited to natural gas and oil below the offshore seabed. The maritime economic zone of the country offers an enormous wealth of fish and seafood. In the British colonial period, Myanmar was the world's largest rice exporter and could move up again at the world's top position. The tourism potential is highly estimated and offers the prospect of tens of thousands of jobs in the service sector.

But despite its abundant resources, Myanmar's exports are still lagging behind as compared to its neighbours. The US led and often self imposed periods of isolation have dealt a blow to the people of Myanmar. The country's unsuccessful economic policies and repression at the hands of the military junta, coupled with periodic economic embargoes have made Myanmar a prototype for the ill effects of military subjugation and isolation. The 2007 uprising against the military regime were symptomatic of not only an ailing civil society infrastructure but more importantly, it was an act of public disobedience against an imposed destitution upon an otherwise well endowed country. The internal unrest in both the region of India as well as Myanmar, has affected border trade and connectivity between the two countries. India signed a border trade agreement in 1994 to open up two trading points along the India-Myanmar border. In an effort to promote the agreement, in 2008 India-Myanmar upgraded bilateral trade relations from Border Trade to Normal Trade, with only two border trade points with Myanmar, at Moreh-Tamu and Zowkhatar-Rhi, and another proposed at Avakhung-Pansat/ Somrai.[17]

The Trilateral Highway among India, Myanmar and Thailand will boost trade, especially between Southeast Asia and our own North Eastern states. It will also facilitate the movement of people, thereby increasing small business trades, skills-building exchanges and pilgrimages. A project with greater potential for India-Myanmar connectivity is the Kaladan Multi-modal Transit Transport Project, which includes rail and port development. India signed a Bilateral Investment Promotion Agreement (BIPA) and Double Tax Avoidance Agreement (DTAA) with Myanmar in 2008. Both countries are signatories to the India-ASEAN Trade in Goods Agreement of August 2009. This will help to achieve our bilateral goals of increasing trade from the current $2 billion to $3 billion by 2015. India signed a MoU in May 2012, during the Prime Minister's visit to Myanmar, to extend a line of credit of $500 million to the government of Myanmar, to be used for infrastructure development projects of the state in agriculture, rail transportation and electric power. As Myanmar is primarily an agricultural economy, the governments have sought greater partnership in developing this sector through initiatives like the Advanced Centre for Agricultural Research and Education.[18]

Myanmar is second golden gateway to ASEAN for India as it is the only country of this group which has a land and maritime boundary with India. With a becoming full dialogue partner of ASEAN since 1995, improved relations with Myanmar will be beneficial in many respects. Myanmar and India are also members of similar sub-regional group such as the BIMSTEC and MGC. These groups are to create an enabling environment for rapid economic development, accelerate social progress in the sub-region and promote active collaboration and mutual assistance on matters of common interests.

Recent Developments in Myanmar: Opportunities for India

Since 2011, the Thein Sein government has ushered in many positive changes—release of political prisoners, greater media freedom and several reforms in the economic, social and administrative spheres. Despite a 25 per cent reservation for the military and the strong presence of Members of Parliament from the military-rooted ruling Union Solidarity and Development Party (USDP), Parliament too has evolved into an active deliberative and lawmaking forum. The changes have brought Myanmar back into the international mainstream after five decades of military rule and its chairmanship of ASEAN this year has gone off quite smoothly. Myanmar is now our most rapidly growing neighbour experiencing eight per cent plus growth rates. There can be mutual benefit if both India and Myanmar can work together to truly transform the evolving connectivity corridors into development corridors, which can also be a demonstration of our 'Act East' policy. Building an interlaced economic partnership across the border can form an enduring bond between the two countries that already enjoy very good political ties. India's AEP should particularly focus in the long run and it must include not only the booming Southeast Asian economies but also Myanmar and countries in the Asia-Pacific such as Vietnam, Laos, Cambodia, North and South Korea. Engaging Japan shall be particularly helpful in honing the counter-China strategies. Unless a proactive realist approach is taken it shall be quite hard to become a permanent or substantial fixture in the East Asian political-economic landscape.

A diversity of foreign direct investment in Myanmar shall certainly be a more desirable option for India than reckoning with an ominous monopoly. Another major reform was passed in November 2012—the introduction of a new Foreign Investment Law aimed at attracting outside companies to establish businesses in Myanmar and provide much-needed employment and infrastructure. The legislation permits fully foreign-owned firms to operate in the country.

Myanmar had invited India to invest in infrastructure. Accordingly, in May 2012 several agreements and MoUs were signed between the two sides to improve connectivity by air, road and multi-modal transport. A year later, post-WEF India has offered Myanmar USD 150 million to establish a Special Economic Zone in Sittwe. It will be linked to Kolkata via sea. Crucially, Myanmar's infrastructure will also link India to Southeast Asia. The infrastructure investment process is aided by India continuing its 2012 deal to provide Myanmar with USD 500 million dollars as a credit line for development projects.

India has been helping Myanmar build institutional capacity and develop areas such as information technology, this often gets overshadowed by assistance from other countries—especially China—with cumulative foreign direct investment in Myanmar reaching $14 billion in June 2014. Chinese trade with Myanmar was $6 billion in 2013, while Indian-Myanmar trade was touching $2 billion, yet it is nowhere near China's investment. There are several other areas where India continues a keen FDI policy with Myanmar. The transitioning economy also desires Indian investments. In June 2013 the government of India announced it had committed investments worth $2.6 billion to Myanmar. India and Myanmar set a bilateral target of increasing trade, worth USD 1.872 billion in 2012, to $3 billion by 2015. To achieve the objective India will have to raise its low exports of only USD 542 million. Increasing exports in goods may be a slow process given Myanmar's young industrial base and low per-capita income. Indian investors have an advantage in service sectors of IT and education. They will support the burgeoning investments in manufacturing, agriculture, automobiles, pharmaceuticals and healthcare.

There are Projects executed by Indian companies in recent years cover a variety of sectors such as roads, railways, telecommunication, automotive, energy and remote sensing. Construction and upgrading of Tamu-Kalemyo-Kalewa road has been completed. RITES has been assisting Myanmar in improving its railway transport system. ISRO set up and subsequently upgraded a data processing centre for remote sensing applications. Tatas have set up a turbo-truck assembly plant with assistance from a line of credit by the Indian government. Earlier, a project for high-speed link in 32 Myanmar cities was completed by the telecommunication company, TCIL. Three leading companies—OVL, GAIL and Essar—have been active in the energy sector. The development of the Tamanthi and Shwezaye hydroelectric power projection Chindwin River valley by NHPC, setting up of a heavy turbo-truck assembly plant by TATA Motors, setting up of India-Myanmar Industrial Training Centre, and Myanmar-India Entrepreneurship Development Centre, India-Myanmar Centre for Enhancement of IT Skills.[19]

A democratising Myanmar offers the Indian government a scope for engagement over wide-ranging issues of governance and institution-building. The democratic India remains the largest and best practicing democracy in its vicinity, possessing decades of experience of managing dissent and diversity. Moreover, a democratising Myanmar bridges the gap between India's normative positions of pro-democracy and its pragmatic approach of constructive engagement with the military leadership. India, despite its engagement with the military-ruled Myanmar, found it difficult to reconcile the domestic support for democratic movements in Myanmar and the strategic imperative of engaging the latter. This reconciliation can allow India to concentrate its resources on developing relations with Myanmar. Finally, a democratising Myanmar allows India to tap onto the biggest resource base of engagement—pro-democracy leaders and support groups operating in India. The return of these exiles to their country can further help India strengthen its constituencies within the political leadership of Myanmar.

India can also get benefit from the possibility of greater coordination and investment of resources and strategies in combating transnational crimes in India's northeast, such as armed insurgency, trafficking in drugs, arms and human beings, and illegal cross-border migration. Moreover, the positive changes in Myanmar may reduce the flow of illegal cross-border movement of people that has proved to be an important carrier and conduit of cross-border trafficking in arms and drugs and overall instability along the border.

In the current scenario, India can engage Myanmar more freely and widen the arena of engagement including defence and security cooperation. Nevertheless, the opening up of Myanmar also poses an important challenge to India's engagement with Myanmar. In the presence of other players, India has to be more attentive to Myanmar's concerns and proactive in its policy initiatives for bilateral and multilateral cooperation. Otherwise, India might see the strategic space being taken over by other players both from the West as well as the East.

Conclusion

India's policies have undergone a change over the last two decades where India strengthened its economic, political, security, and civilisation links with the rest of Asia. To cope with the global financial turmoil, India however should become even more persistent and proficient in deepening its linkages with the rest of Asia, while strengthening its capacities to meet its developmental challenges. To accomplish this task, India will need to develop far greater expertise in geo-economics, an area which has not received the requisite attention. India should also consider establishing a well-funded resources, think-tank for researching, debating, communicating, and influencing foreign policy issues and options. This will also enable India to better communicate its intentions to rest of the world, including its partners in Asia. The AEP is expected to usher in a new era of development for the Northeast through network of pipelines, connectivity, communication and trade. Effective trade and transportation links between India and Myanmar can improve market size for potential investments. Myanmar should be considered India's second golden bridge (after Northeast) to Southeast Asia, and thus a crucial component for its AEP.

India and China share a competitive economic and security interests in Myanmar but there has not yet been any direct challenge to each other's national interest. It is the commonality of aspirations that is resulting into the threat perceptions whereby China's increasing presence in Myanmar is causing uneasiness in the Indian security perspectives. India should equip itself well in the sphere of diplomacy, and his emphasis must be on connectivity and the building of shared values with neighbours has resonance in Myanmar. It remains to be seen whether he can sell India's strengths effectively and infuse the economic and strategic bilateral relationship with a much-needed dose of dynamism.

India has perhaps found its wings as far as building bilateral and multilateral alliances with most ASEAN member states in the commerce, cultural and defence sectors. However, the Policies are not yet on firm footing with Myanmar. In this regard it is worth noting that neither of these countries are conventionally liberal market economies or democracies. Perhaps herein lays a rationalisation for their natural camaraderie and also India's inability to make substantial headway, competitively. In order to have an enduring and fruitful relationship with the ASEAN countries, India should go beyond the institutionalised avenues of ASEAN summits and partake in shrewd real politics. This warrants a competitive streak when it is open for major commercial and defence agreement, especially with regards to a resource rich and strategically well placed country like Myanmar.

REFERENCES

1. Ministry of Development of North Eastern Region, Government of India, "Look East Policy and NER", February 2011, at http://mdoner.gov.in/content/aspects-of-lep (Accessed on 12 sep, 2014)
2. http://thediplomat.com/2014/08/the-strategic-importance-of-myanmar-for-india/ (Accessed on 23 Sep, 2015)
3. Pushpita Das (2013), "India-Myanmar Border Problem: Fencing not only the Solution", IDSA Comments, at http://idsa.in/idsacomments/IndiaMyanmarBorderProblems_pdas_151113
4. R. Bhattacharya (2010), "Does Economic Cooperation Improve Security Situation: The Case of India-Myanmar Relations", *Asia-Pacific Journal of Social Sciences*, Special Issue No.1, p. 74
5. Y. Singh (2007), "India's Myanmar Policy: A Dilemma between Realism and Idealism", *IPCS Special Report*, No. 37, at http://www.ipcs.org/pdf_file/issue/928587478IPCS-Special-Report-37.pdf
6. K. Kinger and H.P. Kaur (2014), "India, China and String of Pearls", *Suraksha Chintan*, Vol. 9(9), p. 167.
7. Jash Amrita (2014), "China in India's Look East-Myanmar: Strategic Interests and Security Concerns", *International Research Journal of Social Sciences*, Vol. 3(6), p. 54.
8. Ibid., 56.
9. SUN, Yun (2012), "China's Strategic Misjudgement on Myanmar", *Journal of Current Southeast Asian Affairs*, 31 (1), 73-96.
10. R. Hariharan (2013), "Sustaining change in Myanmar", South Asia Analysis Group, paper 5439, at http://www.southasiaanalysis.org/node/1218 (Accessed on 09 Sep 2014).
11. Zhiquen Zhu (2010), *China's New Diplomacy: Rational, Strategies and Significance*, Ashgate Publishing Ltd., United Kingdom.
12. Thongkholal Haokip (2010), "India's Look East Policy: Prospects and Challenges for Northeast India", Presidency University, Kolkata.
13. Julien Levesque (2008), Northeast in India's Look East Policy, *Institute of Peace and Conflict Studies*, New Delhi, at http://www.ipcs.org/seminar/india/northeast-in-indias-look-east-policy-633.html (Accessed on 11 Oct, 2014)
14. S.S. Mazumdar, "The Northeast steering India's look east policy", *Manipur online*, 07 January, 2011, at http://manipuronline.com/look-east-policy/the-north-east-steering-indias-look-east-policy/2011/01/07 (Accessed on 05 Nov,2014)
15. A. Wilfried (2011), "Geostrategic importance of Myanmar increasing", Eurasisches Magazin (Germany) at www.eurasischesmagazin.de/artikel/?artikelID=20110805 (Accessed on 25 Oct 2014)

16. Ministry of Health– Government of Myanmar, Country Profile-Natural Resources (2013), at http://www.moh.gov.mm/file/COUNTRY%20PROFILE.pdf
17. Ministry of Development of NER, GOI, Border Trade,(2014) *http://www.mdoner.gov.in/content/border-trade (Accessed on 08 Oct 2014)*
18. S. Ramaswamy & T.S. Maini, "The Strategic importance of Myanmar for India", *The Diplomat,* August 12, 2014 http://thediplomat.com/2014/08/the-strategic-importance-of-myanmar-for-india/ (Accessed on 15 Sep 2014)
19. B.P. Routrey (2011), "India-Myanmar Relations: Triumph of Pragmatism", *Jindal School of International Affairs,* Vol 1(1).

14

India-Nepal Relations: Evaluating Security Implications

Narender Kumar

Introduction

Nepal is emerging as a key nation for India and China to secure their regional and vital strategic interests. Although the Himalayan Kingdom has been traditionally an Indian ally, but the changing strategic and economic realities are indicative of the fact that national interests are permanent and the rest is dynamic in nature. India cannot take Nepal for granted anymore; therefore, it calls for a relook at the future trajectory of friendship which should be based on mutual growth and equality. Nepal needs India as much as India needs Nepal, since economic and security scenario in the subcontinent is changing and has serious implications to the peace and stability of both nations. It is a challenge for India to forge a strong bond of friendship without disturbing the fragile political and economic stability in Nepal. It is also a fact that Nepal will expect economic growth and investment in infrastructure which is not loaded entirely towards India, rather it must also protect their long-term interests in return. Let there be no doubt, Nepal is playing India and China cards well for economic development of the Himalayan Kingdom.

Chanakya had said, "neighbouring states are most relevant in foreign policy". Nepal holds special significance to India, because, it is the second nation with Hindu majority; it is a buffer between India and China; and it continues to secure the flank against any Chinese foray across the Himalayas. Nepal is a geographical paradox in itself. It is a landlocked nation, but blessed by rich natural resources. It is sandwiched between the two nuclear nations and holds strategic significance for India and China. Nepal is water surplus, land surplus, resource surplus, yet it is food deficient, power deficient and infrastructure deficient. Nepal has 42000 MW identified hydro power potential and at the moment state has been able to exploit only 01% potential. Nepal can sustain the national economy by the tourism industry and exporting electricity. It is expected that if both these fields are exploited, Nepal will no more be considered a poor nation.

India shares 1,753 kilometres of open International Borders with Nepal. Five Indian states, Sikkim, West Bengal, Bihar, Uttar Pradesh and Uttarakhand share borders with Nepal. India and Nepal has resolved and demarcated 98% of borders, which does not run along defined geographical landmarks except Kali Nadi in the West. There are two areas of dispute which remains unresolved, Kalapani on the Western flank of Nepal and Susta on the Eastern flank. Notwithstanding the unresolved areas of border, both nations have displayed the maturity and it is unlikely that it will create turbulence in developing strategic partnership between India and Nepal. On the other side Nepal shares its Northern Border with Tibet Autonomous Region (TAR). China was weary of the Tibetan movement from either side, since China perceived that infiltration and ex-filtration of Tibetans may cause instability in TAR. As a result, China is making all possible efforts to maintain passive footprints in Nepal to prevent Nepalese territory being used by Tibetan Diaspora to cause instability in Tibet.

Nepal is second biggest Hindu nation after India. The religious and demographic distribution is, Hindu 81.3%, Buddhist 9%, Muslim 4.4%, Kirant 3.1%, Christian 1.4%, other 0.5%, unspecified 0.2% (2011 EST.).[1] Nepal has been culturally closest to India for centuries, people to people contact, religious affinity, social and family bonds and large ethnically identical population on both sides of the International Border in fact establishes a strong unbroken bond between two nations. For centuries Nepalese people have been coming to India for work and trade, this has integrated the citizens of two nations socially and culturally. Even today the people enjoy unrestricted travel for work on either side.

Nepal was unified by King Prithvinarayan Shah in 1746. He had cautioned his countrymen that they need to be careful since Nepal is sandwiched between two giants. At that time Nepalese chose to come down to India from the mountains for salt and succour. Since then the relationship between India and Nepal has been a roller coaster ride. Sometime gravitating towards India and at times to China. The unwise action of Rajiv Gandhi government to establish economic blockade was not appreciated by Nepal since it hurt people more than the government. The monarchy was slowly drifting away from India and had established a close relationship with China to counter the Indian influence, as India was perceived to have closer relations with democratic forces in Nepal.[2] Nepal has gone through political turmoil and nation has denounced monarchy and adopted democracy. The Communist uprising shook the very foundation of the nation and is slowly emerging out of the shadow of the bloody trail which almost led to a complete chaos and anarchy. This uprising was also a reminder to India that diplomatic influence and passive control of India over Nepal will not be endured for long and it is time that Nepal emerges out of the shadow of India. This has cast a serious question over Indo-Nepal Peace and Friendship Treaty of 1950. Though the treaty has come under severe strain since it is considered unequal by Nepalese political hierarchy, as a result China wanted to fish in troubled water to get the treaty annulled through the Communist Party of Nepal. There maybe a need to take a re-look at the treaty in the light of the fact that Nepal has an alternative for imports of essential commodity, including oil, since, China has developed railroad connectivity to Nepal through Tibet. It has set a scorching pace to reach Kathmandu and is on the way to eliminate total dependence of Nepal on India. This has other ramifications since China willy-nilly will expand its strategic boundaries right up to the banks of river Ganges. Constitution formulation is an important instrument and in the author's opinion will lay down the trajectory of the future relations of Nepal with India. However, it is unwise to overtly advise Nepal what should be the broad framework of the constitution. India should not be seen as an interested party in constitution formulation.

Nepal is a Victim of Component of Modern Instability

An unstable Nepal is more dangerous than a neutral Nepal for India. The predicament is that Nepal is a victim of component of modern instability such as political instability, uncertain economic growth, corruption, the nexus between criminals and drug traffickers, home to non-state actors, poverty and the threat of natural disasters. Under the circumstances Nepal is not in a position to steer through this complex situation on its own. It maybe injudicious to abandon Nepal to fend for itself, therefore, at this juncture, Nepal need assistance and support from India to make a smooth transition from uncontrolled chaos to a stable democratic nation. It is incumbent upon India to prevent Nepal becoming another Afghanistan. Care must be taken that whatever assistance and support India provides to Nepal, should not give an impression of big brother or a favour. India, principally should develop a relationship with Nepal as equal partners.

Uneven Development a Factor for Instability

Nepal is in need of infrastructure development, communication, connectivity and linking geography with the economy. Most of the problems of Nepal are linked to lack of economic empowerment of the people and neglect of rural areas. The social scientists have determined that conflict in Nepal was primarily due to lack of development, but the conflict also became an impediment to development. Nepal has the lowest per capita income among the SAARC nations and one of the primary reasons is the conflict and monarchy. Conflict prevented development and economic outreach and monarchy concentrated all their efforts to keep Kathmandu and few important power centres happy. As a result development was restricted to areas in close proximity to Kathmandu and few city centres and rural Nepal was completely neglected. Nepal is going through political, social and economic instability which is a cause of concern for India. This scenario is allowing state and non-state actors to find safe sanctuary in Nepal. If this trend is not arrested, it will cause turbulence in India, Bhutan and even Nepal itself.

Internal Instability a Turning Point

Nepal has seen political turbulence and transition. The conflict claimed the lives of 17,000 people, displaced an estimated 100,000 and ultimately brought about the abolition of a 240-year-old monarchy.[3] The transition has not been smooth; it has divided the Himalayan Kingdom between extreme left wing ideology and multi-party democratic values. The Comprehensive Peace Agreement of 2006 was designed to create a permanent peace, but, whilst progress has been made, challenges remain; politicians are yet to agree on a new constitution and the country remains plagued by political instability.[4] If Nepal chose to adopt "Left Wing Ideology" it will have deep impact on regional security construct, which has the potential to destabilise Nepal and even India. The civil war maybe over, but Nepal's fragile peace continues to be tested.[5] India favours multi-party democracy than an autocratic state under communists or Monarchy, whereas China would like Nepal to be under communist regime. Nepal's future trajectory has kept India and China on the edge as both nations are jostling for retaining passive control over the Himalayan Kingdom.

Nepal is Emerging as a Security Dilemma for India and China

India and China see the potential of instability in Nepal if the political transition is not smooth. For the time being the political turbulence seems to have calmed down, but can erupt once again if communists perceive they are being sidelined.

(a) Security Challenges to India

- India's insecurity emerges from the rise and support to LWE. Nepal can be a source of material and ideological support to LWE.
- The threat from Jihadi terror is looming large. The ISI has set up various organisations such as Muslim Volunteer Force, Muslim Liberation Front, Islamic United Liberation Army, Islamic Movement of India, Islamic Revolutionary Force and Saddam Baini to operate its subversive activities.[6] The active support of the ISI and its modules operating from Nepal are providing material and ideological support to SIMI, IM and even HUJI of Bangladesh. The geographical proximity of Nepal to Muslim predominant areas of UP and Bihar are vulnerable, since ISI backed modules will not leave any opportunity to create instability in heartland India through Nepal.
- Nepal has become a transit route for the proliferation of fake currency, drug trafficking and safe havens for criminals. That is proving to be a huge challenge to Indian establishment. Porous borders allow criminals and terror modules to move in and out of Nepal to carry out anti national and anti-social activities in India.
- Illegal trade of cheap Chinese goods, narcotics and poaching is emerging as a major pitfall of open and porous border. Though SSB has been deployed as a border guarding force, yet the cross border movement under such circumstances is not an easy task to curb.

(b) Security Challenges to China

As far as China is concerned coercion of the Tibetan population is still a challenge. Nepal is emerging as a route for infiltration and exfiltration of Tibetans activists to avoid Chinese repression in TAR. China perceives that the open borders and considerable population of Tibetans in Nepal is a cause of concern. It appreciates that the cultural, religious and even subversive activities can be initiated from Nepal to ferment instability in TAR. China is conscious of the fact that friendship and strategic relationship with Nepal are imperative to ensure peace and stability in Tibet.

Nepal Vital for India's China and Pakistan Policy

Delhi in the past never considered Nepal relevant for its China and Pakistan policy. This mind-set allowed China and Pakistan to expand their footprint in Nepal. As a consequence ISI started operating from Nepal with impunity and porous border with India gave a perfect platform to Pakistan for the infiltration of Jihadis, proliferation of fake currency, drug trafficking and planning and execution of subversive and terror acts in mainland India. Similarly, China building bridges with Nepal is a cause of concern and has willy-nilly eliminated the prospect of reversal of cultural and religious threat for uprising in Tibet, a leverage which India had against China. In spite of having invested much lesser in developing a friendship with Nepal, China has created an environment to protect their vital interests. Whereas India have been investing much more, yet the interests are getting compromised by the day. Modi Government has realised that in the larger interest of national security and strategic interests, the priority in diplomacy should be given to "neighbours first". India needs to remove the inevitability of asymmetry, mutual suspicions and unease[7] with the old ally to prevent Nepal as a platform for Pakistan and China to create vulnerabilities in the backyard of India.

China's Initiative to Increase Foot Prints in Nepal

The conflict of interests between India and China clashes in Myanmar and Nepal. Nepal has remained a close Indian ally for long, but China slowly manoeuvred into a position where it has made the Indian position unstable. In the last decade or so, China has managed to create Nepal as leverage against India. Increasing footprints of China in Nepal will certainly hurt India in the long run. Nepal has emerged as significant to China as it is to India. Nepal has close to 10% Buddhist population and it has second largest Tibetans refugee population in the world after India. China is concerned about the Tibetan activities and discreet engagement by inimical forces with Tibetans and Buddhists of Nepal. Memories of Khampa rebellion against China from Nepal are still fresh. China may not be worried about the armed struggle through Nepal, but what it fears is cultural and religious uprising which could be initiated from Nepal. China has chosen soft power (cultural and economic) to ensure their interests in Nepal are protected.

(a) Crossing by Tibetan activists from either side was a cause of instability in TAR. Nepal is home to more than 20000 Tibetan refugees and China's main concern is to stifle their anti-China activities. It has succeeded in curbing the Khampa activities, illegal crossings through porous border and anti-China political activities from Nepal. Most recently China has expanded security and police posts along the Nepalese border with Tibet, significantly reducing the number of people crossing the border to seek refuge in Nepal and beyond.[8] China has entered Nepal through trade, communication network and infrastructure development. This will bring Chinese establishment almost in the backyard of India or along the banks of River Ganga and Kali. China is also making inroads through China Study Centres, which are close to the Indian borders. China's interests in Nepal are strategic as well as economic. The improved communication route will give China an access to Nepalese and Indian markets as well as enhance their footprints in the subcontinent by shrinking India's traditional strategic space.

(b) China is building Lhasa Kathmandu railway line at the cost of $ 2.2 billion, which is likely to be ready by 2020. It has undertaken up-gradation and expansion of the Kathmandu Ring Road, the Tatopani Dry Port project and construction of the Upper Trishuli 3A Hydro Power Station.[9] The focus of China is communication development so as to reach every part of Nepal to eliminate India's influence and monitor anti-China activities in Nepal. Prithivi, and Arniko Highway, the Pokhara-Baglung Road and the Narayanghat-Gorkha Highway are other projects which China has undertaken. China is likely to also undertake development of Kathmandu Airport. Next on the line is electronic communication and hydro power projects. Exploitation of hydro potential by China will deprive India an opportunity to generate energy for its power deficient neighbouring states and electronic communication will allow China to capture a huge communication market thus depriving India huge revenue. This will also possibly assist China in monitoring Indian cyber and electromagnetic domain.

Status of Nepal as Buffer State Important

After the loss of Tibet as a buffer state in 1950 when China took control over it, Nepal had become strategically important for both the countries. Nepal is the gateway to the sensitive Tibet Autonomous Region (TAR), which plays an important role in China's South Asia Policy.[10] Geographical location makes it perfect buffer which has secured the Central sector of India, however, this secured flank is contingent to Nepal's posturing. In the recent past Nepal has maintained an equi-distance from India and China to maintain neutrality and unbiased international posture. China has set a scorching pace to reach Kathmandu faster by developing rail and road network which will provide Nepal with alternative access to international market. But at the same time Nepal does not want to lose India as a strategic and economic partner. Nepal is conscious of the consequences of over dependence on China, as a result does not want to become second Tibet.

Way Ahead for India to Keep Nepal as Friend and Ally

India should look at Nepal as an opportunity to maintain internal and external security, a source of hydro-power energy, human resource pool, a consumer market for Indian goods, potential of religious tourism and cultural bond. Similarly, Nepal ought to see India as an enabler for economic growth, partner in the development of Nepal, internal security, employment generation for its diaspora, religious and cultural partner. In the light of this fact, it is imperative that India's assistance and actions should be seen as sincere efforts in the interests of both nations for collective growth. It is a fact that some section of Nepalese population and political parties perceive the Indian foot prints in Nepal with contempt and the big brother syndrome. There is a sense of scepticism about the intent. In the larger interest, it is imperative that India remove those insecurities and assure Nepal of cooperation, non-interference and a partner on whom Nepal and its people can trust.

(a) **Historic, Cultural and Religious Relationship a Bonding Factor.** Cultural, religious and economic integration is a cornerstone of relations with Nepal. Throughout history, the movement of people between Nepal and India was unrestricted.[11] For centuries now Lumbini, Pashupatinath, Bodh Gaya and Chardham are a confluence of civilisation and culture for the people of Nepal and India. Approximately 6,00,000 Indians are living/domiciled in Nepal. These include businessmen, traders, professionals (doctors, engineers, IT personnel) and labourers, who have been living in Nepal for a long time,(including seasonal/migratory in the construction sector).[12] Every Hindu Nepali visit places of worship in India at least once their life time, this connect should not be allowed to get disrupted, but what is significant is that this relationship needs to be nurtured. Governments on both sides should put mechanisms in place to facilitate people to people contact, especially for travel to and from Nepal, suitable arrangements for religious tourism at each of the important places, establishment of liaison offices for assistance and redressal of grievances of the work force on reciprocal basis.

(b) **Cultural Diplomacy a Potent Tool.** Cultural diplomacy is a potent tool, especially where large identical ethnic and religious communities live in two neighbouring nations. Cultural diplomacy can work seamlessly to develop greater interaction between people, community, society, and business organisations to develop common understanding. Teachers, doctors, artists, trade organisations and tourists are informal ambassadors of cultural diplomacy. There is a scope for building greater cooperation with the people of Nepal through cultural diplomacy, which can become an effective track to diplomacy to shape the opinion of the governments on either side.

(c) **Support for Establishment of Democracy.** It is in India's interests to promote and support Nepal to establish a democratic government. That will be far more beneficial to India than any other form of government. Imposition of the type of democracy and formulation of the constitution should be left to the choice and national consensus rather than dictation from Delhi. What India can do at this stage is to allow the Nepalese intellectuals and constituent assembly members to study and interact with the democratic, autonomous and constitutional institutions of India. That will prove to be far more convincing than to impose advice on the constituent assembly.

(d) **Equal Partners in Development**. Nepal is in need of infrastructure and economic development. Impact of political or economic instability in Nepal willy-nilly is likely to impact India as well. Development is an effective tool if it touches the heart and meets the basic necessity of every citizen of the land. Careful identification of projects should be carried out, that can be executed in a given timeframe. It should have utility for the public at large, and the nation as a whole. Development of Nepal ideally should be looked at with four cardinal aspects; **economic development, human development, sustainable development and territorial development**". It ideally should not appear to be a pure business and protection of Indian interests, but should be seen by public as genuine and sincere efforts of India in the development of Nepal. What is significant for Nepal and its people is communication (rail, road and electronic), generation of hydro power (increased availability for domestic consumption and for revenue generation), health services and education. Where India has lagged behind China is in the delivery of projects and quality of work. Poor quality and delay in execution of projects reflect lack of sincerity and purpose.

(e) **Military-to-Military Cooperation**. The Nepalese military is still not coerced by Chinese foray, though the same cannot be said about Nepalese police. The Indian Army (IA) and Nepalese Army (NA) continue to have bilateral military-to-military interaction at all levels. China will not be in a position to use Nepalese territory as long as the IA and NA are in close cooperation with each other. The precedent of giving the honorary rank of General to the Chiefs of the Army of each nation on a reciprocal basis is a good tradition and must continue. India has advantage since the Gorkha Regiment has a fair amount of troops from Nepal which should continue to keep the bond alive.

(f) **Enabling of Nepal Army and Police A Better Option Than Isolating the Border**. Enabling Nepal Army and police is economical and more responsible approach than adopting the strategy of isolation. It must be understood that the Nepal Army and police lacks equipment, vehicles, communication, modern weapon system and resources to control the border region. If they are enabled, Nepal Army and police will deliver. Even if the military hardware support is as an aid or on credit line so be it, but it will be a costly mistake if Nepal Army and police is allowed to look towards China for equipping and training. Therefore, engaging the Nepalese Army and police is cost-effective and mutually beneficial than isolating and building fences.

(g) **Relationship with the State and not with the Political Parties.** India should be seen siding with the State and people of Nepal and not with the political parties. Patronising a political party has pitfalls, especially if the party is discarded by the people. India is facing a similar predicament in Bangladesh, where it is perceived that the Indian establishment is supporting Awami League. As a consequence whenever BNP has come to power in Bangladesh, the terrorists and insurgent groups have found refuge in Bangladesh. Entire ULFA hierarchy operated from Bangladesh for more than a decade. It maybe prudent to ensure that India should not be seen as favouring non-communist government in Nepal, because if that happens Indian interests in Nepal can be compromised as and when the Communists are voted to power. It is very difficult in diplomacy to undo if a long term agreements are signed with far reaching consequences. Case in point is Indo-Nepal treaty of friendship, China is keen to get this treaty annulled and had asked Communists to annul this treaty which could have been a disaster for India.

(h) **Nepal a Disaster Prone Nation.** It is easy to walk into the hearts of the people and government by standing with the people and government at the time of crisis. India should try and be a net security provider to Nepal, especially against natural disasters. It maybe a good idea to pursue to maintain NDRF team and disaster bricks close to Nepal borders so that it can be moved to the ground zero at the shortest possible time. There is a need to earmark dedicated air efforts, emergency medical teams and satellite communication terminals to deal with the disasters. Similarly, India should provide Nepal with the remote sensing pictures, weather predictions, snow blizzards and avalanche warning system to prevent loss of lives and property. Satellite pictures during and post disaster could also be made available to facilitate disaster relief operations. There is also a need to be generous with the aid for recovery and reconstruction to rehabilitate people and auxiliary services.

(j) **Economy as Leverage.** Development of economy has traditionally been seen as the first form of development.[13] Nepal is aware of the fact that development of Nepal has to be in consonance with India, since Nepal is dependent upon India for consumer goods, access to the outside world, access to technology and raw material and supply of oil. Nepal enjoys free trade and transit facilities which in itself is a great concession. India's leverage of economic development should target economic empowerment of youth and rural areas where the bulk of Nepalese live. An environment of integration of Nepalese economy with UP, Uttarakhand and Bihar states are far more plausible solution than to integrate Nepal's economy with the rest of the country. If India is able to generate employment in Nepal for Nepalese citizen, it will restrict the flow of undesirable and unskilled labourers to India. Notwithstanding the above, India is a source of sustainability of the large number of Nepalese population. The economy is a tool which India must exploit to keep Nepal as a strategic partner and it will be a costly mistake if it is construed as an instrument of punitive measure.

(k) **Assistance for Development of Sports.** Engagement of youth in constructive activities is important to shape them favourable. Nepal lacks sports and youth development programme and infrastructure, as a result, a large percentage of youth lose the focus and either get involved in criminal activities or join left wing organisations. It maybe worth experimenting that India should patronise three games which are popular in Nepal such as boxing, football and cricket. Construction of sports centres with these facilities and subsequent integration of their teams with Indian Sports Federation Championships is a good idea to pursue. Even Nepal should be given an offer so that their cricket team can participate in any of the tournament in longer and shorter version of the game. There is no harm if a potential talent in these games is identified and recruited in Indian Army. Even world shooting champion Ritu Rai is a Nepalese citizen recruited into the Indian Army.

(l) **Educational Institutes for Skill Development.** Youth are the future leaders and most appropriate ambassadors of a nation and society. Nepal is short of skill development and higher education institutes. There are two ways through which India can engage the youth and shape their mind-set through educational programs. First is to keep some seats reserve for students of Nepal in various central universities in India and the second option is to open educational and skill development institutes in Nepal where some percentage of Indian students are also trained and educated. This will allow Nepalese students to bond with their Indian counterparts and Nepalese students at a later stage will be Indian ambassadors in Nepal as they grow in the system.

(m) **Effective Border Management Mechanism.** The model which India should adopt for border management is as under:

- **Openness of Borders for Trade and Movement of Persons.** Openness of borders implies free trade and mobility of people as key factors of the border management with full respect for human rights and freedoms.[14]
- **Closing of Borders for all Criminal Activities** and other activities which jeopardize stability in the region.[15] Border management should ensure that smugglers, illegal migrations, terrorist, criminals and anti social elements are not allowed refuge and spilling over from

either side. A holistic mechanism with mutual cooperation is essential to prevent undesirable acts.

Conclusion

There is a need to upgrade the bilateral relations between India and Nepal to a level of strategic partners. India cannot afford to allow Nepal to drift away from it, especially if it is likely to become a Chinese ally. It is in the interest of India and Nepal that both nations chart out a new trajectory of bilateral relations for mutual interests. The governments of the day have initiated the steps to make a new beginning to revitalise the bilateral relations between India and Nepal. Collective growth and respect for the protection of mutual interests is imperative to remove the insecurities and scepticism which have crept into the relationship between two religiously and culturally identical neighbours. Expansion of diplomatic influence is a sign of strategic wisdom and shrinking of influence is a sign of withering power. Strategic space once conceded is near impossible to regain in the present day competitive international environment. China is close on the heels and India can't let go an important ally and strategic partner, especially with a neighbour with whom India has historic cultural, social and religious ties. There is a need to create a conducive environment to promote a lasting friendship with Nepal for protection of mutual interests. Kamal Thapa, the Foreign Minister of Nepal, said, "Today the aid era seems to be replaced by a foreign investment era. Hence, there is a need to use the country's resources as an effective diplomatic tool.[16] India should read the signal and forge a deeper bond with Nepal on the principles of respecting each other's sovereignty, territorial integrity, mutual nonaggression, non-interference in each other's internal affairs, equality, mutual benefit and peaceful coexistence.[17]

REFERENCES

1. Index Mundi, Nepal Demographics Profile 2014, accessed on Nov 29, 2014, http://www.indexmundi.com/nepal/demographics_profile.html.
2. P. Jaiswal, Caught in the India-China Rivalry: Policy Options for Nepal, Institute of Peace and Conflict Studies, Issue Brief 249, March 2014.
3. Nepal: Conflict Profile, Insight on Conflict, accessed on December 09, 2014 from http://www.insightonconflict.org.
4. Ibid.
5. Ibid.
6. S. S. Pattanaik, Indo-Nepal Open Border: Implications for Bilateral Relations and Security, Accessed on December 09, 2014, http://www.idsa-india.org, Jun 2008.

7. A. Upadhyay, Modi's trans-Himalayan link to bring Nepal, India, China together, Accessed on December 09, 2014 from http://www.ekantipur.com.
8. R. Ranjan and D. Malone, A Yam, "Between Two Boulders", in Sebastian von Einsiedel, D. M. Malone, S. Pradhan (ed), *Nepal in Transition: From People's War to Fragile Peace*, Cambridge University Press 2012, p 307.
9. M. Chansoria, "China makes presence felt in Nepal", *The Sunday Guardian*, December 08, 2014.
10. Jaiswal, n 2.
11. Smruti, n 6.
12. India–Nepal Relations, accessed on December 11, 2014 from Government of India MEA Portal http://www.mea.gov.in/Portal/ForeignRelation/Nepal_December_2013.
13. L.G. Bellù, Development and Development Paradigms A (Reasoned) Review of Prevailing Visions, Easy Pol Module 102, May 2011
14. Integrated Border Management Strategy in the Republic of Serbia.
15. Ibid.
16. S. Thapliyal, Changing Trends in India-Nepal Relations, accessed on December 11, 2014 from http://www.idsa-india.org.
17. Hongxia Liu, "The Analysis on New China's Diplomatic Standpoint of the Basic Practical Principles", *Journal of Politics and Law*, June 2008.

15

Maoist Insurgency in India and Nepal: An Analysis

Shekhar Adhikari

The present polemics of Maoism/Left Wing Extremism/Naxalism and the prevailing situation has seriously endangered the security of India and Nepal. Maoism in both the countries has led to huge economic and social disparities, which has created a feeling of deprivation and desperation among the underprivileged classes. Indian and Nepalese societies are characterized by ethnic, religious, logistic and wide gap in the socioeconomic disparities. The emergence of Maoism is primarily due to these reasons. It is interesting to examine the movement in the form of modernization, industrialization and development. We have seen in the past that many countries have faced popular uprisings and movements that challenged the state ideology or its paradigm of development.

In this article, I examined in brief Indo-Nepal outlook, the Naxalite movement in India, and the Maoist insurrection that has led to fundamental changes in Nepal. The central question is why Maoism has continued to inspire violent revolution so long after the Chairman Mao's death. Almost 40 years have passed, Mao Tse Tung still continues to inspire violence in South Asia. From these cases, there emerge three compelling reasons for Maoism's existence and persistence in South Asia: it employs tactically effective methods; it springs from political organizations that are prone to extremist schisms;

and it targets populations that have not tasted the fruits of political and economic development.

Hence, effective dealing with Maoist insurrection in these countries will necessitate the implementation of policies that bring real change to the peasants and rural poor. Policy makers must also be open to new and peaceful avenues that may compel Maoists to contribute to positive change. Until such policies are implemented with vigour and determination the prospects of Maoist violence will continue.

Indo-Nepal Relations

India and Nepal share a long and open border and have similar cultural history. A sizeable population of Indian origin lives in Nepal and vice versa. The 1950 Treaty of Peace and Friendship grants the national of India and Nepal with national treatment as far as certain industrial, economic and commercial activities are concerned. But the nature and scope of this treaty has been the subject of controversy since its conclusion. Critics argue that this treaty is based on the 'Himalayan frontier policy' of India, fundamentally a policy pursued by the British during colonial rule, which should be changed to reflect the current reality.[1]

Nepal views India's attitude towards itself differently. Nepal is virtually land-locked by India and India has tended to view Nepal as its own backyard. But while India is a huge factor in Nepal's international relations, Nepal is an important, though relatively small, factor in India's own foreign policy. India has been critical of the inclination of Nepal's leaders to adopt the role of an irritating neighbour, incapable of understanding the bilateral relationship from a broader perspective. India views its dealings with Nepal in a regional context, while Nepal takes a bilateral view of relations with India.[2]

Nepal's plans for modernisation and economic development on the one hand, and the misperceptions regarding the asymmetric relationship on the other hand have often prevented meaningful cooperation between the two neighbours. For instance, Nepal has huge hydroelectric potential but is yet to take advantage of this resource, largely, because of mistrust towards India, the natural market for power.

There is little balance in the interplay between diplomacy and law in shaping the relations between Nepal and India. As a result, Indo-Nepal relations have become a "laboratory" for testing various principles of international law. While some treaties between the two countries have been unbalanced, inviting inevitable criticism, others, even those concluded ostensibly on the basis of equality, have yet to be implemented because they have also been trained by the old mindset of "unequal" treaties. For instance, Nepal as a land-locked country has a guaranteed right to free access to and from sea through the territory of India under international law, but India had been slow to acknowledge that fact and is often reluctant to honour the right in practice. Furthermore, the very existence of some treaties is contested. Treaties have been concluded between the two countries without being designated in such an order to avoid parliamentary scrutiny.[3]

Indo-Nepal relations are marred by mistrust, confusion and dogmatism. It is necessary to develop an environment in both countries that is conducive to meaningful cooperation. The perception that India sees Nepal as its own backyard causes resentment in Nepal. And Nepal's tendency to denigrate its larger neighbour for any perceived ills is equally unhealthy and may ultimately block any effort by the two countries to work together. Thus, in this context Maoist insurgency in India and Nepal may be critically examined.

Naxalite Movement in India

The first practical attempt to translate the Naxalite movement into practice was made by militant groups of CPI (M) during the United Front regime in West Bengal in May 1967. They started an agitation winning over the local landless peasants and creating a series of activities in Naxalbari, Khairibari, and Phensidewa areas of West Bengal. From 1967-72, the CPI (M) embarked on guerilla activities that became a major concern for the centre and state governments. To understand the reason for this development, one must take into account the border, political, economic and social contexts during this period.

Political Development: From 1966-72 the struggle for political leadership began between Indira Gandhi and Moraji Desai. In this internal fight, Mrs. Gandhi emerged as the head of a coalition of Congress functions, but it became quite problematic for her to fight the national election as effectively as it had in the past. The Congress could manage 40% of the popular vote and barely managed majority in a parliament it had previously dominated.[4] In 1969 the party officially split into two competing camps: Congress (0) under Moraji Desai and Congress (I) under Indira Gandhi. Though Mrs. Indira Gandhi was still a force to reckon with but had to rely on a coalition of leftist parties to give her a working majority, a fact that complicated her ability to respond forcefully to the growing Naxalite movement.

Similarly, we saw the CPI, which for decades, was a unified force, split into two groups in 1964 along the line of the international split between Russian and Chinese policies over the revisionist policies adopted by the Soviet Union after the death of Stalin. The Moscow supported in India came to be known as the CPI (R) and the Peking group CPI (M). Thus, the structural shifts in Indian politics served to facilitate further the emergence and spread of Naxalism in a number of ways. Political upheaval at the centre allowed alternative ideologies to take root and provided breathing room for their more extreme ideological brethren. Concurrently, the new requirements of coalition building diverted political attention from the essential task of ensuring security in their constituencies.[5]

Economic Development: From 1951–66, India was still a predominantly rural agrarian economy. Because of lack of agricultural set up India faced serious problem in the form of severe food shortage in Bihar and Bengal from 1965 to 1967. Lack of proper irrigation facilities and over dependence on the seasonal monsoon caused widespread famine in 1952–53. India, then, had to rely on American aid in 1966 to boost her economic setback.

In the meantime, India's fourth Five Year Plan was implemented and the focus of the plan was to "lay the foundation for breakthrough in agriculture in the countryside. But this kind of development helped large landowners over small farmer. As Edward Duyker pointed out that in the predominantly agrarian Santal tribes in West Bengal, this had immensely benefitted large landholders over small farmers, widening what were already significant income disparities between the two.[6]

Social Development: Looking back into the history of the Indian peasant movement, we notice that their uprising phenomenon was common. During the period from 1783 to 1900 alone, under the British Raj, over 100 such incidents affected the region to greater or lesser degrees and a number of them in the perennially restive province in Bengal.[7] In retrospect, it appears that many of the factors that had encouraged events in the past were present in the late 1960s. As the standard of living deteriorated amongst the peasants, strikes and food riots became more frequent in the later 1960s.[8] In 1967, the poor conditions of rural people forced them to take the extreme step of suicide due to dire economic situation.

A similar situation was witnessed in the urban society. Lack of adequate facilities compelled a number of young people to resort to such undesirable actions like petty theft, criminal activities and other anti-social behavior. Anti-establishment and leftist activities became the order of the day in Bengal. In 1965, the communist faction captured the leadership of the student's union at the Presidency College and embarked on a campaign of disobedience, strikes and prospects. Many of them were violent.

This kind of development in urban and rural areas suited the leaders of the Maoists groups in the CPI (M). To ignite this potent mixture of urban and rural unrest, it provided the much needed spark to arouse the sentiment of the masses.

Internal Characteristic of the Naxalite Movements: The growth of Naxalism in 1967 owes mainly to Charu Mazumdar and Kanu Sanyal who discarded the thesis of conciliatory leaning towards New Delhi and electoral politics. Of the two, Charu Mazumdar was more aggressive in his approach towards obtaining the goal of proletarian revolution. Under the guidance of Charu Mazumdar and Kanu Sanyal, on March 3, 1967, the Naxalite movement in West Bengal was launched from a strategically located territory called "Naxalbari". It was a police station under Siliguri sub-division of Darjeeling district in West Bengal.[9] This northern portion of the State of West Bengal is situated some 30 to 50 miles from Sikkim, Tibet and Bhutan in the North, Nepal in the West and from Bangladesh in the East. The strategic significance of this area of about 100 square miles lies in the fact that it is precisely located at the point of India's narrowest corridor, 13 to 14 miles wide also called the 'chickens neck' that connects the main portion of India's land mass with its north-eastern Assam, North East Frontier Agency, Nagaland, Manipur and Tripura.

Thus, the aim of Naxalite strategy was focused on the elimination of the landlords, money lenders, police and its information. By adopting this strategy, the Naxalite would be in a state to seize political powers in the cities.

Government Responses (Centre and State)

Initially, the Central government did not give much attention to the outbreak of violence in Naxalbari. The government viewed it simply as localized law and order problem. To be fair, the early movement was too weak and even as Naxalism gained momentum in 1968-69, it failed to attract the government responses. However, by 1970, the situation began to change. As the Naxalite movement became more violent, it was difficult for the government to ignore their activities. On Aug 11, 1970, Indira Gandhi stated that the government would fight the Naxalites with "all the strength at its command."[10] The announcement of the early election in 1971 provided an incentive for the deployment of military and paramilitary forces to some of the most Naxal affected districts.[11] In July, 1971, the centre launched, "Operation Steeplechase", a coordinated operation by the Indian Army, the Central Reserve Police Force and local police across contiguous districts in West Bengal, Bihar and Odisha that were affected by the Naxalite violence. This area encompassed West Bengal's Midnapur and Birbhum districts. The Steeplechase Operation achieved some remarkable achievements. Hundreds of Naxalites were arrested, large quantities of weapons were captured and more important, the government succeeded in restoring the confidence among the rural population.

The Central government also tried to appease the rural masses by bringing a number of rural developmental and land reform programmes. The West Bengal Land Reform Act, which was passed in 1970, was one such attempt made by the government. It imposed ceiling on the land and reduced the maximum rent that landlord could charge from the peasant who tilled their land. But, the Central government's effort in this direction could not appeal much to the masses and the Naxalities. However, in spite of interference from the centre the Naxal problem remained a state affair. India's constitution devolved authority over internal security to the states and it was their policies and initiative that mattered most.[12] In case, the state failed in its effort to curb the Naxal violence then there was a constitutional answer for that.

With the deteriorating security situation in the state, the Central government imposed Presidential rule in West Bengal in March 1970 under Article 356 of the constitution and allowed the centre to take executive authority in a state if the ruling government can no longer form a majority in the state legislature. The Centre, after imposing President's rule, took stringent measures and the situation began to improve rapidly. The 1932 Bengal Suppression of Terrorist Outrage Act was quickly revived, giving the police excessive powers of detention. Funding of the state police forces were double and the number of the name and files increased drastically. The state's own police force of nearly 60,000 men was deployed solely against the Naxals. Further, the state's police force was reinforced by bringing about a dozen battalions of CRPF comprising about 6,000 armed policemen.[13] The police forces were posted in the main areas of Naxalite activity, especially Siliguri, Midnapur and Calcutta. In April, coordination and cooperation between military force, CRPF, and state police crushed the Midnapur agitation in a matter of weeks. The presence of all these forces in Calcutta also proved effective. As a result, thousands of Naxal activists and sympathizers were arrested or put to death. By the end of 1971, Mazumdar was forced to abandon the urban operation in the face of increasing casualties and losses. Finally, on July 16, 1972, Charu Mazumdar was arrested from a safe house in the Calcutta suburb of Entally. On July 28, he died in police custody. With his death, the first phase of Naxalite activity in India was over.

Failure of the Naxalite Movement

The Naxalite movement could not succeed because its leaders did not give much attention to the following factors: (1) lack of a strong party organization; (2) failure to build a powerful mass base; (3) not giving much attention to Indian military might; and (4) a formal attitude towards land reforms.

Moreover, much of the responsibility for the ultimate failure of Naxalite movement goes to Charu Mazumdar. Charu Mazumdar's strategy of the armed uprising lacked analytical approach both in application and execution. The Naxalites could not use Charu's strategy at a proper time and against the right persons; there was much confusion among them as to who were to be considered as "class enemies". It was more problematic when they attacked police officials because most of them who died belonged to the lower ranks, like constables. The higher officers were beyond their reach. Another drawback of the strategy was that it affected all those persons who refused to give the demanded money irrespective of the fact whether the amount was small or big. Thus, a large number of persons who were annihilated were not really their class's enemies. Furthermore, Charu's strategy of annihilation camping was seen by most villagers as nothing more than the murder of a co-villagers by strangers. Muzamdar's annihilation programme has been characterized by Sushital Roy Choudhary as "indiscriminate killing". He, however, also agreed that though Mazumdar did not subscribe to it he only went to the extent of suggesting that it should be confined to three classes of the enemy, i.e. the money lenders, the landlord and the police and its informer.[14]

The Present Naxalite Movement

Although the Centre and State government were successful in stopping the

Naxalite activities in 1972, the movement proved to be inspiration for the other states interested in achieving social justice through political, peasant-led violence. The Naxalites of the 21st Century have once again captured the attention of the Central government, with the Former Prime Minister Manmohan Singh labeling them in March 2006 as the "single biggest internal security challenge ever faced by our country."[15]

After West Bengal, Maoist revolution have been most effective in the states of Andhra Pradesh, Bihar, Jharkhand Chhattisgarh, Orissa, Madhya Pradesh, Maharashtra, Uttar Pradesh and Tamil Nadu. They have been credited with increasing the wages and land holding of agricultural workers, as well as attracting development projects. However, these naxals have resorted to such tactics as slitting the throats, kidnapping of children, blowing up vehicles, the hijacking and looting of a passenger train, and murdering.

Today, the question is that Maoism is tactically effective? We have seen that these naxal groups operating in India have been following military and organizational strategy of Mao. This makes it possible for an under-armed, small group of ideologically inspired people to wrest political control of isolated. In late 1970s and 1980 these Naxal groups went underground because of Indira Gandhi's declaration of emergency and harsh step taken to bring down the movement. But in spite of all this there is no indication that groups like Maoist Communist Center and People's War group have been weakened. But rather, in recent years, events such as the murder of rival politicians, the killing of informers, and the destruction of police officers suggests that they are growing.[16] Further, the merging of these two groups into a new Communist Party of India (Maoist) in the autumn of 2004 means they have become the largest left-wing resistance movement in the country, with influence in at least nine states, and alleged international collaboration with Pakistan's Inter Services Intelligence Agency as well as Sri Lanka's Tamil separatist movement.[17]

Another question that arises is the degree to which India's Maoists are true to their namesake. In the tactical sense, the Naxalites have followed the Mao's prescriptions for the effective use of time, space and material against a much larger and stronger enemy. However, Mao was quite clear in warning against the movement becoming the home of bandits and anarchists, and insisted that guerrilla warfare be properly organized.[18] Kidnappings, murdering of civilians, hijacking of a train, and other incidents of terror ascribed to India's Maoists in 2006 indicate that various Naxalite groups are deviating from the course of Mao Tse-Tung thought. Elsewhere, it is even suggested that Maoists are dabbling in lucrative corners of capitalism, becoming involved in the illicit trade of narcotics and counterfeit currency.[19] On the other hand, there may be confusion as to who is responsible for actions that stray from the Maoist path. Are the terrible incidents the work of organised Naxalite parties, or are they violent outlaws operating in the anarchic zones of Naxalite control?

The Naxalite issue had continued in India because it has political utility. In the past, there have been instances where the national government refrained from offering meaningful development and military support to fight them. Instead, they watched as the Maoists took control of rural areas, and then used reports and commissions to highlight the "failing" of their state-level rivals. At the local levels, private armies, such as the infamous Ranvir Sena in Bihar, are wielded by the upper castes as a blunt counterweight to the Naxalites, rival political parties, and the aspirations of the lower castes. The use of violence is legitimised by the activities of Maoists, and the Ranvir Sena has received considerable political support from political parties. Ironically, if the Maoists were to disappear then the upper caste landlords would be obliged to divulge power to lower-caste communities. Allowing the problem to fester, on the other hand, facilitates their continued economic and political hegemony.[20] The following chart shows the fatalities committed by Naxalities from 2005–15.

Fatalities Committed by Naxalities from 2005–15 in India (Year Wise Breakup)

Years	*Civilians*	*Security Force Personnel*	*Maoists*	*Total*
2005	281	150	286	717
2006	266	128	343	737
2007	240	218	192	650
2008	220	214	214	648
2009	391	312	294	997
2010	626	277	277	1180
2011	275	128	199	602
2012	146	104	117	367
2013	159	111	151	421
2014	128	87	99	314
2015	36	30	26	92
Total	2768	1759	2198	6725

Source: http://www.satp.org/satporgtp/countries/india/maoist/data_sheets/fatalitesnaxal 05-11-html.

Maoist Insurgency in Nepal

In Nepal violence played a major role in their politics. To substantiate this, two events were important. First, in 1846, the Kot massacre that led to the establishment of the Rana Dynasty, which reduced the powers of the king, and second, in June 2001, the Royal Palace massacre that in due course ended the monarchy rule in 2008. Maoism in Nepal was inspired by Naxalite Movement of West Bengal. Like India, the movement has roots in the socio-economic conditions of the country, and was born from a fissiparous and idealistic Communist Party. Unlike India, the Maoists have been largely successful in toppling the national government, and have effective control over 80% of the country. Its recent success, however, did not come through military action alone, and required coordination and compromise with Nepal's other political parties.[21]

The Maoist insurgency in Nepal was a consequence of the country's particular economic, political and social circumstances that developed in the 1990s. In the realm of economic expectations among Nepal's young, educated and rural populations far outpaced realities of their country's development. Despite hopes of change after the return of democracy in 1990s, Nepal in 2004 ranked 140th on the Human Development Index, with 82.5% of its population living beneath the poverty line and nearly 20% classified as "undernourished".[22]

Political Development: In politics, Nepal's largest parties failed to consolidate their gains or expand their organisational base into Nepal's vast hinterland. Instead of strengthening up new leadership in rural areas (where 83.4% of the population lives), the first ruling party of new, democratic Nepal appointed the same classes that had ruled under the previous regime to continue to govern the provinces. When a united front of communist parties took control in1994, hopes were high that the parties would address the issues of poverty and injustice, but the disunity and opportunism that they brought with them only contributed to a feeling of malaise.[23]

Social Development: In term of social groups, the period following democracy to the present day has seen a consolidation of elites in the management of the country, most clearly demonstrated by the composition of Nepal's civil service. Since the mid-1980s, the number of civil service employees from the most economically and politically powerful ethnicities in Nepal have risen from 69% to 98%.[24] Another example comes from the other end of the social spectrum. The UNDP's 2004 Human Development Report gives stark details concerning Nepal's Dalit (untouchable) population, with life expectancy, literacy and income that are far below the country's average.

This type of inequality undoubtedly forced radical to resort to violent action, so that social, political and economic order could be set up in Nepal. Deepak Thapa describes this as "hope in a radical solution," and a function of poverty rather than a consequence of Maoist ideology.[25] In Nepal, the peaceful shift that occurred in 1991 to democracy was supposed to bring development but it did not. When the King dissolved parliament in 2002 and consolidated his control over the government in 2005, it only fuelled pessimism.

The pertinent question is why Nepal opted for Maoism and not some other form of radical change? It could be the Chinese ideological influence in certain sections of the Nepalese population. Perhaps of this, Mohan Bikram Singh joined the Communist Party of Nepal (CPN) and by 1957 had risen to a position of prominence. He built a strong communist organization. Like other communist parties in South Asia, later on the CPN went through a series of splits following the Sino–Soviet break in the 1960s, and further splintered with the establishment of the Panchayat ("no party") rule under King Mahendra.

Mohan Bikram Singh demanded elections for a constitutional assembly. He established a radical Maoist party in the mid 1960s that broke into a number of factions, and established his own party in 1983, the Communist Party of Nepal (Masal). He opposed the democracy created in 1991, again calling for a constitutional assembly, but them mellowed, deciding to participate in the elections of 1994. In doing so, he abandoned his district to a more extreme Maoist organisation that capitalised on an impoverished population that had for three decades been indoctrinated against participating in parliamentary politics.[26] The party that learnt much from Singh was the CPN (M). It launched its "Peoples War" in 1996. It was led by Prachanda and Baburam Bhattarai and the movement expanded from its core areas in western Nepal to cover 80% of the country. The CPN (M) is similar to its contemporaries in India in its birth from a fissiparous communist party, and its mobilisation of impoverished rural people frustrated by the working of democracy and inspired by radical methods to change their social, political and economic fortunes. Unlike the Naxalites, the CPN (M) is united by charismatic leadership. It has seized upon popular discontent with national policies, and during its early stage of war targeted "class enemies" (including members of other communist parties) rather than state security forces.[27]

Conflict Zone

The insurgents are conducting violent activities in 68 of the 75 districts that comprise Nepal. Their influence varies between moderate to extreme in these districts. In the districts of Rolpa, Rukum, Jajarkot, Salyan, Pyuthan and Kalikot in mid-western Nepal, Government presence is limited to the district headquarters with the rest of each district under Maoist control. The Nepalese Home Ministry has designated these districts as 'sensitive classes A'. Nine districts, namely Dolakha, Ramechhap, Sindhuli, Karvepalanchowk. Sindhupalchowk, Gorkha, Dang, Surkhet and Achham, are classified as 'Sensitive Class B', while 17 'Sensitive Class C' districts are Khotang, Okhaldhunga, Udaypur, Makwanpur, Lalitpur, Nuwakot, Dhading, Tanahu, Lamjung, Parbat, Baglung, Gulmi, Arghakhachi, Bardiya, Dailekh, Jumla and Dopla.[28]

Government Response

The government of Nepal under King Gyanendra decided to take a tough stand against the Maoist insurgency. In 2001, the deployment of the Royal Nepalese Army to fight the Maoist resulted in cruelty. By the time King Gyandera declared a state of emergency on 1 February 2005, over 3,000 people were detained by the government, and estimates of the number of internally displaced people ranged from 8,000 to 2,000,00.[29] There have been abuses committed from all sides such that Amnesty International has described the war as having "destroyed human rights in the countryside." No doubt, the law-and-order situation in Nepal is still a serious one.

While developed countries have condemned him, the King received overt support from Pakistan, Bangladesh and China in his war against the Maoist insurgency.[30] Although in the past these governments have not had the same leverage as the developed countries in altering Nepal's policies, they appeared willing to provide weapons, training and materials in order to gain influence there.

The King hoped to crush the powers of the Nepali Maoists, but he failed in his attempt. Hence, in November 2005, the Maoists entered into an agreement and called for a constitutional assembly to determine the future structure of a new government. In February 2006, this unlikely coalition successfully boycotted local elections called by the King, and his calls for dialogue with the political parties were promptly dismissed. In mid-March, a CPN(M) blockade of major roads began to take effect, and by early April crowds were gathering in Katmandu to demand the return of democracy and an end to the monarchy. By mid April, a general strike and mass protests began to shake King Gyandera's hold on power, and on 24 April he reinstated the parliament he had dismissed four years earlier.

It was this use of army against the Maoist that made the RNA and the Maoist enemies. There were no indications of hostility between them until the end of the King Birendra's regime in 2001. Initially, the RNA fared badly against the Maoists. It had never been exposed to a resolute and well-organized ideological rebellion. In the 23 operations listed between November 2001 and December 2002, the Maoist claimed success against the RNA in all except three or four.[31] In these operations, they had destroyed the army camps and even captured many of their weapons. The army, therefore, had to be expanded and heavily equipped. Its strength reached almost 100,000 by April 2006, when the Jan Andolan–II eventually brought the Maoist insurgency to an end. But the enhanced strength also did not result in the RNA's victory over the Maoists. At best, it created a stalemate, where army could defend its cantonments only, without stirring out to challenge the Maoists in rural or urban areas. On their part, the Maoists made good use of tactics by paralyzing the movement of goods and people on the main road network of Nepal and created chaos in the country. The hostility between the two precipitated the issues of 'civilian supremacy' and equal treatment of the Maoists people's Liberation Army and the RNA. This issue has vitiated the whole peace process in Nepal and, if not resolved soon, threatens to restart the insurgency.

The leadership also played an important factor in building up the Maoist insurgency and carrying forward their 'people's war'. The Maoist movement began in Nepal in the early 1970s in the context of the Chinese Cultural revolution and the rise of Naxal revolt in India. The Nepalese Maoists were preoccupied with the internal ideological and leadership differences. Most of them still believed that their armed struggle should be waged even on the basis of Marxist–Leninist–Maoist ideas. The present leaders of the Maoist movement are ready to accept the reality of the situation in Nepal. They have ideological resilience and are better educated. The high educational level of this leadership has enabled them to understand the problems, both within and outside Nepal. This in turn had helped them to broaden their approach and imbibe the lessons learnt from this exposure in carrying their movement forward. The present leadership also analysed the failure of the communist movements and learned from them and then tried to evolve a synthesis of the ideal and the real in the classical Marxist sense. Explaining his approach to 'people's war', Prachanda said:

> "...We must also learn war by waging war. The intellectuals' instinctive tendency is that we have to learn all these things, we should read everything...and then we can make war. These kinds of tendencies were there right from the beginning. But we said, no. This is not Maoism. This is not Marxism. This is not dialectical materialism....The issues is of learning through war itself."[32]

Again in 2001, he added:

> "In our opinion, the real key to rapid development of the people's War is the fusion between the science of proletarian revolution, on the one hand, and the needs and fighting spirit of the Nepalese people, on the other."[33]

The new Maoist leadership has to, however, face tensions and rivalries within the organization. These tensions have manifested on issues of ideology and tactics on united front allies and adversaries. There was clear ideological and personality clash between the Maoist Prachanda and Deputy Baburam Bhattarai. There clash has at times threatened to split the movement vertically, but the party has managed to keep the organisational unity largely because Baburam Bhattarai does not believe in personality projection.

The External Factor

Both the countries' insurgency was considerably helped by the external powers. As noted above, the new Maoist leadership was induced to establish wider contacts and learned from their external exposure. In case of Nepal insurgents, their first contacts were with the Indian Naxalites in 1970s. But the new Maoist leadership has explained these contacts and there have been reports that Prachanda played a significant role in facilitating the merger of India's Maoist Community Centre (MCC) and the People's War group. Recent studies say that insured have well-established linkages with international organizations.

Coordination Committee of Maoist Parties and Organisations of South Asia (CCOMPOSA)

The Maoist group of four South Asia countries, India, Nepal, Bangladesh and Sri Lanka have joined hands to form CCOMPOSA to advance "People War" in South Asia. Its objective is to "coordinate the activities of the Maoist parties and organizations in South Asia..., by spreading a protracted people's war in region, in the context of hastening and advancing of the World Proletarian Socialist Revolution."

ISI Links: ISI has been very active in Nepal and Bangladesh since long, especially along the borders. The objective is to encircle India and for this it is giving much needed support to numerous Indian militant groups based in Bangladesh. The rise of Maoist groups in India and Nepal has further served their purpose and they do not hesitate in providing moral and material support to these groups. This bond has been mutually beneficial to both the parties, as Maoist receives weapons and other warlike stores from ISI to be used against the Indian states.

LTTE Links: The Naxalite linkage with LTTE dates back to 1990s when it was estimated by intelligence agencies that PWG used to acquire weapons especially AK–47 rifles from this organization. In the present context, the Naxalite presence in Tamil Nadu with the discovery of a training camp organized by former PWG Naxals in Periyakulam forests, Theni district on 25 June 2007, is also believed to have strong sympathy for LTTE which has led security forces to suspect a renewed nexus between the Naxals and the LTTE.

Revolutionary International Movement (RIM): The Revolutionary International Movement came into existence on March 12, 1984, at the second conference of Marxist–Leninist parties. It is claimed by some that the objective was to overthrow the old system of exploitation and oppression and to bring into effect the revolutionary power of the oppressed led by the proletariat. The constituent groups of the RIM are waging, or preparing to wage a revolutionary war, according to the conditions of their different countries. There were 19 Maoist groups in the RIM at the time of its formation, but now it has been reduced to 13 groups, including MCCI. There is a South Asia chapter of the RIM and these groups meet annually. The members of RIMSA are as follow "CPI (ML) (NB): CPN–M, MCCCI: Proletarian Party of Purbo Bangla Central Committee, PPPB (CC): Proletarian Party of Purbo Bangla-Maobadi Punargathan Kendro, PPPB (MPK); Revolutionary Communist Centre of India (Marxist-Leninist-Maoist), RCCI (MLM): Bangladeshi Samyobadi Dal-Marxist-Leninist, BSD (ML); Communist Party of Bhutan (Marxist-Leninist-Maoist), CPB (MLM).

Creation of Compact Revolutionary Zone: The Naxalite with the support of their Nepal counterpart, had planned to create a "Red Corridor", starting from the border with Nepal and extending up to Kerala. It was in August 2001 that the idea of establishing a Compact Revolution Zone (CRZ) or the Red Corridor came into existence. It extended from the forest tracts of Adilabad (Andhra Pradesh) to Nepal, traversing the forest areas of Maharashtra, Chhattisgarh, Jharkhand, Bihar and Nepal. It was conceptualized at Siliguri in a high level meeting of the Maoist leaders. The notion of CRZ seems to grow as Maoist cadres between 2001 and 2012 in both India and Nepal. The CRZ was essentially seen as a prologue to the further expansion of Maoism in the subcontinent. As of now, while Communist Party of Nepal – Maoist (CPN–M) is now playing active role in the nation's politics, their Maoist counterparts in India have carved over several guerilla zones in different parts of our country. What was once a utopian idea, the concept and reality of CRZ in India had indeed made big strides. The consolidations in West Bengal and Bihar are the key to the achievements of the CRZ. The Naxalites plan to use West Bengal as a corridor between their areas of domination in India and Nepal.[34]

The strategic aim is to have a continuous stretch of territory under their influence and control and the ultimate goal will be to liberate the entire zone. It would provide the Naxal organization to coordinate their operations and extend their area of influence. Once achieved, the CRZ will virtually drive a wedge through the vital areas of the country and would help to crystallize linkages with other Maoist groups operations in South Asia, including the Communist Party of Nepal – Maoist (CPN-M) and the Communist Party of Bhutan – Maoist (CPB–M).[35]

The pertinent question is what are the implications of CRZ? The impact of CRZ could be seen as follows:

(1) **Free Movement:** The Naxalite cadres would be able to move freely throughout the CRZ including crossing over the Nepal. This would enable them to launch joint operations in future. The following regions are reported being used by CPN (Maoist) cadres:

- Uttarakhand—Rauthi, Jhulaghat, Garbygang, Dharchula, Golagad, Baluakot, Sirkha and Banbassa.
- Uttar Pradesh—Tuthibari, Nautanwa, Sonauli and jungle tracks in Philibit, Kheri, Baharaich, Balrampur and Maharajganj districts along the Indo–Nepal border.

- Bihar—Haraiya, Raxaul, Mahuwa, Dhobini, Sikta, Bhaisatlan and Mahadevnath.
- West Bengal Kalimpong, Siliguri and Darjeeling districts.

(2) **Sanctuaries:** Depending upon the role of state's security force, the Maoist cadres can establish safe haven and hideouts for operations, training, medical aid evading prosecution/contact with security forces. CPN (Maoist) cadres are reported to have taken shelter in:-

- Uttarakhand—Pithoragarh, Dharchula, Jhulaghat, Tanakpur and Banbassa.
- Uttar Pradesh—Thulibari, Nichloul, Nautanwa, Dhenera, Baghekhane, Bankati, Sampuran Nagar, Gorakhpur, Varanasi, Kanpur and Lucknow.
- Bihar—Narkatiyagang, Ramnagar, Valmikinagar, Ghorshan, Chhauradano, Bhaisatolan, Gardi, Ramnagar, Sirsamu and Sonbarsa.
- West Bengal—Bijanbai, Mirik, Sukhiya, Pokhri, Manebhangan, Darjeeling, Siliguri and New Jalpaiguri.

(3) **Training**: The Naxalite affected areas being under developed and forested, safe joint training camps can be organized. It has been reported that some Maoists have been possibly trained in West Champaran and Aurangabad districts of Bihar and Palamu and Kodarma districts of Jharkhand. The reports are there that CPI–ML (PW) cadres are imparting specialist training to Maoist of Nepal in Ropla district of Nepal.

Support and Sympathizer: A Nepal Maoist Newsletter *Ankur* is being circulated in India for a price of Re 1. CPN (Maoist) is known to have the following front organizations in India—Akhil Bharatiya Nepali Ekta Samaj, Bharatiya Nepal Ganatantrik Morcha, Mool Pravash Akhil Bharat Nepal Ekta Samaj, Nepali Janadhikar Surkhasa Samiti (Bharat), Bharatiya Gorkha Sangathan, Krantikari Lok Adhikari Sangh in Terai, Nepal Uttan Samaj (Nainital).

Emerging Threats from Nepal Due to China Factor

Most of the insurgent related problems in India have cross-border linkages. Consequently, border management has become an integral component of India's internal security management. The India-Nepal border has assumed significance only in the recent years due to continuing instability in Nepal and increasing Chinese proximity to Nepal. The 1,751 km India-Nepal border runs through 20 districts of five Indian states. Unlike Nepal-China border, which runs mainly through high altitude mountains, most of India-Nepal border runs through plains and rivers. The India-Nepal border is open and there is no visa regime for persons of both the countries. There are 22 agreed routes for mutual trade and 15 for land traffic. Most of the border areas run through undeveloped and populous areas where a high crime rate, poor governance, inadequate infrastructure, and an ill-equipped police force make conditions conducive for various forces inimical to Indian and Nepalese interests to operate. Moreover, there is a high volume of illicit trade in forest products and wildlife. The open border and absence of effective law and enforcement in Nepal have also contributed to drug smuggling. A number of recent reports have indicated that Nepal's Maoist insurgents are involved in smuggling drugs to India to raise money to buy arms.[36]

Drugs and mafia on the India–Nepal border pose a serious challenge to the Indian security apparatus, and most criminals find safe passage to Nepal and a safe refuge too. The Nepalese border has been the passage to haven for smugglers, who have been able to smuggle drugs and arms to India without hindrance.

Expressing apprehension over China's involvement in activities in Nepal, the then Uttarakhand Chief Minister Ramesh Rokhriyal said: "There is an increase in the activities of China in Nepal, Tibet and also Pakistan. We apprehend that there will be increase in anti-India activities on the Indo–Nepal border via Nepal, which will pose a danger to our country in the near future. Uttarakhand shares its border with China and Nepal and shares 350 km of the LoC and 250 km of the International border with the two countries. There is a growing threat to security due to increase in the activities of China in areas bordering the state.[37] Apart from strategic implication, China's effort to develop the rail link to its border with Nepal can reduce Kathmandu's dependence on India as it will enable it to import petroleum products from Beijing. A pro China-Nepal would not be in India's interest.

The Chinese have made its presence in Nepal in a big way. Efforts have been made to remove the Nepalese over dependence on India. China gave aid to Nepal as part of its policy. The road provided a direct strategic connection between China and Nepal through the difficult Tibetan route. To India, these developments were a cause of grave concern.

It is quite clear that China is also trying to make Nepal one of a series of

"Little Dragons" spewing fire at India. Hence, the Maoists-led Nepal will be influenced by China in its foreign policy decision-making. This would mean more space for infiltration of Chinese agents and their clandestine activities against India. Traditionally Chinese leadership still stick to Sun Tzu dictum that "To fight and conquer in all your battles is not supreme excellence; supreme excellence consists in breaking the enemy's resistance without fighting."[38]

Conclusion

With the detailed examination of the various phases of the Maoist activities, now, it becomes important to answer the major analytical question posed at the beginning of the article. Do Maoists in India and Nepal, today and in future pose a qualitatively and qualitatively different and a more serious threat to their security than in the past?

To address this fundamental question, it becomes important to discuss the relevance of Maoism in India and Nepal. In China, Mao Tse Tung's policies have been discredited. But the revolutionary path he has shown is still being followed in South Asia. In India and Nepal, Mao not only combined the Marxist–Leninist's ideology of revolution but also made a comprehensive study of the Chinese situation in overcoming the government policies. Mao puts the peasants at the forefront of his revolutionary formula and made land reforms the central theme on seizing the state power. On violence, Mao stated that "we are advocates of the abolition of war, we do not want war, but war can only be abolished through war and in order to get rid of the gun, it is necessary to take up the gun". One can say, as an ideology, Maoism was both progressive and inspirational, championing economic liberation opposing capitalist imperialism and criticizing revisionisms.

Revolution springs from political organizations that are prone to extremist schisms because it targets population that have not tasted the fruits of political and socio-economic development. The growing concern over the Maoist movement as a security threat does not signify that the movement and its aim to build a new socio-economic and political order is a new or recent phenomenon.

How then the Maoist movement can be ended or at least contained? On the government side, one can urge the governments in India and Nepal to review their current policy perspective and strategy of tackling Maoism with predominant security operations to eliminate the Maoists and instead, reorient it for implementation of a comprehensive agenda of protection and affirmative action which would wean away the tribal from the influence of the Maoists. The development and economic policies which aversely affect the tribal should be reversed and changed. The article is not intended to be presented to its readers as a policy paper but with an analysis of the complete Maoist phenomenon. The insight gained into the nature and danger of the Maoist movement allow for some recommendations.

The government in both the countries must build up political pressures to tackle this serious internal security threat. The governments much initiate diplomatic measures to enlist the support of the neighbouring countries to deny any kind of cooperation between the Maoist organization. Legislative back up, statutory actions, banning of unlawful organizations and setting up of Coordination Centre to deal with the revolutionary extremism must be formed on the basis of the government response to the challenge posed to the Indian and Nepali security.

Talks must be initiated by the centre and state representatives and all militant groups. Ceasefire, if desired, should be carried out in all the affected Maoist states in order to show the united force of the government. There is a need for all political parties to have a united stand on this problem. Moreover, what is more important is the involvement of the people in the fight against the Maoists because it is the people who suffer most. The recent incidents of backlash by the public against the Maoists in some states are a positive indicator.

The central and eastern parts of India and Nepal as a whole are relatively underdeveloped as compared to other parts of the country, both industrially and agriculturally. The areas also lag behind in almost all human development indices. Efforts must be centered around options of hard economics. Hence, efforts must be made by the government to tackle the disparities in the social system on a war footing. Though one cannot think of complete eradication of poverty but this could be reduced to a great extent by the government as to fulfill the demand of development amongst the local masses.

All this could be more effectively done by central schemes with liberal funding. In order to enlist the support of the people, the government must rely on psychological warfare. Here, the government must expose the weaknesses in the Maoist's ideological framework. Then, the restoration of people's faith in the government and efficient use of the mass media to highlight the use of extreme violence and the loss of human life and property are other key areas in the government's strategy. The people should be made more aware of development taking place in international politics, particularly emphasizing the diminishing role of Communism as we saw in the case of the collapse of communism in the USSR. The local people should be enlightened with the idea that Communism deals with the materialism. The leadership of the Maoist movement is in the hands of the upper class, whereas the cardres belong to the lower classes. There should be realization among the masses that we believe in the concept of non-violence. Socialism can be achieved peacefully through the democratic process. It should be noted that many South American and South Asia countries have not progressed despite strong leftist movements. In the age of globalization and liberalization, applying the Maoist's strategy is not so relevant for our country. In any case, China is more capitalist than India and Nepal Furthermore, an attractive and all encompassing surrender-cum-rehabilitation policy will have a great psychological impact on the people, as well on the Maoists who seem to be far removed from their ideology. Giving relief to victims will show the human face of the government.

REFERENCES

1. S. Subedi. 2005. "India, Nepal and the Maoist Conflict: A Nepalese Perspective", *Liberal Democracy Nepal Bulletin*, I(1):, p. 2.
2. Ibid.
3. Ibid.
4. S. Wolpert, *A New History of India*, 7th edition, Oxford University Press, New York, 2004, pp. 382–83.
5. R. Ray, *The Naxalites and their Ideology*, Oxford University Press, Delhi, 1988, p. 115.
6. E. Duyker, *Tribal Guerilla: The Santhals of West Bengal and the Naxalite Movement*, Oxford Press, New Delhi, 1987, pp. 55–57.
7. A. Mehra. 2000. "Naxalism in India: Revolution or Terror, Terrorism and Political Violence", 12 (2): p. 39.
8. Wolpert, op.cit, p. 382.
9. T.C. Johri, *Naxalite Politics in India*, New York, 1972; M. Ram, *Maoism in India*, Vikas Publication, Bombay, 1971; B.D. Gupta, *The Naxalite Movement*, Allied Publisher, Calcutta, 1974.
10. P. Singh, *The Naxalites Movement*, Rupa and Co., Delhi, 1995, p112.
11. S. Ghosh, *The Naxalite Movement*, Calcutta, 1947, p XXII.
12. Liberation, November, 1968, pp. 28-53.
13. S. Ghosh, op.cit, p. XXII
14. B.D. Gupta, op.cit, p. 60.
15. M. Singh, PM's Speech at the Chief Ministers Meet on Naxalism, April 13, 2006.
16. *The Hindu*, 23, 2005.

17. See N. K. Pant, Naxalite Violence and Internal Security, Institute of Peace and Conflict Studies, Article no. 523, July 13, 2001.
18. Mao Tse Tung, *On Guerilla Warfare*, Urbana, University of Illinois Press, 2000, p.45.
19. A. Kamgoj, Naxalism: India's Biggest Security Challenge, Institute of Peace and Conflict Studies, Article 1995, April 20, 2006.
20. S. DeBlieck. 2006. "Why Mao? Maoist Insurgencies in India and Nepal, *Peace Conflict and Development*, Issue 9: p.16.
21. Ibid.
22. United Nations Development Programme, Human Development Report: Cultural Liberty in Today's Diverse World, 2004, 141,148, 162.
23. See S. DeBlieck, op.cit, p.20
24. Thapa and Sajapati, *Kingdom Under Seige: Nepal's Maoist Insurgency*, 1996–2003, p 77.
25. Ibid., pp. 64, 79.
26. Ibid., p. 67.
27. S. DeBlieck, op.cit, p 24.
28. Prakash Singh, "The Naxalite Movement in India" Rupa & Co., New Delhi, 1995,
29. Ibid., p.26.
30. *The Daily News*, March 28, 2005.
31. S.D. Muni, *Maoist Insurgency in Nepal: The Challenge and the Response*, Rupa & Co. New Delhi, 2003 pp 88-89.
32. S.D. Muni, The Maoist Insurgency in Nepal: Origin and Evolution, ISAS Working Paper, No. 111, 28 July2010, p.11.
33. ibid.
34. R.K. Kujur, From CRZ to SEZ: Naxal Reins of Terror, April 21, 2007, www. ipcs.com.
35. Wikipedia Encyclopedia, http://www.wikipedia.org.
36. Nepal, South Asia Monitor, http://www.southasiamonitor.org/nepal/2006.
37. P. Murthy, Nepal Between India and China, World Focus, September,2010.
38. See S. Kondapalli, India–China Relation, 2009-10 World Focus, September 2010.

16

Understanding Extremism in Pakistan

Shalini Chawla

The terrorist attack in the Army Public School (Peshawar) on December 16, 2014, was probably the most horrifying and ghastly terror attack Pakistan has ever witnessed, leading to massive outrage and compelling the leadership to think about its strategic options. Killing of 135 innocent children indeed sparked aggressive reactions and Islamabad has been under tremendous pressure to counter home-grown terrorism. But obviously the question arises, how did Pakistan become an epicentre of terrorism? What led to this growth of ideological extremism in Pakistan? The answers to these questions lie in the study of Pakistan's journey into extremism.

Pakistan has been in existence for now more than six decades but the state has not been able to define its identity till date. Pakistan has struggled with contradictions in its posturing; it shared an ambiguous relationship with Islam; tried to embrace Western notions of modernity at the same time tried retaining the orthodox Islamic identity; has an overpowering and ambitious army which has ruled the nation for more than 30 years directly, and nearly an equal period with a civilian façade in front, but, has still struggled periodically to go back to the democratic order controlled by the fractured political leadership and has suffered a deep national identity crisis. Lack of identity has encouraged rise of ethnicity and pluralism within the Pakistani society. Born as a result of demand for a separate Muslim homeland it eventually stood as the saviour of Islam and in the process the military-led state has adopted policies based on religion which have had severe repercussions for the state. Religion has been used in Pakistan for nation building to strategic security.

Pakistan today has become the breeding ground for terrorism and the extremist elements within Pakistan, have taken a much stronger footing than ever before posing threat to the very existence of the Pakistani state. Today, liberal thinking faces enormous challenges for its survival. But, one has to address the question that did Pakistan fall prey to extremism just as the result of its involvement in the war on terror post-9/11? The answer is clearly 'no'. Pakistan today, is actually facing the blowback of its own policies which it has believed and pursued in the last five decades. Pakistan's reliance on terrorism as foreign policy tool is indeed responsible for its drift into extremism. This paper attempts to study Pakistan's journey towards present state of extremism, which the Pakistani leadership is unable to control posing the most alarming challenge to the stability of the country.

Birth of Pakistan: Jinnah's Dream

Pakistan was born as a demand for a separate homeland for Muslims as the All India Muslim League led by Muhammad Ali Jinnah strongly argued that Muslims had a special identity which would not be able to survive in a Hindu-dominated society, thus, a separate homeland for Muslims was the only solution. But, Jinnah's dream was quite different from what Pakistan actually transformed into. There was lack of consensus over Pakistan's ideological and territorial contours as Ayesha Jalal rightly pointed out:

> "Jinnah's resort to religion was not on ideology to which he was ever committed or even a device to use against rival communities; it was simply a way of giving a semblance of unity and solidarity to his divided Muslim constituents. Jinnah needed a demand that was specifically ambiguous and imprecise to command general support, something specifically Muslim though unspecific in every other respect."[1]

Jinnah in his famous speech before the Constituent Assembly on August 11, 1947 outlined his secular vision:

> "You are free; you are free to go your temples, you are free to go your mosques or to any other place of worship in this state of Pakistan. You may belong to any religion or caste or creed—that has nothing to do with the business of the state.... We are starting with this fundamental principle that

> we are all citizens and equal citizens of one state...In the course of time Hindus would cease to be Hindus and Muslims would cease to be Muslims, not in the religious sense, because that is the personal faith of each individual, but in the political sense as citizens of the State".[2]

Jinnah's dream was a secular state where the Muslim culture and social norms could be promoted. Jinnah's vision was the outcome of different set of circumstances where on the post-colonial movement he visualised an arrangement for the Indian Muslims who could be free in an independent state. But, Pakistan, over the decades completely drifted away from Jinnah's spirit. Pakistan never inherited a uniformed vision and there were contesting ideas, thus, the birth of the nation itself suffered lack of consensus and clarity on the issue of Islam. In the coming years, Pakistan hardly became a beneficiary of committed and visionary leadership. The state was driven differently by different regimes following different objectives. Jinnah passed away on October 11, 1948, and this was indeed a deadly blow to the spirit of Pakistan, and hardly anyone would disagree that his death altered the course of history.

Many of Pakistan's political elites were uncertain about the role of Islam in defining the nation's constitutional foundations. [3] It took the policy makers close to a decade to formalise the constitution of Pakistan which dissolved Jinnah's spirit of secular Islam.

There was persistent confusion and lack of consensus about the interpretation of Islam and this provided the political and military leadership enough space to exploit the factor of religion to serve their own interests. After independence the most daunting task for the Pakistani leadership was to secure Pakistan from the internal and external threats. Internally, Pakistan was fragmented and the two wings West Pakistan and East Pakistan which differed ethnically, culturally and economically, were separated by thousand miles of Indian territory. Not only the issue of East Pakistan but Pakistan also experienced insurgency in Baluchistan in the 1940s itself. The Frontier Province also was opposed to the idea of being a part of Pakistani state. With these internal vulnerabilities was the perceived threat from India, which Pakistanis suspected had hegemonic ambitions, and had been unfair in providing Pakistan with their due share of resources inherited from the British India. Hostility against India was the leading factor which obviously exaggerated with Pakistan's internal struggles.

The Beginning of the Ideological Drift and Pakistan's War for Kashmir

The factor of religion became one of the most critical in Pakistan's strategic security.

The need to control Jammu and Kashmir and incorporate it into Pakistan was felt very strongly in Pakistan since the British declaration of the India's partition. The prime reasons for Pakistan's quest for J& K were economic and strategic factors.

Pakistan launched the first war for Kashmir in 1947–48 in the name of 'tribal revolt'. The Pakistan Army with the consent of the political leadership invoked the tribesmen and the retired and serving army officers in the name of jihad, to raid and seize Kashmir. Islam was leveraged in the very beginning of the state itself to respond to the Indian threat. The government in Pakistan called on religious scholars to issue supportive *fatwas* (religious decrees).[4] The importance of the 1947–48 aggression was that it laid the basic guidelines for the future aggression by Pakistan. This was the beginning of use of religion to forward the state polices and also conduct covert operations backed by the full fledged support by the military.

Internally, Jinnah's dream of a pluralistic society was being challenged and in the early 1950s there were street protests calling for declaration that Ahmedias were non-Muslims.[5] The protests were orchestrated in part to destabalise the ruling polity and resignation of Pakistan's first foreign minister, Sir Zafarullah Khan, an Ahmadi was demanded.[6] In 1974, Ahmadis were officially declared non-Muslims through a constitutional amendment.

On the external front, the Pakistan army's covert activities expanded in Jammu and Kashmir after the 1962 India-China War. A close study of the covert activities indicates that the factor of religion started to gain momentum in the 1960s. Pakistan's covert activities in Kashmir were now gradually moving towards using religion as a driving force to gain support for the disintegration of India.

Another development in the late 1950s and 1960s was Pakistan's entry into a Cold War alliance with the United States. Pakistan entered into military agreements with the US and started to receive massive military aid. The US alliance provided Pakistan with high technology weaponry for their Army, Air Force and Navy. This added to their aggressive instincts to acquire Kashmir. The military establishment and rule was further strengthened in Pakistan with the US assistance and it gave military great confidence to carry on its covert war in Kashmir.

In the 1950s, Pakistan's covert operations in Kashmir valley did not yield results and were adding to frustration and impatience in Pakistan, even leading to the military officer's Rawalpindi Conspiracy against the civilian government. In 1964, Pakistan developed a strategy that came to be known as *Operations Gibraltar* and *Grand Slam*, which is a landmark in the history of both the nations. Although, the initial reasons for annexing Kashmir ceased to exist, the first factor of insecurity, due to the presence of the Indian Army on the western border, was solved as a result of the ceasefire agreement in 1949. The second factor, regarding the waters of rivers which originated from Kashmir was also solved with the Indus Water Treaty signed in 1960 through the good offices of the World Bank during Ayub Khan's regime.

In the late 1960s, a new set of jihadis emerged deriving their inspiration from left wing anti-imperialist struggles. The Pakistan military and political leadership were more and more convinced about the indispensability of covert warfare in their religiously driven strategies towards Jammu and Kashmir. Defeat in 1965 of its aggression only added to the leaning towards Islamic ideology.

1971: Break-Up of Pakistan

In the late 1950s and early 1960s, Pakistan witnessed the rising image of the military in the eyes of the people. General Ayubs' era in fact marked the beginning of military control in the political and civil system of Pakistan. This was important as it eventually led to the splitting up of Pakistan. Ayub's successor General Yahya Khan, talked about Islamic identity of Pakistan and kept defence at the top of its agenda. Yahya Khan, utilised the intelligence agencies to motivate the Islamic parties to work against the two major political parties—the Awami League and the Pakistan's People's Party. These parties were accused of being un-Islamic. The military regime had close ties with Jamaat-e-Islami and also encouraged the mushrooming of other Islamic groups.[7]

In the 1960s military's role expanded and also, political and ethnic tensions increased. The two wings of Pakistan, West and the East were undoubtedly very different. The only common factors between the two wings was *Islam* and *fear of India*. The West Pakistanis never valued or respected this identity of East Pakistan and what was more painful for the East was the discriminating attitude of the Punjabi who treated themselves as a superior class. The tensions in the Eastern Wing resulted in an insurgency and Pakistan's third war with India.

What was most critical was the evolution of Pakistan's grand strategy after 1971 war. The grand strategy incorporated two important objectives which decided the future course of action for the Pakistani leadership:

> First, to expand territory eastward (take Kashmir). This implied rise in covert activities in J&K and added emphasis on radical Islam in the name of jihad. Thus, terrorism was to be adopted as a foreign policy tool.
>
> Second, to expand control westward (to gain leverage in Kabul). This implied creating strategic depth in Afghanistan and also facilitating a Pakistan friendly governance.

Global Rise of Islamic Ideology in the 1970s and 1980s

The 1970s and 1980s witnessed re-emergence of Islam as a potent global force starting with Saudi Wahhabi spread of ideology. The Iranian revolution that shattered the secular basis of nationalist thinking and expectations of modernization and development theories. The revolution drew attention towards the significant changes that were taking place in many Muslim countries across the globe in the 1970s. Ironically, the revival of the Islamic ideology was most prominent in the societies which were modern or in the process of modernisation, possessing well-trained, western oriented, secular elite, for example: countries like, Egypt, Lebanon, Tunisia, Turkey and Algeria.

In Egypt and Malaysia the resurgence of Islam was manifested in people's lives, the conventional religious beliefs and also the state politics. Religion came much more into practice and was reflected in the form of daily prayers, fasting and the way people dressed. Spiritualism was emphasized with the revitalization of Sufism Islamic Ideology. Muslim rulers put stress on Islamic identity to gain legitimacy and Islamic organizations and symbols assumed paramount importance for the state.

Bhutto's turning towards Islam has to be studied taking into account the developments worldwide. He turned towards Islam to counter his Islamic critics and also to strengthen ties with oil-rich nations of the Arabian Gulf.

Bhutto's Islamic Socialism

The idea of an Islamic Pakistan was pronounced by Bhutto and then subsequently nurtured and developed by Zia, who used religion aggressively in controlling the state. Bhutto took forward the idea of *Islamic Socialism* and thus, enforced Islam as a major factor in statecraft. Stephen Cohen points out, "If the Pakistan movement and the first twenty-five years of the history of Pakistan can be characterized as a struggle to turn Indian Muslims into Pakistanis, the years since 1972 have been an extension of the process; a struggle to turn Pakistanis into good Muslims."[8] Bhutto's Islamic Socialism was considered insincere and it was seen more to establish the non-Indian identity of Pakistan.[9] Zia put the state at the services of Islam and took steps to inculcate the Islamic practices within state by banning alcohol and gambling, and declaring Friday as a non-working day. In 1976, Bhutto, appointed Zia-ul-Haq as the new Army Chief and allocated him the responsibility to Islamize the Pakistan Army. It was during this period "Jihad" was included as the motto for Pakistan Army apart from "Iman" and "Taqwa".

General Zia's pursuit of Islamisation

General Zia systematically reinforced the *Islamisation of Pakistan* which was propagated by his predecessor, Zulfikar Ali Bhutto. Zia's vision came out very clearly in his words:

> "Pakistan, which was created in the name of Islam, will continue to survive only if it sticks to Islam. That is why I consider the introduction of Islamic system as an essential prerequisite for the country."[10]

Zia introduced "Islamic Reforms" in various aspects of the Pakistani society and economy. Number of banking and commercial practices based on Islam were introduced, dress code in accordance with Islamic norms were stressed, new women's universities were proposed and strict regulations were laid on the sale and consumption of alcoholic beverages.[11] During General Zia's regime Islamic practices in the day-to-day life were made mandatory by the state. Pakistan Army in this period developed close links with the various Islamists groups and religion was used more and more in strategic thinking. Zia, in the process of reinforcing the Islamization of Pakistan and introducing Islamic reforms, allowed the Tablighi Jama'at (an Islamic missionary society) to operate freely within the Army. Zia was also the first army chief and the first politician in Pakistan to appear before the Tablighi's annual convention at Raiwind.[12]

Zia was entrusted with the task of Islamisation of the Pakistan Army when he took over as the army chief. Bhutto saw Zia as the right man to take the Pakistani military to the next stage of its evolution as the guarantor of an anti-India, Islamic ideology.[13] Zia, even as a Corps Commander distributed books written by Jamaat-e-Islami's founder, Maulana Sayyid Abdul Ala Maududi, as rewards for the officers who proved their calibre in various fields in his garrison. Adherence to the Islamic practices emerged as a major criteria for selection in the Army. According to Zia, a soldier had to be a true Muslim before he takes the responsibility of defending the Islamic Republic. In the armed forces the status of the religious teachers was raised to the level of a commissioned officer. This became a major attraction for the qualified individuals from the universities and religious institutions.

Pakistan under Zia's regime, started to practice Islamic practices much more as compared to earlier political or military regimes in the country. The state was now being run on the values interpreted on the basis of religion. The number of mosques were increased in the country. The education system was deeply influenced and Islamiat and Pakistan studies became compulsory for the B.A., Engineering, Medical, Commerce and Law students.

The Islamist parties and especially groups like Tablighi Jamat linked to the Deobandi tradition got much more access to the military officials. Zia encouraged the Islamist parties to counter the political forces. The Islamist parties did receive a favourable treatment form the ruling militia and members from Jamaat-i-Islami were offered senior positions in the important ministries. The judicial system of the state was Islamised and a Shariat Council consisting of Ulema was established to look into the constitutional and legal matters pertaining to the state, which were to be conducted in accordance with the Islamic thought.

It was during this process of *Islamisation* that Afghan War came into picture and altered the total dynamics of Pakistan's political, military and strategic policies.

The Afghan War in the 1980s

Following the Soviet invasion of Afghanistan Pakistan became the front-line for the United States in the fight against communism. Pakistan had already been a party to the destabilization of Afghanistan which increased with Soviet intervention and its reaction by US and Pakistan as its frontline state. The most significant developments as the outcome of Afghan war were:

1. The US war in Afghanistan led to structural and organizational development of the factor of *religion in war*. The soldiers for war were being trained to fight in a "holy war" in the name of God. The declaration of "jihad" in Afghanistan led to the legitimized structural development of institutions preparing young fighters. Religious belief that made the Mujahideen formidable warriors to defeat.[14]
2. Pakistan became a training ground for the guerilla fighters. The leadership agreed to support the guerrilla warfare with arms, ammunition, money, intelligence, training and operational advice. Pakistan offered the border areas of the NWFP (now Khyber Pakhtunkhwa) as a secure base for the Mujahideen guerrilla fighters.[15]
3. This major strategic development placed Pakistan in a position where it could demand the latest military weapons. Pakistan received an enormous military aid from the US. It also received unlimited funds from Saudi Arabia and Gulf countries to finance the US weaponry, which, Pakistan opted to procure in the 1980s.
4. The US intelligence services followed a strategy of supplying enormous amounts of arms and ammunition to Mujahideen leaders and commanders in the field.
5. The development of the narcotics trade on the frontier borders of Pakistan flourished with CIA assistance to fund the covert operations.

Rise in Terrorism in the 1980s and 1990s

In Kashmir, in the 1980s religious resurgence coupled with increasing alienation of the youth for diverse reasons started to grow in Kashmir and Pakistan's strategy of covert war through terrorism began to concretize. What was happening in Afghanistan and also simultaneously in Khalistan (with Pakistan's active assistance), had direct impact in the valley. Thus, in the mid-1980s, disturbances in Kashmir were growing with the unusual amount of Jamaat activity, processions and resentment against the Hindus and the communal divide had started to be a major disturbing factor. Pakistan continued its covert war and the year 1984 witnessed substantive escalation of violent acts in the Jammu and Kashmir. In the late 1980s and 1990s Pakistan became much more active in sponsoring terrorism in J&K. The ISI encouraged young Kashmiris to come to Pakistan for training. The ISI initially trained the secular groups in Kashmir and eventually shifted to training of the groups linked to Pakistan's own Islamic parties. [16]

The weapons used by the terrorist had undergone a change as Pakistan had acquired modern arms in the 1980s to equip the covert fighters in Afghanistan. On one side, Pakistan had equipment for the Afghan Mujahideen which could be easily smuggled into Kashmir, on the other side, Pakistan also acquired modern weapon system including F-16s from the US during this period and thus, was emotionally stronger to carry the covert strategy in Kashmir. But the most important factor for escalating the covert war in Punjab and Jammu and Kashmir was the acquisition of the nuclear weapons by Pakistan which it perceived as the security guarantee against a robust Indian military response.

Development of the Nuclear Weapons: Shield against Terrorism

Pakistan accelerated its nuclear programme in the 1980s under Zia. The military regime in Pakistan tried to exploit the India "threat" and acquisition of nuclear capability to acquire domestic legitimacy. It was under Zia's rule that Pakistan became a nuclear state and defined a coherent nuclear strategy. By 1987 it is believed that Pakistan could carry out a full nuclear explosion. By 1992, Pakistan declared officially that it possessed the cores of nuclear weapons and in 1998 Pakistan nuclear tests followed India's new posture of a nuclear state.

The acquisition of nuclear capability enhanced Pakistan's capability to wage and escalate the covert war in Kashmir as nuclear weapons were believed to deter India from responding with conventional military retaliation. Policy makers in Pakistan seem to be convinced that they will be able to carry on or rather accelerate their activities in Kashmir with the threat of using nuclear weapons if required and this would control India's strategic moves in the valley. This thought process seems to have grown with Pakistan's "first use policy". Pakistan claimed that it had the capability of a nuclear bomb in 1987, and it is noteworthy, that during the late 1980s the activities in the valley also witnessed a shift. The terrorist acts increased significantly in numbers and were planned in a more organised manner making the job of India security forces difficult.

Pakistan became more vocal about the possession of nuclear weapons in the late 1980s and then in the 1990s in order to create an impression of the fact that any radical move from Indian side might be retaliated with the *Islamic bomb*. Pakistan's strategy has been to use the nuclear card for aggressive militancy in Kashmir and thus Pakistan military now had the nuclear umbrella to shield them from the Indian military response. *Jihad*, now had the protection of the nuclear bomb for Pakistan. There is a clear correlation between progress in acquisition of nuclear weapons and launch of covert war during last 25 years.

1990s: Political Tug of War

After Zia's death Pakistan faced innumerable challenges. The nation had been under the military rule for a long period and thus getting back to democracy was a challenge, economic downslide had started to show signs, jihadi culture took firm roots in the country and U.S. alliance had just ended and Pakistan stood isolated internationally. The democratic regimes between 1988 and 1999 were unstable and changed frequently, especially, if the agenda of the elected governments challenged the power and functioning of the Army. During this period there were four elections and both Benazir Bhutto and Nawaz Sharif returned to power twice. There were four caretaker governments in between as neither of the elected governments could complete its term.

The ISI became an important centre of power on account of its role in the Afghan war and its involvement with the Americans. Although, the fundamentalists and Islamists appeared to have lost in the elections, their influence continued to grow, especially, among the intelligence agencies, military officers and emerging middle class in Pakistan. The ISI also managed to create and sustain the differences between the political parties which hampered the evolution of a mature democratic set up in Pakistan and contributed to the frequent changes on the political front. The intelligence encouraged and utilised the Islamist parties to counter the political groups which went against the military's interests.

On the external front, there were two developments in this decade. Both these developments were the continuation of Pakistan's existing polices. The leadership in Pakistan intensified its terrorist activities on the Indian soil through their proxies and anti-India terrorist organisations became much more active in the valley and other parts of India. The ISI was not a fully trained and equipped organisation with a ready infrastructure for jihad which was now fully diverted towards India to continue Pakistan's strategy of 'bleed India through thousand cuts'. By 2002, Pakistan became home for more than two dozen militant groups operating in neighbourhood and pursuing their agenda which was looked at by the state in its favour. The largest among them were LeT, JeM, Harkat-ul-Mujahidden (HuM) and Harkat-al-Jihad-al-Islami (HJI).

All of these organisations shared a similar source and pursued similar goals. These organisations had state's patronage and funds have never been a problem. The state's patronage in fact helped the jihadi organisations to raise funds in the public places.

On the Western front, Pakistan was keen to create its strategic depth and not to have a hostile government. The Army, ISI along with the political leadership came together to support a new class of warriors—*Taliban*. In 1994, Afghanistan saw the outbreak of Taliban, which was composed of the younger generation of Pakistani-Afghans. Talban were mainly the Afghans who grew in the Pakistani refugee camps and were products of Madrassas which were encouraged during Zia's time and were funded by the Saudi money. Maulan-Fazl-ul-Rahman, leader of the Jamait-i-Ulems-i-Islam-F (JUI-F) supported Taliban and being a close ally of Benazir he played a critical role in facilitating communications between Pakistan and Taliban.[17] The Pakistani leadership extended full-fledged support to Taliban and added to their strength from Pakistani Madrassas. Taliban, began to take over one province after another in Afghanistan and brought the whole of Afghanistan under their control in less than five years. [18]

Musharraf's Coup and US led War on Terror Post-9/11

Military under the leadership of General Musharraf assumed control of the state in 1999 and, even though the coup was condemned by most of the world leaders, it was mostly supported by the Pakistani populace. Pakistan once again witnessed a major strategic development and entered into a third alliance with the US post-9/11. Once again, Pakistan arrived at a critical crossroads. Musharraf attempted to project a path of moderation and publicly announced on 12 January 2002, that Pakistani territory will not be used for (jihadi) terrorism. In 2004, he announced his plea for *Enlightened Moderation* which could provide an answer to Pakistan's identity and its relationship with Islam. Defining the Enlightened Moderation he said:

> "The strategy of enlightened moderation ... involve a win-win situation for the whole of the world as well as for the Muslim countries. This is a two-pronged strategy. One prong is to be delivered by the Muslim world itself by shunning militancy and extremism and adopting the path of socioeconomic uplift to achieve its own emancipation. The other prong is meant to be delivered by the West, and the United States in particular, to determinedly resolve with justice all political disputes in which Muslims

> are engaged and also assist in the socioeconomic betterment of the deprived Muslim world....The time have come to re-think our position. What we need is a renaissance....We have to concentrate on human resource development, and the best way for that is through poverty alleviation, greater education, better health and assured social justice.... We have to adopt the path of moderation, a conciliatory approach, a pacific approach, in order to cleanse ourselves of the charge that Islam is a religion of militancy and is averse to modernization, democracy and secularism."[19]

Although, Musharraf talked about the moderate, secular path which included rejection of extremism, but the actual strategies which military pursued were certainly not in sync with the announced enlightened moderation. It was more to appease the West and project an image of Pakistan as a moderate Islamic nation which believed in countering extremism and was more focused on the socio-economic development.

The military regime came under immense pressure by the Bush administration to act against the terrorist organisations and Musharraf did issue orders to ban some of the key militant outfits and also registering of the Madrassas. These efforts failed to provide results and the popular consensus has been that military's flawed approach towards the war on terror has been responsible for rising extremism and flourishing insurgency on Pakistan's frontier borders, NWFP (now Khyber Pakhtunkhwa – KPK) and FATA. These have been troublesome regions in even the most peaceful times and are now engaged in a full blooded insurgency. Pakistan for the first time is facing terrorist attacks within its own territories. The military has a history of waging insurgencies (in the name of Jihad) since the time of its creation in 1947, and, post-9/11 has been compelled to take a reversal role of counter-insurgency. Military has been flagrantly discriminate in dealing with various terrorist groups and has not given up its jihadi terrorism as state policy.

Pakistan military did conduct numerous operations to target the Taliban and Al Qaeda, but the top leadership of these groups was not targeted, which was very clearly demonstrated by the fact that Osama bin Laden was comfortably living in Abbottabad before getting killed in 2012, in the operation conducted by the US Naval Seals.

The military has continued to jurture the terrorist groups which have been working in coordination with the Pakistan Army and the ISI against India, such as, Lashkar-e-Taiba, Jaish-e-Muhammad, and the Harkat-ul-Mujahideen. These are the terrorists groups which Pakistan army has trained, encouraged and financed to carry out the covert war in Jammu and Kashmir and rest of India since 1980s. These groups are the "strategic assets" of the military and are an extension of Pakistan's military strategy to continue the sub conventional war against India. Although, some of these organisations, including the most prominent Lashkar-e-Taiba was banned in 2002, they have continued to functions. Jamaat-ud-Dawa is the front organistaion for Lashkar and JuD chief, Hafiz Saeed with a bounty of 10$ million is treated as a hero by the Pakistanis.

Taliban Insurgency: Emergence of the Tehreek-e-Taliban Pakistan (TTP)

The Taliban insurgency began as early as 2003 when the Al-Qaeda and the Afghan Taliban fighters were flushed out of Afghanistan by the US Armed forces. In 2007, the Tehreek-e-Taliban Pakistan (TTP) emerged as an entity in the context of series of military operations (that took place post 9/11)—Pakistani military operations in FATA as well as U.S. unmanned aerial vehicle (UAV) strikes in FATA. Until then, most of the component groups of TTP were loosely organised with ties to the Afghan Taliban. The TTP started to professionally organize itself when Abdullah Mehsud of Afghan Taliban returned to Waziristan from the Guantanamo Bay camp. He blew himself in Pishin, Balochistan during a siege by Pakistani forces in 2006.[20] After Abdullah Mehsud's death, Baitullah Mehsud, a leading member of the Afghan Taliban, organised all the groups operating in FATA who professed similar ideologies and knit them into one of the most dangerous terrorist/insurgent group called the TTP.

The organisation consists of a number of militant groups (around 20 of them) and is rooted in the tribal belt of Pakistan. TTP's creation in December 2007 marked a new development arising out of the realisation among the local and foreign militants that a central command is required in order to attain their objectives, and Baitullah Mehsud provided them the unifying force. Main objectives of TTP are: (i) foreign troops must leave Afghanistan; (ii) Pakistan must end its cooperation with the US and NATO forces; and (iii) sharia must replace the existing legal system. TTP has adopted a strictly anti-state and specifically anti-military agenda and has been conveying its message by consistently attacking the government/military offices. In other words, TTP has organised itself as a true insurgency, ideologically as well as organisationally.

TTP draws its ideological guidance from al-Qaeda and also, provides safe haven to the al-Qaeda allies in FATA. Given the mutual cooperation between the two organisations it would not be wrong to state that the TTP is a force multiplier for al-Qaeda.[21] TTP has launched numerous attacks against US, NATO and Pakistani targets. The organisation regards the Pakistani state as enemy of Islam for siding with the US. TTP has adopted an anti-state posture and has claimed responsibility for most of the terrorist attacks including assassination of Benazir Bhutto. The organisation is growing in influence among young and unemployed youth and is using *shariah* to promote its political and ideological agenda.

Conclusion

Presently, Pakistan is a facing a broad landscape of militancy. Variety of terrorist groups with varying agenda operate from Pakistan and share varied relationship with the state. Some of these organisations like the TTP regard the state as enemy of Islam for joining hands with the West and killing their own people. On the other side are the deadly groups like the Jamaat-ud-Dawa, which are flourishing in the heart of Pakistan and are under the state patronage. For the first time, militancy has managed to penetrate in the interiors of Punjab and Sindh, and the Army GHQ became one of the terror targets in the recent past. In fact, bases of all the three forces have been attacked, and the air force bases have become frequent targets The impact of Afghan war has allowed the al-Qaeda, Haqqani network and the Taliban inside Pakistan where they have been expanding their influence. Pakistan military and the ISI have nurtured some of the terrorist organisation which it categorically grades as their "strategic assets" and is clearly not willing to act against them. These so called "friendly"[22] groups as Ayesha Siddiqua Agha terms it include: the Good Taliban, Lashkar-e-Taiba (LeT), Jamaat-ud-Dawa (JuD), and Jaish-e-Muhammad. The Haqqani network which has strongholds in the bordering Afghan districts of Paktia and Khost and is involved in the anti-US and anti-NATO operations has enjoyed the state patronage for long.[23] The military has desisted from acting against these groups and has been "selective and partial" in its counter-terrorism approach, which has been the root cause for the lack of success in the war on terror.

The frontier borders—NWFP and KPK have become the breeding ground for terrorism and the region presents a conglomeration of various insurgents and terrorists groups to the Pakistani military and the NATO forces.

Al-Qaeda, Haqqani and Taliban have established their sanctuaries in these area. Insurgency in Baluchistan, which became active in 2004 has aggravated much more after killing of Akhbar Bugti in 2007. Added to this deadly mix of extremist fact is the TTP. Pakistani Taliban has posed real danger to the sate and they are in a way extension of Sunni Deobandi militancy. The Pakistani Taliban has absorbed members of radical Sunni organisations. This has also further exaggerated the problem of Shia-Sunni violence not only on the tribal belt but also other parts of Pakistan.

Islam has remained extremely critical for Pakistan in its domestic and foreign policy. But the interpretation of Islam has varied under different regimes. Jinnah's vision was of that of a secular nation where Muslim culture and norms could be protected and practiced freely by the Muslims. Obviously, his vision was shaped up under different set of circumstances, and eventually, as one can see the state adopted different interpretations of Islam completely deviating away from Jinnah's spirit. Religion under Zia, found its most extremist expression and Pakistan's ideological posture was reshaped. The underlying problem is that the state has but been able to define its relationship with Islam till date. Pakistani leadership cannot allow itself to be entangled in contradictions, where it talks about enlightened moderation on one side, and simultaneously, patronise the terrorist outfits which brain wash the young Pakistani minds to join hands in fighting a holy war in the neighbourhood. Pakistan is facing a deadly jihadi blowback of its own long stated policies based on terrorism, threatening the survival of state. Leadership in Pakistan needs to seriously reconsider its strategic calculus and restrain from using terrorism legitimised by religion as a foreign policy tool.

REFERENCES

1. A. Jalal, *The State of Martial Rule* (Cambridge, Cambridge University Press, 1990) p. 16.
2. *Quaid-i-Azam Mohammad Ali Jinnah's Speeches as Governor-General of Pakistan 1947-48*, (Karachi, Government of Pakistan, 1964).
3. Farzana Shaikh, *Making Sense of Pakistan* (London, Foundation books, 2009) p. 5.
4. Z. Haider, "Ideological Adrift", ed. Maleeha Lodhi, *Pakistan Beyond the Crisis State* (New Delhi, Rupa Publications, 2011) p. 116.
5. Ahmedis are followers of an alleged nineteenth century messiah called Mirza Ghulam Ahmed.
6. Z. Haider, n 4, p. 116.
7. Ibid., p. 118.
8. S.P. Cohen, *The Pakistan Army* (Karachi, Oxford University Press, 1998), p. 89.
9. See, S.P. Cohen, *The Idea of Pakistan*, (New York, Oxford University Press, 2005), p. 170.
10. "General Zia ul-Haq's Address to the Nation on July 5, 1977", quoted in Hasan Askari Rizvi, *The Military and Politics in Pakistan 1947-1986*, (Lahore, Progressive Publishers, 1986), pp. 289-93.

11. S.P. Cohen, *The Pakistan Army*, (Kaeachi, Oxford University Press, 1998), p. 91.
12. S.P. Cohen, *The Idea of Pakistan*, (New York, Oxford University Press, 2005), p. 113.
13. Husain Haqqani, *Pakistan: Between Mosque and Military*, (Lahore, Vanguard Books, 2005), p. 112.
14. Brigadier M. Yousaf and Major M. Adkin, *The Bear Trap* (Lahore, Jang Publishers, 1992), p. 32.
15. Ibid., p. 49.
16. R. Ahmed, *Descent into Chaos* (London, Penguin Group, 2008), p. 111.
17. Hassan Abbas, *Pakistan's Drift Into Extremism: Allah, the Army and America's War on Terror*, (New York, M.E. Sharpe, 2005) p. 154.
18. Ibid., p.155.
19. Speech by General Musharraf, "OIC Challenge and Response: Enlightened Moderation", 1 June 2004, at http://presidentmusharraf.wordpress.com/2005/01/18/musharraf-oic-enlightened-moderation/
20. I. Gul, *The Al Qaeda Connection: the Taliban and Terror in Pakistan's Tribal Areas*, (New Delhi, Penguin books, 2009) p. 51.
21. "Tehrik-e-Tliban Is a Terror Group", *VOANEWS.com Policy*, July 9, 2010, at http://www.voanews.com/policy/editorials/Tehrik-e-Taliban-Is-A-Terror-Group-102393269.html
22. A.S. Agha, "Pakistan's Counterterrorism strategy: Separating Friends from Enemies", *The Washington Quarterly*, Winter 2011, pp. 149–62.
23. Ibid.

17

The Emerging Patterns in India-Pakistan Conflict

Rajpal Budania

The twenty-first century is being termed as the Asian century as the region has become the epicenter of international geo-politics. Within Asia, South Asia is being termed as the most dangerous area in the world. South Asia has attracted the attention of the world as never before. The international security studies are dominated by the issues relating to South Asia. India-Pakistan conflict is one of the most talked about issues in international security studies. The world has changed and moved towards cooperative regimes. In contrast, South Asia is one region which has not seen emergence of a successful cooperative regime. The Indo-Pakistan conflict has entered a new phase and has acquired new dimensions.

This article is an attempt to take note of the emerging patterns in India-Pakistan conflict. The article focuses on five main perceptible patterns in India-Pakistan conflict. *One*, India and Pakistan relations have been predominantly marked by confrontationist policies since the days of the partition. But now there is a marked desire for cooperation, to develop structures of cooperation and manage issues in conflict through a dialogue mechanism. *Two*, there has been transformation of strategies on the most contentious issues of Kashmir and terrorism. Pakistan has come round to the position that there can be no military solution to the issue of Kashmir. On the issue of terrorism both the countries believe that there has to be a common understanding and development of durable structures for combating terrorism. *Three*, there is a clear trend of taking peace initiatives so that issues are managed and negative developments are not allowed to turn into major crises. *Four*, the international community is playing a responsible role in understanding the key issues of terrorism and Kashmir. On the issues Pakistan had won many sympathizers to its policies, particularly the United States of America and its allies. But today, all of them are supportive of India's stand that Kashmir is a bilateral issue and it needs to be resolved peacefully by both the countries. The international community has put Pakistan under a scanner for its policies on sponsored terrorism. The international alliance against terrorism has brought unprecedented positive consequences for not only India but the entire South Asian region. *Five*, India-Pakistan conflict is witnessing a new and more dangerous trend reflecting competitive security in the field of strategic rivalry. In this strategic rivalry, Cold War alignments stand altered and now the U.S. strategic cooperation with India is a new factor in the regional balance of power. China has stepped its strategic cooperation with Pakistan. Moreover, Russia is contemplating defence cooperation with Pakistan and thus causing security concerns to India. This article reflects in detail on all these emerging trends in India-Pakistan conflict.

Dialogue Process and Peace Initiatives

A pattern of dialogue in a structured manner on all the contentious issues has emerged between India and Pakistan. India-Pakistan relations have witnessed a new trend of managing conflicts in a structured manner through a mechanism of dialogue and concrete peace initiatives. All the contentious issues between India and Pakistan have been included in the composite dialogue process initiated in 1997. It covered eight baskets of issues: Jammu and Kashmir (J&K); Siachen; Tulbul Navigation Project/Wular Barrage; Sir Creek; Terrorism and Drug Trafficking; Economic and Commercial Cooperation; Peace and Security; and Promotion of Friendly Exchanges in various fields. The composite dialogue process remained disrupted from end-1998 to June 2004. The dialogue could not make headway because of India's insistence that an end to Pakistan-sponsored terrorism must precede any dialogue. The dialogue process was resumed in the aftermath of India's peace initiative in 2003. Since then several rounds of talks have been held on all the issues covered under the composite dialogue.

India-Pakistan beleaguered relations witnessed considerable improvement in the aftermath of India's peace initiative in April 2003. During his visit to the beleaguered state of Jammu and Kashmir, Indian Prime Minister Atal Bihari Vajpayee, on 18 April 2003, made peace overtures to Pakistan by announcing restoration of diplomatic relations and cross-border transport links, severed after 13 December 2001 terrorist attack on Indian Parliament. India's peace initiative was welcomed in Pakistan. Critics in India believed that Pakistan will not be able to restrain the terrorists; a condition on which the success of the peace process depended. A day after the peace initiative, Vajpayee himself clarified that a meaningful dialogue would be possible only if Islamabad stopped supporting cross-border terrorism. [1] The initiatives are a result of pressure on both sides to manage the conflicts peacefully and prepare a ground for their final settlement. The two governments have held regular talks on all the contentious issues and developed institutional mechanisms to resolve them. Restoration of democracy in Pakistan after the February 2008 general elections, and further successful conduct of general elections in 2013 when Nawaz Sharif became the prime minister of Pakistan, has generated a positive dynamic in the management and resolution of India-Pakistan conflict. The international community, particularly the major powers, has welcomed the India-Pakistan peace process and their bilateral efforts for resolving disputes.

India has officially acknowledged that the peace process has produced positive results.[2] Situation in Kashmir has improved as a result of diminishing incidence of terrorist violence. The ceasefire along the international boundary, the Line of Control (LoC) and the Actual Ground Position Line (AGPL) in Siachen in force since November 2003 set a new milestone in the peace process.[3] The LoC remained peaceful and hardly witnessed any major violation until the last couple of years.

Pakistan has come up with several proposals on Kashmir. In December 2006 President Musharraf made a four-point proposal for settling the Kashmir issue.[4] The four-point formula included: making borders irrelevant, demilitarization, self-governance, and joint management. He also said that Pakistan would give up its claim on the state if India too did the same for resolving the issue.[5] India said that it was not ready to a joint management of J&K as proposed by Pakistan.[6] It also did not agree to the Pakistani concept of self-governance in the state. India believes that the state already enjoys it by having a popular government. India, however, is supportive of the idea of softening of LoC, particularly to allow trade relations.

For the need for increasing cooperation for combating terrorism, the India-Pakistan joint statement made during the SAARC summit in January 2004 in Islamabad is historic. The joint statement of January 6, 2004, by Indian Prime Minister Atal Behari Vajpayee and Pakistani President Pervez Musharraf highlighted that in order to take forward and sustain the dialogue process, violence, hostility and terrorism must be prevented.[7] President Musharraf pledged that "he will not permit any territory under Pakistan's control to be used to support terrorism in any manner."[8]

During their meeting in Havana, Cuba, on 16 September 2006, during the Non-aligned Movement (NAM) summit, the Indian Prime Minister Manmohan Singh and Pakistani President Pervez Musharraf agreed upon the establishment of a joint India-Pakistan anti-terrorism mechanism.

Over the years, India has maintained that normalisation of relations between the two countries is largely dependent on Pakistan completely discarding its policy of using terrorism as a state policy against India in all of its manifestations. Vajpayee government, however, had adopted a harder approach on the issue when it insisted that there could not be any dialogue with Pakistan until it completely stopped sponsored terrorism against India. During the UPA (United Progressive Alliance) regime, there was a nuanced departure from that approach and India insisted that terrorism was the main stumbling block and dialogue might go on but also emphasised that it would not bear the desired fruit until Pakistan put in a sincere effort to terminate terrorism in its entirety. Prime Minister Manmohan Singh elaborated India's approach thus: "People-to-people contacts have gone up, trade relations have shown improvement...but there cannot be normalisation of relations between our two countries unless and until terror machine, which is still active in Pakistan is brought under control. This has been our policy during the nine years we have been in office. It is the same approach which can guide us in dealing with Pakistan in years to come."[9] After the NDA (National Democratic Alliance) formed government in May 2014, the Narendra Modi-led government has adopted a hard position on the issue of terrorism and now India is insisting that dialogue can take place only when Pakistan stops all kinds of support to terrorism. The BJP national executive passed a resolution on foreign policy at its meet at Benagluru on 3 April 2015, which says: "We have laid out a clear policy for building peaceful and friendly relations with Pakistan, predicated on an end to terrorism. ...There can be no compromise with terrorism. There can't be any duplicity towards a problem that has become a regional crisis and is fast becoming an international nightmare...All outstanding issues with Pakistan can be resolved through bilateral dialogue in an atmosphere free from terror and violence."[10] Furthermore, the resolution also said that India's engagement with Pakistan would be based on strategic interests.[11] For India, terrorism is the key issue in its relations with Pakistan and tackling it amounts to serve its key security interests vis-à-vis Pakistan.

Nuclearisation of South Asia has imposed an obligation on both India and Pakistan to manage the disputes, crises, or issues through political means and initiatives. Understanding the diplomatic need and strategic compulsions of the time, India took the initiative for concluding the Lahore declaration after the nuclear tests. Prime Minister Atal Behari Vajpayee visited Pakistan and signed on 21st February 1999 the Lahore declaration and the memorandum of understanding (MoU) with the Pakistani Prime Minister Nawaz Sharif. Both the documents bind India and Pakistan on the process of dialogue on a range of issues. These have been considered important steps towards initiating a political process for building peace by undertaking confidence and security building measures in conventional and nuclear fields.

The Lahore declaration and the MoU spell the framework in which the nuclear risk reduction measures can be undertaken and a peace process strengthened. The MoU says: "The two sides shall engage in bilateral consultations on security concepts and nuclear doctrines with a view to developing confidence-building measures in the nuclear and conventional fields, aimed at avoidance of conflict.... The two sides shall engage in bilateral consultations on security, disarmament and non-proliferation issues within the context of negotiations on these issues in multilateral fora."[12] The two sides decided to take measures and inform each other of any "accidental, unauthorized or unexplained incident" in the nuclear field.[13] Advance notification of ballistic missile tests by the two countries was also included in the MoU. Both the countries have developed synergy on the issues of nuclear disarmament and non-proliferation in international fora.[14] Both the countries have held several rounds of talks so far on nuclear CBMs. Both the sides have reaffirmed their commitment to unilateral moratorium on further nuclear testing.

New Tactics on Terrorism and the Kashmir Issue

India-Pakistan relations have entered a new phase wherein both the states are claiming success in their respective positions on the contentious issues of Kashmir and terrorism. India and Pakistan have fought several wars over the

Kashmir issue. Apart from this, Pakistan has also used proxy war or state-sponsored terrorism against India over the issue. During the Cold War period, the issue got intensely internationalized and Pakistan largely succeeded in making Kashmir a core issue in its relations with India. The very strategies Pakistan employed for weakening India have today turned Pakistan into a failing and unstable state. Apart from being a sponsor of terrorism, Pakistan has become a victim of terrorism. After 9/11, India has achieved significant success in convincing the world public opinion on the factor of Pakistan-sponsored terrorism as a major stumbling block in the resolution of the Kashmir issue.

India has achieved substantial success in addressing the internal dimensions of the problem. The elections to the assembly of Jammu and Kashmir in 2014 have indicated that domestic variables of J&K are slowly and gradually becoming more favourable to India's approach to resolving the issue by promoting the participation of the people of Kashmir in the democratic process. The political and military establishment of Pakistan has not been happy at the gains India has made by curbing insurgency and restoring popular government in Jammu and Kashmir. Pakistan has attempted several ploys for thwarting India's efforts at consolidating democratic process in J&K by conducting elections at all levels, namely for the Lok Sabha, state assembly and even local bodies on a regular basis since the elections of 1996. It has called them farce. Allegations were made that Indian security forces played big role in these elections. The separatist parties were motivated to compel people to boycott elections. Terrorist attacks and threats have been made several times against the democratic process in J&K. Even the representatives of the local bodies were killed and pressurised to resign from their posts. Pakistan along with the separatist forces in Kashmir has worked against the success of democratic process in the state as a matter of policy.

New patterns are emerging in India-Pakistan conflict over the Kashmir issue. Both India and Pakistan have adopted new approaches and tactics on the complex issue of Kashmir. Pakistan's strategy on the Kashmir issue has acquired a nuclear context. Pakistan has made concerted efforts in creating an impression on the international community that India and Pakistan might witness a nuclear clash on the Kashmir issue. Pakistan's strategy has been focused on nuclear blackmail to gain politico-military advantage in Kashmir. To India's discomfiture, it has suited the Western powers to talk of Kashmir as a nuclear flashpoint. In the post-nuclearisation period, Pakistan has attempted to use cross border infiltration, and even intrusion as was witnessed during the Kargil crisis, and the consequent clashes across the LoC as a leverage to convince the U.S. and other powers that such clashes could escalate into a nuclear conflict, and, therefore, they should intervene on the Kashmir issue. Hence, after the overt nuclearisation of South Asia India is under pressure and facing a dilemma over Pakistan's ploys for making Kashmir as a nuclear flashpoint. Now as both India and Pakistan have access to nuclear arms, what one fears the most is the possibility of military conflict as a means of achieving policy goals. Pakistan perceives any situation of Kashmiri disenchantment with Indian political-security establishment as an opportunity to achieve its sinister designs in Kashmir. The Kargil conflict showed that nuclear factor had emboldened Pakistan to redefine its policy on the Kashmir issue by questioning sanctity of the LoC. In December 2013, Nawaz Sharif said that "Kashmir is a flashpoint and can trigger a fourth war between the two nuclear powers any time."[15] To further increase pressure on India, Pakistan also considered the idea of linking the solution of terrorism and even Afghanistan conflict with resolution of the Kashmir issue.[16] It believes that if the Kashmir is resolved according to the wishes of the Pakistani establishment, the problem of terrorism will automatically be resolved as Kashmir provides raison d'être to terrorism in Pakistan.

Though differences over the approach to solving the problem are gaining ground in the domestic politics of India, there still prevails a broad consensus on the security imperative of India's Kashmir policy and the Shimla accord as a framework for the solution of bilateral inter-state problems.

India's democratic polity has provided peaceful alternatives to state terrorism of one kind or another for resolving such conflicts within the system through negotiations. Notwithstanding the mistakes Indian political leadership has made on Kashmir as a centre-state issue in India's domestic politics, India's policy on Kashmir based on political means has proved to be more effective than that of Pakistan based on war, interference and internationalization of the issue. But now in the aftermath of radicalization of the people of Kashmir Valley, it is being argued that India need to review its certain internal mechanisms for dealing with the problem. During the run-up to the general elections to the Lok Sabha in 2014 and also during the election to the J&K Assembly elections in 2014, the BJP proposed in its election manifesto for abolition of the special status to the state of Jammu and Kashmir as granted under the Article 370 of the Indian Constitution to emotionally, politically and economically integrate the state with India.

India has become more assertive in maintaining its traditional policy of status quo in Jammu and Kashmir. India has pronounced that there is no religious or territorial solution to the Kashmir problem and the boundaries between India and Pakistan cannot be redrawn.[17] In November 2009, Prime Minister Manmohan Singh reiterated India's position: "I have publicly stated that there can be no redrawing of borders (in Jammu and Kashmir)... but our two countries can work together to ensure that these are borders of peace, that people-to-people contacts grow in a manner in which people do not even worry whether they are located on this side of the border or that side."[18] The Indian Prime Minister Manmohan Singh while addressing the UN General Assembly on 28 October 2013 categorically stated that Jammu and Kashmir is an integral part of India and there can never ever be any compromise on India's territorial integrity.[19] India, therefore, believes that the Kashmir issue requires change of Pakistani policy of irredentism based on two-nation theory and completely stopping any kind of support to terrorism against India. India has engaged all the parties and groups of all shades of opinion in talks for a peaceful internal resolution of the issue.[20]

One major change in the perception of Pakistan on the method of resolution of the Kashmir problem has become more palpable in recent years. Of late, Pakistan has come round to the view that the Kashmir issue cannot be resolved through military means or war. This was echoed by President Musharraf, while addressing the Foreign Affairs committee of the Spanish Congress in Madrid on 25th April 2007, when he observed that military solution was not an answer to resolve the Kashmir issue as the option of using force to settle bilateral disputes between India and Pakistan never worked in the past.[21] Similar sentiments have been expressed by the leadership which followed Musharraf. President Asif Ali Zardari opined that Kashmir cannot be resolved through military means. The present Pakistan Prime Minister Nawaz Sharif has also echoed similar line. After the victory of his party in the general elections of 2013, Nawaz Sharif stated that issues between India and Pakistan cannot be resolved through guns and bullets; Pakistan must never allow its territory to be used for terrorist activities against India; the issue of Kashmir needs be resolved peacefully to the satisfaction of all the parties, India, Pakistan and the people of Kashmir.[22] He rather optimistically stated: "The message to my friends in India that we have a lot of love and affection for you all. We must become good friends and hold each other's hands… let us make a new beginning, let us sit down together and let us resolve that we will from now onwards resolve all our outstanding issues peacefully and in a very friendly manner, in a very friendly atmosphere."[23]

The successive governments in India, whether the earlier UPA government or the present NDA government, have had a common perception on the issue of tackling Pakistan sponsored terrorism. India believes that until Pakistan takes effective steps to curb state-terrorism in its entirety, the dialogue on the resolution of the Kashmir issue will not bring concrete results. The developments in this regard indicate a change of approaches on both sides. Both India and Pakistan have developed a common perception that terrorism must be eliminated and both the countries have become insecure due to the menace of terrorism. In a major departure from the past, India believes that though Pakistan is the epicenter of terrorism, yet it has also become a victim of terrorism.

Deepening Strategic Rivalry

The strategic rivalry between India and Pakistan had entered a new phase which is qualitatively different from the earlier period. The strategic rivalry not only endangers them bilaterally but it has become a major threat for international security as Pakistan is turning into a failed state and there are serious doubts about the safety of its nuclear arsenal. The assumption that two nuclear powers cannot go to war has been quite substantially proved wrong when Pakistan carried out a limited aggression against India in the Kargil-Drass sectors of J&K in 1999. Moreover, Pakistan carried out this adventure under its nuclear umbrella. Despite its claim of having 'credible' minimum deterrence, India was subjected to a case of nuclear blackmail and as a result India could not take recourse to optimal military defence onslaught and it had to fight the war within its territory.

Paul Bracken has argued that the second nuclear age as witnessed in Asia, or for that matter in Pakistan, is very alarming as the weaponisation is sought on the basis of acute nationalism and in a very clandestine manner. Moreover, the nuclear weaponisation in Asia is characterised by multi-pronged rivalries, command and control uncertainties, affordability factors, and pursuit of weaponisation by non-democratic and instable regimes.[24] Pakistan is increasing its nuclear warheads at a disconcerting pace. In fact, Pakistan has been termed as having the fastest growing nuclear arsenal. It is believed to be having more nuclear weapons than India. The estimates put India's nuclear warheads between 90 and 110, whereas Pakistan's are put at 100-120.[25] At the present pace Pakistan will overtake other nuclear weapon states in terms of numerical strength of its nuclear warheads.[26] There are two plausible rationales for Pakistan's growing nuclear arsenal. One, because of India's superior capabilities and two, the evolving U.S. distrust of Pakistan and the belief that the U.S. might intervene in Pakistan for the purpose of eliminating its nuclear weapons.

The missile race between India and Pakistan has entered a strategic superiority realm. Both India and Pakistan have been developing their missile delivery systems. India bestowed with indigenous capabilities has overtaken an ambitious missile development programme which includes both offensive and defensive missile systems. It has successfully tested the Inter-continental Ballistic Missile (ICBM) *Agni*-V with a range of 5,000 km. India has taken missile race to a new level by also testing defensive missiles along with the offensive missiles. It is working on a two-tier—lower tier and high altitude—defence shields to intercept incoming missiles. India has been concerned at the development of ballistic missiles by Pakistan and China. The 23 November 2012 Advanced Air Defence (AAD) tests by India demonstrated its capability to intercept ballistic missiles with a range of 1500 km.[27] In response to this, on 28 November 2012, Pakistan successfully tested a ballistic missile *Hatf*-5 with a range of 1300 km. Pakistan at the moment is not developing a defensive shield. It is confident that its cruise and ballistic missiles provide credibility to its nuclear deterrence. In fact, when Pakistan tested its short-range ballistic missile *Nasr* in February 2013, it highlighted the point that *Nasr* was designed to defeat all known anti-tactical missile defence systems and furthermore, Pakistan hoped to eventually bring that technology to its long-range missile programme.[28] Moreover, India has successfully tested sea-launched version of the hypersonic cruise missile, BrahMos. India has made progress on developing a submarine-launched ballistic missile (SLBM) by successfully completing developmental trials of a medium-range ballistic missile K-15 Sagarika, having a range of 700 kilometres. [29] India has also succeeded in developing an indigenous nuclear submarine *Arihant* when the atomic reactor on-board the submarine went critical on 10 August 2013. This shows that India is leaving Pakistan behind in the race for strategic superiority.

Changing Perceptions of Major Powers

The Cold War dynamics of external support to India-Pakistan strategic rivalry stand altered. During the entire Cold War, the U.S. and also China supplied arms and weapons systems to Pakistan with a view to establishing regional balance. After the end of the Cold War, the U.S. policy of parity between India and Pakistan on strategic matters has changed. During the Cold War, Russia played a key role in bolstering India's defence capabilities and also giving India support on the issue Kashmir. In the post-Cold War South Asia, the Russian role has become peripheral. In order to acquire relevance in South Asia, Russia is attempting to redefine its policies towards India and Pakistan. The U.S. is no more giving Pakistan military help to counter India. But now China has stepped in and giving strategic assistance with a view to countering India. India's security dilemma has become more alive due to the China's role in seeking to balance India's power by collaborating with Pakistan in its nuclear weaponisation programme as well as giving conventional arms to it beyond its legitimate needs. India's rationale for acquiring credible defence capabilities and posture can be found in its concern over China's continued support to Pakistan's nuclear and missile programmes. India's policy makers have remained under constant strategic pressure due to China emerging as the largest arms supplier to Pakistan in recent years.[30]

Perceptions of the major powers of the world towards South Asia have changed in the twenty-first century. Almost all major powers have welcomed the peace process between India and Pakistan. Most of them have appreciated India's perception of the conflict, based on bilateralism and peaceful resolution of contentious issues, and stopping all kinds of support to terrorism. During the Cold War period, the U.S., Soviet Union and China had affected the security environment of South Asia in a critical manner. Their policies were instrumental in abating the conflictual relations between India and Pakistan. After end of the Cold War the roles of these extra-regional powers are being redefined. Today, their policies and roles are becoming a crucial variable for Indo-Pakistan cooperation and also the conflict.

The U.S. is considered as the most important global player in the South Asian regional security. In fact, the U.S. considers that both India and the U.S. can work together for promoting peace and democracy in the region. Both believe that evolution of Pakistan as a moderate Islamic state will help in maintaining peace and stability in the region. There has been a view in India that the U.S. policy of regional balance or equating India with Pakistan has emboldened Pakistan to be aggressive against India and create an atmosphere of hostility in the region. India has believed that in the past the U.S. arms to Pakistan had encouraged it to resolve disputes with India through military approach. However, in recent years, the Indo-U.S. strategic partnership is indicative of the U.S. willingness to no more treat India and

Pakistan on parity. Their relationship has entered a historic phase after the July 18, 2005 agreement for having a civilian nuclear deal and its final conclusion in October 2008. India has become a key player in the international security strategy of the United States.[31] Now the U.S. considers India as a responsible nuclear power, which has a significant role in the U.S. goal of nuclear non-proliferation. The U.S. has not granted the same status to Pakistan.

India and U.S. are engaged in a structured annual strategic dialogue since 2009 with a view to deepening their strategic and commercial cooperation. When the U.S. President Barack Obama visited India in January 2015, Indo-U.S. Joint Declaration stated: "Reflecting the close ties between our two great democracies, India and the United States agree to elevate our long-standing strategic partnership, with a Declaration of Friendship that strengthens and expands the relationship between our two countries." [32] Furthermore, during the visit both the countries signed a joint strategic vision for the Asia-Pacific region stating: "As the leaders of the world's two largest democracies that bridge the Asia-Pacific and Indian Ocean region and reflecting our agreement that a closer partnership between the United States and India is indispensable to promoting peace, prosperity and stability in those regions, we have agreed on a Joint Strategic Vision for the region." That shows that the India-U.S. relations have irrevocably moved beyond the Cold War mindset.[33]

Till the end of the twentieth century, the U.S. was mainly concerned about managing the India-Pakistan conflict over Kashmir and defusing potential nuclear crises.[34] India-U.S. relations started witnessing a paradigm shift in the aftermath of the Kargil crisis when the U.S. openly blamed Pakistan for the crisis and aggression and sided with India for defusing the crisis. After 9/11 events, the Indo-U.S. relationship has acquired further momentum. The U.S. now largely supports India's considered position terrorism and has put pressure on Pakistan to stop sponsoring terrorism directed against India or any other country. The U.S. has, in fact, put pressure on Pakistan to ensure that its soil is not used for terrorist activities. The U.S. is getting frustrated with Pakistan on a range of issues, particularly on its dubious role in the fight against extremism and terrorism. Whether on terrorism or nuclear proliferation or democracy in Pakistan, the Pakistan-watchers in the U.S. have started thinking of a new approach towards Pakistan, which would serve the U.S. interests, but also affect the Indo-Pakistan conflict positively.

Russia's role is becoming a challenge for India. As India has moved closer to the U.S., Russia is opening up to Pakistan. India is worried about the possibility of Russia's defence cooperation with Pakistan. Russia signed a military cooperation agreement with Pakistan in Islamabad on November 20, 2014. The stated objective of the agreement is: "exchanging information on politico-military issues, strengthening collaboration in the defence and counter-terrorism sectors, sharing similar views on developments in Afghanistan and doing business with each other."[35] It is rightly observed that "Russia-Pakistan military cooperation agreement is a matter of concern for India. The Russian Defence Minister spoke about coordinating 'regional security policies' and 'doing business with Pakistan'—indicating that weapons sales and joint military exercises can be on the agenda."[36] Furthermore, during the visit of Pakistan defence minister Khawaja Asif to Russia in April 2015, a concrete step was taken to increase defence cooperation, which includes conducting joint military exercises between the two countries. The two sides also agreed to increase defence cooperation in training and import of arms and equipment.[37]

However, Russia has welcomed the dialogue process between India and Pakistan. The Russian President Vladimir Putin has believed that the peace process would add to the development of the region and resolution of the bilateral problems.[38] Russia has always supported India's stand on Kashmir and its resolution according to the Shimla Agreement. Russia considers India as an important player for promoting Asian security. Both India and Russia have similarity of perceptions on transnational security threats like international terrorism and religious extremism. Apart from Russia, the U.S., China and other countries are also concerned on these issues, and hence they have a mutuality of interests. The convergence of interests between India and other major powers on these issues will put pressure on Pakistan for mending its policies on Kashmir and transnational terrorism.

China's role in promoting peace and stability in South Asia is the most contentious one. China is still helping Pakistan with a view to keeping India under strategic pressure, and it does not want to see India increasing its power, stature, and profile within the South Asian region or beyond South Asia.[39] China's ever growing strategic relationship with Pakistan puts a severe constraint on China's claims of promoting peace and stability in South Asia. Lasting peace in South Asia is possible only when China resolves its problems with India, particularly the border issue and does not cooperate with Pakistan with a view to pose a security threat to India. China's strategy to regionally balance India through Pakistan will only compel India to bolster its strategic forces and strengthen its strategic cooperation with the U.S. for balancing China. However, China is not supporting Pakistani game plan of internationalization of the Kashmir issue and has supported the resolution of bilateral disputes between India and Pakistan through bilateral negotiations. It has adopted a careful stand on the Kashmir issue. When the Chinese President Jiang Zemin paid a state visit to India in 1996, he suggested that both India and Pakistan put the Kashmir issue on the backburner and devote more time to cooperating in other areas.[40] Such an approach suits India's policy on the contentious issue of Kashmir. It also means that Pakistan has lost China's political support on the issue of Kashmir in terms of internationalization and proxy war or radicalization or even its position that Pakistan cannot promote its relations with India in other fields until Kashmir is resolved first.

Conclusion

Both India and Pakistan are having competitive policies and strategies on a range of issues, particularly Kashmir, state-sponsored terrorism and armaments. All these issues in India-Pakistan conflict are witnessing new trends. Both India and Pakistan are states with nuclear weapons and both the states understand the realities of nuclear deterrence. After the Kargil conflict, Pakistan's nuclear weapons programme has come under increased international scrutiny. Pakistan is not likely to repeat the mistake of the past as it did in the case of initiating the Kargil conflict. Military approach to resolving the conflict over Kashmir with India is becoming less prominent in the pronouncements of political leadership in Pakistan. After 9/11, the entire international community feels threatened from the extremism and terrorism existing in Pakistan. Now Kashmir issue and terrorism are more objectively understood by the international community and India's approach of bilateralism and pacific settlement of all outstanding issues between the two states is being appreciated by all the major powers of the world. Consequently, terrorism has emerged as a core issue in India-Pakistan conflict as well as South Asian regional security. India has started asserting that terrorism is the key threat to its security and also the security of rest of the world, and for peaceful management of the India-Pakistan conflict terrorism must be uprooted in all of its dimensions. India, therefore, has even made a policy upgradation and it feels that Pakistan has also become a victim of terrorism, and both the states have undertaken several bilateral initiatives for combating terrorism. Terrorism and Pakistan's nuclear weapons are global concerns now and there is increased international cooperation on these issues. All this has put pressure on Pakistan to renounce its policy of militarism and state-sponsored terrorism against India.

The need of the hour is to make the comprehensive process of interaction result oriented. One tacit consequence of several peace initiatives and mechanisms has been that India and Pakistan can be credited with not allowing crises turn into large scale military confrontations. For instance, the standoff after the terrorist attack on Indian Parliament in December 2001, the 2008 crisis after the terrorist attacks in Mumbai and killing of Indian soldiers along LoC have not been allowed to escalate. One factor which can transform India-Pakistan conflict is related to structural transformation in Pakistan. India has a vested interest in strengthening of democracy in Pakistan and a democratically elected government having control over foreign policy-making and independence for taking critical decisions on managing relations with India.

The post-Cold War world order is entirely different from the Cold War period. India has emerged as strong political, economic and military power at the global stage. In contrast, Pakistan is being labeled as a failing state, which poses serious threat to South Asian and international security. The major powers see opportunities in developing cooperative relations with India, whereas they feel threatened the way Pakistan is placed today in terms of its internal chaos, radicalization of its society and polity, and its dubious role in nuclear proliferation and state-sponsored terrorism.

REFERENCES

1. See "We'll talk if Pak stops exporting terror: PM," *Hindustan Times*, April 20, 2003.
2. "Situation improving in Kashmir: Peace process has produced some success, says Antony," *The Hindu*, July 29, 2007.
3. Ministry of Defence, Government of India, *Annual Report, 2005-2006*, p. 6.
4. "Musharraf faces criticism for Kashmir proposal," *The Hindu*, December 7, 2006.
5. *Ibid.*
6. "India not ready for joint management of Kashmir," *Hindustan Times*, January 12, 2007.
7. "Joint Press Statement on PM's Visit to Pakistan (January 2004)," *Strategic Digest*, Vol. 34, No. 2, February 2004, pp. 113-114.
8. *Ibid.*, p. 114.
9. "Normal ties with Pak after terror machine shut: PM," *The Times of India*, March 9, 2013.
10. "Terror and talks cannot go together", *The Hindu*, April 4, 2015.
11. *Ibid.*
12. A. Baruah, "Bus to Pakistan," *Frontline*, February 27, 1999, p. 5.

13. "View from Lahore," *Hindustan Times*, February 23, 1999.
14. "India rejects Pak proposal for nuke restraint regime," *The Tribune*, October 20, 2007.
15. "Kashmir is a flashpoint for another India-Pak War: Sharif," *The Times of India*, December 5, 2013.
16. R.R. Barnett and R. Ahmed, "From Great Game to Grand Bargain: Ending Chaos in Afghanistan and Pakistan," *Foreign Affairs*, Vol. 87, No. 6, November-December 2008.
17. "Borders cannot be redrawn but we can work towards making them irrelevant," *The Indian Express*, March 25, 2006, <http://www.indianexpress.com/news/-borders-cannot-be-redrawn-but-we-can-work-towards-making-them-irrelevant-/1073/0>
18. "PM says borders in Kashmir cannot be redrawn, Pak protests," *The Hindustan Times*, November 23, 2009, < http://www.hindustantimes.com/News-Feed/India/PM-says-borders-in-Kashmir-cannot-be-redrawn-Pak-protests/Article1-479297.aspx>
19. "Epicentre of terror is in Pakistan: PM," *The Hindu*, September 29, 2013.
20. Several round table Conferences have been held to put together all shades of opinion. One recommendation that has emerged out of these conferences is aimed at enhancing cross-border linkages.
21. "Kashmir issue will be resolved soon: Pervez," *Hindustan Times*, April 27, 2007.
22. "We have a lot of love for India," An interview with Karan Thapar, *The Hindu*, May 14, 2013.
23. *Ibid.*
24. B. Paul, "The Structure of the Second Nuclear Age," *Orbis*, Vol. 47, No. 3, Summer 2003, pp. 399-413.
25. *SIPRI Yearbook 2013: Armaments, Disarmaments and International Security* (New York: Oxford University Press, 2013)
26. Pervez Hoodbhoy, "Pakistan's rush for more weapons – why?" *The Express Tribune*, January 29, 2012, <http://tribune.com.pk/story/328922/pakistans-rU.S.h-for-more-bombs—why/>
27. A. Eric, "Indian Missile Defense Program Advances," *Arms Control Today*, January/February 2013, <http://www.armscontrol.org/act/2013_01-02/Indian-Missile-Defense-Program-Advances>
28. C.K. Chumley, "Pakistan conducts ballistic missile test," *The Washington Times*, February 12, 2013, <http://www.washingtontimes.com/news/2013/feb/12/pakistan-conducts-own-nuclear-missile-test/>
29. "Indian Navy's K-15 SLBM successfully completes development trials," January 29, 2013, <http://www.naval-technology.com/news/newsindian-navys-k-15-slbm-successfully-completes-development-trials>
30. Ministry of Defence, Government of India, *Annual Report, 2008-09.*
31. P.R. Lavoy, "India in 2006: A New Emphasis on Engagement," *Asian Survey* 47:1 (January-February 2007), p. 115.
32. "India-U.S. Delhi Declaration of Friendship," (January 25, 2015), at <http://www.mea.gov.in/bilateral-documents.htm?dtl/24727/IndiaUS_Delhi_Declaration_of_Friendship>
33. "US-India Joint Strategic Vision for the Asia-Pacific and Indian Ocean Region," (January 25, 2015), at <http://www.mea.gov.in/bilateral-documents.htm?dtl/24728/USIndia_Joint_Strategic_Vision_for_the_AsiaPacific_and_Indian_Ocean_Region>
34. Daniel Drezner, "The New World Order," *Foreign Affairs* 86:2 (March-April 2007), p. 41.
35. R. Roy, "Russia's Military Cooperation Agreement with Pakistan: An Assessment," (IDSA Comment, 15 December 2014), at <http://www.idsa.in/idsacomments/RussiasMilitaryCooperationAgreement_rroy_151212.html>.

36. *Ibid.*
37. "Defence Union: Pakistan, Russia to conduct joint military drills," *The Express Tribune*, April 16, 2015, at < http://tribune.com.pk/story/870725/defence-union-pakistan-russia-to-conduct-joint-military-drills/>
38. "Dangers to construct world on unipolar principles: Putin," *The Hindu*, December 4, 2006.
39. M. Malik, "The China Factor in the India-Pakistan Conflict," *Parameters* 33:1 (Spring 2003), p. 43.
40. J. Cherian, "Zhu Rongji in India," *Frontline*, February 15, 2002, p. 122–23.

18

Indo-Pacific Region: India's Strategic Vision

Hari Saran

Introduction

The strategic scenario of the globe has changed in the post-Cold War era due to the sudden rise of China as an economic and military power and as well as non-traditional security threats like terrorism and piracy. In this changed strategic environment, Asia-Pacific regions become more important than Trans-Atlantic region. In this century Asia-Pacific has been transformed into Indo-Pacific region. It encompasses the region of Indian Ocean and Pacific Ocean. Now, Indo-Pacific arc from Persian Gulf to East China Sea has become the centre of gravity due to various economic and military considerations.[1] Major economic and military powers of this region are India, Australia, Japan, South Korea and China. Chinese economy has now become the largest economy of the globe. Chinese military and maritime might is growing with alarming pace. Even US is very cautious about China's growing power and influence in this region. China has serious maritime disputes with her Pacific neighbours. Pacific countries are mostly developed ones and have sufficient maritime power and connection to face any Chinese pressure and aggression. They have got the unconditional security support from America. While, Indian Ocean regional countries are mostly developing states and they are in need of external economic, technical and military assistance. That is why

China has strategically consolidated her maritime power and developed friendly relations with almost all countries of the Indian Ocean region during the past decades. The main objective of this paper is to assess and analyze the changing strategic scenario of Indo-Pacific region due to growing maritime and economic power of China in relation to our maritime, economic and strategic interests in the region. Some suggestions and recommendations have also made here to develop India's strategic capability to check the Chinese naval movement towards Indian Ocean region in any crisis period.

As we are well aware that Indo-Pacific region is the home of most nuclear powers, centre of trade and nearly half of the world's population. In Asia, only Chinese economic and military capabilities are sufficient to alter the geopolitical and geostrategic conditions of Indo-Pacific region. The major powers of this region are India, ASEAN countries, Australia, Japan, South Korea and US. All are cautious by Chinese developments and intentions. China has a number of land border/territory disputes with India and maritime boundary/territorial disputes with Vietnam, the Philippines, Malaysia, Indonesia, Japan, Taiwan and South Korea. The US is cautious about growing China's influence in the region. The region was previously under the dominance of America. In this century, US has increased its relations with other powers of the region to rebalance the giant China. The US administration has declared that US will act as a net security provider in Indo-Pacific region by adopting cooperative measures with all key countries of the region.[2] President Obama started eight day tour of Japan, South Korea, the Philippines and Malaysia from 23 April 2014. The tour had a great strategic value. The aim was to reassure these countries that US will not going to leave this region in the hands of China. The US has firm intention to keep the whole region free from Chinese threat and pressure.

Indo-Pacific region is also very important for India's future development and security. Being the regional maritime power of Indian Ocean, it is India's responsibility to utilize the economic and strategic opportunities of Pacific Ocean also.

Basic Assumptions: These are as follows:

- Indo-Pacific region currently forms the epicenter of world affairs.
- The emergence of China as a major economic and maritime power was seen as the most important factor in shaping the new strategic environment of Indo-Pacific region.
- China is not very comfortable in the Pacific water region. On the

other hand, China has been successful in increasing its political, economic, technical and maritime relations with almost all countries of Indian Ocean during the post Cold War period.

- The US still dominates Indo-Pacific region by money and power. It has a number of economic and strategic interests and allies in this region.
- India's future growth and development is closely linked with Indo-Pacific region. To protect and promote these national interests, India must have strategic vision and capability to project her as a major power of the region.

Some of the **commonly agreed** upon facts related to the region are as follows:

1. Indo-Pacific region accounts for two-thirds of total oceanic space, home to nearly 3 billion people and a GDP of nearly $ 20 trillion.
2. There is an unabated region-wide drive for economic development and cooperation in Indo-Pacific countries.
3. The region is going through an exciting era, where all countries have embarked in the pursuit of a new paradigm of peace, prosperity and stability.
4. There are no major ideological differences in the regional powers.
5. The region is troubled with many conflicts and unsettled maritime disputes that have the potential to trigger wars.
6. High priority areas of Indo-Pacific region are—
   - Energy Security
   - Maritime dispute resolution (through legal, cooperative and political means)
   - Trade security
   - Maritime Security (Security of sea lanes of communication)
7. The region is now clearly divided between China and America. China had been well connected with almost all the countries of the region. USA is pursuing the policy of cooperative strategy in managing regional affairs.
8. ASEAN and APEC are the two important political and economic organizations of this region.
9. APEC (Asia Pacific Economic Cooperation) members account for about 40 per cent of world's population, 54 per cent of the world's Gross Domestic Product (GDP) and 44 per cent of the world's trade.

10. ASEAN countries are like connecting bridge between these two regions. ASEAN (Association of South East Asian Nations) members account for about 8.8% of world's population and 3% of the total land area of the Earth. The maritime jurisdiction of ASEAN is about three times larger than its land counterpart. The total GDP was US $2.403 trillion in 2013.[3]
11. In the present scenario, Indo-Pacific region is an area of geopolitical and geostrategic rivalry between US, China and India. All the other major powers of this region are also cautious about China's policies and intentions. One cannot rule out the possibility of a future conflict and competition in the region.
12. China, India, Japan, Australia, Taiwan, South Korea and virtually all of the middle ranking regional powers are engaged in expanding and modernizing their navies. China has spearheaded this naval arm race, saying that it should have naval capabilities to match its economic might. Now, China's GDP has reached almost parallel to US and China wants to have a Navy parallel to US Navy.

Strategic Environment of Indo-Pacific Region

The major players of Indo-Pacific region are as follows:

China

The two major economies of this region are China and India. The arc from Bay of Bengal to East China Sea has now become the most volatile area of Indo-Pacific region. China has now become the biggest economic and military power of the region. This arc water region is clearly under the power pressure of China. China wants to enjoy the economic and military/maritime freedom in the whole region. The only obstacle in this endeavourer is America and India.

In this century, China's maritime strategy is aimed to acquire anti-access capability in the Pacific, consolidation in the South China Sea and expansionism in the Indian Ocean region. China has released its first 'Blue Book' on the Indian Ocean region in June 2013. In this book, China has for the first time spelled out its strategy to secure its interests in the IOR that are basically commercial rather than military. China has declared that it wants to deepen its economic relations with IOR littoral states. In this book, China has made it clear that if countries like India, the US and China failed to engage with each other more constructively as their interests begin to overlap, the Ocean could end up "as an ocean of conflict and trouble". This is a clear warning for India and America.

Recently, China's Foreign Affairs Office has informed Indian Foreign Ministry that its SSN has taken a long trip in the Indian Ocean water between Dec. 13, 2013 and Feb. 12, 2014. This initiative has changed the strategic environment of IOR and seriously aggravated India's security concerns and perceptions. Now it has been proved that Chinese SSN are working perfectly and has become capable enough to take independent long voyage without any base support. The second important thing is now visible that in near future Chinese can deploy PLAN vessels (Carrier Battle Group) in the Indian Ocean region. One can easily visualize that the strategic scenario of the IOR has changed now and is poised to become more serious in near future. *China has already deployed its 'Xia' class nuclear submarines with SLBMs in South China Sea. In any crisis situation, these deadly platforms can reach northwest quadrant of the Indian Ocean in a very short period via Strait of Malacca or Sunda.* China has adopted various measures to acquire permanent presence like facilities in the IOR countries through anti-piracy operations, establishing port facilities, giving financial and technical support to different infrastructural projects, providing medical aid through hospital ships and developing defence relationships during this century.

Now in this 21st century, China is the world's fastest growing superpower. It is building energy relationship worldwide especially in Central Asia, Russia, Africa, and the Middle East and in Gulf countries. Over 70 per cent of China's imports come from West Asia and Africa and all of this is transported by sea. The International Energy Agency (IEA) predicts that by 2020, China will become the world's second largest oil importer. China is creating a strategic petroleum reserve and is building a fleet of super-tankers for the transport of energy to China.

China has adopted the policy of economic liberalization in 1978. After the reintegration of Hong-Kong in 1997 and Macao in 1999, China became economically more powerful and stable. Due to growing global trade, China wants to dominate the major sea lines of communication of the region. According to the 2004, Defence White Paper of China, Beijing clearly acknowledged a shift from China's traditional land power to a maritime power for winning command of the high sea and for conducting counter-strikes.

According to World Bank report, China overtook the US in 2009 to become the world's largest energy user. China has displaced Japan as the world's second largest builder of long haul tankers. China handles more than one-fifth of the world's container traffic. [4]

The growing maritime power of PLAN could deny or complicate US control over Indo-Pacific region. According to China's National Defence White Paper 2008, the Chinese Navy will become a global power by 2040. PLAN wants to increase its maritime strategic depth capability. The development of aircraft carrier has been initiated and intensified by China during this century to attain strategic depth capability. Presently the PLAN has become the third most powerful force of the globe. PLAN has been working on an aggressive expansion plan to be the second powerful force of the world by 2040. PLAN has decided to focus on its submarine force especially on nuclear powered and diesel electric submarines. Chinese engineers and technicians are working hard to improve the speed of their nuclear submarines. [5]It is the only Asian Navy with SLBM capability. The major aim of PLAN is to enhance China's national security, safeguard maritime security and consolidate its status as a world power.

China has islands related old disputes with Japan in East China Sea region. These islands are Diaoyu and Senkakus. In the South China Sea water region, China has maritime jurisdiction and Spratly island disputes with Brunei, Taiwan, Indonesia, Malaysia, the Philippines and Vietnam. The question of Taiwan is also a very difficult and serious matter of this region. In the past China has made several attempts to impose restrictions on the disputed matter. The former US President Clinton had sent two aircraft carrier battle groups to the Taiwan region to deter China, when it took proactive military actions prior to a Taiwan Presidential election in 1996. China has declared 'air defence identification zone' over an area that includes islands—Senkaku controlled by Japan but claimed by China in the East China Sea. China has warned that it will adopt defensive emergency measures to respond to aircraft that do not cooperate in the identification or refuse to follow the instructions. Against this Japan has said that,' Japan could never accept the zone set up by China as it is our island.'[6] On this disputed issue, Chinese President Xi Jinping had retaliated and said that, "We are strongly committed to safeguarding the country's sovereignty and security, and defending our territorial integrity."In response the Japanese PM Shinzo Abe said that, "Provocations against Japan's sovereign sea and land are continuing, but they must not be tolerated."

China's String of Pearls Strategy

China has initiated a drive to develop strategic relationship and setting up bases along the sea lanes from the Middle East to South China Sea not simply to protect its growing energy interests but also to enhance its broader strategic objectives. [7]

America

Presently the security structure of Indo-Pacific region is solely dominated by America. Majority of regional states are cooperating America to manage the growing Chinese might in this region. These powers are India, Australia, Taiwan, Vietnam, the Philippines, Japan, South Korea and ASEAN states. The power balances of the region are still in the hands of US. US has developed and engaged almost all the powers of region to maintain the regional peace and stability. America has stationed her fifth fleet in Indian Ocean at Bahrain and seventh fleet in Pacific Ocean at Japan to cover the entire Indo-Pacific region. In addition, American has developed a strong air and naval base at Diego-Garcia, Busan and Guan Island. America has also engaged India and ASEAN countries in various maritime security affairs. American naval might is capable enough to take any challenge of the region without any active port support. The whole world has witnessed the US naval military capability during the operations of Afghanistan and Iraq. Chinese are well aware of the fact and are rigorously working hard to improve her strategic reach naval capability.

The US administration has declared its Indo-Pacific policy at various platforms and time that US will act as the main security provider of this region with cooperative measures to all key powers of the region. [8] The US has acknowledged the strategic linkage between the Indian and Pacific Oceans. To boost the confidence and morale of her regional allies, US Navy has shown power demonstration by naval exercises and port visits regularly. US President Clinton had sent two aircraft carrier battle groups to the Taiwan region to deter China, when it took provocative military actions prior to Taiwan Presidential election in 1996. In June 2006, the US had conducted its largest Pacific Ocean exercise since the Vietnam War. It involved 22000 personnel, 280 aircrafts (including B-2, B-52) and 30 warships (three US aircraft carrier battle groups). Again in 2007, US conducted a very big naval exercise in the Bay of Bengal near Straits of Malacca along with warships of India, Japan and Australia. In mid-2010, three ballistic missile submarines reconfigured for cruise missile attack surfaced simultaneously in Diego-Garcia (Indian Ocean), Busan (South Korea) and Subic Bay (the Philippines).[9]

President Obama visited Australia in Nov. 2011 and said that, "the US will play a larger and long-term role in shaping this region and its future, by upholding core and friends." In January 2012, US Administration has confirmed her policy of Asia-Pacific region by saying that," US economic and security interests are inextricably linked to developments in the arc extending from the Western Pacific and East Asia into the Indian Ocean region and South Asia, creating a mix of evolving challenges and opportunities. Accordingly, while the US military will continue to contribute to security globally, we will do the necessary rebalance toward the Asia-Pacific region.[10]

The US administration knows it very well that growing maritime strength of PLAN could deny or complicate US control over Indo-Pacific region. In response, after Yongsan base (South Korea) and Okinawa base (Japan), US is developing a new strategic base at Guam. The new port at Changi (Singapore) is capable enough to support US aircraft carriers. The US will station its littoral combat ships at Singapore in the near future. The US has also increased its relations with all major powers of this region including Vietnam and India. The US is also planning to access the facilities of Vietnamese port-Cam Ranh Bay. The US has made significant adjustments to bring more regional maritime facilities closer to her side.

The US President Obama visited the Philippines in 2014. At a joint press conference in Manila, President Obama said that, "Our goal is not to counter China. Our goal is not to contain China. Our goal is to make sure that international rules and norms are respected in the area of international disputes."[11]

India

Indian policy makers have also acknowledged the importance of changing strategic scenario of Indo-Pacific region. India with its size, resource potential, and strategic location is being increasingly seen as a regional maritime power poised on the threshold of emerging as a centre of power in the Indo-Pacific region. India has also enhanced its economic and defence capabilities in the past years. Nuclear, space and missile development programme have also enhanced India's regional image and capability. India has constructed aircraft carrier and nuclear submarine indigenously. By 2020, Indian Navy will have SLBM and regional navigation satellite system (IRNSS) capability.

Due to economic development, India is poised to play an increasingly larger role in the Indo-Pacific region in the coming decades. India wants a secure and peaceful Indo-Pacific region. India's future growth, development, security and progress all are closely intertwined with countries of Indo-Pacific region. Keeping in view the whole scenario India has taken a prudent approach to develop better relations with almost all countries of Indo-Pacific region during the past decade.

The Indian Maritime Doctrine 2004 states that India has now become the regional maritime power by all means. The revised Indian Maritime Doctrine 2009 clearly states that India wants to built a Blue Water Navy capable of not only defending the homeland, but of protecting its wider security and economic interests in the Indo-Pacific region and beyond. Keeping in view the strategic scenario of Indo-Pacific region, it was decided that Indian Navy should be capable enough to perform four major roles, i.e. nuclear deterrence, economic and energy security, forward presence and naval diplomacy. Visualizing the economic and strategic importance of South East Asia and South China Sea region, the first regional theatre command-Andaman and Nicobar command (Tri-service command) was created in 2001 at Port Blair.

India has made it clear that it has strategic and economic interests in the South China Sea and beyond. ONGC Videsh Ltd has oil fields in Russian Sakhalin region. Vietnam has allotted two more gas exploration blocks to Indian company ONGC Videsh Ltd for which the agreements were signed during the official visit of President Mr. Pranab Mukherjee to Vietnam in September 2014.[12] India wants to protect her economic, commercial and navigational interests in the Indo-Pacific water region. In the present geo-political and strategic environment, it has become necessary for India to have blue water navy with credible amphibious and nuclear deterrence capability.

During the post-Cold War period, India has made an impressive progress in increasing its relations with the countries of Indo-Pacific region. In this region only Pakistan and China can pose conventional security threats to India. Both are true friend and have serious land border disputes with India. China is far ahead of India in the field of economic and maritime power. The other major powers of the region are also very cautious about the rising economic, military and maritime power of China. In the present scenario, economic engagement is necessary for national security. China has emerged as India's largest trading partner with prospects of bilateral trade target of US $100 billion by 2015.[13] In the next five years, China is going to invest US $ 100 billion in India.[14]

India's Strategic Compulsions

1. In Asia only China can pose a direct military threat to India's security.
2. China is presently far ahead of India in terms of economic and military capabilities.
3. In any crisis period, Chinese land, air and naval forces can create a massive challenge to our security.
4. India has about a 3000 km long land border with China.
5. China has developed air fields and deployed various types of missiles in Tibet region of China.
6. Fortunately, China has no maritime border or jurisdiction in the Indian Ocean region.
7. Chinese navy will certainly use Straits of Malacca and Singapore to reach in the Indian Ocean region in any crisis period.
8. In such scenario, the Andaman and Nicobar Islands will be our forward base to check the Chinese movements towards Indian Ocean water and bases.
9. The majority of Indian Ocean region are in favor of China and in any crisis period Chinese naval forces can use their port, harbor and shore facilities.
10. India's military might and especially overall maritime power should be capable enough to address Chinese aggression at any time. India's maritime power on Andaman and Nicobar islands should be strong enough to check the Chinese advancement towards Bay of Bengal and Indian Ocean. These islands will act as a forward base to protect our economic and strategic interests in Malacca Region, Pacific Region, South China Sea, East China Sea and beyond. [15]

India's Strategic Vision

In the present scenario, Indo-Pacific has become India's geo-economic and geo-strategic region. India's economic resurgence has now been started on a massive scale. India has also started a major drive to strengthen its maritime power and projection. India has successfully crafted a pragmatic foreign policy to increase and strengthen its relations with the major players of this part of the globe. For future development and stability, India must have true blue water navy with strategic reach capability and legs. Indian Navy has initiated a major modernization and expansion program to develop such capability during this century. If all goes well, Indian Navy will certainly attain underwater nuclear power projection capability by 2025. By that time, Indian Navy will have a network-centric approach and land attack assistance capability. The Indian Regional Navigation Satellite System (IRNSS) is going to be operational by the end of 2016. It will provide positional information of about 1500 km. around the Indian mainland.

America has changed her perception regarding India's capabilities and role in the Indo-Pacific region and stated the following points on several occasions. These are:

- India is a major developing economy of the Indo-Pacific region in general and in IOR in particular.
- India has a large and potent maritime power and capability in the IOR.
- Having the largest naval power in the IOR, India has now become the net security provider in the IOR.
- India will be a potent partner in the US security architecture of Indo-Pacific region during the years ahead.
- Indo-US maritime relations should be strengthened to balance the growing Chinese influence and presence in the IOR.

Conclusion

In order to counter Chinese initiatives in this region, India and America have also intensified their naval diplomacy during the past decade. India is well aware of the fact that in future, after the US, China will be the only country that could disturb the balance of power equation in the Indo-Pacific region in general and Indian Ocean region in particular. India too is modernizing its navy and has a good growth rate during the past decades. The Navy's new acquisition projects and plans in the pipeline, add up to well over Rs 300000 crore over the next 15 years.

Chinese knows it very well that only US can constrain its emergence as a potential rival in IOR. Therefore, China continues to strengthen its relations with IOR-RIM countries in all spheres—economic, political, diplomatic and military in the post-Cold War era. It has established a surveillance post in the Bay of Bengal to monitor the sea-borne movements of this region. It has been continuously increasing its influence and presence in the IOR. Through Pakistan and Myanmar, its forces can reach the warm waters of Indian Ocean in any emergency. It can avail the naval support facilities in several littoral countries of IOR in any crisis period. The growing Chinese influence in the IOR is very significant and alarming because it left behind the influence of India to a great extent.

In the present strategic world scenario, India's destiny is interlinked with Indo-Pacific region. India wants peace and stability in the Indo-Pacific region for future economic growth and prosperity. It will be achieved only by—

(a) strategic partnership
(b) strategic vision and maritime power
(c) Indian Navy must have sound strategic reach and endurance capability based on SSBNs and satellite navigation and ranging system.

The following suggestions may have some relevance in this national endeavor:

1. India should follow the policy of cooperation and comprehensive strategic economic partnership with Pacific Ocean countries in the years ahead. These countries are economically and technically very developed. India wants to be a part of 'Global Supply Chains' by the help of major economic powers of this region.
   India should try to help the Indian Ocean regional countries in building institutions, infrastructure, defence and maritime power, credit line, etc., through soft power diplomatic efforts. These countries are weak, small and developing. India should try to utilize all possible opportunities of this region through pragmatic economic, technical and military assistance.
2. India should construct and develop medical hospital ships to provide medical assistance to littoral states of Indian Ocean. Presently Indian Navy has not even a single medical ship. This platform could also be utilized in disaster relief operation. In Indo-Pacific region, US and China has a number of medium and big size hospital ships.
3. All the ongoing maritime development projects should be completed on top priority. Maritime power is necessary to be a major player of Indo-Pacific region.

REFERENCES

1. In the Defence White Paper 2013, PM Julia Gillard of Australia has used the word 'Indo-Pacific Strategic Arc' rather than Asia-Pacific. *The Indian Express*, May 10, 2013.
2. The US carried out a remarkable demonstration of naval power in mid 2010, when three

ballistic missile submarines reconfigured for cruise missile attack surfaced simultaneously in Diego-Garcia (Indian Ocean), Busan (South Korea) and Subic Bay (The Philippines). (M. Thompson, "US Missiles Deployed Near China Send a Message", *TIME*, July 2010) US Secretary of Defence Leon Panetta visited India in June 2012 and said, "We will expand our military partnerships and our presence in the arc extending from the Western Pacific and East Asia into the Indian Ocean region and South Asia. (US Department of Defence, "Panetta Says US-India Relations Must Deepen, Grow for Peace", New Delhi, India, June 6, 2012) President Obama started eight day tour of Japan, South Korea, the Philippines and Malaysia from 23 April 2014. The tour had a great strategic value. The aim was to reassure these countries that US will not leave this region in the hands of China. The US has firm intention to keep the whole region free from Chinese threat and pressure.

3. www.asean.org/asean-member-states.
4. P.K. Gautam, Mapping Chinese Oil and Gas Pipelines and Sea Routes', *Strategic Analysis*, Vol. 35, No. 4, July 2011, p. 595.
5. *Defence News*, Sep. 11, 2006.
6. *The Times of India*, Varanasi, Nov. 24, 2013, On this disputed issue, Chinese President Xi Jinping had retaliated and said that, "We are strongly committed to safeguarding the country's sovereignty and security, and defending our territorial integrity." In response the Japanese PM Shinzo Abe said that, "Provocations against Japan's sovereign sea and land are continuing, but they must not be tolerated." http://www.cfr.org/asia-and-pacific/chinas-maritime-disputes/p31345).
7. G. Khurana, "China's String of Pearls in the Indian Ocean and its Security Implications" *Strategic Analysis* 32 (1), January 2008, p. 11.
8. R.G. Sutter, M.E. Brown and Timothy J.A. Adamson, "Balancing Acts: The US Rebalance and Asia-Pacific Stability', The George Washington University, August 2013.
9. M. Thompson, "US Missiles Deployed Near China Send a Message", *TIME*, July 8, 2010
10. US Department of Defence,' Sustaining US Global Leadership: Priorities for 21st century Defence, Washington DC.US Dept. of Defence, January 2012, 2.
11. http://time.com/78779/obama-philippines-china.
12. *The Times of India*, New Delhi, 14 September, 2014.
13. *Strategic Digest*,Dec.2011, pp.1253.
14. *The Hindu*, New Delhi, 14 September 2014.
15. Recently, China's Foreign Affairs Office has informed Indian Foreign Ministry that its SSN has taken a long trip in the Indian Ocean water between Dec. 13, 2013 and Feb. 12, 20114. This has changed the strategic environment of IOR and seriously aggravated India's security concerns and perceptions. By this, one thing is clear that now Chinese SSN are working perfectly and has become capable enough to take independent long voyage without any base support. The other thing which is now visible is that in the near future Chinese will be in a sound position to deploy PLAN vessels (Carrier Battle Group) in the Indian Ocean region. One can easily visualize that the strategic scenario of the IOR is poised to change in the near future. "Exclusive: Indian Navy headless as Chinese nuclear sub prowls Indian Ocean", Sandeep Unnithan, *India Today*, New Delhi, March 21, 2014.

19

Chorus or Cacophony: Varied Voices in Indo-Sri Lankan Relations

S. Utham Kumar Jamadhagni

Introduction

The significance of Narendra Modi's foreign and security policies have been influenced by the neighbourhood first approach. He outlined his vision for the region by stating that "the future of any country is influenced by the state of its neighbourhood". Similarly, Sirisena, the Sri Lanka President, since his election, has also given several indications of wanting to restore the warmth that once existed in India–Sri Lanka relations. He even sent foreign Minister Mangala Samaraweera to New Delhi on 18 January, 2015, and the President himself visited India in February, 2015 on his first visit abroad. The Sri Lanka President had seen strains development of earlier Indo–Sri Lanka relationship and tilt towards China. The India Prime Minister Narendra Modi visited Sri Lanka in the month of March 2015 and addressed the parliament. Modi urged the new Sri Lankan government with his words—"historic opportunity to win the hearts and heal the wounds across all sections of society", a reference to bridge the gap between the Tamil minority and the Sinhalese majority. Modi further added "diversity can be a source of strength for nations. When we accommodate the aspirations of all sections of our society, the nation gets the strength of every individual."

One is well aware of the fact that Sri Lanka is an island neighbour and relation with this proximate country is inevitable. Though earlier the ties were smooth, be it the ancient links when the Indian emperor Asoka sent his son and daughter in a proselytisation drive to the "tear drop" of Indian Ocean, or that during and after independence, the ethnic conflict has vitiated the atmosphere. At first, India aided the Tamil rebels, offering them training and safe haven which later led to opposition to the LTTE which firmed up with the assassination of India's Prime Minister. Thus, by the end of the war, India was ably supporting the Sri Lankan cause of opposing the rebels. There have also been evidences of supply of arms and equipment in building up an offensive against the Tamil Tigers especially in the closing stages of the civil war.

Here, the constraints in India's relations with her close neighbour would be looked at from the viewpoint of differing perceptions among significant stakeholders. The domestic Tamil community possesses linguistic and filial connection with the Tamils of Northern Sri Lanka. Thus, the fate of the Tamil community in Sri Lanka is a simmering political topic in this state. All political parties focus on the Sri Lankan Tamil issue in a variety of ways. While some emphasise on nurturing the secessionist claim there are others who demand greater autonomy for the Tamil majority areas. The post war relief and rehabilitation of displaced Tamils is another issue of concern. The Indian government has time and again impressed upon the Sri Lankan establishment that relief and rehabilitation must be taken up more vigorously.

The Indian Central Government and the state of Tamil Nadu differ significantly in their stand on the issues of war crimes, the crossing of the International Maritime Boundary and the sovereignty of the ceded Katchativu Island. While Tamil activists and separatist supporters accuse the Lankan government of being involved in massive human rights violations, the Indian government has desisted from voting against the island country in international fora like UN. The protests have varied from objection to training Sri Lankan defence personnel in India to demanding boycott of international events held in Sri Lanka. In fact, during the 2013 CHOGM meeting the Prime Minister of India did not attend.

Vote Bank politics has played truant in both countries as the Buddhist majority Sri Lankan electorate is shown the "hard hand" against terrorism, while local and national elections in India warrant a hardening of "anti-Sri Lanka" stance. The implementation of the 13th Amendment of the Sri Lankan constitution that offers greater autonomy to the northern areas is another sticking point. Of late, the capture of Indian fishermen allegedly crossing the international waters has been a principal point of contention. With the LTTE threat gone, the Sri Lankan fishermen want to resume fishing in their waters. However, Indian fishermen in search of more fertile fishing grounds transgress the maritime borders regularly. This warrants stern reaction from the Sri Lankan Navy which confiscates their boats and applies the due process of law landing the fishermen in prison. Massive protests occur in Tamil Nadu against Sri Lankan brutality and call for reclaiming the control over the uninhabited Katchativu Island.

The resolutions brought against Sri Lanka in international fora are applauded by Tamil groups in India but the response from the Indian government is much more guarded. At times both these are contradictory with India at times even desisting from voting against her island neighbour. Not only is the action–reaction phenomenon affecting the peace and security of India, but so also do the role of powers like China whose aim is to increase its strategic foothold in the Indian Ocean region and Pakistan–Lankan relations and the problems it entails. While China is involved in significant infrastructure projects in the island nation recently, India has maintained this relation for long. It has included laying of the longest railroad in the island and prompt assistance during the 2004 tsunami. However, India must be wary of Chinese inroads into areas of strategic importance.

The stakes, stance and actions of various constituencies often at variance with each other further complicates the approach to a peaceful and secure big power in the region of South Asia. The attempt here is to look at a few of the specific issues and highlight their import in challenging India's peace and security.

Sri Lanka is India's nearest island neighbour. Relations with this small power in South Asia have been mercurial. The recently restored Yal Devi Express railway line that connects Colombo and Jaffna with the help of India deploying 400 skilled labourers out of a total of 4000 personnel for the project is a sign of continued cooperation with Sri Lanka.[1] This 339 km line is the longest track in Sri Lanka and was built in 1894. During the ethnic war period the trains were suspended. This is one instance of India's sustained engagement with the island nation despite simmering discontent and open disapproval by other stakeholders.

Early Relations

Roots of migration to Sri Lanka can be traced to erstwhile Kalinga and Bengal or the newly name-altered Odisha and West Bengal states. Though, such information courts controversy these days, the Indian connection with the tear-drop island cannot be overlooked.[2] It is said that the present day Sinhalese are descendants of King Vijaya who ruled parts of Bengal and sailed to Sri Lanka with a few hundred of his people to establish the Sinhala kingdom.[3] There are also theories of the probable Indian origin of the Sinhalese language script which is based on the Brahmi script[4]. In fact, the Sinhala chronicle *Mahavamsa* was written in Pali which was in vogue in Eastern India in the ancient period. Religious links date back to the age of one of the most famous emperors of India, Ashoka the Great. It is said that he despatched ships of citizens led by his daughter Sangamitra and son Mahinda to the island nation to spread Buddhism.[5] Buddhism continues to be Sri Lanka's most popular religion.

Issues and Interests

The post-independence period saw both countries adopting inward looking economic strategies hindering increased trade between neighbours.[6] Also, the one-language policy adopted in the early years of Sri Lankan independence and the repeated promises and failures to adhere to them estranged the Tamil population culminating in a bloody conflict that spanned over three decades. With close affinity to the Tamils of southern India, the internal issue of Sri Lanka took on international dimensions with first covert and later overt support by India's regional political parties. Political parties in Tamil Nadu owed allegiance to the formation of a separate state or Eelam until the fall of the LTTE and now pitch for greater autonomy for the Tamils under the Sri Lankan constitution. The Tamil Nadu constituency varies greatly from the Central government's view on a variety of issues including the fishermen's problem, Katchchativu issue, the implementation of the 13th amendment, alleged human rights violations during the closing stages of the civil war.

Perhaps the Sri Lankan Tamil issue determined the overall health of the Indo–Sri Lankan relations for some time. Other areas of interaction including trade suffered. Only after the economic reforms of the 1990s and the 1998 agreement of free trade (ISLFTA) have the trade ties firmed up. The improvement in business relations has had positive impact on the political issues too. India is among Sri Lanka's biggest trading partners.

Setting the Stage

Earlier the relations were a little uneasy during the 1980s. The decision to involve India in Sri Lankan security problems including the ill-advised policy of sending the IPKF into Sri Lanka only proved counter-productive. The debate on the power of the Prime Minister's Secretariat overriding concerns of the External Affairs ministry and even the army continue to this day.[7] The withdrawal of the IPKF and the Rajiv Gandhi assassination saw a lull in India's involvement in Sri Lankan affairs. With the end of the civil war, there are now efforts at rejuvenating ties between India and Sri Lanka. However, this has been punctuated by several constraints brought about by differing perceptions of the various stakeholders on a variety of issues.

Federation or Nation?

The concept of federalism and the status of centre–state relations have had a significant impact on Indo-Sri Lankan relations. This has occurred on both sides as the Tamils who populate the southern Indian state of Tamil Nadu identifies closely with the Tamils of Northern Sri Lanka. There was a general sympathy and understanding of the struggle for self determination attempted by their Sri Lankan brethren. Thus the fate of the Tamil community in Sri Lanka is a simmering political topic in this state. This has also meant pressure on the central government to oppose Sri Lankan government on various issues. Such pressure has worked in many scenarios. The protest from the Tamil parties with a looming election forced India's Prime Minister to refrain from attending the CHOGM (Commonwealth Heads of Government) meeting hosted by Colombo in November 2013.[8] Repeated protests against the presence of Sri Lankan Army officers especially in Tamil Nadu resulted in withdrawal in some occasions.[9]

Rehabilitation

All political parties focus on the Sri Lankan Tamil issue in a variety of ways. While some emphasise on nurturing the secessionist claim there are others who demand greater autonomy for the Tamil majority areas. The post-war relief and rehabilitation of displaced Tamils is another issue of concern. The Indian government has time and again impressed upon the Sri Lankan establishment that relief and rehabilitation must be taken up more vigorously. In fact, in the increased budgetary allocation of Rs 500 crores last year to Sri

Lanka the main concentration is on the building of 50,000 houses for internally displaced persons.[10] There has also been a raise in aid for Sri Lanka from Rs 290 crores in 2012–13.

Stand on 13th Amendment

As for opinion on the 13th amendment to the Sri Lankan constitution that seeks to offer greater autonomy to Tamils of the north, the centre and the Tamil Nadu state and other constituencies span the gamut from insistence to opposition. In the case of the Indian Prime Minister Modi, he has emphasised that the 13th Amendment must form the basis of a political solution carved out when all stakeholders "engage constructively, in a spirit of partnership and mutual accommodation".[11] A fall out of the Indo-Sri Lankan accord, the 13th amendment enacted in 1987 sought to devolve more powers to the provinces.[12] However, some Tamil hardliners even in Sri Lanka feel that the pitch for stronger autonomy within the Sri Lankan constitutional framework would spell doom to the idea of a separate homeland for the Tamils namely, Tamil Eelam.

Fishing in Troubled Waters

Currently, the festering issue in Indo–Sri Lankan relations is the capture of Indian fishermen straying across the International Maritime Boundary line (IMBL) and confiscating their boats. Hundreds of fishermen from the southern districts of Tamil Nadu regularly enter international waters in search of "catch" everyday. During the ethnic crisis, the Sri Lankan Tamil fishermen were barred from fishing. Now they can't fish as the Indian boats come very close to the Sri Lankan shores to fish. Also some Indian fishermen using bottom trawling technique severely affects marine resources and damages the nets of the Sri Lankan brothers.[13] From the External Affairs Minister, Sushma Swaraj's recent message urging Indian fishermen not to cross the IMBL it is clear where the blame lies. Not only are the Indian fishermen accused of crossing maritime boundaries, Sri Lankan fishermen cross Maldives waters to net the tuna that are available in abundance there.[14]

The Tamil political parties are up in arms over alleged mistreatment of fisherfolk arrested by Sri Lankan Navy personnel. The Chief Minister of Tamil Nadu has regularly written to the Prime Minister requesting his intervention in the release of imprisoned fishermen totalling 744 this year alone. Another problem is the impounding of trawlers by the Sri Lankan authorities. Some are also damaged forcing the fishermen to seek compensation too. In the case of five fishermen who received death sentence on charges of drug trafficking, it was the efforts of the Prime Minister Modi and diplomatic means that culminated in President Rajapaksa's use of executive powers to commute the punishment.[15] This may be seen as an example of convergence of Tamil Nadu political parties and the Central government on an Indo-Sri Lankan issue.

To Cede or not to Cede

The other fishing related problem, however, has seen varied approaches. The Katchchativu Island is an uninhabited mile-long island that houses a church dedicated to St. Anthony. In March of every year the Indian and Sri Lankan fishermen congregate here for a religious festival. By the 1974 agreement India recognised Sri Lanka's sovereignty over the island. With continued problems for Tamil Nadu fishermen, Tamil political leaders including the then Chief Minister demanded that India redeem the island. There was even a resolution passed in the Tamil Nadu State Assembly to this effect.[16] The Union Government of India considers the sovereignty of the island a done deal.

At Loggerheads

However, there have also been other instances of the central government acting against the wishes of the Tamil political groups. For example, in the case of a US-sponsored resolution on human rights at the United Nations to begin an international investigation into alleged war crimes in March 2014, India abstained from voting in favour of the resolution.[17] Tamil political parties launched protests against this and other union government actions like invitation to President Mahinda Rajapaksa to attend the swearing-in ceremony of Prime Minister Narendra Modi.[18] Earlier, the Tamil Nadu members of parliament also refused to be a part of a delegation of MPs from various political parties that visited the island country in April 2012 to oversee developmental projects and emphasise on the need for a political solution to the Tamil issue.[19]

Termed the IV Eelam War, the final conflict between the Sri Lankan government and LTTE ended with the complete annihilation of the leadership and cadres in a brutal and bloody massive assault. There were fears of blatant human rights violation with the killing of thousands of innocent civilians. The international media has periodically released gruesome pictures of torture and ill treatment that has created a stir and even a European Union backed resolution on alleged war crimes of Sri Lankan government. The island nation has successfully warded off international pressure seeking independent investigation over such violations. The visit of the UNHCR chief, Navi Pillay in 2013, courted controversy when the UN official stated that the country was heading in an authoritarian direction.[20] The rejection of the UNHCR's recommendation of an investigative panel by Sri Lanka proved further proof of the government's reluctance to submit itself to international investigation citing reasons of sovereignty.[21] Significantly countries including India, China have supported Sri Lanka's contention on international investigation. The state of Tamil Nadu differs from the Central government's stand in seeking to declare President Rajapaksa, a war criminal and strong opposition to India's decision to abstain from voting against Sri Lanka on the issue.

Action-reaction Chain

Several happenings have punctuated Indo-Sri Lankan relations after the end of the ethnic conflict in 2009 with intense reactions over Sri Lankan omissions on Tamil related issues. In 2012 Sri Lankan pilgrims visiting Tamil Nadu were mobbed and harassed, Buddhist monks visiting Gaya were attacked and a series of protests were made over the presence of Sri Lankan football teams, Air Force and Army personnel who were training at DSSC (Defence Services Staff College, Wellington) and Tambaram Air Force Station.[22] In 2013, a memorial was inaugurated to remember the sacrifices made by Tamils including the Mullivaikkal tragedy during the ethnic conflict.[23] Some of these actions pressured the Indian government to transfer the defence personnel elsewhere to complete their training and even sending back the football team.

Looming Red

Not only are there domestic constraints in Indo–Sri Lankan relations but there is an international angle as well. This is specifically regarding the rise in Chinese influence and presence in Sri Lanka in the name of developmental projects and the like. The warming of relations between the two countries has extended from economy, trade, infrastructure development, defence to political support in the international arena.[24] China is now Sri Lanka's biggest foreign investor. Nearly 24% of all foreign investment is Chinese.[25] The Free Trade Agreement between the two nations comes into effect in 2015. China has been involved in major port and road development projects like the $500 million Colombo Port International Container Terminal that would serve as a hub between Singapore and Dubai and join a select league of mega ports.[26] In the case of Hambantota, the port development work was initially offered to India who did not take it up.[27] Chinese have built the port and there are plans to expand it further. China has also completed the laying of the island's first ever four-lane expressway linking Colombo with Katunayake with a length of about 25.8 km with major funding by Exim Bank of China. The new national theatre called the Lotus Pond has also been built with massive 80% Chinese capital.

Other than this there are other areas that are raising the hackles for India.[28] China is also growing strategically closer to Sri Lanka with the smaller power expressing willingness to join the Maritime Silk Road.[29] This is a Chinese initiative proposed in 2013 by President Xi Jinping to establish a sea-based infrastructure corridor.[30] The docking of nuclear submarines at Colombo port and frequent visits by other Chinese ships like an amphibious landing ship and a frigate are looked at in India with some concern as being steps to increase the Asian power's presence in the Indian Ocean.[31] There are also reports of China setting up an Aircraft Maintenance Centre in Trincomalee to cater to 44 Chinese aircraft used by the Sri Lankan Air Force.[32] In 2013 the two countries sought to "upgrade their relations to a strategic cooperative partnership".[33] Apart from overt military assistance, the establishment of telecommunications network and a GPS service providing telecommunications centre in Kandy could increase fears of eavesdropping on Indian systems. During the last years of the ethnic war, China had provided Sri Lanka with a variety of military equipment including 3D radars, fighter jets, anti-tank guided missiles, Rocket launchers and shoulder-fired surface-to-air missiles. China also sold artillery armour mortars, security equipment, tanks, jets, naval vessels, radars, communication equipment to the Sri Lankan military.[34] China thus continues to be one of Sri Lanka's largest arms suppliers. In contrast to India which offered aid for rehabilitation, China helped in building army training camps in the North and East of Sri Lanka with $100 million aid.[35]

Long Distance Friend

Pakistan is another power whose close relations with Sri Lanka are a concern to India. The two countries have had strong ties since their independence. During the 1971 Bangladesh liberation, Pakistan was allowed to refuel at the Bandaranaike airport, an act that is not forgotten to this day by the grateful Pakistanis.[36] The relations have only deepened in the last two decades. Like

China, Pakistan has also been supplying Sri Lanka with arms especially during the last stages of the Eelam War IV. In fact, by 2009 defence equipment volume almost tripled from the initial 1999 figures[37]. Pakistan also offers training to Sri Lankan military personnel. Naval ships travel frequently from Pakistan to Sri Lanka. In July last year, Sri Lanka highlighted the area of nuclear technology as a principal area of cooperation with her SAARC friend.[38] Interestingly, India had made an offer earlier to forge civil nuclear ties which was rejected. Another reason for Pakistan's affinity is the large Muslim population in the island country. Islam is the third largest religion in Sri Lanka. The more worrisome feature of the close relations for India is the overt and covert intelligence operations launched from Sri Lankan spies trained and sponsored by the ISI. Principally aimed at gathering information on sensitive defence and nuclear facilities, the scheme was uncovered with the arrest of three of them till date.[39] With future plans for establishment of a Naval Strategic Force (PNSF) an access to the Indian Ocean through Sri Lanka would pose a significant strategic challenge to India.

Indian Attempts

India's involvement in Sri Lanka's infrastructure development cannot be underestimated. While some have been completed many have been bogged down by delays. In 2012 India cleared the Kankesanthurai harbour which lies in the Jaffna peninsula in the northern part of Sri Lanka of ship wrecks and worked towards dredging which was accomplished in 2013[40] and breakwater rehabilitation.[41] India has also restored the Pallai-Kankesanthurai rail line at a cost of about $149 million.[42] Indian assistance was sought to develop the Palali airstrip in Jaffna into an international airport.[43] The foundation for renovating the Jaffna Duraiappa stadium was laid by Minster for Economic Development Basil Rajapaksa, taken up with a 145 million rupee grant from the Indian government.[44] Yet another instance of Indian assistance to bring industrial development to Jaffna peninsula is the opening of the Achchuvely Industrial Estate on August 27, 2014.[45] It seeks to provide a platform for industrial infrastructure in the Northern Province focussing on textiles, plastic and leather products, oil and fibre products, food processing units, and agro-based industries. It is expected to initially create 2000 jobs directly and 10000 indirectly. India has given 270 million Sri Lankan Rupees for the project. Restoration of the Thiruketheeswaram Temple in Mannar has been taken up by the Department of Archaeology of Sri Lanka with assistance from Archaeological Survey of India (ASI) and the College of

Architecture and Sculpture, Mamallapuram.[46] In the Central province India has undertaken the building of a 150-bed hospital in Dickoya at a cost of Rs 50 crores. India is also setting up a $512 million coal power plant in Sampur in joint partnership[47]. India is also planning to construct a new Cultural Centre in Jaffna[48]. India's line of credit is about USD $1.8 billion, although the figure is roughly half of China's current line of credit which stands at roughly USD $3.4 billion.[49]

In March 2015 the Indian Prime Minister Narendra Modi visited Sri Lanka while addressing the Parliament of Sri Lanka he considered the Sri Lankan Parliament to be one of the most vibrant in Asia. Modi expressed his delight to have got the chance to visit Sri Lanka so early in his term. Believing Sri Lanka to be an inspiration for human development, he assumed it to be home for existence, skill and extraordinary intellectual heritage. He expressed that how without having any land boundary the two nations have been the closest neighbours. The Prime Minister stated his vision of an ideal neighbourhood where trade, investments, technology, ideas and people flow easily across borders. He assured India's full commitment and support in development partnership with Sri Lanka.

Furthermore, the Indian Prime Minister stated that India's economic growth had picked up with the world looking towards India as "the new frontier of economic opportunity". Sri Lanka has the potential to be our strongest economic partner and will work to boost trade and make it more balanced. He said the pact between customs authorities of the two countries "will simplify trade and reduce non-tariff barriers on both sides." He announced a new line of credit of $318 million for Sri Lankan railways.[50]

In another important step, The Reserve Bank of India and the Central Bank of Sri Lanka have agreed to enter into a currency swap agreement of $ 1.5 billion – a move to keep the Sri Lankan rupee stable. The pact assumes significance as the Sri Lankan rupees has been under pressure for quite some time. Despite attempts made by the central bank, the currency has been losing value since the beginning of this year. At the current valuation, one Indian rupees is equivalent to 2.12 Sri Lankan rupees. In the area of energy cooperation, Indian Oil Crop Ltd's Sri Lankan subsidiary, Lanka IOC Plc. And Ceylon Petroleum Crop. have agreed to jointly develop the upper tank farm of the China Bay installation in Trincomalee on mutually agreed terms. Modi further said that a joint task force would be constituted "soon" to work out modalities. Modi said that India is ready to help Trincomalee to become a "regional petroleum hub". This is a departure from the Rajapakse government's position of threatening to take back 99 oil storage tanks leased by Lanka IOC more than a year ago. The China Bay Tank farm has 99 storage tanks worth a capacity of 12,000 kilometers each. Only 15 of these tanks are operational.[51]

Conclusion

India and Sri Lanka have a curious relationship. While commonality of nation, language and religion can be identified, there are now vast differences among the perceptions, expectations and actions of the constituencies, namely the Tamil political parties in India, the Tamil Nadu Government and the Union government of India. At times, the central Indian government succumbed to the pressures of the sympathisers of the Tamil cause in Sri Lanka and reacted to topical events. Here states were seen to be more powerful than federal system. When the Union government was at variance with the Southern state's sentiments it often met with protests, resolutions and even violence. Thus, while all stakeholders are united on the idea of better conditions of life and livelihood for the Tamils of Northern Sri Lanka, the approach and solutions thought of, differ widely. Changing foreign policy stance saw overt and covert assistance to the cause of self determination convert to opposition to the "terror outfit" of LTTE. Support for the separatist movement was no longer welcome and leaders of Tamil outfits were repeatedly arrested or condemned for pro-LTTE stance. The end of the ethnic war brought glaring differences in the individual state of Tamil Nadu and the country-level response. There were allegations of arms supply by India to Sri Lanka that sought to decimate the Tamils. Allegations of blatant war crimes led to outrage in Tamil Nadu but the Indian government desisted from voting against Sri Lanka over the human rights issue. While the Indian government is emphasising on speeding up of rehabilitation works not much could be forced on the Sri Lankan side. The fishermen crossing the IMBL and the Katchchathivu problems clearly place the Tamil Nadu opinion makers and the Indian government at diametrically opposite ends of the opinion spectrum. The periodic transgressing of the maritime border between the two countries cannot be supported by the union government. Reneging on international agreements could set a bad precedent in a region already beset with a host of intractable problems. Thus, the stakes, stance and actions of various constituencies often at variance with each other further complicates the approach to a peaceful and smooth relation between a big power in the region of South Asia and its smaller neighbour. While the welfare of the Tamils evinces a chorus, the actions and reactions certainly exhibit marked difference ending in cacophony of the various stakeholders in Indo–Sri Lankan relations.

REFERENCES

1. India puts Jaffna train back on rails, *The Hindu*, October 7, 2014 http://www.thehindu.com/news/international/south-asia/india-puts-jaffna-train-back-on-rails/article6476395.ece
2. G.C. Shekhar, Lanka plays Bengal card—Envoy links Sinhalese to eastern states, TN groups fume, *The Telegraph*, March 29, 2013, http://www.telegraphindia.com/1130329/jsp/nation/story_16723882.jsp#.VIfoqPmUeT8 (accessed Dec 10, 2014)
3. King Vijaya (B.C 543-504) and his successors, (http://www.angelfire.com/ak/Maithri/Short_History_of_Sri_Lanka.pdf (accessed Dec 10, 2014)
4. http://www.omniglot.com/writing/sinhala.htm
5. For a detailed account of the visit refer H.R. Perera, Buddhism in Sri Lanka: A Short History", Access to Insight (Legacy Edition), 1 December 2013 http://www.accesstoinsight.org/lib/authors/perera/wheel100.html#sect-06 (accessed Dec 10, 2014)
6. Brian Orland, *India's relations with Sri Lanka*, in David Scott, ed., Handbook of India's International Relations, Routledge, 2011, p.102
7. Vernon Hewitt's article *Prime Minister and Parliament* in James Manor ed., Nehru to the Nineties: The changing office of Prime Minster in India, UBC Press, Vancouver, 1994 p.60
8. Can't attend CHOGM: PM tells Lankan President, Khurshid to lead India, *The Indian Express*, November 10, 2013 http://archive.indianexpress.com/news/cant-attend-chogm-pm-tells-lankan-president-khurshid-to-lead-india/1193162/
9. Lankan Military officers withdrawn from India, *Ceylon Today*, June 25, 2013 http://www.ceylontoday.lk/16-35956-news-detail-lankan-military-officers-withdrawn-from-india.html (accessed Dec 11, 2014)
10. *Outcome Budget 2013-2014*, GoI, MEA, New Delhi, p.16, http://www.mea.gov.in/Uploads/PublicationDocs/21546_MEA_Outcome_Budget_2013-14_English.pdf
11. Why Narendra Modi insists on 13th Amendment for Sri Lanka, Daily Mirror, August 30, 2014 http://www.dailymirror.lk/opinion/dbsjeyaraj-column/51737-why-narendra-modi-insists-on-13th-amendment-for-sri-lanka.html (accessed Dec 11, 2014)
12. 'Obsession' with 13th Amendment won't help, say Tamil politicians, *The Hindu*, April 12, 2013 http://tamilnadu.indiaeveryday.in/fullnews-obsession-with-13th-amendment-wont-help-say-tamil-1128-5314321.htm
13. For a detailed discussion of the issue from both sides see, Sea of Discord, *The Hindu*, Weekly edition 2, November 30, 2014
14. Adluri Subramanyam Raju, 'India's Security in the Palk Straits', in Goplaji Malviya (ed.), *Security Dimensions of Peninsular India*, Centre for Security Analysis, Chennai, 2005, p. 71.
15. Fishermen on death row freed, *The Hindu*, November 19, 2014 http://www.thehindu.com/news/national/sri-lanka-releases-indian-fishermen/article6614883.ece
16. Retrieve Katchativu, save fishermen, *The New Indian Express*, May 4, 2013 http://www.newindianexpress.com/states/tamil_nadu/Retrieve-Katchativu-save-fishermen/2013/05/04/article1574019.ece?service=print
17. India sits on the fence over Sri Lanka, *The Wall Street Journal*, March 28, 2014
18. Row over invite to Rajapaksa for Modi's swearing-in, *Hindustan Times*, May 24, 2014 http://www.hindustantimes.com/elections2014/election-beat/clamour-grows-over-invite-to-

rajapaksa-for-narendra-modi-s-swearing-in-ceremony/article1-1222342.aspx (accessed Dec 11, 2014)

19. Indian MPs led by Sushma Swaraj on Sri Lanka visit, *The Times of India*, April 16, 2012 http://timesofindia.indiatimes.com/india/Indian-MPs-led-by-Sushma-Swaraj-on-Sri-Lanka-visit/articleshow/12691881.cms
20. http://www.abc.net.au/worldtoday/content/2013/s3838854.htm
21. Lanka Government needs to do more for reconciliation: UNHCR chief, *ANI News*, September 23, 2014 http://aninews.in/newsdetail4/story184654/lanka-government-needs-to-do-more-for-reconciliation-unhcr-chief.html
22. http://www.ndtv.com/article/cheat-sheet/sri-lankan-pilgrims-attacked-in-tamil-nadu-10-developments-262909
23. 'Nedumaran inaugurates Mullivaikkal memorial', *The Hindu*, November 6, 2013 http://www.thehindu.com/news/national/tamil-nadu/mullivaikkal-memorial-declared-open/article5321273.ece
24. J. Goodman, 'Sri Lanka's growing links with China', *The Diplomat*, March 16, 2014 http://thediplomat.com/2014/03/sri-lankas-growing-links-with-china/
25. Funds from China boosts roads, ports in Sri Lanka, *China Invests Overseas*, 22 September, 2014 http://www.china-invests.net/20140922/34209.aspx (accessed December 14, 2014)
26. CICT elevates Colombo to mega port status, Sri Lanka Ports Authority, http://www.slpa.lk/news_events_13040.asp
27. India refused to build Hambantota port: Rajapaksa, March 18, 2010 http://www.rediff.com/news/report/what-mahinda-rajapaksa-says-about-indo-lanka-ties/20100318.htm (accessed 14 December 2014)
28. India perturbed over Beijing's 'warming relations' with Sri Lanka, China, *The Times of India*, November 3, 2014, http://timesofindia.indiatimes.com/india/India-perturbed-over-Beijings-warming-relations-with-Sri-Lanka-China-says/articleshow/45023296.cms
29. Sri Lanka backs China's plan to build Maritime Silk Road, February 13, 2014 http://zeenews.india.com/news/south-asia/sri-lanka-backs-chinas-plan-to-build-maritime-silk-road_911219.html
30. A. Singh, 'China's Maritime Silk Route: Implications for India', *IDSA Comment*, July 16, 2014 http://www.idsa.in/idsacomments/ChinasMaritimeSilkRoute_AbhijitSingh_160714.html
31. Sri-Lanka-snubs-India-opens-port-to-Chinese-submarine-again, *The Times of India*, November 2, 2014 http://timesofindia.indiatimes.com/india/Sri-Lanka-snubs-India-opens-port-to-Chinese-submarine-again/articleshow/45008757.cms
32. Chinese aircraft maintenance centre in Trinco, *Ceylon Today*, July 23, 2014 http://www.ceylontoday.lk/51-68802-news-detail-chinese-aircraft-maintenance-centre-in-trinco.html
33. China's strategic presence in Sri Lanka, *Colombo Telegraph*, https://www.colombotelegraph.com/index.php/chinas-strategic-presence-in-sri-lanka/
34. H. Gardner, China's aid revealed in Sri Lanka's victory parade, *The National*, June 9, 2009, http://www.thenational.ae/news/world/south-asia/chinas-aid-revealed-in-sri-lankas-victory-parade#full
35. R. Hariharan, Chinese Defence Minsiter's visit to Sri Lanka: An Indian perspective, Chennai Centre for China Studies Paper No: 1029, September 11, 2012 http://www.c3sindia.org/southasia/3052
36. S. Shrivastava, 1971, 'India Pakistan War: Role of Russia, China, America and Britain', The World Reporter, October 30, 2011 http://www.theworldreporter.com/2011/10/1971-india-pakistan-war-role-of-russia.html (accessed December 14, 2014)

37. http://www.merinews.com/article/pakistan-sri-lanka-relations-their-long-distance-amiability/15900858.shtml
38. http://indiatoday.intoday.in/story/pak-help-to-lanka-for-n—plant-alarms-india/1/209895.html
39. *The Times of India*, September 13, 2014 http://timesofindia.indiatimes.com/india/ISI-spy-was-bartender-in-2009-Army-party-in-Chennai/articleshow/42391713.cms
40. http://www.sagarsandesh.in/news/dci-completes-dredging-of-kankesanthurai-kks-harbour-in-n-sri-lanka/
41. 'Kankesanthurai Harbour wreck removal complete', *The Hindu*, January 18, 2012 http://www.thehindu.com/news/international/kankesanthurai-harbour-wreck-removal-complete/article2811550.ece
42. http://www.railway-technology.com/news/newsindia-to-help-sri-lanka-rebuild-pallai-kankesanthurai-railway-line
43. Palali airport to be upgraded to international level, *Daily News*, March 15, 2013 http://archives.dailynews.lk/2013/03/15/bus01.asp
44. Jaffna Duraiappa Stadium To Be Developed Into An International Sports, *Target*, Stadiumhttp://www.target.lk/article.php?article=3637
45. http://www.news.lk/news/business/item/2615-minister-basil-inaugurates-achchuvely-industrial-estate-in-jaffna
46. India-Sri Lanka Joint Declaration, June 9, 2010, Ministry of external Affairs, GoI, http://mea.gov.in/bilateral-documents.htm?dtl/4087/IndiaSri+Lanka+Joint+Declaration
47. Sri Lanka speeds up work on power project after Rajapaksa-Modi meet, May 30, 2014 http://www.oneindia.com/new-delhi/sri-lanka-speeds-up-work-on-power-project-after-rajapaksa-modi-meet-1456347.html
48. India to build cultural centre in Jaffna, *The Hindu*, June 10, 2014 http://www.thehindu.com/news/international/south-asia/india-to-build-cultural-centre-in-jaffna/article6098460.ece
49. N. Manoharan, China and its Peripheries: Beijing and India-Sri Lanka Relations, Issue Brief #217, May 2013, IPCS, p.5 http://www.ipcs.org/issue-brief/china/china-and-its-peripheries-beijing-and-india-sri-lanka-relations-217.html
50. http://www.livemint.com/Polotics/BXAww21DgFW7nCQLaBJou/Narendra-Modi-arrives-in-Sri-Lanka-as-Final-Stop-oF-his-3na.html.
51. Ibid.

20

India's External Security Conundrum: Complexities of Securing Peace in South Asia

Nanda Kishor M S

Most of the discourses on India's security, for a long time have begun with the phrase 'in the post-cold war era' and then there was a major event that shook the world and changed the academic discourses on security to 'after 9/11' dramatically. Needless to say, this is seen regularly even now as most of the asymmetric threats emerge from the violent non-state actors across the spectrum, who have redefined the concept of security to a large extent. The new millennium in all possible ways is likely to sustain more transformational, innovative and challenging trends than any other century in the past as there are no signs of wars among states. Though the concept of states fighting each other is slowly becoming irrelevant yet staggeringly the states are in arms race and preponderance of power remains the aim of several nations. The larger threat animatedly threatening the nations and keeping them it on tenterhooks is the transnational form of terrorism. This is in a way an intricate challenge for the states as the preparation to deal with the enemy is two-fold: adversarial state/s and violent non-state actors. Some in the academia believe this as an opportunity after a long time for several nations with different ideologies and traits to come together on a single platform to fight this phenomenon, whereas on the other, there seems to be a greater difficulty in defining the new enemy, understanding them fully for executing a successful strategy. Irrespective of the stature of a nation in the world political system, it has pushed nations to converge and come to terms in managing the enemy if not eliminating. In reality, it is an implicit factor that terrorist groups or networks cannot operate in vacuum. The terrorist groups need 'sponsors', a term popularly used in counterterrorism literature referring to a nation allowing its territory to be used for carrying out terrorist activities. Sponsoring is of two types, firstly, the country and its leadership willingly and knowingly supports or does not disrupt terrorist groups and its activities. Secondly, the country is avert to terrorist activities but unable to eliminate them and continues to be a place of operation for the network. In either of the case it is called as sponsoring, as inability to act against is essentially considered as sponsoring. To discuss India's security in the region, both types of sponsoring are important. A multifaceted problem of violent non-state actors and state together posing problem to the security apparatus is a grave threat India faces in its region. Though China is on India's high security radar and falls under the larger ambit of Southern Asia, this research would limit it to South Asia as there is vast amount of literature being written about Sino-Indian security issues. Given this backdrop, to understand the precarious security scenario in which India resides needs meticulous inspection of its location, strength, weakness and status in the region.

India by her own actions or due to strategically forced actions, has to deal with the harsh reality of facing two important nations Pakistan and Bangladesh that emerged from its territory in the post-colonial twentieth century. It is far from doubt that these two share extremely uneasy relations with India. The very birth of these states has something to do with instability in the region and preparing ground for extra regional powers to play their power politics. One cannot blame these nations for the instances solely as the then international security environment also played a major role in shaping what they are today. The remaining states of the region also do not share a great rapport with India due to its geographical dominance, military strength, economic prosperity and global recognition which have invariably labeled it as a regional hegemony. Several scholars reflect the same opinion existing in the region by asserting that the sheer geopolitical size of India has "given rise to negative perceptions about India as a selfish hegemony, seeking to maximise its power at the cost of others in the neighbourhood".[1] India's new-found strength in economic sphere coupled with credentials of turning out to be one of the strongest knowledge economy is being shadowed by the precarious security scenario. India is not the only example in the world, nor is it only unique to the subcontinent but a common problem being faced by many nations across the world when the above mentioned attributes are identical. It becomes unique for the fact that due to time and energy it invests in resolving its regional problems is humongous and at times seen as a farfetched one. Stanley Weiss terms it as tyranny of geography.[2]

The recent histories of nations such as Afghanistan, Pakistan, Nepal, Bangladesh, Sri Lanka and even Maldives in the region has not been pleasant and they have been in news for all wrong reasons in international affairs. This scenario has direct implications on India's security in one or the other way. If Afghanistan is in the limelight due to Taliban and Al-Qaida leading to war on terror, Pakistan is known for being a safe heaven for terrorists and equally becoming a victim of the terrorist activities, Nepal has been in turmoil over its domestic conditions and also known for its cross border terrorist networks, Bangladesh for infighting with regard to the 1971 war memory and subsequent radical groups trying to destabilise a democratically elected party in power as it is against extreme radicalization and demonizing India, Sri Lanka for fresh religious intolerance by Sinhala groups after long struggles between LTTE and the government and Maldives for the coup and attempts to move towards radical Islam. The only exception has been Bhutan though it suffered being the land for training of some of the radical elements from the state of Assam. It would not be an exaggeration to take up terrorism as the first component of major security threat for India in the present South Asian scenario to discuss.

Terrorism and Militant Groups

It is often not surprising at all to note that since last 15 years the topic of terrorism has overtaken the state itself in the international arena. This is more so with regard to South Asia, as the shift of gravity to the East has not been limited to economy but also to security. Though the region had few groups which were internationally known such as LTTE, they could not move beyond a particular territory and were never given the title transnational in the present sense of the term. The language and ethnic related issues also limited its outreach of operations. With the advent of Taliban rule in Afghanistan and subsequent Al-Qaeda expansion to several parts of the world at once attracted the attention of the world including the Unites States. The attention garnered can be attributed to two reasons: firstly, the group dared attacking the United

States which never imagined to be attacked when formerly USSR could not do so. Secondly, the mix of religion and terrorist activity took it to a different level altogether. The usage of Islam and Islamic hermeneutics to justify their acts did not allow several countries to brutally attack the terrorist group unlike how they dealt with the left backed groups across the world.

Unfortunately, India has been a victim of terrorist activities for a long time but the United States accepted it only when its own soil was attacked. Pakistan has long cultivated and deployed numerous so-called Kashmiri *tanzeems* (organizations) to pressure India to resolve the ongoing Kashmir dispute in Pakistan's favor.[3] Pakistan based Lashkar-e-Taiba (LeT) and Jaish-e-Mohammed are the two terrorists groups that have proven themselves the most capable and motivated to carry out attacks in India.[4] Apart from this, Pakistan continues to be the place of origin and operation for several other groups that include militant groups such as Harkat-ul-Jihadi-al-Islami (HuJI), Harkat-ul-Mujahideen (HuM), Lashkar-e-Taiba (LeT), Jaish-e-Mohammad (JeM).[5] Unfortunately, many terrorist groups in Pakistan and Bangladesh have their ideological base in Pakistan and receive either active or passive help from the agencies that are within the military and other security establishments of the Pakistan government. One of the noted scholars on terrorism literature Jay Millan defines terrorism as a substitute of overt warfare and when diplomats fail, soldier take over, when soldier fail, terrorists take over. This is an apt situation in which Pakistan is placed right now. The nuclear conundrum post 1998 and post Kargil defeat, Pakistan has resorted to asymmetric warfare in the form of promoting terrorist organisations. These terrorist groups are also involved in supporting the groups having role in "hawala" transactions and extortion for profit like that of Dawood Ibrahim have been given sanctuary in Pakistan and are linked up with the ISI to finance terror strikes in India[6] and these proxy networks of significance include groups like the Harkat-ul-Ansar, LeT, JeM, and the Harkat-ul-Jihad-Islami (HuJI).[7] What makes it more problematic and difficult to handle many a times is that of the ties of organisation like LeT with the religious, missionary organisation now known as Jamaat-ul Dawa (JuD). The nature of attacks by LeT on Indian soil such as December 2000 Delhi's Red Fort to the November 2008 Mumbai has not only shaken Indian civilians but also the visitors to India. Being aware of the mighty forces India possesses, LeT tried to prove its capabilities, its linkages and outreach by attacking the financial capital of India in turn affecting the financial security of the country. The organization also carried a very definitive message from the Pakistani establishment that when they are unable to take on India directly, asymmetric warfare will be the strength of the contemporary battlefield to move closer to achieving its objectives. What puts India on high security alert and its forces is the fact that there is likely to be an increase in terrorist violence emanating from the world's epicenter of terrorism, and a good deal of it is likely to be directed towards India.[8]

According to Husain Haqqani, the Lashkar is determined in carrying out the mission laid out in their booklet 'Why We Are Waging Jihad?'. The eight goals are: eliminating evil and facilitating conversion to Islam; ensuring Islam's ascendance; forcing non-Muslims to pay the jaziya (historically, a tax paid by non-Muslims to Muslim rulers); assisting the weak and powerless; avenging Muslims who have been wronged; punishing the enemies of Islam for breaking promises and treaties; defending a Muslim state; and liberating what were historically Muslim territories during the Caliphate era.[9] These are sort of apocalyptic views being put forward by a group and using religion to entice the civilian population. This is a grave security concern for India in the South Asian region essentially emanating from Pakistan. Every attack on Indian soil would be considered as a success irrespective of all the terrorists getting killed in the action as intrusion itself is consider as success in terrorism and counter-terrorism literature with regard to India. The immediate danger is the plan that has been hatched by LeT for quite some time now is the operations by Indian Mujahedeen. Indian government has to deal with a twofold problem of managing terrorist groups externally and managing homegrown terrorism. The Student Islamic Movement of India (SIMI) and the IM both have been used by LeT to create a reign of terror within India in recent times. LeT has understood that the Indian forces have become alert after 2008 Mumbai blast and it is not easy to intrude to India and carry out attacks. It has been using some of the organization in India by providing financial assistance and training to attack. The IM leader Yasin Bhatkal took over as the head on the IM after both of his brothers, Iqbal Bhatkal and Riaz Bhatkal escaped to Pakistan in 2008. He has been successful in indoctrinating Muslim youth and recruiting them in the IM and carrying out several blasts including Delhi High Court in September 2011, Mumbai in July 2011, Chinaswamy Stadium in Bengaluru in April 2010, German Bakery in February 2010, Ahmedabad in 2008 and twin blasts in Hyderabad in August 2007 amongst others.[10] Bhatkal has been arrested and his arrest has opened up a can of worms which essentially establish Pakistan's project to destabilize India's security and induce threat.

It will be interesting to note that a country like Nepal which is culturally close to India has been one of the biggest security threats to India. This is not in comparison to the type of role played by Pakistan but Nepal has been used as a transit point for most of the people who are recruited by Pakistani terrorist organisations. The free border arrangement between Nepal and India has been thoroughly used by Pakistani terrorist organisations. The geopolitical conditions of Terai is favorable to facilitating criminal smuggling activities and hosting safe havens; conditions that have attracted the interest and followers of LeT.[11] Without a stable government and decision making process, Nepal has figured in the failed state list produced by the United States government. After LeT was implicated in the November 2008 Mumbai attacks, attention turned to their Terai operations. Based upon the confession of the sole surviving attacker, India demanded that Nepal take swift action against several of the traders. Aslam Ansari (Pakistan) and Nasim Ansari (Nepal) were arrested in the border town of Birgunj in December 2008 by police due to pressure from India and Interpol for their suspected roles in funding LeT. With the arrest of Yasin Bhatkal on 28 August 2013 by the Bihar Police in a joint operation with the National Investigation Agency (NIA) and Abdul Karim Tunda of the Lashkar-e-Taiba (LeT) from the India-Nepal border on 16 August 2013 has only proved the point beyond doubt that Nepal has ended up becoming a sponsor of terrorism.

The case of Bangladesh is much more peculiar as the terrorist activities go up depending on the regime in rule. It has been recorded and accepted widely that whenever BNP has been in power the radical groups have advantage. This has been evident on several occasions and Sriradha Dutta opines that the violent outburst against Hindus, who are mainly supporters of the Awami League, in the aftermath of the BNP coalition victory in the 2001 election, reflected not only the underlying tension that prevailed between the two main political parties in Bangladesh but also with India. Though on several occasions Prime Minister Sheikh Hasina had raised the concern of *Talibanisation* of Bangladesh, her intervention could not achieve anything as the then ruling party was in favour of radical groups. To prove this point beyond doubt, the Bangladesh Nationalist Party (BNP)-led coalition government, headed by Khaleda Zia, provided safe heavens to Indian insurgent groups in the North-East India with a view to keeping India internally engaged. It is only after Sheik Hasina has been in power that India has been in a much more comfortable position. Needless to say, even now when the Bangladeshi government is making all its attempts to cooperate with India, there are radical groups which have strong nexus with Pakistan and are waiting for opportunities to attack India. Bangladesh continues to be a greater threat to security of India as the pro Al-Qaeda organizations of Pakistani originsupported by the ISI such as the LeT, HuJI, and Harkat ul Mujahideen (HuM) try operating through Bangladesh, help illegal migration into Assam and West Bengal, and arrange the flow of funds from Wahabi charity organizations in Saudi Arabia to the radical groups. Several militant Islamist groups that exist in Bangladesh, like Jam'atul Mujahideen Bangladesh (JMB), the Jagrata Muslim Janata Bangladesh (JMJB), the Harkatul-Jihad-Islami (HuJI), the Islami Chhatra Shibir, and the Hizb-ut-Tahri, are always a threat to India. The Sheikh Hasina government is a great support to the Indian Government but sustaining her in the seat of power is not India's duty but it can facilitate by taking positive decisions concerning Bangladesh from migration, water sharing, and construction of dams to addressing climate changes issues amicably.

Other Security Concern

Apart from terrorism, there are several other security issues India needs to divert its attention to. Though the change of guard in Sri Lanka is a welcome scenario for India compared to that of a strong headed Rajapaksa, there is no guarantee that it would work in favour of India. Rajapaksa was seen as a person who would play the China card whenever there would be an adversarial decision taken against Sri Lanka by India. There have been numerous incidents in the Palk Strait of the Sri Lankan Navy firing and imprisoning Indian fisherman who use mechanized trawlers and practice illegal fishing methods that destroy Sri Lankan fishing boats. Sri Lankan Prime Minister Ranil Wickramasinghe has come up with an unusually hard and provocative statement suggesting that Indian fishermen would be shot if they were to intrude into Sri Lankan waters.[12] India wants an amicable solution to the fishermen problem in the traditional waters of Palk Bay as it has all the potential to disturb the internal politics of India. The internal political dilemma is in much better condition compared to that of the previous regime of Manmohan Singh. The recent special committee and a cabinet subcommittee set up by Prime Minister Ranil Wikremasinghe on the Chinese funded US$ 1.5 billion Colombo Port City Project has been a welcome gesture as India had its own security concerns as a large portion of cargoes bound for India are transshipped through Colombo port. During the previous Sri Lankan administration, mistrust between India and Sri Lanka on regional security increased as there was an increased Chinese infrastructural investment and subsequent support for a maritime trade route that would permit Chinese submarines to dock along the Sri Lankan coastline was expected. The Chinese entry has changed regional security scenario and India would not want this government to go too close to China. The main concern is the possibility of use of infrastructure put in place by China against Indian interests. In the Annexure of the India-Sri Lanka Accord of 1987 India and Sri Lanka have agreed that "Trincomalee or any other port in Sri Lanka would not be made available for military use to any country in a manner which is prejudicial to India's interest." India trusts that Colombo would abide by this provision seriously.[13] As it is too early to assess the behavioural pattern of the new government, Sri Lanka continues to be a security concern for India.

Afghanistan is another security concern for India even though India has a better image among Afghanis due to its development activities. The last instance of attacking the Indian consulate in Herat on 23 May 2014 came as a shocking one. India would go through a real problematic situation once the withdrawal of the US and NATO led troops take place completely. Though several academicians and experts opine that such complete withdrawal will not happen, if happens then certainly it is not in India's interest. Due to the West led groups keeping vigilance, some of the Pakistan based militant groups are unable to operate in Kashmir through Afghan groups. The new president, Ashraf Ghani Ahmadzai, though not avert to India, he is also not seen as a great friend of India compared to his predecessor Karzai. His visits to Saudi Arabia and Pakistan only assert that he is much into reconciliation than confronting the real problems of his country. A series of Pakistani officials visited Kabul including the army chief, Gen. Raheel Sharif and Lt. Gen. Rizwan Akhtar, the new head of the Inter-Services Intelligence directorate, the powerful military spy agency. If Ashraf Ghani is making effort to reduce visibility of Taliban through Pakistan, nothing can be equivalent to that of his irrationality. Even the Afghan people know the intentions of Pakistan in long run. These events only put India in a difficult situation. Some assert that Pakistan's ultimate goal is that Afghanistan provides Pakistan strategic depth against India. Pakistan's Defense Secretary stated in January 2014 that they would not accept a robust role for India in Afghanistan as international forces wind down involvement in Afghanistan. India's goals are to deny Pakistan "strategic depth" in Afghanistan, to deny Pakistan the ability to block India from trade and other connections to Central Asia and beyond, and to prevent militants in Afghanistan from attacking Indian targets in Afghanistan.[14] India's energy security demands a better relation with

Afghanistan. Even if all the countries decide to go ahead with the project, there is always a threat during the operational part by extremist groups.

Maldives is another significant country in India's maritime security. If India wants its footprint in a firm manner in the region, greater attention needs to be given to the Maldives archipelago. For India, Maldives' location in the Indian Ocean and close to its southern tip makes it a strategically significant country. The report of increasing Chinese presence in the Maldives is a matter of anxiety for India. Both the countries have agreed to "strengthen cooperation to enhance maritime safety and security in the Indian Ocean Region through joint patrolling and aerial and maritime surveillance, exchange of information, capacity building and the development of an effective legal framework against piracy".[15] The internal politics and the coup tendency is a real security concern for India. It has serious implications on India's economic interest too. The GMR issue was one such example of strained relations. The trilateral cooperation between India-Maldives-Sri Lanka can be best served if the security issues in the Indian Ocean Region are solved amicably and for that Maldives becomes one of the primordial interests for India. A stable democracy in Maldives is in India's interest and for this to happen, India needs regularly interact with the island nation. India also needs to make sure that Maldives does not become safe heaven for jihadi activities. It was known for long that Maldivian students had been enticed into attending madarsas in Pakistan since the late seventies-or from around the time the ISI began its 'zero option' unconventional war on India.[16] Recent visit of the Maldivian president is a welcome sign and his gesture of India first would help in India taking adequate measures to secure its position in the Indian Ocean.

Apart from terrorist networks and attacks on India, there are other security concerns for India with regard to Pakistan. India has non-traditional security issues with Pakistan with regard to the river sharing. The energy demands of India has been driving it to go for hydroelectric projects on the Jhelum and Chenab rivers and also the much needed Kishanganga project. All of these have been opposed by Pakistan. Pakistan had moved for arbitration against India under the provisions of the Indus Waters Treaty 1960 that regulates the use of waters in the shared rivers on 17 May 2010. There were three major appeals filed by Pakistan at International Court of Arbitration (ICA): first, the flow of water to be at a minimum of 10 to ideally 100 cumecs towards Pakistan's Neelum-Jhelum River; second, to permit Pakistan to have an access of monitoring of water; and last, restrict India to divert the water to its hydroelectric project near Bonar Nullah. The Hague-based International

Court of Arbitration has allowed India to go ahead with construction of the 330-MW Kishanganga hydro-electric project in North Kashmir which was under dispute with Pakistan. Pakistan has serious concerns with regard to the design of the project. Pakistan also claims that India is exploiting its base in Afghanistan to cause problems in Baluchistan and in Pakistan's restless tribal areas along the Pakistan–Afghanistan border. Similar accusations proliferate about India's expanding presence in Iran, especially its 'listening post' in Zahedan in Iran's Sistan-o-Baluchistan province, abutting Pakistan's own restive Baluch province.[17] Though many of the allegations are made against India due to the frustration Pakistan is being unable to handle of the firm footprint of India in Afghanistan and Central Asia, it has the ability to disturb India's peace by resorting to asymmetric methods on which India needs to be cautious.

With regard to Bangladesh, illegal immigration continues to be a perennial problem. The illegal migration poses multidimensional problem. Most of the academicians are of the opinion that there is a possibility that between 10 and 35 million Bangladeshis are illegally residing in India. The Centre for Women and Children Studies based in Bangladesh estimated in 1998 that 27,000 Bangladeshis had been forced into prostitution in India. This is one of the major security concerns for India as it leads to considerable economic burden for India and equally endangers national security in a severely threatened global atmosphere of terrorism. Though often it is criticized that the illegal immigration situation is overemphasized with the security discourse due to intelligent agencies, one cannot deny the role of some illegal migrants in several blasts that have taken place in India due strong radicalization process by Pakistan in Bangladesh. There are several internal security issues that are related to the illegal immigrant problem such as the ongoing conflict between Bodos and Bengali speaking Muslims from Bangladesh. It is essentially political, economic and security concerned issues. Between 2007 and 2012, Muslim immigrants had migrated in large numbers from Dhubri to Kokrajhar district especially to Gosaigaon sub-division. This created enormous pressures on agriculture land, one of the vital means of livelihood for indigenous communities.[18] The external problems with Bangladesh have direct influence on some of the major problematic regions of India and internal security issues. The extremist groups from the northeast found safe heavens in Bangladesh for a long time. It was only during Sheik Hasina's era that things have become better due to her pro-India policies which led Bangladesh handing over, Ranjan Daimary, the 'president' of the anti-talks faction of the National Democratic

Front of Bodoland (NDFB-ATF) to India. In similar fashion a number of United Liberation Front of Asom (ULFA) leaders were arrested and subsequently handed over to the Indian authorities. Some of the top ULFA leaders who were handed over to the Indian authorities were 'general secretary', Arbinda Rajkhowa, deputy commander in-chief Raju Baruah, 'foreign secretary' Sasadhar Choudhury, and 'finance secretary' Chitraban Hazarika on 1 May 2010.[19] To sum it up, the security concerns with Bangladesh range from illegal migration, child and women trafficking, drug trafficking and support to Indian extremists by providing safe place to stay.

In case of Nepal, there are serious issues of anti-India feeling among the people. India had to go through a typical dilemma of being suspected by monarchy for supporting groups favouring democratic regime in Nepal and on the other hand being accused of supporting the monarchy clandestinely to come back to power. India has been constantly accused of working for an instable Nepal. The open border between the nations has been a major issue of security concern as it is used by terrorists, smugglers, drug peddlers (*ganja* from Nepal and *charas* from India), smuggling of small arms from both sides, etc. Illegal armed groups operating in the Madheshi region, and organised criminal gangs take advantage of the open border and take shelter on either side to evade the law enforcement agencies of respective countries. Apart from that, of late, some religious fundamentalist groups have increased their activities along the border region. This could pose a serious security challenge both to India and Nepal in future.[20] The recent visit of Prime Minister Modi to Nepal has charted a fresh chapter in Indo-Nepal relations. Both countries endorsed new developmental projects, showed their willingness to improve the peace and security at border, promised to improve border infrastructure, and expressed concern over the slow pace of implementation of many projects.[21] As these developments are too early to judge, the security concerns have to be taken up by India with Nepal regularly.

Bhutan being a landlocked Himalayan country, has been one of the most important strategic location to India. Though 'Operation All Clear' against ULFA, NDFB and KLO was most successful in 2003, the story has not ended there. According to some reports, United Liberation Front of Assam (ULFA) and National Democratic Front of Bodoland (NDFB) have been training the Communist Party of Bhutan (MLM) and its two wings, Bhutan Tiger Force and United Revolutionary Youth of Bhutan. CPB-MLM aims to overthrow the regime in Bhutan, and has opposed the democratic elections in Bhutan. Moreover, the militant groups are reportedly using the Southern jungles of Bhutan as a transit route to enter Arunachal Pradesh.[22] The Chinese assertion along the Bhutan border is also equally alarming. The amalgamation of security threats posed by extremist groups from India and China using Bhutan's territory is the real concern for India.

It is rightly pointed out that there are causal relations between managing a region and global aspirations of becoming a major power for India. India aspires to be a power that has to be recognized with its economic might assisted with larger population being youth. India certainly needs to move beyond managing its neighbour to lead its neighbours. Its strategic vision has to overcome some of its inherited problems of clinging onto wait and watch approach to 'be first and lead'. It's far from doubt that India has never imposed its credential of being the largest democracy on its South Asian neighbours and that image restrains it from taking bolder steps. It is high time that India advocates some of its credentials to its neighbours and equally learn important ones from others. From security point of view, India needs to be pro-active as signaling alone will not fetch anything. One of the important examples of action-oriented decision is that of calling off the foreign secretary level talks with Pakistan after Pakistani High Commissioner Abdul Basit's meeting with Hurriyat leader Shabir Shah was a grave concern for India. This sent a strong message in action which was not anticipated by Pakistan. One cannot agree with statements implying that India does not want to get stuck with South Asia's unending problems but moved ahead and play a larger global role. However problematic it is, India should first give its priority to its South Asian neighbours as it is not only a security issue but also a moral duty. If India wants to be part of setting normative standards in international politics, then it has to carry its South Asian neighbours all along. Shying away from a problem is certainly not the character of a major power but to reconcile and work on newer solutions with new approaches to the problem. Except for Pakistan, in the present scenario of 2015 South Asia, India is expected to lead and carve a place for South Asia as a region in the world politics. There is a fresh confidence that has come in the South Asian neighbours with the election of Narendra Modi to the government and his clear policy of 'South Asia first'.

The time is ripe to think of a regional security complex and remove the fears long persisting among neighbours on India as a nuclear nation with superior military power. The regular issue of non-cooperation from Pakistan would surface for sure, but one can hope that by taking other remaining nations in the region into confidence and making them partners in the progress is the only way to coerce Pakistan to fall in line. India's security also essentially depends on how it deals with its neighbours with mutual trust and respect. The ad-hoc fashion of dealing with neighbours needs to be transformed into 3C's: Communicate, Cooperate and Converge. India is capable of helping and subsequently presenting its concerns, priorities and expectations from the South Asian neighbours. So far, India has been waiting for conducive regimes to come in the neighbourhood to be in a better position, but the time has come to create advantageous environment through its forward looking decisions and support to convert any regime to a conducive one. If India's national security and interest is the high priority to have peace in India, the best option is to lead from the front, rework on the economic model to bring prosperity to the region and place a consensual model of progress to place South Asia distinctly on the world map. There is a necessity for India to move beyond the rhetoric's to action if it is serious in securing peace.

REFERENCES

1. M. Bisht, "India-Bhutan relations in the next two decades," In Rumel Dahiya, & Ashok K Behuria (eds.), *India's Neighbourhood: Challenges in the Next Two Decades*, New Delhi: Pentagon Press, 2012, pp. 137–62.
2. B. Chellaney, 'India: Regional Security Challenges', in Wilhelm Hofmeister (ed.), *Security Politics in Asia and Europe* (pp.157-176). Singapore: Konrad-Adenauer-Stiftung, 2010.
3. C. Fair, Insights from a Database of Lashkar-e-Taiba and Hizb-ul-Mujahideen Militants, *The Journal of Strategic Studies*, 37 (2), 2013, pp. 259–90.
4. M. Daniel, *Terrorism and Indo-Pakistani Escalation*. The United States of America: Council on Foreign Relations, 2010.
5. Sharma, S.K., & Behera, A., *Militant Groups in South Asia*, New Delhi: Pentagon Press, 2014, p. 320.
6. P. Swami, *India, Pakistan and the Secret Jihad*. New York: Routledge, 2007.
7. A. Rashid, *Descent Into Chaos*. London: Allen Lane, 2008.
8. S. Kalyanaraman, Asymmetric Warfare: A View from India, *Strategic Analysis*, 36(2), 2012, pp. 193-197.
9. H. Haqqani, The Ideology of South Asian Jihadi Groups. In Hillel Fradkin, Husain Haqqani, & Eric Brown (Eds.), *Current Trends in Islamist Ideology*, 1, Washington, DC: Hudson Institute, 2005.
10. A. Behera, Deradicalisation in Bangladesh: Challenges Ahead. *Journal of Defence Studies*, 5(2), 2011, pp. 138, 146.
11. J. Miklian, *Illicit Trading in Nepal: Fueling South Asian Terrorism*. Oslo: International Peace Research Institute, 2009.
12. Sharma, S.K., & Behera, A., *Militant Groups in South Asia*, New Delhi: Pentagon Press, 2014, p. 320.
13. N. Manohran, *China and its Peripheries: Beijing and India-Sri Lanka Relations*, 2013, Retrieved March 10, 2015, from http://www.ipcs.org/issue-brief/china/china-and-its-peripheries-beijing-and-india-sri-lanka-relations-217.html

14. K. Katzman, *Afghanistan: Post-Taliban Governance, Security, and U.S. Policy*, 2015, Retrieved March 10, 2015, from http://fas.org/sgp/crs/row/RL30588.pdf
15. G. Arvind, India and Maldives: Ties Must Be Consolidated, 2014, Retrieved March 10, 2015, from http://www.idsa.in/policybrief/IndiaandMaldives_agupta_130113.html
16. S. Moorthy, India and Maldives Towards Consolidation, 2010, Retrieved March 10, 2015, from http://www.ipcs.org/pdf_file/issue/IB145-Maldives-Sathiyamoorthi.pdf.
17. C. Fair, Insights from a Database of Lashkar-e-Taiba and Hizb-ul-Mujahideen Militants, *The Journal of Strategic Studies*, 37(2), 2013, pp. 259–90.
18. N. Goswami, Bodo violence: Contest for power and territory, 2014, Retrieved March 10, 2015, from http://www.idsa.in/idsacomments/Bodoviolence_ngoswami_090514.html
19. A. Behera, Deradicalisation in Bangladesh: Challenges Ahead, *Journal of Defence Studies*, 5(2), 2011, pp. 138–146.
20. Nihar Nayak, Issues and Concerns in India-Nepal Relations. In Rumel Dahiya, & Ashok K Behuria (Eds.), *India's Neighbourhood: Challenges in the Next Two Decades*, New Delhi: Pentagon Press, 2012, pp. 137–62.
21. T.R. Wani, India's Prime Minister Narendra Modi Visit to Nepal: Renewing Relations. *International Journal of Scientific and Research Publications*, 5(2), 2015, pp. 1-2.
22. M. Bisht, India-Bhutan relations in the next two decades. In Rumel Dahiya, & Ashok K Behuria (Eds.), *India's Neighbourhood: Challenges in the Next Two Decades*, New Delhi: Pentagon Press, 2012, pp. 137–62.

Index

Abbot, Tony, Australian Prime Minister, 3, 29
Act East Policy (AEP), 18, 27-28, 99, 183, 186, 189, 192
Actual Ground Position Line (AGPL), 250
Adhikari, Shekhar, 209
Advanced Air Defence (AAD), 257
Afghan Civil War, 41
Afghan War, 33, 238
Afghanistan, 32, 33, 34, 35, 36, 37, 38, 39, 41, 42, 43, 198, 238, 295, 300
    Pakistan Double Game in, 38
AfPak, 41
    Talibanisation, 41
Agni-V, 257
ahimsa, 138
al Qaeda, 33, 38, 147, 173, 245, 295, 299
Algeria, 236
All Party Hurriyat Conference (APHC), 150
Alliance of Small Island States (AOSIS), 165
Andaman Nicobar Command (ANC), 169
Antony, A.K., former defence minister, 4
APEC (Asia Pacific Economic Cooperation), 24, 126
AQIS, 147
Arabian Gulf, 236
Arabian Sea, 126, 149
ASEAN Regional Forum (ARF), 126
ASEAN, 5, 130, 142, 182, 184, 189, 192, 271
ASEAN-India vision document 2020, 186
ASEM (Asia-Europe Summit Meeting), 126
Asia, 10, 26-27, 103, 106, 124-25, 129-30, 133-35, 139, 141, 159, 169, 187, 192, 248, 256, 266, 274, 288
Asia-Pacific, 130-32, 134, 189, 259, 265, 272
Australia, 4, 19, 265-66, 268, 271-72
Automatic Identification System (AIS), 170

B4B ('Bharat for Bhutan' and 'Bhutan for Bharat'), 88
Bangladesh Border Guard (BGB), 69
Bangladesh Nationalist Party (BNP), 298
Bangladesh, 35, 47-48, 51, 52, 54, 56, 58, 181, 182, 222, 295
    Arsenic Contamination, 56
    Climate Change, 60
    Cyclones and Storm Surges, 60
    Drought and Salinity, 55
    Flood, 54
    Pollution, 59
    Population and Poverty, 52
    Trans-boundary Water Sharing Issue, 57
    Water Crisis, 53
    Wetlands, 57
Bazaraguru chhu, 83
BCIM, 11
Bhadauria, Sanjeev, 124
Bhartiya Janata Party (BJP), 9, 18, 77
Bhutan, 2, 18, 78, 81, 159, 303
    102nd National Day, 82
Bhutan-China border, 83, 86
    11th Five Year Plan, 88
Bhutto, Benazir, 241
Bhutto, Zulfikar Ali, 236-37
    Islamic Socialism, 237
Bilateral Investment Promotion Agreement (BIPA), 188
BIMSTEC, 80, 82, 87, 126, 189

Border Defence Cooperation Agreement (BDCA), 101, 120
Border Management, 206
Border Security Force (BSF), 62, 69
Brahma Chellany, 7
Brazil, 4
Bremmer, Ian
  'J curve' phenomenon, 178
BRICS, 3, 5
Budania, Rajpal, 248
Bush, George W., 23

Cambodia, 189
Canada, 17, 28
Central Asia, 4, 11, 36, 41, 44, 133, 269, 300, 302
Central Asian Republics (CARs), 39, 41, 149
Central Tibetan Administration (CTA), 113, 115
chalein saath saath, 15
Chanakya, 195
Chawla, Shalini, 231
Chin National Front (CNF), 183
China Development Bank (CDB), 7
China Study Centres, 201
  Security Challenges to, 200
China, 4, 7-9, 12, 17, 19, 24, 26, 41, 42, 54, 82, 84, 107, 149, 160, 175, 176, 181-82, 187, 190, 192, 196, 197, 257-58, 260, 265, 268, 269, 280
  Defence White Paper 2004, 269
  National Defence White Paper 2008, 270
  Peoples' Liberation Army (PLA), 111
  South Asia Policy, 202
  String of Pearls Strategy, 130-31, 133, 160, 271
Claim over Arunachal Pradesh, 96-97
China's Win, India's Loss, 100-01
China-Myanmar Strained Relations, 185
Chinese Navy, 131
Choe-Yon relationship, 109
Clinton, Bill, the then US President, 23, 271
Cold War, 28, 32-34, 39, 47-48, 122, 132, 141, 143, 159, 165, 234, 249, 253, 257-59, 262
Colombo Port City Project, 299
Colonel Young Husband, 118
  expedition, 109
Commission of National Inquiry (CoNI), 156
Communist Party of Bhutan (MLM), 303
Communist Party of India (Maoist), 216
Communist Party of Nepal (CPN), 219
Compact Revolution Zone (CRZ), 224
Compendium of Environment Statistics of Bangladesh, 52
Coordination Committee of Maoist Parties and Organisations of South Asia (CCOMPOSA), 222
Cross-border migration, 50
Curtis, Lisa, 15-16

Dalai Lama
  Role, 113-16
  Sino-Indian Relations, 116
Dawn, 37
Deepening Strategic Rivalry, 256
Dogra invaders, 109
DOSTI (friendship) exercises, 169
Double Tax Avoidance Agreement (DTAA), 188
Drugs, 148, 226
  smuggling, 50
Durand line, 35

East Asia, 27, 130, 181-82, 272
East China Sea, 265, 268, 270, 274
East of the Suez, 159
Economic Development, 212
Ecosystem integrity, 51
Egypt, 236
Eighth Dalai Lama, 108
Ekueuvrin, 168
El-Nino-Southern Oscillation (ENSO), 52
Enlightened Moderation, 242
Environment-threat-vulnerability nexus, 51
European Union (EU), 21, 145, 284
Exim Bank of China, 286

Faculty of Engineering Technology (FET), 175
FADs (Fish Aggregation Devices), 175
FATA, 39, 243
Fifth Dalai Lama, 115, 120
Fiji, 19
First World War, 139
Foreign Direct Investment (FDI), 88-89, 157
Fourteenth Dalai Lama, 98, 111, 114-15, 117
Fourth Dalai Lama, 117
France, 17, 28
Free Movement, 224

G-20, 5, 16, 19
Gandhi, Indira, 21, 15
Gandhi, Rajiv, 11, 25
Gandhi, Sanjay, 25
Gandhi, Sonia, Congress President, 10
Ganges Water Treaty, 57
GBM (Ganges, Brahmaputra and Meghna), 54
Gen. B.M. Kaul, 94
Gen. Huang, 110
Gen. Kayani, former army Chief, 37
Germany, 17, 28
Ghar Wapsi, 23
Global Supply Chains, 276
Global Times, 6
Global Times, Chinese daily, 26
GMR, 161-62, 171
Good Taliban, 245
Gopal, S., 79
Grand Slam, 235
Grare, Frederic, 14
Great Game, 134
Gujral Doctrine, 21
Gurkhas, 109

Hamilton, Booz Allen, 130
Haqqani Network, 43
Harish, P.S., 137
Harkar-ul-Mujahidden (HuM), 241
Harkat-ul-Jihadi-al-Islami (HuJI), 241, 296, 299
Harkat-ul-Mujahideen (HuM), 243, 296, 299
Harper, Stephen, Canadian Prime Minister, 29
Hashmi, Sana, 91
Hatf-5, 257
Hindi Chini Bhai Bhai, 92-93
Hindu, 16
Hindustan Aeronautics Ltd (HAL), 169
Hindustan Times, 14
HIV/AIDS, 50
Hizb-e-Islami, 43
Hollande, Francois, French President, 29
Human Development Report, 49, 219
Human trafficking, 50

IMF, 78
IMTRAT, 80
India and Tibet, 117
India and USA, 13
India and West, 28
India Today, 1
India, 3, 5, 13, 36, 40, 41, 54, 58, 130, 142, 157, 161, 177, 187, 190, 196, 197, 207, 222, 258, 260, 265, 271, 298
  fourth Five Year Plan, 212
  Naxalite Movement, 211-12
    Government Responses, 213
    Failure, 215
    Present, 215
  North-eastern Border
      Infrastructural Development, 99-100
  Post-Independence Period, 140
  Security Challenges, 199
  Strategic Compulsions, 274
  Strategic Vision, 274
India's Maoist Community Centre (MCC), 222
India-Afghanistan
  relations, 35
India-Africa forum summit, 28
India-ASEAN
  Car rally, 186
  Trade in Goods Agreement, 188
India-Bangladesh Land Boundary Agreement (LBA), 68
India-Bangladesh Land Boundary Agreement, 66-74
  Cross-Border Security Cooperation, 71
  Economic Interactions, 70-71
  Proposed Deal, 69
India-Bhutan Relations: 1949-2007, 79-81
  China as a Factor, 82-89
India-China
  Border, 10, 26, 92
  Burgeoning US-India Friendship, 95
  Forward Policy, 94
  Relations, 27, 92
  Tibet Factor, 94-95
India's Influence, 95-96
  Strategic Importance of Tawang, 98-99
India-China-Pakistan relations, 127
India-Maldives Relations
  Maritime Security Cooperation, 166
  Robust Engagements, 167
Increased Strategic Cooperation, 168
  Political Relations, 170
  Environmental Cooperation, 176
India-Myanmar relationship, 182
Indian Army (IA), 37, 99, 142, 146, 168, 204, 206, 214, 235
Indian Maritime Doctrine 2004, 273

Indian Navy, 160, 162, 166-67, 169-170, 272-76
Indian Navy-MNDF exercises, 169
Indian Ocean, 11, 17, 28-29, 128, 131, 134, 139, 142, 155, 158-59, 163, 165-67, 169, 172, 177-78, 184-85, 187, 259, 265-69, 271-72, 274-76, 279-80, 286-87, 301
Indian Regional Navigation Satellite System (IRNSS), 273, 275
India-Nepal Peace and Friendship Treaty of 1950, 197
India-Pakistan
War, 146
Conflict, 248
Dialogue Process and Peace Initiatives, 249
India-Sri Lanka Accord of 1987, 300
India-Sri Lankan Relations
Action-reaction Chain, 285
At Loggerheads, 284
Cede or not Cede, 284
Fishing in Troubled Waters, 283
Long Distance Friend, 286
Looming Red, 285
Rehabilitation, 282
India-US
Civil Nuclear deal, 16
Engagement, 23
Relationship, 21
Strategic partnership, 129
Ties, 142
Indonesia, 142, 266
Indo-Pacific Region
Strategic Environment, 268
Indus Water Treaty, 235, 301
Industrial Extension Bureau (INDEXTB), 7
Inner Mongolia, 112
Inner Tibet, 118
Inter-continental Ballistic Missile (ICBM), 257
International Energy Agency (IEA), 269
International Maritime Boundary line (IMBL), 283
IOR, 269, 275
IOR-RIM, 275
IPCC, 177
IPKF, 282
Iran, 4, 33, 34, 41-43, 149, 175, 302
Iraq, 4, 33, 43, 271
ISAF, 37
Islamic
bomb, 240
reforms, 237
socialism, 237
Islamic Ideology
Global Rise, 236
Islamic State of Iraq and Syria (ISIS), 43, 150-50
ISLFTA, 281
Israel, 21
IV Eelam War, 284

J&K
Interference of Foreign Elements, 145-53
Jagrata Muslim Janata Bangladesh (JMJB), 299
Jaish-e-Mohammad (JeM), 147, 150-51, 241, 243, 246, 296
Jalal, Ayesha, 232
Jam'atul Mujahideen Bangladesh (JMB), 299
Jamaat-ud-Dawa (JuD), 246296
Jamadhagni, S. Utham Kumar, 278
Jamait-i-Ulems-i-Islam-F (JUI-F), 242
Jammu and Kashmir, Maharaja Hari Singh, 146
Japan, 3, 4, 6, 8, 10, 12, 17, 21, 24, 28, 89, 127, 130, 133-35, 175, 187, 189, 265-66, 268, 270-72
Japanese War, 111
Jihad, 152, 234, 237, 239, 241
Jinnah, Muhammad Ali, 232-33
Joint Intelligence Bureau (JIB), 148
Joint naval exercises, 142
Joint Working Group (JWG), 102

Kachin Independent Army (KIA), 183
Kailash Mansarovar, 9
Karakoram Highway (KKH), 149-50
Karthikheyan, T.C., 165
Kashmir valley, 148
Kashmiri American Council (KAC), 148
Kashmiriyat, 146
Kaul, B.M., 80
Kaushik, Diwakar, 1
Kautilya's Arthasastra, 138
Kerry, John, 3
Kharat, Rajesh S, 77
Khurshid, Salman, former External Affairs Minister, 9
Khyber-Pakhtunkhwa, 35
King Prithvinarayan Shah, 196

Kinger, Kamal, 181
Kishor M S, Nand, 293
KLO, 303
KPK, 243
Kumar, Ashok, 181
Kumar, Narender, 195
Kurote Dzongkhang, 83

Laos, 182, 184, 186, 189
Lashkar-e-Taiba (LeT), 43, 147, 150-51, 241, 243, 246, 296, 298-99
LBA (Land Boundary Agreement), 26
Lebanon, 236
Left Wing Ideology, 198
Li Keqiang, Chinese Premier, 102
Line of Actual Control (LAC), 126
Line of Control (LoC), 250
Little Dragons, 227
Long Range Identification and Tracking (LRIT), 170
Look East Policy, 22, 99, 130, 143, 183
LTTE, 126, 223, 279-81, 284, 295

Madhav, Ram, 18
Madhyam Marg, 78
Malay Peninsula, 182
Malaysia, 142, 236, 266
Maldives Institute of Technical Education (MITE), 175
Maldives National Defence Force (MNDF), 174
Maldives National University, 175
Maldives, 154, 158, 159, 160, 161, 162, 165, 166, 173, 176, 177, 295, 301
  Geo-strategic Location, 158
  India's Economic Assistance, 174
  Rising Challenges to Democracy, 173
  Second Poll, 156
  Strategic Ties vs. Economic Engagement, 162
Maldivian Democratic Party (MDP), 155
Maldivian EEZ, 175
Maldivian National Defence Forces (MDNF), 168
Malé, 156-57, 160-61, 171-72, 174
Mandala theory, 138
Manivasakan, S., 154
Maritime Domain Awareness (MDA), 162, 169
Maritime Silk Road, 9
Marxist-Leninist-Maoist ideas, 221
Mauritius, 28, 160, 162
McMahon Line, 92, 96, 97, 103
Mekong-Ganges Cooperation (MGC), 126, 189
Memorandum of Understanding (MoU), 7, 142, 188, 252
Merchant Ship Information System (MSIS), 170
Merkal, Angela, German Chancellor, 29
Middle East, 43, 130, 139, 187, 269, 271
Middle Way of Autonomy, 117
Military Implications, 120
Ming Dynasty, 108
Mishra, Aditya, 47
Mongolia, 26, 27
Moon, Ban Ki, UN Secretary General, 13
Mukherjee Mr. Pranab President of India, 2, 273
Musharraf, Gen. Pervez, Pakistani President, 242-43, 250-251, 255
Myanmar, 16-19, 54, 99, 126, 133, 181-93, 200, 275
  Economic Opportunity, 187
  Development, 189

NAM, 80, 87, 251
Narayanan, Sripathi, 154
Narendra, Modi, Prime Minister, 2-3, 8, 13, 15, 16, 18, 19, 20, 23, 24, 25, 26, 27, 77, 284
  64th birthday, 6
  US diplomacy, 25
Nathu La Pass, 9, 80
National Democratic Front of Bodoland (NDFB), 303
National Investigation Agency (NIA), 173
National Socialist Council of Nagaland-Isak-Muviah, 183
National Socialist Council of Nagaland-Khaplang (N, 183
NATO forces, 37, 147, 244
Natural disasters, 50
Nav pe charcha, 28
Naxalbari, 213
Naxalism, growth of, 213
NDA government, 2
Necklace of friendship, 131
NEFA, 94, 97
Nehru, Jawaharlal, 1, 21, 79-80, 91-95, 100-1, 140-41, 143
Nehru-Noon agreement, 68
Neighbours first, 200
Nepal, 2, 18, 54, 77-78, 81, 87, 100, 126, 159,

182, 195-207, 209-11, 218-229, 295, 297-98, 303
a Disaster Prone Nation, 205
Conflict Zone, 220
External Factor, 222
Government Response, 220
Maoist Insurgency, 218
Nepalese Army (NA), 204
NGO Maldivian Democracy Network, 173
Non-Alignment, 4, 141
Non-traditional Security Threats (NTST), 49, 50
Noorani, A.G.
Credulity and Negligence, 101
North Eastern Region (NER), 181, 187
North Korea, 189
North West Bangladesh, 55
Northeast Asia, 8
Northern Alliance, 41
Nuclear Suppliers Group (NSG), 28
Nuclear Weapons, Development, 240
NWFP, 35, 239, 243, 245,

Obama, Barack, President of United States, 16-17, 22-23, 29, 33, 259, 272
ONGC Videsh Ltd., 273
Operation All Clear, 303
Operation Cactus, 159, 163, 167
Operation Enduring Freedom, 33-34, 38, 43
Operation Steeplechase, 214
Operations Gibraltar, 235
Organisation of Islamic Conference (OIC), 145, 150
Outer Mongolia, 112
Outer Tibet, 118

Pakistan, 18, 24, 33, 34, 35, 36, 38, 41, 148, 238, 240, 258, 260, 275, 295
army, 234, 237
Inter Services Intelligence (ISI), 36-37, 39, 40, 147-48, 199-200, 223, 239, 241-43, 245, 287, 296, 299, 301
1971: Break-Up, 235
Pakistan's War for Kashmir
Beginning of the Ideological Drift, 234
Panchsheel, 27, 79, 141
Pang La, 86
PDP (People's Democratic Party), 86
Penn Complex, 14
People War, 223
People's Daily, 6
People's Liberation Army (PLA), 93, 149
People's Liberation Army, 129
People's Liberation Organisation of Tamil Eelam (PLOTE), 159
People's Republic of China (PRC), 85, 91, 113, 117
People's War, 222
Persian Gulf, 265
Philippines, 5, 266, 271
PLA, 6, 86, 112, 120, 121, 128
PLAN, 269-70
Pokhran II nuclear tests, 23
Political Development, 211, 218
post-Cold War, 48, 49, 273, 275
Power Struggle, 125
Prachanda, 219, 222
Putin, Vladimir, Russian President, 29, 260

Qing Dynasty, 108-9, 115
Quetta Shura, 43

Radcliffe Award, 67
Rana Dynasty, 218
Rao, PV Narasimha, former Prime Minister, 142
Rao, P. Muralidhar, 18
Red Corridor, 224
Republic Day, 21
Revolutionary International Movement (RIM), 223
Rijiju, Kiren, Union Minister of State for Home, 9
Rio+20, 84
Russia, 5, 17, 21, 24, 28, 39, 41-43, 118, 249, 258-260, 269
Russia-India-China, 5

Saagar Mala, 28
Saagar Yatra, 28
SAARC, 1, 2, 20-22, 77, 80, 82, 87, 162, 174, 198, 251
Sanctuaries, 225
Saran, Hari, 265
Saudi Arabia, 4
Sea Lines of Communications (SLOCs), 125, 133
Second World War, 139, 140
Security, 121

Seychelles, 160, 162
SEZs, 88
Shafi, Kamran, Pakistani Journalist, 36
Shah, Amit, 25
Shahi, Shivendra, 66
Shanghai Cooperation Organisation (SCO), 126
Shanghai Cooperation Organisation, 5, 11
Sharif, Nawaz, Pakistani Prime Minister, 1, 13, 22-24, 241, 250, 252, 254-55
Shinzo Abe, 3
Sibal, Kanwal, 14
Singapore, 4, 17, 142, 272
Singh, Amar, 66
Singh, Jaibans, 145
Singh, K. Natwar, Former External Affairs Minister, 3
    My China Diary, 116
Singh, Manmohan, the then Indian Prime Minister, 3, 10, 17-18, 23, 69, 98, 216, 251, 255, 299
Singh, Tej Pratap, 32
Sino-Bhutan boundary disputes, 87
Sino-India
    Border, 80
    Chinese Challenge, 125
    Cooperation, 4, 6
    Dynamics, 124
    Positive Developments, 126
    Potential for Discord, 127
    Relationship, 26
    Struggle for Power, 125
Sino-Tibetan tensions, 119
Sixth Dalai Lama, 97
SLBM, 273
Social Development, 212, 218
Social media, 151
Somalia, 40
South Africa, 4
South Asia Free Trade Area, 20
South Asia, 14, 17, 20, 24, 36, 44, 48, 71, 77, 130, 155, 163, 181, 209, 219, 223-24, 227, 229, 248, 254, 258, 260, 272, 280, 289, 294-95, 304-5
    Nuclearisation, 252
South China Sea, 5, 8, 128, 130, 268-71, 273-74
South Korea, 26-28, 187, 189, 265-66, 268, 271-72
Southeast Asia, 8, 99, 130-31, 133, 143, 181-84, 186-88, 190, 273
Soviet Union, 25, 32, 37, 159, 212, 258
Sri Lanka, 19, 28, 71, 126, 142, 154-55, 159-62, 169, 170, 175, 177, 179, 223, 278-83, 285-89, 295, 299
Sri Lankan Air Force, 286
Student Islamic Movement of India (SIMI), 297
Submarine-Launched Ballistic Missile (SLBM), 257
Sufism Islamic Ideology, 236
Swaraj, Sushma, External Affairs Minister of India, 2, 24

Taiwan, 127, 266, 271
Taliban insurgency, 244
Taliban, 38, 242, 295
Tamu-Kalemyo-Kalewa road, 190
Tehreek-e-Taliban Pakistan (TTP), 39, 244-46
Terrorism
    and Militant Groups, 295
    New Tactics, 252
    Rise, 239
Thailand, 89, 142, 175, 182, 186
The SAARC Yatra, 24
The Wahhabi Invasion, 147
Third World, 27
Thirteenth Dalai Lama, 110, 115
Tibet and China, 107
    Pre-1911, 108-9
    Post-1911, 109-11
    Post 1949, 111-13
Tibet Autonomous Region (TAR), 99, 106-7, 112, 120, 122, 196, 200-2
Tibet, 9, 82
Tibetan
    Army, 110
    Plateau, 182
Tillanchang, 167
Time magazine, 29
Times of India, 86
Tonga, 19
Transnational organized crime, 50
Tunisia, 236
Turkey, 236

ULFA, 303
UN Security Council, 85, 126
UNCLOS, 5
UNDCP, 149

UNDP, 49, 219
UNICEF, 56
United Liberation Front of Asom (ULFA), 183, 303
United Nation (UN), 50, 80, 87
United Nations Drug Control Program (UNDCP), 148
United Nations Framework Convention on Climate Change, 176
United Nations Security Council (UNSC), 4, 23, 129
United States (US), 7, 12-13, 15-17, 21, 24-25, 33-34, 37, 40, 42-43, 127, 129-30, 141, 147-48, 160, 234, 238, 244, 249, 259-60, 265-69, 271-72, 275, 295-96, 300
    costliest war in history, 32
    Navy, 271
Unmanned Aerial Vehicle (UAV), 244
UPA-II Government, 2
US Federal Bureau of Investigation (FBI), 148
US-China alliance, 141
US-India partnership, 15
US-Russia
    relations over Ukraine crisis, 39
    rivalry, 39

Vajpayee, Atal Behari, the then Prime Minister of India, 252
Vanuatu, 19
Vietnam, 3, 5, 8, 33, 142, 189, 266, 271
Virk, Simrat Kaur, 106
Vyaktipuja, 24

War on Terror, 34, 38, 43
Water Sharing, 121
Wen Jiabao, Chinese Premier 97
West Asia, 36, 44, 147, 269
West Asian Non-Alignment, 4
World Bank, 59, 78, 235, 270
WTO, 3, 5, 17, 22

Xi Jinping, Chinese President, 3-13, 19, 27, 29, 114, 161, 163, 270, 286
Xinhua News Agency, 114
Xinjiang, 112

Yal Devi Express railway line, 280
Yuan Dynasty, 108
Yugoslavia, 40

Zamini Haqeeqat, 73
Zardari, Asif Ali, Pakistani President, 255
Zia-ul-Haq, 237-38
    Islamisation of Pakistan, 237